THE FIRST AMENDMENT

THE ESTABLISHMENT OF RELIGION CLAUSE

BILL OF RIGHTS SERIES

THE FIRST AMENDMENT
THE ESTABLISHMENT OF RELIGION CLAUSE

Its Constitutional History and the Contemporary Debate

EDITED BY ALAN BROWNSTEIN

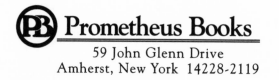

Prometheus Books

59 John Glenn Drive
Amherst, New York 14228-2119

Published 2008 by Prometheus Books

Inquiries should be addressed to
Prometheus Books
59 John Glenn Drive
Amherst, New York 14228–2119
VOICE: 716–691–0133, ext. 210
FAX: 716–691–0137
WWW.PROMETHEUSBOOKS.COM

12 11 10 09 08   5 4 3 2 1

Library of Congress Cataloging-in-Publication Data

The establishment of religion clause : the First Amendment : its constitutional history and the contemporary debate / edited by Alan Brownstein. — 1st American paperback ed.
        p. cm.
    Includes bibliographical references.
    ISBN 978–1–59102–517–7
    1. Church and state—United States—History. 2. Freedom of religion—United States. 3. United States. Constitution. 1st Amendment. 4. Established churches—United States. I. Brownstein, Alan.

KF4865.E849 2007
342,7308'42—dc22

                                                                2007011065

Printed in the United States of America on acid-free paper

CONTENTS

Series Preface   11
   David B. Oppenheimer

Editor's Introduction   15

SECTION I: THE HISTORY OF THE
ESTABLISHMENT CLAUSE

CHAPTER 1: SUPREME COURT JUSTICES ON THE HISTORY
OF THE ESTABLISHMENT CLAUSE   **31**

Everson v. Board of Education of the Township of Ewing, et al.   31

Wallace, Governor of Alabama, et al. v. Jaffree, et al.   43

Elk Grove Unified School District v. Newdow   53

5

CHAPTER 2: THE NONPREFERENTIALISM DEBATE — 56

Church-State Separation: Restoring the "No Preference" Doctrine
of the First Amendment — 56
Robert L. Cord

"Nonpreferential" Aid to Religion: A False Claim about Original Intent — 65
Douglas Laycock

CHAPTER 3: THE ESTABLISHMENT CLAUSE
AS A FEDERALISM MANDATE — 76

Toward a General Theory of the Establishment Clause — 76
Daniel O. Conkle

The Intellectual Origins of the Establishment Clause — 83
Noah Feldman

The Bill of Rights: Creation and Reconstruction — 90
Akhil Reed Amar

The Second Adoption of the Establishment Clause:
The Rise of the Nonestablishment Principle — 97
Kurt T. Lash

CHAPTER 4: THE COMPLEX BACKGROUND
OF THE ESTABLISHMENT CLAUSE — 104

The Essential Rights and Liberties of Religion
in the American Constitutional Experiment — 104
John Witte Jr.

The Separation of the Religious and the Secular:
A Foundational Challenge to First Amendment Theory — 118
Laura Underkuffler-Freund

SECTION II: GOVERNMENT FUNDING OF RELIGIOUS INSTITUTIONS AND RELIGIOUS ACTIVITIES

Editor's Introduction: Supreme Court Cases Adjudicating
Government Funding of Religious Institutions and Activities   131

CHAPTER 5: DIRECT AID   **136**

Religious Freedom at a Crossroads   136
   Michael W. McConnell

Federal Funds for Parochial Schools? No.   142
   Leo Pfeffer

Public Aid to Parochial Schools   151
   Paul A. Freund

The Establishment Clause and Aid to Parochial Schools   157
   Jesse H. Choper

CHAPTER 6: INDIRECT AID OR VOUCHERS   **167**

The Increasingly Anachronistic Case against School Vouchers   167
   Ira C. Lupu

The Price of Vouchers for Religious Freedom   174
   Laura S. Underkuffler

School Vouchers and Religious Liberty: Seven Questions
from Madison's "Memorial and Remonstrance"   183
   Vincent Blasi

Evaluating School Voucher Programs through a
Liberty, Equality, and Free Speech Matrix   194
   Alan E. Brownstein

Vouchers and Religious Schools: The New Constitutional Questions   208
   Thomas C. Berg

CHAPTER 7: CHARITABLE CHOICE AND SOCIAL WELFARE SERVICES BY FAITH-BASED PROVIDERS **216**

A Constitutional Case for Governmental Cooperation
with Faith-Based Social Service Providers 216
Carl H. Esbeck

Interpreting the Religion Clauses in Terms of Liberty, Equality,
and Free Speech Values—A Critical Analysis of
"Neutrality Theory" and Charitable Choice 226
Alan E. Brownstein

Remembering the Values of Separatism and State Funding of
Religious Organizations (Charitable Choice):
To Aid Is Not Necessarily to Protect 235
William P. Marshall

**SECTION III: GOVERNMENT PROMOTION OR
EXPRESSION OF RELIGIOUS BELIEFS**

Editor's Introduction: Supreme Court Cases Evaluating
Government Promotion or Expression of Religious Beliefs 245

CHAPTER 8: GOVERNMENT, RELIGION, AND CULTURE: AN OVERVIEW **250**

Religious Freedom at a Crossroads 250
Michael W. McConnell

Religious Liberty as Liberty 256
Douglas Laycock

CHAPTER 9: RELIGIOUS EQUALITY AND RELIGIOUS ENDORSEMENTS **266**

From Liberty to Equality: The Transformation
of the Establishment Clause 266
Noah Feldman

Harmonizing the Heavenly and Earthly Spheres:
The Fragmentation and Synthesis of Religion,
Equality, and Speech in the Constitution 279
   Alan E. Brownstein

Symbols, Perceptions, and Doctrinal Illusions:
Establishment Neutrality and the "No Endorsement" Test 292
   Steven D. Smith

Secular Purpose 302
   Andrew Koppelman

The Pledge of Allegiance and the Limited State 314
   Thomas C. Berg

CHAPTER 10: COERCION AND ESTABLISHMENT **324**

Coercion: The Lost Element of Establishment 324
   Michael W. McConnell

"Noncoercive" Support for Religion: Another False Claim
about the Establishment Clause 331
   Douglas Laycock

Religious Coercion and the Establishment Clause 340
   Steven G. Gey

Lemon Is Dead 348
   Michael Stokes Paulsen

CONSTITUTION OF THE UNITED STATES OF AMERICA **357**

The Amendments to the Constitution 373

BILL OF RIGHTS SERIES
EDITOR'S PREFACE

Abortion; the death penalty; school prayer; the pledge of allegiance; torture; surveillance; tort reform; jury trials; preventative detention; firearm registration; censorship; privacy; police misconduct; birth control; school vouchers; prison crowding; taking property by public domain. These issues, torn from the headlines, cover many, if not most, of the major public disputes arising today, in the dawn of the twenty-first century. Yet they are resolved by our courts based on a document fewer than five hundred words long, drafted in the eighteenth century, and regarded by many at the time of its drafting as unnecessary. The Bill of Rights, the name we give the first ten amendments to the United States Constitution, is our basic source of law for resolving these issues. This series of books, of which this is the first volume, is intended to help us improve our understanding of the debates that gave rise to these rights, and of the continuing controversy about their meaning today.

When our Constitution was drafted, the framers were concerned with defining the structure and powers of our new federal government and balancing its three branches. They did not initially focus on the question of individual rights. The drafters organized the Constitution into seven sections, termed "Articles," each concerned with a specific area of federal authority. Article I sets forth the legislative powers of the Congress; Article II the executive powers of the President; and Article III the judicial power of the federal courts. Article V governs the process for amending the Constitution. Article VI declares the supremacy of federal law on those subjects under federal jurisdiction, while Article VII provides the process for ratification. Only Article IV is concerned with individual rights, and only in a single sentence requiring states to give citizens of other states the same rights they provide to their own citizens. (Article IV also provides for the return of runaway slaves, a provision repealed in 1865 by the Thirteenth Amendment).

When the Constitutional convention completed its work in 1787, it sent the Constitution to the states for adoption. The opponents of ratification, known as the "Anti-Federalists" because they opposed the strong federal government envisioned in the Constitution, argued that without a Bill of Rights the federal government would be a danger to liberty. The "Federalists," principally Alexander Hamilton, James Madison, and John Jay, responded in a series of anonymous newspaper articles now known as the "Federalist Papers." The Federalists initially argued that there was no need for a federal Bill of Rights, because most states (seven) had a state Bill of Rights, and because the proposed Constitution limited the power of the federal government to only those areas specifically enumerated, leaving all remaining powers to the States or the people. But in time, Madison would become the great proponent and drafter of the Bill of Rights.

The proposed Constitution was sent to the States for ratification on September 17, 1787. Delaware was the first State to assent, followed rapidly by Pennsylvania, New Jersey, Georgia, and Connecticut. But when the Massachusetts Legislature met in January 1788 to debate ratification, several vocal members took up the objection that without a Bill of Rights the proposed Constitution endangered individual liberty. A compromise was brokered, with the Federalists agreeing to support amending the Constitution to add a Bill of Rights following ratification. The Anti-Federalists, led by John Adams and John Hancock, agreed, and Massachusetts ratified. When Maryland, South Carolina, and New Hampshire followed, the requisite nine States had signed on. Virginia and New York quickly followed, with North Carolina ratifying in 1789 and Rhode Island in 1790. In addition to Massachusetts, New Hampshire's, Virginia's, and New York's ratifying conventions conditioned their acceptance on the understanding that a Bill of Rights would be added.

The first Congress met in New York City in March 1789 and, among its first acts, began debating and drafting the Bill of Rights. Federalist Congressman James Madison took responsibility for drafting the bill, having by then concluded it would strengthen the legitimacy of the new government. He relied heavily on the state constitutions, especially the Virginia Declaration of Rights, in setting out those individual rights that should be protected from federal interference.

Madison steered seventeen proposed amendments through the House, of which the Senate agreed to twelve. On September 2, 1789, President Washington sent them to the States for ratification. Of the twelve, two, concerning Congressional representation and Congressional pay, failed to achieve ratification by over three-quarters of the states. (The Congressional Pay Amendment was finally ratified in 1992.) The remaining ten were ratified and, with the vote of Virginia on December 15, 1791, became the first ten amendments to the Constitution, or the "Bill of Rights."

The Bill of Rights as originally adopted only applied to the federal government. Its purpose was to restrict Congress from interfering with rights reserved to the people. Thus, under the First Amendment the Congress could not establish a national religion, but the States could establish State support for selected religions, as seven States to some extent did (Connecticut, Georgia, Maryland, Massachusetts, New Hampshire, South Carolina, and Vermont). Madison had proposed that the States also be bound by the Bill of Rights, and the House agreed, but the Senate rejected the proposal.

Although the Declaration of Independence provided that "We hold these truths to be self-evident, that all men are created equal," the Constitution and Bill of Rights are conspicuously silent on the question of equality, because the agreement that made the Constitution possible was the North/South compromise permitting the continuation of slavery. Thus, today's issues like affirmative action, race and sex discrimination, school segregation, and same-sex marriage cannot be resolved through application of the Bill of Rights. This omission of a guarantee of equality led to the Civil War, and in turn to the post-Civil War Fourteenth Amendment that made the newly freed slaves US and State citizens and prohibited the States from denying equal protection of the laws or due process of law to any citizen. In light of this Amendment, the Supreme Court began developing the "incorporation doctrine," holding that the Fourteenth Amendment extended the Bill of Rights so that it applied to all government action. By applying the Bill of Rights so expansively, the legal and social landscape of America was fundamentally changed.

In the aftermath of the Civil War and with the ratification of the Fourteenth Amendment, the Supreme Court slowly began applying the Bill of

Rights to state and local governments. The result has been that the debates of 1787–1791 have become more and more important to modern life. Could a high school principal begin a graduation ceremony by asking a minister (or a student leader) to say a prayer? Could a State require a girl under the age of 16 to secure her parent's permission to have an abortion? Could a prison warden deny a pain medication to a prisoner between midnight and 7:00 a.m.? Could a college president censor an article in a student newspaper? These questions required the courts to examine the debates of the eighteenth century to determine what the framers intended when they drafted the Bill of Rights. They also raised the related and hotly disputed question of whether the intent of the framers was even relevant, or whether a "living" Constitution required solely contemporary, not historical, analysis.

Hence this series. Our intent is to select the very best essays from law and history and the most important judicial opinions and to edit them, making the leading views of the framers' intentions and of how we should interpret the Bill of Rights accessible to today's reader. If you find yourself passionately agreeing with some of the views expressed, angrily disagreeing with others, and appreciating how the essays selected have examined these questions with depth and lucidity, we will have succeeded.

David B. Oppenheimer
Professor of Law and Associate Dean for Faculty Development
Golden Gate University School of Law
San Francisco

EDITOR'S INTRODUCTION

Congress shall make no law respecting an establishment of religion, or prohibiting the free exercise thereof...

A. Controversy and Conflict

There are few areas of constitutional law that are as controversial and unsettled as the interpretation of the Establishment Clause of the First Amendment. The case law interpreting and applying the Establishment Clause is routinely condemned as arbitrary, incoherent, and inconsistent. Legal commentary critiquing Establishment Clause doctrine is similarly fragmented and reflects sharply divergent views among church-state scholars. Moreover, debate about the Establishment Clause extends beyond courtrooms and the academy. Disputes relating to the relationship between church and state contribute to the political polarization of American society. Establishment Clause constraints on government are hot button sociopolitical issues that are argued with intense emotional fervor. From the school prayer decisions forty years ago to contemporary conflicts about attempts to remove the phrase "under God" from the Pledge of Allegiance, or proposals to allow school vouchers to be used to subsidize religious schools, or the President's Faith-Based Initiative to facilitate government funding of religious organizations providing social services, competing claims about the meaning of the Establishment Clause have provoked serious disagreements in our public discourse.

Of course, disagreements about the meaning and application of constitutional provisions are hardly unusual. Constitutional arguments are as old as the document itself. But debate about the understanding of the Establishment Clause seems unique because of the depth and breadth of the fault lines undercutting current doctrine. With other complex constitutional mandates such as those protecting freedom of speech or guaranteeing the equal protection of the laws, there is a strong core of agreement on basic purposes and seminal judicial decisions are rarely challenged. With the Establishment Clause, however, there is virtually no consensus on even the most basic understanding of what this part of the First Amendment requires. The continuum of discussion ranges from the contention that the Establishment Clause mandates a rigorously enforced separation of church and state to the argument that the Establishment Clause has no substantive content at all—because its sole, original goal was to prevent federal interference with state laws establishing religion.

The purpose of this book is to provide a foundation for understanding these constitutional arguments. It is a collection of articles that focus on ideas and principles rather than particular cases or doctrinal analysis. Ultimately, Establishment Clause controversies reflect a clash of constitutional values. Only by examining these core disagreements can readers develop a sense of what the fight over the meaning of the Establishment Clause is all about.

Obviously, however, the articles I have chosen for this anthology will also discuss Supreme Court cases as well as the tests the Court has employed in adjudicating church-state issues to some extent. The Establishment Clause cannot be examined in abstract isolation from the case law. I have endeavored, however (with a few exceptions), to avoid materials that provide a detailed analysis of specific cases or that evaluate the consistency of decisions with prior precedent. Even with regard to the tests the Court utilizes, such as Justice O'Connor's "Endorsement Test," I have tried to select articles that discuss the core principles underlying the test and explain and evaluate the test's purpose and implementation—rather than those that consider its application to specific disputes.

I have also endeavored to avoid suggesting my own answer to the many questions posed by the articles in this volume by providing an editor's overview or perspective. The authors whose work is presented in this anthology speak for themselves, and I leave it to the reader to evaluate their arguments without my assistance. I include my own voice in these debates only as one of many writers whose work is included here—on the same playing field as the other scholars whose work is presented in these pages. The goal of this book is for readers to develop a deeper appreciation of the source and content of the debates about the meaning of the Establishment Clause. It is formally agnostic on how those issues should be resolved.

Given the lack of consensus in Establishment Clause jurisprudence and scholarship, I encountered some tension in editing this volume between the goal of providing readers a range of perspectives reflecting a balanced array of viewpoints on contentious issues and my desire to address the many disputes about the meaning and application of the Establishment Clause that have arisen over the last fifty years. By emphasizing core ideas and values, rather than specific cases and shifts in doctrine, however, I have been able, I believe, to offer readers an unusually varied and balanced set of perspectives that will provide them a solid foundation for understanding and evaluating many of the core debates in this area of constitutional law.

That does not mean, however, that for every article in this anthology there is an analytic counterpoint refuting its arguments. The balance achieved is more holistic than that. Alternative perspectives are not always directly contradictory to each other. Moreover, in some instances, the balance provided in an overall section is not reflected in each chapter. In the section on Government Funding of Religious Institutions and Religious Activities, for example, the materials supporting government aid to religion in different chapters may seem stronger or weaker than the materials opposing such funding arrangements. Critics of the "No Aid" position may have the edge in the Direct Aid chapter while the pendulum may tilt the other way in the chapter on Charitable Choice. Taken in its entirety, however, the section presents balanced perspectives—even if particular chapters may marginally favor one side of the debate over the other.

B. The Free Exercise Clause and the Establishment Clause

The subject of this anthology is the Establishment Clause of the First Amendment. It is the first volume of a set of books on the Bill of Rights that Prometheus Books is publishing. The next volume in the series will focus on the Free Exercise Clause. The decision to divide the discussion of rights into individual books may cause only modest difficulties in determining the substantive contours of most of the books in this series, but it is a major problem for the two anthologies discussing the religion clauses. The line between Free Exercise and Establishment Clause issues is not a clear one. Sometimes these clauses overlap each other. In other circumstances, they seem to be in tension with each other. In both situations, it is difficult to discuss one clause without reference to the other. For example, one argument that is raised against interpreting the Establishment Clause to permit the government to fund both religious organizations and secular organizations on an equal basis is that doing so will undermine the argument that religious organizations should be treated differently than their secular counterparts for Free Exercise purposes. If there is no legitimate basis for singling out religious grantees and limiting their access to government support under the Establishment Clause, because secular and religious grantees are fungible and entitled to equal treatment, then there may be no legitimate basis for singling out religious organizations (or individuals for that matter) under the Free Exercise Clause and providing them exemptions from regulatory burdens that their secular counterparts must obey.

Because of issues like these, it is not possible to discuss either of the religion clauses entirely in isolation. Therefore, readers should not be surprised to discover that some articles in this anthology will refer to Free Exercise concerns at least as a backdrop to their discussion of Establishment Clause issues. Some cross discussion of the other religion clause simply cannot be avoided.

One particular area that requires special mention because it straddles both clauses is the question of whether a legislative accommodation exempting religious organizations or individuals from regulatory burdens so unfairly privileges religion that it violates the Establishment Clause. As a technical doctrinal matter, this is clearly an Establishment Clause issue. The substance of any discussion of this issue, however, goes to the core of debates about the meaning of the Free Exercise Clause. A central concern in interpreting the Free Exercise Clause is whether it is necessary for the judiciary to protect religious practices against governmental interference as a matter of constitutional law or, in the alternative, whether we can rely on the legislature to accommodate religious practices through the political process. Because of the primacy of this question to free exercise jurisprudence, Thomas C. Berg, the editor of the Free Exercise volume, and I agreed that materials discussing Establishment Clause constraints on legislative accommodations of religion should be included in the Free Exercise anthology.

C. The Meaning of the Establishment Clause

This volume is divided into three Sections: The History of the Establishment Clause, Government Funding of Religious Institutions and Religious Activities, and Government Promotion or Expression of Religious Beliefs.

The History section begins with a chapter describing three starkly divergent accounts of the origin of the Establishment Clause in language taken directly from Supreme Court opinions. Justice Black's majority opinion in *Everson v. Board of Education* provided the foundation for the Court's Establishment Clause jurisprudence for several decades. To Justice Black, indeed to the entire Court at this time, the Establishment Clause prohibition against government funding of religious organizations and activities is grounded on a historically recognized constitutional commitment to the separation of church and state. (I have included James Madison's "Memorial and Remonstrance Against Religious Assessments" from the appendix to *Everson* here as well, on the assumption that no discussion of the Establishment Clause can avoid grappling with this seminal statement on the relationship of government and religion.)

Justice Rehnquist's dissenting opinion in *Wallace v. Jaffree* directly challenges the historical account presented in *Everson* and presents an alternative description of the purpose and application of the Establishment Clause. According to Justice Rehnquist, the Establishment Clause does not require government to distance itself from religion. Instead, it permits government to support religion as long as it does not provide preferential treatment to any faith, tradition, or denomination.

Justice Thomas's brief dissenting opinion in *Newdow v. United States* offers an entirely different perspective that challenges the entire development of Establishment Clause doctrine over the last fifty years. He argues that the original purpose of the Establishment Clause was to prevent federal interference with state religious establishments. Pursuant to this understanding, the Establishment Clause does not protect the substantive rights of individuals. As a structural limit on federal power, it could not be incorporated into the Fourteenth Amendment as were other First Amendment guarantees, such as freedom of speech, and it does not operate as a constraint on the actions of state and local government.

Chapter 2 presents conflicting evaluations of the thesis (endorsed by Justice Rehnquist in *Wallace v. Jaffree*) that the Establishment Clause was intended to prohibit preferential treatment of one faith over others, but did not restrict evenhanded government support of religion. Robert L. Cord's article, "Church-State Separation: Restoring the 'No Preference' Doctrine of the First Amendment," argues that an antipreferentialist interpretation of the Establishment Clause most accurately reflects our constitutional history. Douglas Laycock's piece, "'Nonpreferential' Aid to Religion: A False Claim about Original Intent," contends that the Establishment Clause was understood more broadly and prohibited even nonpreferential state support of religion.

Chapter 3 focuses on the federalism question referenced in Justice Thomas's dissent in *Newdow*. Was the Establishment Clause intended to do no more than prohibit the federal government from interfering with each individual state's framework for working out the relationship between government and religion within its borders—including state establishments of religion? Here, four distinct perspectives are presented. In a brief excerpt from his lengthy work, "Toward a General Theory of the Establishment Clause," Daniel O. Conkle suggests that at the time of the drafting and adoption of the Bill of Rights, the substantial differences among the various states with regard to church-state relationships compels the conclusion that no consensus could have developed on any substantive content for the Establishment Clause. Accordingly, the only understanding of the Establishment Clause that could have garnered support was one grounded on federalism and the protection of state rights regarding religion against federal interference. Noah Feldman's article, "The Intellectual Origins of the Establishment Clause," challenges the premise of Conkle's analysis by arguing that there was a common goal that motivated proponents of the Establishment Clause—protecting freedom of conscience—that provided it substantive meaning.

The two other pieces in this chapter focus on the incorporation of the Establishment Clause into the Bill of Rights and its applicability to state governments. An excerpt from Akhil Reed Amar's book, *The Bill of Rights*, construes the Establishment Clause, in historical terms, as a structural constraint on federal power that cannot be meaningfully incorporated into the Fourteenth Amendment and made applicable to the states. Kurt T. Lash's article, "The Second Adoption of the Establishment Clause: The Rise of the Nonestablishment Principle," acknowledges that the original understanding of the Establishment Clause served federalism purposes. Lash argues, however, that by the time of the adoption of the Fourteenth Amendment, the language of the Establishment Clause had developed substantive meaning—and it was this latter understanding of the Clause that was intended to be part of the restrictions on state governments imposed by the Fourteenth Amendment.

Chapter 4 includes two articles that view the history of the Establishment Clause as less certain and more complicated than other writers have suggested. In "The Essential Rights and Liberties of Religion in the American Constitutional Experiment," John Witte Jr. describes a range of overlapping principles that influenced the American polity at the time of the adoption of the Bill of Rights including liberty of conscience, the free exercise of religion, pluralism, equality, separationism, and disestablishment. All of these values played a role in the developing understanding of how church-state relationships should be structured. No single principle, Witte suggests, was adequate to resolve the varying problems presented by religion and government. Laura Underkuffler-Freund also recognizes the complex political and cultural milieu out of which the Establishment Clause developed in "The Separation of the Religious and the Secular: A Foundational Challenge to First Amendment Theory." She rejects more conventional distinctions (such as antipreferentialism or the separation of the religious and the secular) to focus on what she concludes were the two controlling themes of the period: the protection of freedom of conscience and the prevention of aggregations of power arising out of institutional alliances between church and state.

The second section of this anthology addresses Government Funding of Religious Institutions and Religious Activities. It is divided into three chapters: Direct Aid, Indirect Aid or Vouchers, and Charitable Choice and Social Welfare Services by Faith-Based Providers.

Chapter 5, Direct Aid, begins with an excerpt from Michael W. McConnell's article, "Religious Freedom at a Crossroads." McConnell provides an overview of the issue of government funding of religious institutions. He concludes that in the context of a welfare state, the "no aid" position is no longer tenable because it requires faith-based organizations to surrender their religious identities and beliefs in order to be eligible for generally available government subsidies. In contrast to McConnell's arguments, in a much earlier piece, "Federal Funds for Parochial Schools? No," Leo Pfeffer sets out the traditional arguments against aid to religious schools. The constitutional goal of protecting religious liberty does not require the state to subsidize the exercise of religion, Pfeffer argues. Indeed, tax-funded religious education burdens the liberty interests of taxpayers who are forced to subsidize the teaching of religious tenets that they reject.

Paul A. Freund's article, "Public Aid to Parochial Schools," complements Pfeffer's analysis in arguing that forcing taxpayers to contribute to the support of religious schools violates the principle of voluntarism in religious matters which underlies both religion clauses of the First Amendment. Freund also suggests that government financial support of religious education can never be neutral in effect and inevitably entangles the state in religious decisions and politicizes religious differences.

In the final essay in this chapter, "The Establishment Clause and Aid to Parochial Schools," Jesse H. Choper distinguishes between the use of government funds for religious purposes, which the Establishment Clause prohibits, and government grants to religious organizations that are used for secular purposes. As long as the government receives appropriate secular educational value for the funds it contributes to religious schools, Choper argues, the Establishment Clause principle prohibiting taxation and subsidies for religious purposes is not violated.

Chapter 6 focuses on Indirect Aid or Vouchers. Notwithstanding their emphasis on vouchers, however, many of the arguments presented in the five articles included in this chapter would be relevant to the discussion of direct aid as well. The first two articles, "The Increasingly Anachronistic Case against School Vouchers" by Ira C. Lupu and "The Price of Vouchers for Religious Freedom" by Laura S. Underkuffler, complement each other in important respects. Both writers address the real world value of vouchers in personal terms but reach different conclusions as to the cost of such programs. To Lupu, restrictions on indirect aid to religious organizations serve no important purpose today. They are the product of outdated religious demographics in our society and an overreading of Madison's historic challenge to government assessments for religious purposes in Virginia. Underkuffler argues, to the contrary, that a constitutional rule permitting the public funding of religious institutions on the same terms as their secular counterparts will have serious consequences for religious liberty. The argument that there is nothing special about religion that justifies prohibiting the use of tax revenue for religious purposes will seriously undermine the core principle that there is something unique about religion that warrants providing it special constitutional protection against state interference.

The next two articles, "School Vouchers and Religious Liberty: Seven Questions from Madison's *Memorial and Remonstrance*" by Vincent Blasi and "Evaluating School Voucher Programs through a Liberty, Equality, and Free

Speech Matrix" by Alan E. Brownstein, also approach the voucher issue from somewhat parallel perspectives. Both writers consider a range of factors in evaluating the constitutionality of voucher programs including concerns about religious institutions becoming dependent on state vouchers, the unequal level of state financial support that different religious communities will receive from voucher programs, and the extent to which state funding will promote the fragmentation of public services (such as education) along religious lines. They also are somewhat tentative in their conclusions. But, on balance, for Blasi, voucher programs should withstand constitutional challenge, while, for Brownstein, the constitutionality of many voucher programs would be problematic.

The last article in the chapter is an excerpt from Thomas C. Berg's work, "Vouchers and Religious Schools: The New Constitutional Questions." Berg describes and defends the Supreme Court's recent decision in *Zelman v. Simmons-Harris*, which upholds a voucher program providing subsidies to religious schools against an Establishment Clause challenge.

Chapter 7 focuses on "charitable choice" laws authorizing government aid to religious organizations that provide various kinds of social welfare services to their clients. The first article in this chapter, "A Constitutional Case for Governmental Cooperation with Faith-Based Social Service Providers" by Carl H. Esbeck, defends the constitutionality of such programs under the rubric of "neutrality theory." This model for interpreting the Establishment Clause suggests that government must not distinguish between religious and nonreligious grantees for the purpose of funding the providers of social services, but government may accommodate these state subsidized religious organizations by providing them exemptions from regulatory requirements—even when those exemptions are not available to their secular counterparts. Alan E. Brownstein's article, "Interpreting the Religion Clauses in Terms of Liberty, Equality, and Free Speech Values—A Critical Analysis of 'Neutrality Theory' and Charitable Choice," criticizes the "neutrality theory" justification for charitable choice laws. Brownstein argues that these laws do not operate neutrally in the real world and that by fragmenting the provision of publicly funded social services on religious lines, charitable choice laws will often disadvantage members of minority faiths. In the final piece in this chapter, "Remembering the Values of Separatism and State Funding of Religious Organizations (Charitable Choice): To Aid Is not Necessarily to Protect," William P. Marshall argues that while many charitable choice laws would be upheld as constitutional, such laws are not necessarily beneficial for religion. They endanger the integrity and autonomy of religious organizations by creating a dependency on government financial support and will inevitably entangle government and religion when the state monitors and evaluates the work of religious grantees.

The next section of the anthology addresses questions about the government's promotion of religious beliefs and its expression of religious messages. Chapter 8 begins the section by presenting divergent perspectives on the role of government in fostering, acknowledging, or promoting religious beliefs. In a second excerpt from "Religious Freedom at a Crossroads," Michael W. McConnell argues that it is impossible for government to be strictly neutral with regard to religious beliefs and that a constitutional mandate requiring government silence on religious issues would unfairly secularize American society. The approach he supports would permit government to communicate religious messages in a way that reflects or "mirrors" the diversity of religious beliefs in the community. In contrast, Douglas Laycock's article, "Religious Liberty as Liberty," contends that government should stay out of the business of sponsoring religious messages while maintaining full and open opportunities for the private expression of religious beliefs. To Laycock, religion is far more important to individuals than it is to government. Thus, permitting government involvement in religious debate does little to further government's legitimate goals, while it exacerbates fears that government is attempting to influence the religious beliefs of citizens in the service of dominant religious factions.

Chapter 9 addresses the problem of religious equality and the Establishment Clause test that most strongly reflects a constitutional concern about the equal status of religious groups in American communities, Justice O'Connor's Endorsement Test. The first two articles in this chapter discuss whether there is any basis for interpreting the Establishment Clause to protect religious equality as well as religious liberty. Noah Feldman, in his article "From Liberty to Equality: The Transformation of the Establishment Clause," argues that there is nothing distinctive about religion or religious minorities as a class that justifies protecting their identity against symbolic harms as a constitutional matter. To Feldman, the government's conveying a message of political inequality to non-Christians raises no more serious a constitutional question than the government's conveying a similar message to political minorities. In direct contrast to Feldman's thesis, in "Harmonizing the Heavenly and Earthly Spheres: The Fragmentation and Synthesis of Religion, Equality, and Speech in the Constitution," Alan E. Brownstein contends that religious minorities deserve constitutional protection against status harms under the Establishment Clause for many of the same reasons that racial and ethnic minorities are protected against stigmatic injuries by the Equal Protection Clause.

The next two articles present divergent perspectives on the issue of whether the Establishment Clause restricts the government's ability to endorse religious beliefs. In "Symbols, Perceptions, and Doctrinal Illusions: Establishment Neutrality and the 'No Endorsement' Test," Steven D. Smith suggests that the concept of endorsing religion is too indeterminate to be employed as a constitutional standard limiting government action. Further, Smith maintains that concerns about the alienation of religious groups, or increased divisiveness among religious groups, do not provide an adequate justification for prohibiting religious endorsements. Conversely, Andrew Koppelman argues in his article, "Secular Purpose," that a bedrock principle of the Establishment Clause must be that the state cannot declare religious truth. While there may be some close cases, Koppelman maintains that there are also many cases where the message the state is communicating clearly expresses or endorses the truth of a religious belief—and in these cases, the state's action should be struck down as unconstitutional.

The final article in this chapter is "The Pledge of Allegiance and the Limited State" by Thomas C. Berg. Berg critically evaluates the arguments raised on both sides of the controversial Establishment Clause challenge to including the phrase "under God" in the Pledge of Allegiance. He concludes that the strongest argument for allowing "under God" to be part of the Pledge is that it should be permissible for government to identify the religious rationale for a limited state—since that idea serves as the foundation for many of the rights the Constitution protects. Berg also recognizes, however, that by calling on citizens to affirm the message of the Pledge, the state may be doing much more than offering a religious rationale for the protection of liberty and justice for all. It is this aspect of the Pledge that provides the strongest basis for holding it to be unconstitutional.

Chapter 10 explores an alternative understanding of the Establishment Clause—one that focuses on coercion rather the endorsement of religion. The first article in this chapter, "Coercion: The Lost Element of Establishment" by Michael W. McConnell, suggests that, as an historical matter, the problems that prompted the framers to adopt the Establishment Clause involved government coercion and compulsion. McConnell contends that if protection against coercion was recognized to be an essential element of Establishment Clause claims, doctrine in this area would be both improved and simplified. Douglas Laycock's article, "'Noncoercive' Support for Religion: Another False Claim about the Establishment Clause," disputes the contention that the framers distinguished between coercive and noncoercive support of religion. Further, Laycock argues, there are sound reasons to prohibit even noncoercive government support of religious beliefs. These state promotions of religion either denigrate religious minorities, or, in an attempt not to do so, communicate a watered down version of religion that is unacceptable to the devout and of little value to everyone else.

The final two articles in this chapter debate the merits of a coercion test for the Establishment Clause in the context of discussing the Supreme Court's decision in *Lee v. Weisman*, the case that struck down state-sponsored school prayers offered at high school graduation ceremonies. Steven G. Gey argues in "Religious Coercion and the Establishment Clause" that the Court's opinion in *Lee v. Weisman* demonstrates the inadequacy of a coercion test. Although the majority opinion claims to be applying a coercion standard, Gey suggests that it actually retreats from any serious commitment to that approach because limiting the Establishment Clause to situations involving actual coercion by government would so obviously lead to unacceptable and unfair results. While acknowledging in "*Lemon* Is Dead" that there are some flaws in the majority's analysis in *Lee v. Weisman*, Michael Stokes Paulsen's article supports both the adoption of the coercion test and its use to strike down state-sponsored prayers at graduation ceremonies. According to Paulsen, states cannot compel high school students to attend even brief religious services by conditioning the benefit of participating in their graduation ceremony on their doing so.

D. Logistical Choices and Exercises of Editorial Discretion

Although the editorial parameters of this anthology may be self-evident to some readers, let me explain some of the editorial considerations employed in the production of this book. First, many of the articles presented have been aggressively edited. In some cases, they are very brief excerpts of much longer works. Given the length of much of the scholarly writing on church-state issues, heavy editing of most works was unavoidable. I have tried to maintain the integrity of the author's arguments, but in doing so I have often had to eliminate examples and tangential discussions that added considerably to the persuasiveness and value of their work. Interested readers should consult the original articles in their entirety to obtain the full flavor and content of each writer's work.

Similarly, I have taken a minimalist approach to footnotes and only include citations to named cases or quotations. Again, the original articles contain a wealth of references that authoritatively support the arguments presented in the text, and I urge readers to examine these articles directly to evaluate the underlying foundations of the various authors' arguments.

While my goal with this work was to provide readers a range of balanced perspectives, I did not feel obliged to maximize the number of authors whose work I included in this anthology. Accordingly, several scholars have more than one article included in this volume. Sometimes, this was a fortuitous consequence of my attempt to provide balanced commentary on a specific issue. Certain articles simply complemented each other in a particularly effective way. In other cases, these decisions reflect the stature of particular scholars and the quality of their work. It should come as no surprise to anyone conversant in the literature in this area, for example, to learn that Douglas Laycock and Michael McConnell have multiple articles included in an anthology on the Establishment Clause.

Needless to say, there are many excellent articles by distinguished scholars that I could not include in this volume because of page limitations. The content of the cutting room floor from this book could have easily provided materials for another volume of comparable size and quality. The wealth of valuable scholarship on the meaning of the Establishment Clause made the task of compiling this anthology a formidable challenge and a humbling experience.

SECTION I

THE HISTORY OF THE ESTABLISHMENT CLAUSE

CHAPTER 1

SUPREME COURT JUSTICES ON THE HISTORY OF THE ESTABLISHMENT CLAUSE

EVERSON V. BOARD OF EDUCATION OF THE TOWNSHIP OF EWING, ET AL.

330 U.S. 1 (1946)

MR. JUSTICE BLACK delivered the opinion of the Court.

A New Jersey statute authorizes its local school districts to make rules and contracts for the transportation of children to and from schools. The appellee, a township board of education, acting pursuant to this statute, authorized reimbursement to parents of money expended by them for the bus transportation of their children on regular busses operated by the public transportation system. Part of this money was for the payment of transportation of some children in the community to Catholic parochial schools. These church schools give their students, in addition to secular education, regular religious instruction conforming to the religious tenets and modes of worship of the Catholic Faith. The superintendent of these schools is a Catholic priest.

Everson v. Board of Education of the Township of Ewing, et al., in "Cases Adjudged in the Supreme Court of the United States at October Term, 1946": 3, 8–13, 15–18, 63–72.

***

The New Jersey statute is challenged as a "law respecting an establishment of religion." The First Amendment, as made applicable to the states by the Fourteenth... commands that a state "shall make no law respecting an establishment of religion, or prohibiting the free exercise thereof...." These words of the First Amendment reflected in the minds of early Americans a vivid mental picture of conditions and practices which they fervently wished to stamp out in order to preserve liberty for themselves and for their posterity. ... Whether this New Jersey law is one respecting an "establishment of religion" requires an understanding of the meaning of that language, particularly with respect to the imposition of taxes.... [T]herefore, it is not inappropriate briefly to review the background and environment of the period in which that constitutional language was fashioned and adopted.

A large proportion of the early settlers of this country came here from Europe to escape the bondage of laws which compelled them to support and attend government-favored churches. The centuries immediately before and contemporaneous with the colonization of America had been filled with turmoil, civil strife, and persecutions, generated in large part by established sects determined to maintain their absolute political and religious supremacy. With the power of government supporting them, at various times and places, Catholics had persecuted Protestants, Protestants had persecuted Catholics, Protestant sects had persecuted other Protestant sects, Catholics of one shade of belief had persecuted Catholics of another shade of belief, and all of these had from time to time persecuted Jews. In efforts to force loyalty to whatever religious group happened to be on top and in league with the government of a particular time and place, men and women had been fined, cast in jail, cruelly tortured, and killed. Among the offenses for which these punishments had been inflicted were such things as speaking disrespectfully of the views of ministers of government-established churches, non-attendance at those churches, expressions of nonbelief in their doctrines, and failure to pay taxes and tithes to support them.

These practices of the old world were transplanted to and began to thrive in the soil of the new America.... Catholics found themselves hounded and proscribed because of their faith; Quakers who followed their conscience went to jail; Baptists were peculiarly obnoxious to certain dominant Protestant sects; men and women of varied faiths who happened to be in a minority in a particular locality were persecuted because they steadfastly persisted in worshipping God only as their own consciences dictated. And all of these dissenters were compelled to pay tithes and taxes to support government-sponsored churches whose ministers preached inflammatory sermons designed to strengthen and consolidate the established faith by generating a burning hatred against dissenters.

These practices became so commonplace as to shock the freedom-loving colonials into a feeling of abhorrence. The imposition of taxes to pay ministers' salaries and to build and maintain churches and church property aroused their indignation. It was these feelings which found expression in the First Amendment. No one locality and no one group throughout the Colonies can rightly be given entire credit for having aroused the sentiment that culminated in adoption of the Bill of Rights' provisions embracing religious liberty. But Virginia, where the established church had achieved a dominant influence in political affairs and where many excesses attracted wide public attention, provided a great stimulus and able leadership for the movement. The people there, as elsewhere, reached the conviction that individual religious liberty could be achieved best under a government which was stripped of all power to tax, to support, or otherwise to assist any or all religions, or to interfere with the beliefs of any religious individual or group.

The movement toward this end reached its dramatic climax in Virginia in 1785–86 when the Virginia legislative body was about to renew Virginia's tax levy for the support of the established church. Thomas Jefferson and James Madison led the fight against this tax. Madison wrote his great Memorial and Remonstrance against the law. In it, he eloquently argued that a true religion did not need the support of law; that no person, either believer or non-believer, should be taxed to support a religious institution of any kind; that the best interest of a society required that the minds of men always be wholly free; and that cruel persecutions were the inevitable result of government-established religions. Madison's Remonstrance received strong support throughout Virginia, and the Assembly postponed consideration of the proposed tax measure until its next session. When the proposal came up for consideration at that session, it not only died in committee, but the Assembly enacted the famous "Virginia Bill for Religious Liberty" originally written by Thomas Jefferson. The preamble to that Bill stated among other things that

> Almighty God hath created the mind free; that all attempts to influence it by
> temporal punishments or burthens, or by civil incapacitations, tend only to

beget habits of hypocrisy and meanness, and are a departure from the plan of the Holy author of our religion, who being Lord both of body and mind, yet chose not to propagate it by coercions on either…; that to compel a man to furnish contributions of money for the propagation of opinions which he disbelieves, is sinful and tyrannical; that even the forcing him to support this or that teacher of his own religious persuasion, is depriving him of the comfortable liberty of giving his contributions to the particular pastor, whose morals he would make his pattern.…

And the statute itself enacted

[t]hat no man shall be compelled to frequent or support any religious worship, place, or ministry whatsoever, nor shall be enforced, restrained, molested, or burthened in his body or goods, nor shall otherwise suffer on account of his religious opinions or belief.…

This Court has previously recognized that the provisions of the First Amendment, in the drafting and adoption of which Madison and Jefferson played such leading roles, had the same objective and were intended to provide the same protection against governmental intrusion on religious liberty as the Virginia statute.

**

The "establishment of religion" clause of the First Amendment means at least this: Neither a state nor the Federal Government can set up a church. Neither can pass laws which aid one religion, aid all religions, or prefer one religion over another. Neither can force nor influence a person to go to or to remain away from church against his will or force him to profess a belief or disbelief in any religion. No person can be punished for entertaining or professing religious beliefs or disbeliefs, for church attendance or non-attendance. No tax in any amount, large or small, can be levied to support any religious activities or institutions, whatever they may be called, or whatever form they may adopt to teach or practice religion. Neither a state nor the Federal Government can, openly or secretly, participate in the affairs of any religious organizations or groups and vice versa. In the words of Jefferson, the clause against establishment of religion by law was intended to erect "a wall of separation between church and State." *Reynolds v. United States,* [98 U.S. 145] at 164.

We must consider the New Jersey statute in accordance with the fore-going limitations imposed by the First Amendment. But we must not strike that state statute down if it is within the State's constitutional power even though it approaches the verge of that power. New Jersey cannot consistently with the "establishment of religion" clause of the First Amendment con-tribute tax-raised funds to the support of an institution which teaches the tenets and faith of any church. On the other hand, other language of the amendment commands that New Jersey cannot hamper its citizens in the free exercise of their own religion. Consequently, it cannot exclude individual Catholics, Lutherans, Mohammedans, Baptists, Jews, Methodists, Non-believers, Presbyterians, or the members of any other faith, because of their faith, or lack of it, from receiving the benefits of public welfare legislation. While we do not mean to intimate that a state could not provide transporta-tion only to children attending public schools, we must be careful, in pro-tecting the citizens of New Jersey against state-established churches, to be sure that we do not inadvertently prohibit New Jersey from extending its gen-eral state law benefits to all its citizens without regard to their religious belief.

Measured by these standards, we cannot say that the First Amendment prohibits New Jersey from spending tax-raised funds to pay the bus fares of parochial school pupils as a part of a general program under which it pays the fares of pupils attending public and other schools. It is undoubtedly true that children are helped to get to church schools. There is even a possibility that some of the children might not be sent to the church schools if the parents were compelled to pay their children's bus fares out of their own pockets when transportation to a public school would have been paid for by the State. The same possibility exists where the state requires a local transit company to provide reduced fares to school children including those attending parochial schools, or where a municipally owned transportation system undertakes to carry all school children free of charge. Moreover, state-paid policemen, detailed to protect children going to and from church schools from the very real hazards of traffic, would serve much the same purpose and accomplish much the same result as state provisions intended to guarantee free trans-portation of a kind which the state deems to be best for the school children's welfare. And parents might refuse to risk their children to the serious danger of traffic accidents going to and from parochial schools, the approaches to which were not protected by policemen. Similarly, parents might be reluctant to permit their children to attend schools which the state had cut off from such general government services as ordinary police and fire protection, connections for sewage disposal, public highways, and sidewalks. Of course, cutting off church schools from these services, so separate and so indisputably marked off from the religious function, would make it far more difficult for the schools to operate. But such is obviously not the purpose of the First Amendment. That Amendment requires the state to be a neutral in its relations with groups of religious believers and non-believers; it does not require the state to be their adversary. State power is no more to be used so as to handicap religions than it is to favor them.

This Court has said that parents may, in the discharge of their duty under state compulsory education laws, send their children to a religious rather than a public school if the school meets the secular educational requirements which the state has power to impose. It appears that these parochial schools meet New Jersey's requirements. The State contributes no money to the schools. It does not support them. Its legislation, as applied, does no more than provide a general program to help parents get their children, regardless of their religion, safely and expeditiously to and from accredited schools.

The First Amendment has erected a wall between church and state. That wall must be kept high and impregnable. We could not approve the slightest breach. New Jersey has not breached it here.

***

APPENDIX [CITATIONS OMITTED]

MEMORIAL AND REMONSTRANCE
AGAINST RELIGIOUS ASSESSMENTS.

To THE HONORABLE THE GENERAL ASSEMBLY

OF THE COMMONWEALTH OF VIRGINIA.

A MEMORIAL AND REMONSTRANCE.

We, the subscribers, citizens of the said Commonwealth, having taken into serious consideration, a Bill printed by order of the last Session of General Assembly, entitled "A Bill Establishing a Provision for Teachers of the Christian Religion," and conceiving that the same, if finally armed with the sanctions of a law, will be a dangerous abuse of power, are bound as faithful members of a free State, to remonstrate against it, and to declare the reasons by which we are determined. We remonstrate against the said Bill,

1. Because we hold it for a fundamental and undeniable truth, "that Religion or the duty which we owe to our Creator and the Manner of discharging it, can be directed only by reason and conviction, not by force or violence." The Religion then of every man must be left to the conviction and conscience of every man; and it is the right of every man to exercise it as these may dictate. This right is in its nature an unalienable right. It is unalienable; because the opinions of men, depending only on the evidence contemplated by their own minds, cannot follow the dictates of other men: It is unalienable also; because what is here a right towards men, is a duty towards the Creator. It is the duty of every man to render to the Creator such homage, and such only, as he believes to be acceptable to him. This duty is precedent both in order of time and degree of obligation, to the claims of Civil Society. Before any man can be considered as a member of Civil Society, he must be considered as a subject of the Governor of the Universe: And if a member of Civil Society, who enters into any subordinate Association, must always do it with a reservation of his duty to the general authority; much more must every man who becomes a member of any particular Civil Society, do it with a saving of his allegiance to the Universal Sovereign. We maintain therefore that in matters of Religion, no man's right is abridged by the institution of Civil Society, and that Religion is wholly exempt from its cognizance. True it is, that no other rule exists, by which any question which may divide a Society, can be ultimately determined, but the will of the majority; but it is also true, that the majority may trespass on the rights of the minority.

2. Because if religion be exempt from the authority of the Society at large, still less can it be subject to that of the Legislative Body. The latter are but the creatures and vicegerents of the former. Their jurisdiction is both derivative and limited: it is limited with regard to the coordinate departments, more necessarily is it limited with regard to the constituents. The preservation of a free government requires not merely, that the metes and bounds which separate each department of power may be invariably maintained; but more especially, that neither of them be suffered to overleap the great Barrier which defends the rights of the people. The Rulers who are guilty of such an encroachment, exceed the commission from which they derive their authority, and are Tyrants. The People who submit to it are governed by laws made neither by themselves, nor by an authority derived from them, and are slaves.

3. Because it is proper to take alarm at the first experiment on our liberties. We hold this prudent jealousy to be the first duty of citizens, and one of [the] noblest characteristics of the late Revolution. The freemen of America did not wait till usurped power had strengthened itself by exercise, and entangled the question in precedents. They saw all the consequences in the principle, and they avoided the consequences by denying the principle. We revere this lesson too much, soon to forget it. Who does not see that the same authority which can establish Christianity, in exclusion of all other Religions, may establish with the same ease any particular sect of Christians, in exclusion of all other Sects? That the same authority which can force a citizen to contribute three pence only of his property for the support of any one establishment, may force him to conform to any other establishment in all cases whatsoever?

4. Because the bill violates that equality which ought to be the basis of every law, and which is more indispensable, in proportion as the validity or expediency of any law is more liable to be impeached. If "all men are by nature equally free and independent," all men are to be considered as entering into Society on equal conditions; as relinquishing no more, and therefore retaining no less, one than another, of their natural rights. Above all are they to be considered as retaining an "equal title to the free exercise of Religion according to the dictates of conscience." Whilst we assert for ourselves a freedom to embrace, to profess and to observe the Religion which we believe to be of divine origin, we cannot deny an equal freedom to those whose minds have not yet yielded to the evidence which has convinced us. If this freedom be abused, it is an offense against God, not against man: To God, therefore, not to men, must an account of it be rendered. As the Bill violates equality by subjecting some to peculiar burdens; so it violates the same principle, by granting to others peculiar exemptions. Are the Quakers and Menonists the only sects who think a compulsive support of their religions unnecessary and unwarrantable? Can their piety alone be entrusted with the care of public worship? Ought their Religions to be endowed above all others, with extraordinary privileges, by which proselytes may be enticed from all others? We think too favorably of the justice and good sense of these denominations, to believe that they either covet pre-eminencies over their fellow citizens, or that they will be seduced by them, from the common opposition to the measure.

5. Because the bill implies either that the Civil Magistrate is a competent Judge of Religious truth; or that he may employ Religion as an engine of Civil

policy. The first is an arrogant pretension falsified by the contradictory opinions of Rulers in all ages, and throughout the world: The second an unhallowed perversion of the means of salvation.

6. Because the establishment proposed by the Bill is not requisite for the support of the Christian Religion. To say that it is, is a contradiction to the Christian Religion itself; for every page of it disavows a dependence on the powers of this world: it is a contradiction to fact; for it is known that this Religion both existed and flourished, not only without the support of human laws, but in spite of every opposition from them; and not only during the period of miraculous aid, but long after it had been left to its own evidence, and the ordinary care of Providence: Nay, it is a contradiction in terms; for a Religion not invented by human policy, must have pre-existed and been supported, before it was established by human policy. It is moreover to weaken in those who profess this Religion a pious confidence in its innate excellence, and the patronage of its Author; and to foster in those who still reject it, a suspicion that its friends are too conscious of its fallacies, to trust it to its own merits.

7. Because experience witnesses that ecclesiastical establishments, instead of maintaining the purity and efficacy of Religion, have had a contrary operation. During almost fifteen centuries, has the legal establishment of Christianity been on trial. What have been its fruits? More or less in all places, pride and indolence in the Clergy; ignorance and servility in the laity; in both, superstition, bigotry, and persecution. Enquire of the Teachers of Christianity for the ages in which it appeared in its greatest luster; those of every sect, point to the ages prior to its incorporation with Civil policy. Propose a restoration of this primitive state in which its Teachers depended on the voluntary rewards of their flocks; many of them predict its downfall. On which side ought their testimony to have greatest weight, when for or when against their interest?

8. Because the establishment in question is not necessary for the support of Civil Government. If it be urged as necessary for the support of Civil Government only as it is a means of supporting Religion, and it be not necessary for the latter purpose, it cannot be necessary for the former. If Religion be not within [the] cognizance of Civil Government, how can its legal establishment be said to be necessary to Civil Government? What influence in fact have ecclesiastical establishments had on Civil Society? In some instances they have been seen to erect a spiritual tyranny on the ruins of Civil authority; in many instances they have been seen upholding the thrones of political

tyranny; in no instance have they been seen the guardians of the liberties of the people. Rulers who wished to subvert the public liberty, may have found an established clergy convenient auxiliaries. A just government, instituted to secure and perpetuate it, needs them not. Such a government will be best supported by protecting every citizen in the enjoyment of his Religion with the same equal hand which protects his person and his property; by neither invading the equal rights of any Sect, nor suffering any Sect to invade those of another.

9. Because the proposed establishment is a departure from that generous policy, which, offering an asylum to the persecuted and oppressed of every Nation and Religion, promised a luster to our country, and an accession to the number of its citizens. What a melancholy mark is the Bill of sudden degeneracy? Instead of holding forth, an asylum to the persecuted, it is itself a signal of persecution. It degrades from the equal rank of Citizens all those whose opinions in Religion do not bend to those of the Legislative authority. Distant as it may be, in its present form, from the Inquisition it differs from it only in degree. The one is the first step, the other the last in the career of intolerance. The magnanimous sufferer under this cruel scourge in foreign Regions, must view the Bill as a Beacon on our Coast, warning him to seek some other haven, where liberty and philanthrophy in their due extent may offer a more certain repose from his troubles.

10. Because it will have a like tendency to banish our Citizens. The allurements presented by other situations are every day thinning their number. To superadd a fresh motive to emigration, by revoking the liberty which they now enjoy, would be the same species of folly which has dishonored and depopulated flourishing kingdoms.

11. Because it will destroy that moderation and harmony which the forbearance of our laws to intermeddle with Religion, has produced amongst its several sects. Torrents of blood have been spilt in the old world, by vain attempts of the secular arm to extinguish Religious discord, by proscribing all difference in Religious opinions. Time has at length revealed the true remedy. Every relaxation of narrow and rigorous policy, wherever it has been tried, has been found to assuage the disease. The American Theatre has exhibited proofs, that equal and compleat liberty, if it does not wholly eradicate it, sufficiently destroys its malignant influence on the health and prosperity of the State. If with the salutary effects of this system under our own eyes, we begin to contract the bonds of Religious freedom, we know no name that will too

severely reproach our folly. At least let warning be taken at the first fruits of the threatened innovation. The very appearance of the Bill has transformed that "Christian forbearance, love and charity," which of late mutually prevailed, into animosities and jealousies, which may not soon be appeased. What mischiefs may not be dreaded should this enemy to the public quiet be armed with the force of a law?

12. Because the policy of the bill is adverse to the diffusion of the light of Christianity. The first wish of those who enjoy this precious gift, ought to be that it may be imparted to the whole race of mankind. Compare the number of those who have as yet received it with the number still remaining under the dominion of false Religions; and how small is the former! Does the policy of the Bill tend to lessen the disproportion? No; it at once discourages those who are strangers to the light of [revelation] from coming into the Region of it; and countenances, by example the nations who continue in darkness, in shutting out those who might convey it to them. Instead of leveling as far as possible, every obstacle to the victorious progress of truth, the Bill with an ignoble and unchristian timidity would circumscribe it, with a wall of defense, against the encroachments of error.

13. Because attempts to enforce by legal sanctions, acts obnoxious to so great a proportion of Citizens, tend to enervate the laws in general, and to slacken the bands of Society. If it be difficult to execute any law which is not generally deemed necessary or salutary, what must be the case where it is deemed invalid and dangerous? And what may be the effect of so striking an example of impotency in the Government, on its general authority.

14. Because a measure of such singular magnitude and delicacy ought not to be imposed, without the clearest evidence that it is called for by a majority of citizens: and no satisfactory method is yet proposed by which the voice of the majority in this case may be determined, or its influence secured. "The people of the respective counties are indeed requested to signify their opinion respecting the adoption of the Bill to the next Session of Assembly." But the representation must be made equal, before the voice either of the Representatives or of the Counties, will be that of the people. Our hope is that neither of the former will, after due consideration, espouse the dangerous principle of the Bill. Should the event disappoint us, it will still leave us in full confidence, that a fair appeal to the latter will reverse the sentence against our liberties.

15. Because, finally, "the equal right of every citizen to the free exercise of his Religion according to the dictates of conscience" is held by the same

tenure with all our other rights. If we recur to its origin, it is equally the gift of nature; if we weigh its importance, it cannot be less dear to us; if we consult the Declaration of those rights which pertain to the good people of Virginia, as the "basis and foundation of Government," it is enumerated with equal solemnity, or rather studied emphasis. Either then, we must say, that the will of the Legislature is the only measure of their authority; and that in the plenitude of this authority, they may sweep away all our fundamental rights; or, that they are bound to leave this particular right untouched and sacred. Either we must say, that they may control the freedom of the press, may abolish the trial by jury, may swallow up the Executive and Judiciary Powers of the State; nay that they may despoil us of our very right of suffrage, and erect themselves into an independent and hereditary assembly; or we must say, that they have no authority to enact into law the Bill under consideration. We the subscribers say, that the General Assembly of this Commonwealth have no such authority: And that no effort may be omitted on our part against so dangerous an usurpation, we oppose to it, this remonstrance; earnestly praying, as we are in duty bound, that the Supreme Lawgiver of the Universe, by illuminating those to whom it is addressed, may on the one hand, turn their councils from every act which would affront his holy prerogative, or violate the trust committed to them; and on the other, guide them into every measure which may be worthy of his [blessing, may re]dound to their own praise, and may establish more firmly the liberties, the prosperity, and the Happiness of the Commonwealth.

WALLACE, GOVERNOR OF ALABAMA, ET AL. V. JAFFREE, ET AL.

472 U.S. 38 (1985)

JUSTICE REHNQUIST, dissenting.

Thirty-eight years ago this Court, in *Everson v. Board of Education*, 330 U.S. 1, 16 (1947), summarized its exegesis of Establishment Clause doctrine thus:

> In the words of Jefferson, the clause against establishment of religion by law was intended to erect "a wall of separation between church and State." *Reynolds v. United States*, [98 U. S. 145, 164 (1879)].

This language from *Reynolds*, a case involving the Free Exercise Clause of the First Amendment rather than the Establishment Clause, quoted from Thomas

---

Wallace, Governor of Alabama, et al. v. Jaffree, et al., in "Cases Adjudged in the Supreme Court of the United States at October Term, 1984": 91–92, 95–95, 98–106, 108, 110–13.

43

Jefferson's letter to the Danbury Baptist Association the phrase, "I contemplate with sovereign reverence that act of the whole American people which declared that their legislature should 'make no law respecting an establishment of religion, or prohibiting the free exercise thereof,' thus building a wall of separation between church and State." 8 Writings of Thomas Jefferson 113 (H. Washington ed. 1861).

It is impossible to build sound constitutional doctrine upon a mistaken understanding of constitutional history, but unfortunately the Establishment Clause has been expressly freighted with Jefferson's misleading metaphor for nearly 40 years. Thomas Jefferson was of course in France at the time the constitutional Amendments known as the Bill of Rights were passed by Congress and ratified by the States. His letter to the Danbury Baptist Association was a short note of courtesy, written 14 years after the Amendments were passed by Congress. He would seem to any detached observer as a less than ideal source of contemporary history as to the meaning of the Religion Clauses of the First Amendment.

Jefferson's fellow Virginian, James Madison, with whom he was joined in the battle for the enactment of the Virginia Statute of Religious Liberty of 1786, did play as large a part as anyone in the drafting of the Bill of Rights. He had two advantages over Jefferson in this regard: he was present in the United States, and he was a leading Member of the First Congress. But when we turn to the record of the proceedings in the First Congress leading up to the adoption of the Establishment Clause of the Constitution, including Madison's significant contributions thereto, we see a far different picture of its purpose than the highly simplified "wall of separation between church and State."

***

The language Madison proposed for what ultimately became the Religion Clauses of the First Amendment was this:

> The civil rights of none shall be abridged on account of religious belief or worship, nor shall any national religion be established, nor shall the full and equal rights of conscience be in any manner, or on any pretext, infringed. [1 *Annals of Congress* 434]

On the same day that Madison proposed them, the amendments which formed the basis for the Bill of Rights were referred by the House to a Committee of the Whole, and after several weeks' delay were then referred to a Select Committee consisting of Madison and 10 others. The Committee revised Madison's proposal regarding the establishment of religion to read:

> No religion shall be established by law, nor shall the equal rights of conscience be infringed. Ibid., at 729.

***

On the basis of the record of [the] proceedings in the House of Representatives [discussing the First Amendment], James Madison was undoubtedly the most important architect among the Members of the House of the Amendments which became the Bill of Rights, but it was James Madison speaking as an advocate of sensible legislative compromise, not as an advocate of incorporating the Virginia Statute of Religious Liberty into the United States Constitution. During the ratification debate in the Virginia Convention, Madison had actually opposed the idea of any Bill of Rights. His sponsorship of the Amendments in the House was obviously not that of a zealous believer in the necessity of the Religion Clauses, but of one who felt it might do some good, could do no harm, and would satisfy those who had ratified the Constitution on the condition that Congress propose a Bill of Rights. His original language "nor shall any national religion be established" obviously does not conform to the "wall of separation" between church and State idea which latter-day commentators have ascribed to him....

It seems indisputable from [what we can learn of Madison's thinking from his comments on the floor of the House] in 1789, that he saw the Amendment as designed to prohibit the establishment of a national religion, and perhaps to prevent discrimination among sects. He did not see it as requiring neutrality on the part of government between religion and irreligion. Thus the Court's opinion in *Everson*—while correct in bracketing Madison and Jefferson together in their exertions in their home State leading to the enactment of the Virginia Statute of Religious Liberty—is totally incorrect in suggesting that Madison carried these views onto the floor of the United States House of Representatives when he proposed the language which would ultimately become the Bill of Rights.

***

None of the other Members of Congress who spoke during the...debate [about the First Amendment] expressed the slightest indication that they thought the language before them from the Select Committee, or the evil to be aimed at, would require that the Government be absolutely neutral as between religion and irreligion. The evil to be aimed at, so far as those who spoke were concerned, appears to have been the establishment of a national church, and perhaps the preference of one religious sect over another; but it was definitely not concerned about whether the Government might aid all religions evenhandedly....

The actions of the First Congress, which reenacted the Northwest Ordinance for the governance of the Northwest Territory in 1789, confirm the view that Congress did not mean that the Government should be neutral between religion and irreligion. The House of Representatives took up the Northwest Ordinance on the same day as Madison introduced his proposed amendments which became the Bill of Rights; while at that time the Federal Government was of course not bound by draft amendments to the Constitution which had not yet been proposed by Congress, say nothing of ratified by the States, it seems highly unlikely that the House of Representatives would simultaneously consider proposed amendments to the Constitution and enact an important piece of territorial legislation which conflicted with the intent of those proposals. The Northwest Ordinance, 1 Stat. 50, reenacted the Northwest Ordinance of 1787 and provided that "[r]eligion, morality, and knowledge, being necessary to good government and the happiness of mankind, schools and the means of education shall forever be encouraged." Ibid., at 52, n. (*a*). Land grants for schools in the Northwest Territory were not limited to public schools. It was not until 1845 that Congress limited land grants in the new States and Territories to nonsectarian schools. 5 Stat. 788; C. Antieau, A. Downey, and E. Roberts, *Freedom from Federal Establishment* 163 (1964).

On the day after the House of Representatives voted to adopt the form of the First Amendment Religion Clauses which was ultimately proposed and ratified, Representative Elias Boudinot proposed a resolution asking President George Washington to issue a Thanksgiving Day Proclamation. Boudinot said he "could not think of letting the session pass over without offering an opportunity to all the citizens of the United States of joining with one voice, in returning to Almighty God their sincere thanks for the many blessings he had poured down upon them." 1 *Annals of Congress* 914 (1789)....

Boudinot's resolution was carried in the affirmative on September 25, 1789....

Within two weeks of this action by the House, George Washington responded to the Joint Resolution which by now had been changed to include the language that the President "recommend to the people of the United States a day of public thanksgiving and prayer, to be observed by acknowledging with grateful hearts the many and signal favors of Almighty God, especially by affording them an opportunity peaceably to establish a form of government for their safety and happiness." 1 J. Richardson, *Messages and Papers of the Presidents, 1789–1897*, p. 64 (1897). The Presidential Proclamation was couched in these words:

> Now, therefore, I do recommend and assign Thursday, the 26th day of November next, to be devoted by the people of these States to the service of that great and glorious Being who is the beneficent author of all the good that was, that is, or that will be; that we may then all unite in rendering unto Him our sincere and humble thanks for His kind care and protection of the people of this country previous to their becoming a nation; for the signal and manifold mercies and the favorable interpositions of His providence in the course and conclusion of the late war; for the great degree of tranquillity, union, and plenty which we have since enjoyed; for the peaceable and rational manner in which we have been enabled to establish constitutions of government for our safety and happiness, and particularly the national one now lately instituted; for the civil and religious liberty with which we are blessed, and the means we have of acquiring and diffusing useful knowledge; and, in general, for all the great and various favors which He has been pleased to confer upon us.

***

George Washington, John Adams, and James Madison all issued Thanksgiving Proclamations; Thomas Jefferson did not, saying:

> Fasting and prayer are religious exercises; the enjoining them an act of discipline. Every religious society has a right to determine for itself the times for these exercises, and the objects proper for them, according to their own

particular tenets; and this right can never be safer than in their own hands, where the Constitution has deposited it. 11 *Writings of Thomas Jefferson* 429 (A. Lipscomb, ed., 1904).

As the United States moved from the 18th into the 19th century, Congress appropriated time and again public moneys in support of sectarian Indian education carried on by religious organizations. Typical of these was Jefferson's treaty with the Kaskaskia Indians, which provided annual cash support for the Tribe's Roman Catholic priest and church. It was not until 1897, when aid to sectarian education for Indians had reached $500,000 annually, that Congress decided thereafter to cease appropriating money for education in sectarian schools.... This history shows the fallacy of the notion found in *Everson* that "no tax in any amount" may be levied for religious activities in any form. 330 U. S., at 15–16.

Joseph Story, a Member of this Court from 1811 to 1845, and during much of that time a professor at the Harvard Law School, published by far the most comprehensive treatise on the United States Constitution that had then appeared. Volume 2 of *Story's Commentaries on the Constitution of the United States* 630–632 (5th ed. 1891) discussed the meaning of the Establishment Clause of the First Amendment this way:

> Probably at the time of the adoption of the Constitution, and of the amendment to it now under consideration [First Amendment], the general if not the universal sentiment in America was, that Christianity ought to receive encouragement from the State so far as was not incompatible with the private rights of conscience and the freedom of religious worship. An attempt to level all religions, and to make it a matter of state policy to hold all in utter indifference, would have created universal disapprobation, if not universal indignation. The real object of the [First] [A]mendment was not to countenance, much less to advance, Mahometanism, or Judaism, or infidelity, by prostrating Christianity; but to exclude all rivalry among Christian sects, and to prevent any national ecclesiastical establishment which should give to a hierarchy the exclusive patronage of the national government. It thus cut off the means of religious persecution (the vice and pest of former ages), and of the subversion of the rights of conscience in matters of religion, which had been trampled upon almost from the days of the Apostles to the present age.... (Footnotes omitted.)

Thomas Cooley's eminence as a legal authority rivaled that of Story. Cooley stated in his treatise...that aid to a particular religious sect was prohibited by the United States Constitution, but he went on to say:

> But while thus careful to establish, protect, and defend religious freedom and equality, the American constitutions contain no provisions which prohibit the authorities from such solemn recognition of a superintending Providence in public transactions and exercises as the general religious sentiment of mankind inspires, and as seems meet and proper in finite and dependent beings. Whatever may be the shades of religious belief, all must acknowledge the fitness of recognizing in important human affairs the superintending care and control of the Great Governor of the Universe, and of acknowledging with thanksgiving his boundless favors, or bowing in contrition when visited with the penalties of his broken laws. No principle of constitutional law is violated when thanksgiving or fast days are appointed; when chaplains are designated for the army and navy; when legislative sessions are opened with prayer or the reading of the Scriptures, or when religious teaching is encouraged by a general exemption of the houses of religious worship from taxation for the support of State government. Undoubtedly the spirit of the Constitution will require, in all these cases, that care be taken to avoid discrimination in favor of or against any one religious denomination or sect; but the power to do any of these things does not become unconstitutional simply because of its susceptibility to abuse.... *Ibid.*, at *470–*471.

***

It would seem from this evidence that the Establishment Clause of the First Amendment had acquired a well-accepted meaning: it forbade establishment of a national religion, and forbade preference among religious sects or denominations.... The Establishment Clause did not require government neutrality between religion and irreligion nor did it prohibit the Federal Government from providing nondiscriminatory aid to religion. There is simply no historical foundation for the proposition that the Framers intended to build the "wall of separation" that was constitutionalized in *Everson.*

***

The Court has...recently attempted to add some mortar to Everson's wall through the three-part test of *Lemon v. Kurtzman*...which served at first to offer a more useful test for purposes of the Establishment Clause than did the "wall" metaphor. Generally stated, the *Lemon* test proscribes state action that has a sectarian purpose or effect, or causes an impermissible governmental entanglement with religion.

***

[The many problems courts experience with this test] arise because the *Lemon* test has no more grounding in the history of the First Amendment than does the wall theory upon which it rests. The three-part test represents a determined effort to craft a workable rule from a historically faulty doctrine; but the rule can only be as sound as the doctrine it attempts to service. The three-part test has simply not provided adequate standards for deciding Establishment Clause cases, as this Court has slowly come to realize....The results from our school services cases show the difficulty we have encountered in making the *Lemon* test yield principled results.

For example, a State may lend to parochial school children geography textbooks that contain maps of the United States, but the State may not lend maps of the United States for use in geography class. A State may lend textbooks on American colonial history, but it may not lend a film on George Washington, or a film projector to show it in history class. A State may lend classroom workbooks, but may not lend workbooks in which the parochial school children write, thus rendering them nonreusable. A State may pay for bus transportation to religious schools but may not pay for bus transportation from the parochial school to the public zoo or natural history museum for a field trip. A State may pay for diagnostic services conducted in the parochial school but therapeutic services must be given in a different building; speech and hearing "services" conducted by the State inside the sectarian school are forbidden...but the State may conduct speech and hearing diagnostic testing inside the sectarian school....Exceptional parochial school students may receive counseling, but it must take place outside of the parochial school, such as in a trailer parked down the street....A State may give cash to a parochial school to pay for the administration of state-written tests and state-ordered reporting services, but it may not provide funds for teacher-prepared tests on secular subjects. Religious instruction may not be given in public school, but the public school may release students during the day for religion classes elsewhere, and may enforce attendance at those classes with its truancy laws.

These results violate the historically sound principle "that the Establishment Clause does not forbid governments to [provide] general welfare under which benefits are distributed to private individuals, even though many of those individuals may elect to use those benefits in ways that 'aid' religious instruction or worship." *Committee for Public Education & Religious Liberty v. Nyquist,* 413 U.S. 756, 799 (1973) (Burger, C. J., concurring in part and dissenting in part). It is not surprising in the light of this record that our most recent opinions have expressed doubt on the usefulness of the Lemon test.

***

If a constitutional theory has no basis in the history of the amendment it seeks to interpret, is difficult to apply and yields unprincipled results, I see little use in it.... We have done much straining since 1947, but still we admit that we can only "dimly perceive" the *Everson* wall.... Our perception has been clouded not by the Constitution but by the mists of an unnecessary metaphor.

The true meaning of the Establishment Clause can only be seen in its history.... As drafters of our Bill of Rights, the Framers inscribed the principles that control today. Any deviation from their intentions frustrates the permanence of that Charter and will only lead to the type of unprincipled decision making that has plagued our Establishment Clause cases since *Everson.*

The Framers intended the Establishment Clause to prohibit the designation of any church as a "national" one. The Clause was also designed to stop the Federal Government from asserting a preference for one religious denomination or sect over others. Given the "incorporation" of the Establishment Clause as against the States via the Fourteenth Amendment in *Everson,* States are prohibited as well from establishing a religion or discriminating between sects. As its history abundantly shows, however, nothing in the Establishment Clause requires government to be strictly neutral between religion and irreligion, nor does that Clause prohibit Congress or the States from pursuing legitimate secular ends through nondiscriminatory sectarian means.

The Court strikes down the Alabama statute because the State wished to "characterize prayer as a favored practice."... It would come as much of a shock to those who drafted the Bill of Rights as it will to a large number of thoughtful Americans today to learn that the Constitution, as construed by the majority, prohibits the Alabama Legislature from "endorsing" prayer. George Washington himself, at the request of the very Congress which passed the Bill of Rights, proclaimed a day of "public thanksgiving and prayer, to be observed by acknowledging with grateful hearts the many and signal favors of Almighty God." History must judge whether it was the Father of his Country in 1789, or a majority of the Court today, which has strayed from the meaning of the Establishment Clause.

ELK GROVE UNIFIED SCHOOL DISTRICT V. NEWDOW

542 U.S. 45 (2004)

JUSTICE THOMAS, concurring.

II

I accept that the Free Exercise Clause, which clearly protects an individual right, applies against the States through the Fourteenth Amendment. See *Zelman* [*v. Simmons-Harris*], 536 U.S., at 679, and n. 4 (Thomas, J., concurring). But the Establishment Clause is another matter. The text and history of the Establishment Clause strongly suggest that it is a federalism provision intended to prevent Congress from interfering with state establishments. Thus, unlike the Free Exercise Clause, which does protect an individual right, it makes little sense to incorporate the Establishment Clause. In any case, I do not believe that the Pledge policy infringes any religious liberty right that

Elk Grove Unified School District v. Newdow, in "Cases Adjudged in the Supreme Court of the United States at October Term, 2003": 49–52.

would arise from incorporation of the Clause. Because the Pledge policy also does not infringe any free-exercise rights, I conclude that it is constitutional.

A

The Establishment Clause provides that "Congress shall make no law respecting an establishment of religion." Amdt. 1. As a textual matter, this Clause probably prohibits Congress from establishing a national religion.... Perhaps more importantly, the Clause made clear that Congress could not interfere with state establishments, notwithstanding any argument that could be made based on Congress' power under the Necessary and Proper Clause....

Nothing in the text of the Clause suggests that it reaches any further. The Establishment Clause does not purport to protect individual rights. By contrast, the Free Exercise Clause plainly protects individuals against congressional interference with the right to exercise their religion, and the remaining Clauses within the First Amendment expressly disable Congress from "abridging [particular] *freedom*[*s*]." (Emphasis added.) This textual analysis is consistent with the prevailing view that the Constitution left religion to the States.... History also supports this understanding: At the founding, at least six States had established religions.... Nor has this federalism point escaped the notice of Members of this Court....

Quite simply, the Establishment Clause is best understood as a federalism provision—it protects state establishments from federal interference but does not protect any individual right. These two features independently make incorporation of the Clause difficult to understand. The best argument in favor of incorporation would be that, by disabling Congress from establishing a national religion, the Clause protected an individual right, enforceable against the Federal Government, to be free from coercive federal establishments. Incorporation of this individual right, the argument goes, makes sense. I have alluded to this possibility before. See *Zelman, supra,* at 679 (Thomas, concurring) ("States may pass laws that include or touch on religious matters so long as these laws do not impede free exercise rights *or any other individual liberty interest"* [emphasis added]).

But even assuming that the Establishment Clause precludes the Federal Government from establishing a national religion, it does not follow that the Clause created or protects any individual right. For the reasons discussed above, it is more likely that States and only States were the direct beneficiaries....

Moreover, incorporation of this putative individual right leads to a peculiar outcome: It would prohibit precisely what the Establishment Clause was intended to protect—state establishments of religion. See [*School District of Abington Township v.*] *Schempp*, 374 U.S. at 310 (Stewart, J., dissenting) (noting that "the Fourteenth Amendment has somehow absorbed the Establishment Clause, although it is not without irony that a constitutional provision evidently designed to leave the States free to go their own way should now have become a restriction upon their autonomy"). Nevertheless, the potential right against federal establishments is the only candidate for incorporation.

I would welcome the opportunity to consider more fully the difficult questions whether and how the Establishment Clause applies against the States. One observation suffices for now: As strange as it sounds, an incorporated Establishment Clause prohibits exactly what the Establishment Clause protected—state practices that pertain to "an establishment of religion." At the very least, the burden of persuasion rests with anyone who claims that the term took on a different meaning upon incorporation. We must therefore determine whether the Pledge policy pertains to an "establishment of religion."

CHAPTER 2

THE NONPREFERENTIALISM DEBATE

CHURCH-STATE SEPARATION:
RESTORING THE "NO PREFERENCE" DOCTRINE
OF THE FIRST AMENDMENT

ROBERT L. CORD

I. INTRODUCTION

For almost four decades, since *Everson v. Board of Education* was decided in 1947,[1] the United States Supreme Court has sought with historical scholarship to justify its interpretation of the First Amendment injunction: "Congress shall make no law respecting an establishment of religion." While the Supreme Court has, on other occasions and subjects, employed a variety of arguments to justify its holdings, in Church-State cases the Court has, for the most part, consistently relied on what it has said is the historical intent and mandate of the "founding fathers," especially Thomas Jefferson and James Madison.

***

Harvard Journal of Law and Public Policy 9, no. 1 (1986): 129, 133–48.

III. The "High and Impregnable Wall" Theory

[In *Everson*] Justice Black's "review" for the Court included, as background, a discussion of religious intolerance in Europe and the transplanting of that evil in the American colonies. The inequities of religious establishments in America eventually engendered a movement for religious toleration, nowhere stronger than in Virginia, under the leadership of Thomas Jefferson and James Madison. According to Justice Black, "[t]he people there, as elsewhere, reached the conviction that individual religious liberty could be achieved best under a government which was stripped of all power to tax, to support, or otherwise to assist any *or all religions*, or to interfere with the beliefs of any religious individual or group."[2] As a result, in 1785 and 1786, Madison fought and won his battle in the Virginia Assembly against the renewal of "Virginia's tax levy for the support of the established church."[3] In fighting that tax, Madison not only wrote his famous *Memorial and Remonstrance Against Religious Assessments* but, additionally, created the atmosphere in which the Assembly enacted Jefferson's famous Statute of Virginia for Religious Freedom.

It should be carefully noted that Justice Black and the Court majority in *Everson* show no reluctance whatsoever in declaring what were the objectives and the intentions of the Framers of the First Amendment. "This Court," wrote Black, "has previously recognized that the provisions of the First Amendment, in the drafting and adoption of which Madison and Jefferson played such leading roles, *had the same objective and were intended to provide* the same protection against governmental intrusion on religious liberty as the Virginia statute."[4]

Although *Everson* was decided by a vote of five to four, there appears to have been unanimity on the Court about: (1) the minimal prohibitions that the Clause imposed on government; and (2) the method by which those restraints were ascertainable. In using history as their guide to identifying the objectives and intentions of the Framers of the Establishment Clause, the *Everson* dissenters were at one with the opinion of the Court....

Many of these prohibitions, equated with the Establishment Clause by Justice Black, are verifiable by historical documentation. Regrettably, some significant ones are not. Likely more by design than by chance, Justice Black's opinion and both dissents omit any reference to words or deeds that would have run counter to the Court's final conclusion—that the First Amendment was intended by its Framers to erect a "high and impregnable wall" between

Church and State.[5] A clear example of this history by omission is the Court's discussion of the events in the Virginia Assembly of 1785 and 1786.

Although the Court's opinion discusses at length Madison's *Memorial and Remonstrance* and Jefferson's Statute of Virginia for Religious Freedom, virtually nothing is said about other events that occurred in that Virginia legislative session. While it is true that on October 31, 1785, Madison, acting as Jefferson's surrogate, introduced his "Bill for Religious Liberty"[6] in the Virginia Assembly, it is equally true that on the same day Madison also introduced Jefferson's bill for punishing—among other undesirable behavior—"sabbath breaking."[7] *Both* of these bills were enacted into Virginia law in 1786. Additionally, there is no mention in *Everson* of another bill attributed to Jefferson which called for "Appointing Days of Public Fasting and Thanksgiving."[8] Madison also introduced this bill but it did not become law. When all of these Madison-Jefferson actions are considered together, they hardly make a convincing case for the *Everson* Court's "high and impregnable wall" theory. Instead these bills, taken together with Madison's *Memorial and Remonstrance*, lend support to an understanding of Church-State separation different from that of the *Everson* Court—one of state religious non-preference. Additional historical documents, generated in other states, as well as Virginia, during the constitutional ratification process, support the universality, as well as the substance, of this "no preference" interpretation.

IV. THE "NO PREFERENCE" DOCTRINE
AND THE ESTABLISHMENT CLAUSE'S ORIGIN

The words that the First Congress eventually shaped into the First Amendment and its Establishment Clause were proposed by James Madison in the House of Representatives on June 8, 1789, four years after he wrote the *Memorial and Remonstrance*. Madison—fully aware that several states had ratified the Constitution with the understanding that a series of constitutional amendments would be added to safeguard certain human rights from encroachment by the national government—called upon the House to act with swiftness tempered by reasonable care.

Although several of the state ratifying conventions urged the protection of diverse individual rights, amendments guaranteeing freedom of religion were commonly suggested. On their face, these suggestions indicate that the States wanted to prevent the establishment of a national religion or the elevation of a particular religious sect to a preferred status and to prohibit interference by the national government with an individual's freedom of religious belief. Specifically, the Maryland ratifying convention proposed an amendment stating: "That there be no national religion established by law; but that all persons be equally entitled to protection in their religious liberty."[9] The Virginia ratifying convention proposed a "Declaration or Bill of Rights" as amendments to the Constitution, of which Article Twenty stated, among other things, "that no particular religious sect or society ought to be favored or established, by law, in preference to others."[10] [Other conventions expressed similar sentiments.]...

Madison's first draft of what ultimately became the Establishment Clause clearly shows this same "no preference" intent: "The Civil rights of none shall be abridged on account of religious belief or worship, nor shall any national religion be established...."[11] Even after Madison's draft was changed by congressional committee deliberations, when asked in debate on the House floor what the re-worded clause meant, Madison said that he "apprehended the meaning of the words to be, that Congress should not establish a religion, and enforce the legal observation of it by law, nor compel men to worship God in any manner contrary to their conscience... to prevent these effects he presumed the amendment was intended, and he thought it as well expressed as the nature of the language would admit."[12]

The resolutions passed by the Maryland, Virginia, New York, North Carolina, and Rhode Island ratifying conventions, the original draft of Madison's religion amendment, the debate within the first House and Senate, and Madison's final statement on the floor of the first House of Representatives support the "no preference" interpretation. In other words, insofar as religious establishment was concerned, the First Amendment was intended by its framers to constitutionally forbid the establishment of a national church or religion, or the placing of any one religious sect, denomination, or tradition, into a preferred legal status—a status that was the essential characteristic of religious establishments....

V. THE *EVERSON* MAJORITY AS AMERICAN HISTORIANS

Government actions during the formative years of the Republic also lend support to the "no preference" interpretation of the Establishment Clause's prohibitions. They do not make credible the *Everson* Court's "high and impregnable wall" theory. For instance, none of the opinions in *Everson* explains the incongruity between what the Court says are the "least" commands of the Establishment Clause and the institution of the congressional chaplain system by the very Congress that wrote the First Amendment and recommended it to the States for ratification....

A. Financing Religious Activities: Chaplains

The Court's opinion in *Everson* has the Establishment Clause precluding as unconstitutional, at a minimum, any government financial support for religious activities: "No tax in any amount, large or small, can be levied to support any religious activities or institutions, whatever they may be called, or whatever form they may adopt to teach or practice religion."[13] While I readily concede that such a position certainly follows from, and is reasonable in keeping with, the *Everson* Court's "high and impregnable wall" concept, it is historically clear that this was *not* part of the interpretation of Church-State separation embraced by Congressman James Madison and the other authors of the First Amendment. During the early days of the First Congress, a joint House-Senate Committee considered establishing a congressional chaplain system. James Madison was one of the six members of the Committee. "The result of their consultation was a recommendation to appoint two chaplains of different denominations—one by the Senate and one by the House—to interchange weekly."[14] ...

If the Establishment Clause means, as the Supreme Court in *Everson* claims, that no tax money in any amount large or small can be used to support "any religious activities or institutions, whatever they may be called, or whatever form they may adopt to teach or practice religion," then we are forced to the ludicrous conclusion that the First Congress—including Representative Madison—either recommended to the States a proposed constitutional amendment, the substance of which they then immediately proceeded to violate, or did not understand what the proposed amendment, which they had authored, meant....

B. Financing Religion for Public Policy Purposes: The Use of Treaties

Federal financial support of religious activities was not limited to the appropriation of money to meet the salaries of Congressional and military chaplains. The *Everson* "high and impregnable wall" theory also cannot be squared with the history of financing of religious institutions to meet valid public policy objectives. Frequently, this took the form of Indian treaty obligations proposed and assumed by the new federal government of the United States.

In 1794, only three years after ratification of the First Amendment, President Washington concluded a treaty—proclaimed January 21, 1795—with the Oneida, Tuscarora, and Stockbridge Indians. The treaty obligated the United States to pay "one thousand dollars, to be applied in building a convenient church at Oneida."[15] The church would replace one that the British had burned during the Revolutionary War. Would church building through treaty pass constitutional muster under the *Everson* decision?

Washington was not alone in church building through treaty. On October 31, 1803, President Jefferson presented to the Senate for its advice and consent, a proposed treaty that his representative had negotiated "with the Kaskaskia Indians for the transfer of their country [to the United States] under certain reservations and conditions."[16] The treaty pledged the United States to supply funds to help build a church and to support a Catholic priest in his priestly duties....

***

In assuming these [and other] treaty obligations, not only was religion financed or otherwise aided by federal tax dollars, but those presidents and congresses closest to—and in some instances responsible for—the addition of the Establishment Clause to our Constitution did not interpret it as being a bar against the use of sectarian means to achieve what would otherwise be construed as constitutionally permissible secular ends.

C. Financing Religion for Policy Purposes: Land Grants and Federal Monies

Providing federal funds to support certain religious activity was not the only way that our early presidents and congresses aided sectarian institutions while using them to promote secular objectives. Large grants of land, as well as federal subsidies, were provided to religious societies that acted as federal government surrogates in educating and "civilizing" the Indians. Madison and Jefferson were well aware of, and participated in, these practices.

***

In 1796, eight years after the ratification of the federal Constitution and five years after the addition of the First Amendment, the Fourth Congress passed "An Act regulating the grants of land appropriated for Military services and for the Society of the United Brethren, for propagating the Gospel among the Heathen."[17] As its name suggests, the Society was interested in more than simply managing the land set aside for Indians already converted to Christianity. While governing this trust in the interests of the Christian Indians living on parts of this land, the Society also used some of the resources, derived from the cultivation of the lands and from the sale of land leases to white tenant farmers, to send out missionaries to convert souls "from among the neighboring heathen."[18]

Under the terms of the original federal statute, the opportunity to receive a land grant for the services specified in the Act was to expire on January 1, 1800. The Fifth Congress extended the deadline to January 1, 1802, by amending the law. Subsequently, the cut-off date was, by further legislative enactments extended...until finally set as April 1, 1805. Even though these laws in effect paid, with enormous land grants held in a controlling trust, an evangelical Christian sect to spread and maintain Christianity among the Indians in the Ohio Territory, none were vetoed or challenged by the incumbent presidents as violating the degree of Church-State separation required by the First Amendment. Instead, the original bill was approved by President Washington, the next two were approved by President Adams, and the last three became federal law upon the approval and signature of President Jefferson.

Later presidents, through treaties with Indian tribes, also provided grants of federal lands to sectarian organizations, thereby supporting their religious activities....

Additionally, despite Justice Black's *Everson* interpretation, that no tax money can—consistent with the Establishment Clause—be used "to support any religious activities or institutions, whatever they may be called, or whatever form they may adopt to teach or practice religion,"[19] the facts show that the United States directly subsidized many church schools, which were engaged in the federal government's program to teach, "civilize," and otherwise improve the Indians.[20] During the years from 1824 through 1831 alone, the *Annual Reports of the Commissioner of Indian Affairs* substantiate that federal tax revenues supported religious schools run by...[various religious societies]. This policy, of federal financing of church schools, continued throughout the nineteenth century until Congress ended it by statute in 1896.

… [D]id many presidents and congresses violate the *supposedly* "high and impregnable" wall between Church and State imposed by the Establishment Clause of the First Amendment, when they authorized the granting of Federal lands and monies to religious organizations that they might spread "the Gospel among the Heathen?" Or did Washington, Jefferson, Madison, their contemporaries, and many succeeding presidents and congresses have a far different view of the proper constitutional relationship between government and religion than did Justice Black and the entire *Everson* Court? Merely to pose these questions is to answer them. A thorough reading of early American history manifests that the Framers of the First Amendment did not intend to preclude every significant relationship between the federal government and religion. Their goal was to avoid what in part the *Everson* Court rightly declared were the "cruel persecutions [that] were the inevitable result of government-established religions."[21] But, unlike the *Everson* Court, for the Framers—as the original Madison draft of the Establishment Clause manifests—an established religion connoted a religion, or religious tradition, that was favored and placed in a preferred status by the government. It was this "evil" that the Framers sought to prevent.

***

While the historical acts of collaboration between government and religion—documented and discussed above—are incompatible with the *Everson* Court's interpretation of the Establishment Clause, that is not the case when one assigns the "no-preference" meaning to the Clause. This very fact lends further support to the position that the "no-preference" interpretation of Church-State separation is the one that the Framers intended and the Founding Fathers embraced. Interpretations of the First Amendment that would prohibit *non-discriminatory* governmental aid to religion, especially in pursuit of a secular goal, are of a distinctly modern origin. In light of primary historical documents, it is faulty to attribute these interpretations—as the *Everson* Court did—to Madison, Jefferson, and the other Founding Fathers.

***

NOTES

The note number from the original article is shown in the parenthesis at the end of each citation.

1. *Everson v. Board of Education of the Township of Ewing, et al.*, 330 U.S. 1 (1946) [Hereinafter 330 U.S.]. (1)

2. Ibid., p. 11 (emphasis added). (21)

3. Ibid. (22)

4. Ibid., p. 13 (emphasis added). (24)

5. Ibid., p. 18. (27)

6. Julian P. Boyd, ed., *The Papers of Thomas Jefferson*, vol. 2 (Princeton, NJ: Princeton University Press, 1950), pp. 545–47. (29)

7. Ibid., pp. 555–56. (30)

8. Ibid., bill no. 85. (32)

9. J. Elliot, *Debates on the Federal Constitution*, vol. 2 (1901), p. 553. [Hereinafter cited as *Debates*]. (37)

10. Elliot, *Debates*, vol. 3, p. 659. (38)

11. Joseph. Gales, ed., *Annals of Congress*, vol. 1 (1834), p. 434. (42)

12. Ibid., p. 730. (43)

13. 330 U.S. 16. (48)

14. "Chaplains in Congress and in the Army and Navy," in *Reports of Committees of the House of Representatives* HR doc. no. 124, 33d Cong., 1st sess., 1854. (51)

15. R. Peters, ed., *The Public Statutes at Large of the United States of America*, vol. 7 (Boston: Charles C. Little and James Brown, 1861), pp. 47, 48. (58)

16. J. Richardson, ed., *A Compilation of the Messages and Papers of the Presidents: 1789–1897*, vol. 1 (Washington: Government Printing Office, 1901), p. 363. (59)

17. See 4th Cong., 1st sess. (1796), chap. 46, in Peters, ed., *The Public Statutes at Large*, p. 490. (68)

18. "Progress of the Society of the United Brethren in Propagating the Gospel among the Indians," S. doc. no. 189, 17th Cong., 2d sess. (1822), in *American State Papers: Indian Affairs*, vol. 2 (1834), pp. 376–77. (69)

19. 330 U.S. 16. (75)

20. *Report of the Condition of the Several Indian Tribes*, HR doc. no. 182, 17th Cong., 2d sess. (1822), in *American State Papers: Indian Affairs*, p. 275. (76)

21. 330 U.S. 12. (80)

"NONPREFERENTIAL" AID TO RELIGION:
A FALSE CLAIM ABOUT ORIGINAL INTENT

Douglas Laycock

***

...[M]y own review of the relevant history...refutes one important claim about the Establishment Clause—that the Framers specifically intended to permit government aid to religion so long as that aid does not prefer one religion over others.

***

The prominence and longevity of the nonpreferential aid theory is remarkable in light of the weak evidence supporting it and the quite strong evidence against it. I do not mean to overstate what we know about the Establishment Clause. Neither its history nor its text offers us a single unambiguous

---

William and Mary Law Review 27 (1985/1986): 875, 877–83, 913–19, 922–23.

meaning. But they can eliminate some possible meanings, and to do that is real progress. So long as the debate is dominated by a false claim, it is hard to discuss the real issues.

***

I. THE NONPREFERENTIAL AID CLAIM

There are several versions of the nonpreferential aid argument, but all reach substantially the same conclusion. The claim is that the framers of the religion clauses intended a specific meaning with respect to the problems now treated under the Establishment Clause: government may not prefer one religion over others, but it may aid all religions evenhandedly. Under this view, the Supreme Court's more expansive interpretation is a usurpation that remains illegitimate no matter how long the Court adheres to it.

This claim is false. The framers of the religion clauses certainly did not consciously intend to permit nonpreferential aid, and those of them who thought about the question probably intended to forbid it. In fact, substantial evidence suggests that the Framers expressly considered the question and that they believed that nonpreferential aid would establish religion. To assert the opposite as historical fact, and to charge the Supreme Court with usurpation without acknowledging the substantial evidence that supports the Court's position, is to mislead the American people.

The fact is that the First Congress repeatedly rejected versions of the Establishment Clause that would have permitted nonpreferential aid, and nothing in the sparse legislative history gives much support to the view that the Framers intended to permit nonpreferential aid. Proposals for nonpreferential financial aid were squarely rejected in Maryland and Virginia in 1785 and 1786, amidst much public debate. No state offered nonpreferential aid to churches, and only Maryland and Virginia seriously proposed such aid. Some of the New England states provided financial aid to more than one church, but these systems were preferential in practice and were the source of bitter religious strife. There is no evidence that those schemes were the model for the Establishment Clause.

The Framers also had a second, less considered intention. Both the states and the federal government openly endorsed Protestantism and provided a variety of preferential, nonfinancial aid to Protestants. This aid was wholly noncontroversial, because the nation was so uniformly Protestant and hostile to other faiths. The early preference for Protestantism is not a precedent for nonpreferential aid, and it is not an attractive model for Establishment Clause interpretation. The Framers' generation thought about Establishment Clause issues in the context of financial aid; they did not think about those issues in connection with nonfinancial aid. We can make better sense of the Establishment Clause if we follow what the Framers did when they were thinking about establishment. Thus, to the extent that the Framers' intent is thought to matter, the relevant intent is their analysis of financial aid to churches.

II. THE BEST EVIDENCE OF THE FRAMERS' INTENT: THE TEXT OF THE ESTABLISHMENT CLAUSE

A. The Rejected Drafts

... [T]he most important fact concealed by the proponents of nonpreferential aid [is this]: the First Congress considered and rejected at least four drafts of the Establishment Clause that explicitly stated the "no preference" view. So far as we can tell from the legislative journal, the issue was squarely posed in the Senate and again in the Conference Committee.

The House of Representatives sent to the Senate a draft of the Establishment Clause somewhat like the version ultimately ratified:

Congress shall make no law establishing religion, or prohibiting the free exercise thereof, nor shall the rights of conscience be infringed.[1]

The first motion in the Senate clearly presented the "no preference" position. The motion was to strike out "religion, or prohibiting the free exercise thereof," and to insert, "one religious sect or society in preference to others."[2] The motion was first rejected, and then passed. The proposal on the floor then read:

Congress shall make no law establishing one religious sect or society in preference to others, nor shall the rights of conscience be infringed.[3]

Next, the Senate rejected two substantively similar substitutes. First, the Senate rejected language providing:

> Congress shall not make any law, infringing the rights of conscience, or establishing any Religious Sect or Society.[4]

Second, it rejected an alternative that stated:

> Congress shall make no law establishing any particular denomination of religion in preference to another, or prohibiting the free exercise thereof, nor shall the rights of conscience be infringed.[5]

The two motions to amend by substitution appear to have presented stylistic choices. But the first vote appears to have been substantive. At the very least, these three drafts show that if the First Congress intended to forbid only preferential establishments, its failure to do so explicitly was not for want of acceptable wording. The Senate had before it three very clear and felicitous ways of making the point.

Still later the same day, the Senate appears to have abandoned the "no preference" position. It adopted a draft that spoke of all religion generically:

> Congress shall make no law establishing religion, or prohibiting the free exercise thereof.[6]

A week later, the Senate again changed its mind and adopted the narrowest version of the Establishment Clause considered by either House:

> Congress shall make no law establishing articles of faith or a mode of worship, or prohibiting the free exercise of religion....[7]

The House of Representatives rejected this version. James Madison and two others represented the House on the Conference Committee that produced the version of the Establishment Clause ultimately ratified:

> Congress shall make no law respecting an establishment of religion, or prohibiting the free exercise thereof.[8]

The Establishment Clause actually adopted is one of the broadest versions considered by either House. It forbids not only establishments, but also any law respecting or relating to an establishment. Most important, it forbids any law respecting an establishment of "religion." It does not say "*a* religion," "a national religion," "one sect or society," or "any particular denomination of religion." It is religion generically that may not be established.

***

The nonpreferentialists tend not to mention the rejected drafts, or to pass over the drafts as insignificant. Some nonpreferentialists rely heavily on similar resolutions from the state ratifying conventions. The Virginia, North Carolina, and New York conventions proposed Establishment Clauses similar to the rejected Senate drafts. James Madison's original bill in the First Congress provided: "nor shall any national religion be established."[9] Like the Senate drafts, however, all of these proposals were rejected.

An approach to interpretation that disregards the ratified amendment and derives meaning exclusively from rejected proposals is strange indeed. The "no preference" position requires a premise that the Framers were extraordinarily bad drafters—that they believed one thing but adopted language that said something substantially different, and that they did so after repeatedly attending to the choice of language.

Perhaps the Framers did not understand what they were doing and viewed the textual choices as stylistic. All sorts of things become possible once one begins to speculate about what the Framers might have thought instead of giving primary weight to what they enacted. But responsible constitutional interpretation does not allow us to assume a mistake of this magnitude. When the record reflects a textual choice as clear as this one, only extraordinarily clear contrary evidence should persuade us not to follow the text.

***

IV. THE DEBATES IN THE REVOLUTIONARY STATES

Independence was an occasion for reviewing church-state relations in the revolutionary states. In the states with established Anglican churches, the King was the head of both the church and the state, and the question of succession extended to both his secular and his religious authority. Several states wrote constitutions in the wake of independence, and they addressed church-state questions in their bills of rights....

For obvious reasons, the debates in the states are not direct evidence of the meaning of the federal religion clauses. Nothing in these debates was offered as an explanation of those clauses, and the Framers could support one regime of church-state relations for their respective states and a quite different regime of church-state relations for the new federal government.…

Thus, I do not offer the state debates as legislative history in anything like the usual sense. Instead, I offer them as intellectual history. The state debates help show how the concept of establishment was understood in the Framers' generation. Learning how that generation understood the concept may be more informative than the brief and unfocused debate in the House. If the Framers generally understood the concept in a certain way, and if nothing indicates that they used the word in an unusual sense in the First Amendment, then we can fairly assume that the Framers used the word in accordance with their general understanding of the concept.

A. Votes Against Nonpreferential Aid

For several reasons, the debates in Virginia were most important. First, the arguments were developed most fully in Virginia. Second, Madison led the winning coalition, and he played a dominant role in the adoption of the Establishment Clause three years later. Third, the debates in Virginia may have been the best known. I am not sure of that, and the subject deserves further investigation, but most of the national figures from Virginia were involved, some in leadership roles on each side. Further, the debate dragged on for ten years. It would be surprising if the leading Virginians had said nothing to their correspondents in other states.…

The Virginia fight came to a head in 1785 and 1786. The defenders of establishment offered a compromise known as a general assessment, under which all Christian churches could receive tax money and every taxpayer could designate a church to receive his tax. The bill would have included Catholics, and it tried to accommodate Quaker and Mennonite objections to paid clergy. Any taxpayer could refuse to designate a church, with undesignated church taxes going to a fund for schools.… Supporters of the bill invoked the slogan "Equal Right and Equal Liberty," and argued that it imposed not "the smallest coercion" to contribute to the support of religion.

Madison's *Memorial and Remonstrance Against Religious Assessments* was published to rally the citizenry against this nonpreferential establishment. Many similar petitions also were circulated, especially by Presbyterians and Baptists, and support for establishment collapsed. The assessment bill died without a vote, and the legislature enacted Jefferson's Act for Establishing Religious Freedom instead. Thus, the great debate about disestablishment in Virginia culminated in a decisive vote against nonpreferential aid.

[Proponents of the nonpreferential aid argument] try to make this choice go away by showing that Madison considered the general assessment bill preferential. Madison and others were able to imagine the bill's effects on Jews, Muslims, and other non-Christians, and Madison also objected that Quakers and Mennonites were not the only religious groups that needed or deserved partial exemption. Both of these objections tended to show that the proposal was not quite as nonpreferential as its supporters claimed. Consequently, according to [this argument], some of the votes against the bill may have been votes against these preferential features rather than votes against a pure system of nonpreferential aid.

That is conceivable, but it is wholly unrealistic. It is anachronistic to view aid to all denominations of Christians as preferential in 1786. There were hardly any Jews in the United States at that time, and no other non-Christians to speak of.... That some Virginians could imagine the effects of establishment on non-Christians only shows how far Virginians had thought through the problem. No public figure had talked that way since Roger Williams.

The provision for Quakers and Mennonites in the general assessment bill was facially preferential, but it was an attempt to make the bill less preferential in its impact. The bill would have been more objectionable without this provision. Madison did not want the Quakers and Mennonites compelled to conform; he wanted everyone to be exempt.

Virginians understood the vote against the bill as a rejection of any form of financial aid to churches. The proof of that is that the ten-year-old controversy died with this bill. No one at the time perceived that only preferential aid had been rejected; no one proposed a new bill that included non-Christians and eliminated the exemptions for Quakers and Mennonites. Instead, the Act for Establishing Religious Freedom provided that "no man shall be compelled to frequent or support any religious worship, place, or ministry whatsoever"[10]—language comprehensive enough to ban taxes for either preferential or nonpreferential aid. The Act also declared that any subsequent bill narrowing its terms would be a violation of natural right.

An equally clear vote occurred in Maryland. Supporters of establishment there proposed a tax even less preferential than the tax proposed in Virginia. Non-Christians were exempt, and Christians could pay either a minister of their choice or a fund for the poor. The proposal was defeated in 1785 after substantial public debate.

The votes in Virginia and Maryland show that whenever a choice between nonpreferential aid and no aid was squarely posed, Americans in the 1780s voted for no aid. When they focused on the question, they concluded that nonpreferential aid was a form of establishment and inconsistent with religious liberty.

***

VI. THE FRAMERS' OTHER INTENTION: NONFINANCIAL AID TO RELIGION

The state debates concerning establishment centered on financial aid. Nonfinancial government support for Protestantism was rampant and largely noncontroversial. Nonpreferentialists also invoke these practices in support of their theory. Supporters of government aid to religion also make the more general claim that the Establishment Clause does not forbid anything analogous to a practice that was common in 1791. The crèche case and especially the legislative prayer case are based on that claim.

The argument cannot be merely that anything the Framers did is constitutional. The unstated premise of *that* argument is that the Framers fully thought through everything they did and had every constitutional principle constantly in mind, so that all their acts fit together in a great mosaic that is absolutely consistent, even if modern observers cannot understand the organizing principle. That is not a plausible premise. Of course the state and federal Establishment Clauses did not abruptly end all customs in tension with their implications. No innovation ever does. Momentum is a powerful force in human affairs, and the Framers were busy building a nation and creating a government. Their failure to spend time examining every possible Establishment Clause issue is hardly surprising. The Framers did not think that everything they did was constitutional.... Madison [observed in 1787] ... that many of the state bills of rights were widely violated. Indeed, one of the arguments against the federal Bill of Rights was that the state bills of rights had been ineffectual.

Those who would rely on early government aid to religion must identify some principled distinction between the practices the Framers accepted and those they rejected. We can then consider whether we are bound by, or are willing to adopt for ourselves, the implicit principle on which they appear to have acted. The search for patterns requires a brief review of the kinds of aid to religion that the Framers supported or at least tolerated.

The Constitutional Convention did not appoint a chaplain, but the First Congress appointed chaplains, and even Madison apparently acquiesced. Presidents Washington, Adams, and Madison issued Thanksgiving proclamations, although Madison did so only in time of war and at the request of Congress, and his proclamations merely invited citizens so disposed to unite their prayers on a single day. President Jefferson refused to issue Thanksgiving proclamations, believing them to be an establishment. In retirement, Madison concluded that both the congressional chaplains and the Thanksgiving proclamations had violated the Establishment Clause. He said he had never approved of the decision to appoint a chaplain.

Congress also subsidized missionary work among the Indians, and even Jefferson signed a treaty agreeing to build a church and supply a Catholic priest in exchange for tribal lands of the Kaskaskias. Congress continued to support sectarian education on Indian reservations until 1898.

***

These examples undoubtedly evidence support for religion, but they are hard to explain as nonpreferential. Supplying a Catholic priest to a tribe of Catholic Indians may be a cheap way to buy land, but it is not a form of non-preferential aid. A missionary or a church-run school inevitably represented a particular denomination, whatever that denomination might be. So did the congressional chaplain. Congress did not hire a chaplain from every faith, or even one from every faith represented by a Congressman. I assume that most of the Framers saw no constitutional problem with a chaplain, but I doubt that they rationalized the practice on the ground that it was nonpreferential.

***

State aid to religion was both preferential and coercive. The states continued practices that no one would defend today. All but two states had religious qualifications for holding public office, and at least five states denied full civil rights to Catholics. Blasphemy was commonly a crime; in Vermont blasphemy against the Trinity was a capital offense, although it presumably was not enforced as such. Observance of the Christian Sabbath was widely enforced, with little in the way of fictitious explanations about a neutrally selected day for families to be together. These laws aroused little controversy, and almost no one thought them inconsistent with constitutional guarantees of religious liberty. Yet tax support for churches was deeply controversial and widely thought inconsistent with religious liberty.

***

In 1791, almost no one thought that government support of Protestantism was inconsistent with religious liberty, because almost no one could imagine a more broadly pluralist state. Protestantism ran so deep among such overwhelming numbers of people that almost no one could see that his principles on church taxes might have implications for other kinds of government support for religion. The exclusion of non-Protestants from pronouncements of religious liberty was not nearly so thorough or so cruel as the exclusion of slaves from pronouncements that all men were created equal, but both blind spots were species of the same genus.

In short, the appeal to the Framers' practice of nonpreferential aid to religion is an appeal to unreflective bigotry. It does not show what the Framers meant by disestablishment; it shows what they did without thinking about establishment at all. I believe that the relevant intention of the Framers is the one they thought about. But if that view is rejected—if both the considered and the unconsidered intentions of the Framers are binding—then the result would not be to approve nonpreferential aid. The Framers' implicit distinction was between financial aid and other aid. If both their intentions are followed, all financial aid will be forbidden, whether or not preferential. But unlimited [non]financial aid will be permitted even if it is preferential and coercive. Few nonpreferentialists would defend that.

***

VIII. Conclusion

The principle that best makes sense of the Establishment Clause is the principle of the most nearly perfect neutrality toward religion and among religions. I do not mean neutrality in the formal sense of a ban on religious classifications, but in the substantive sense of government conduct that insofar as possible neither encourages nor discourages religious belief or practice. This is the principle that maximizes religious liberty in a pluralistic society, and this is the principle that the Framers identified in the context of tax support for churches. They did not substitute nonpreferential taxes for preferential taxes; they rejected all taxes. They did not substitute small taxes for large taxes; three pence was as bad as any larger sum. The principle was what mattered. With respect to money, religion was to be wholly voluntary. Churches either would support themselves or they would not, but the government would neither help nor interfere.

That is what disestablishment meant to the Framers in the context in which they thought about it. They applied the principle only in that context—only to tax support. Their society was so homogeneous that they had no occasion to think about other kinds of support. Now that we have thought about it, we are not unfaithful to the Framers' intent when we apply their principle to analogous problems. Congress cannot impose civil disabilities on non-Protestants or ban blasphemy against the Trinity just because the Framers did it. It is no more able to endorse the predominant religion just because the Framers did it. Our task is not to perpetuate the Framers' blind spots, but to implement their vision.

NOTES

The note number from the original article is shown in the parenthesis at the end of each citation.

1. L. de Pauw, ed., *Documentary History of the First Federal Congress of the United States of America*, vol. 3 (1972), pp. 159, 166. (27)
2. L. de Pauw, ed., *Documentary History of the First Federal Congress of the United States of America* (*Senate Journal*), vol. 1, p. 151. (28)
3. Ibid. (30)
4. Ibid. (31)
5. Ibid. (32)
6. Ibid. (33)
7. Ibid., p. 166. (34)
8. U.S. Constitution, amend. 1. (36)
9. Joseph Gales, ed., *Annals of Congress*, vol. 1 (1834), p. 434. (42)
10. William Waller Hening, *Statutes at Large*, vol. 12 (1823), pp. 84, 86. (120)

CHAPTER 3

THE ESTABLISHMENT CLAUSE AS A FEDERALISM MANDATE

TOWARD A GENERAL THEORY OF THE ESTABLISHMENT CLAUSE

Daniel O. Conkle

***

III. THE ESTABLISHMENT CLAUSE AND THE
LESS ACTIVIST MODELS OF JUDICIAL REVIEW

***

Properly conceived, the issue that separates Justice Rehnquist from *Everson*'s historical analysis concerns the collective intentions of the framers and ratifiers. According to Rehnquist, they intended merely to prohibit certain forms of government aid for particular religions to the exclusion of others. The *Everson* Court, by contrast, found a broader intention to prevent government from furthering religion generally, even in the absence of discrimination among religions.

Northwestern University Law Review 82, no. 4 (Summer 1988): 1129, 1131–42.

Needless to say, it can be exceedingly difficult, if not impossible, to determine the original understanding of a provision in the Bill of Rights. The evidentiary materials are woefully incomplete, and it is difficult to determine the relevance and relative weight of the various types of evidence that do exist. The historical question addressed in the *Everson*-Rehnquist debate is one that falls prey to these evidentiary and analytical problems; as a result, it is difficult to say whether the framers and ratifiers of the Establishment Clause intended to adopt a broad or a more narrow prohibition on congressional action. In this instance, however, the framers' and ratifiers' lack of clarity is quite understandable, for the issue that separates Rehnquist from the *Everson* Court was of only secondary importance to those who supported the Establishment Clause. Indeed, to focus on this issue is to ignore the motivating reason for the clause and thereby to misapprehend its original meaning.

At the time of the First Amendment's adoption, the newly created American states reflected divergent views concerning the appropriate relationship between religion and government. Virginia had recently expressed a separationist philosophy in its Bill for Religious Liberty, and six other states also embraced antiestablishment policies. The remaining six states, however, continued to maintain or authorize established religions. In these latter states, at least, the prevailing political philosophy thus permitted the use of public power for the support and furtherance of religion.

Given this widespread and deep division, how could Congress and the ratifying state legislatures have reached agreement on the Establishment Clause? It was supported, after all, both by separationists and by those who were committed to programs of state-sponsored religion. These various political actors simply could not have agreed on a general principle governing the relationship of religion and government, whether it be the principle endorsed in *Everson* or any other. If the Establishment Clause had embraced such a principle, it would not have been enacted. What united the representatives of all the states, both in Congress and in the ratifying legislatures, was a much more narrow purpose: to make it plain that *Congress* was not to legislate on the subject of religion, thereby leaving the matter of church-state relations to the individual states. This purpose honored the antiestablishment policies of states such as Virginia, but it also protected the existing state establishments from congressional interference. The appropriate breadth—or at least the appropriate phrasing—of the Establishment Clause was a matter that received considerable attention in the First Congress, but primarily as an issue concerning the appropriate *means* for effecting a policy of federalism on questions of church and state.

When the original Constitution was proposed and ratified, it was widely understood that, even without the First Amendment, the newly created national government would have no power on the subject of religion. James Madison himself, for example, believed that there was "not a shadow of right in the general government to intermeddle with religion" and that the "least interference with it would be a most flagrant usurpation."[1] The national government was conceived as a government of limited and enumerated powers, and these powers did not extend to matters of religion.

The Bill of Rights was designed, in the words of Madison, "to extinguish from the bosom of every member of the community" any fear that the national government would exceed its stated powers and thereby encroach upon the rights of individuals and of the states.[2] On many of the subjects addressed—freedom of expression and the rights of the criminally accused, for example—the framers and ratifiers may have formulated and agreed upon general principles concerning the role of government and the rights of individuals, principles as suitable for application to the states as to the federal government. Because there was no fear of encroachment by state government, there was no need to make the Bill of Rights enforceable against the states. But many of its principles would have been widely endorsed by the framers and ratifiers as principles to which each state should adhere.

The Establishment Clause, by contrast, could not have reflected such a general principle, for the framers and ratifiers could not have agreed on its content. Instead, perhaps more than any other provision in the first eight amendments, it was designed to restrain the national government because it *was* the national government, not because the national government might violate principles that needed no further protection in the states. As a statement of general principle, the Establishment Clause would not have been enacted. As a statement of federalism, it was widely supported.

The Establishment Clause, as originally understood, thus was animated by the policy of federalism. This conclusion does not resolve the *Everson*-Rehnquist debate, but it may help explain the historical arguments that have been advanced. The issue for the framers and ratifiers was, in essence, how to effectuate the basic policy of federalism on which they all agreed. If they intended the more narrow prohibition suggested by Justice Rehnquist in *Jaffree*, they did so because they were satisfied that such a prohibition would resolve their federalism concerns. If, on the other hand, they intended the broader prohibition identified by the Court in *Everson*, it was because they embraced an even stronger policy of federalism, one that would remove from Congress and preserve to the states an even broader segment of legislative power.

As applied to congressional legislation, the original understanding of the Establishment Clause depends on a resolution of the *Everson*-Rehnquist debate. Although Justice Rehnquist's arguments are not without merit, the *Everson* Court's position is at least equally forceful. The resolution of this debate, however, is of limited importance, because the Court's Establishment Clause cases typically address state, not federal, government policies. Even assuming that *Everson* correctly identified the original understanding of the Establishment Clause as applied to federal action, the historical premise for applying this prohibition to the states remains to be examined.

2. *The Fourteenth Amendment.*—In his dissenting opinion in *Jaffree*, Justice Rehnquist took the *Everson* Court to task for its reading of the history of the First Amendment. At the same time, however, he accepted without challenge the *Everson* Court's "'incorporation' of the Establishment Clause as against the States via the Fourteenth Amendment."[3] But if the historical evidence is mixed concerning *Everson*'s First Amendment conclusions, the evidence concerning "incorporation" points clearly against the Court's position. That evidence strongly suggests that the Fourteenth Amendment, as originally understood, did not incorporate the Establishment Clause for application to state government action.

***

... [I]t is not clear that the Fourteenth Amendment was originally intended to make *any* of the Bill of Rights applicable against the states. In any event, there is more specific evidence that the framers and ratifiers of the Fourteenth Amendment, whatever their intentions with respect to the Bill of Rights generally, at least did not intend to incorporate *the Establishment Clause* for application to the states. In 1875 and 1876, *after* the adoption of the Fourteenth Amendment, Congress considered, but rejected, a resolution that was specifically designed to make the religion clauses of the First Amendment applicable to the states. The proposed "Blaine Amendment" would have provided that "[n]o State shall make any law respecting an establishment of religion or prohibiting the free exercise thereof."[4] The Blaine Amendment received considerable attention in Congress, and it passed in the House of Representatives before being defeated in the Senate.

Post-ratification congressional action or inaction is ordinarily a hazardous basis for determining the original meaning of a constitutional amendment. The Congress that considered the Blaine Amendment was not the Thirty-Ninth Congress, which had proposed the Fourteenth Amendment, and, in any event, Congress's rejection of the Blaine Amendment could have been grounded on a belief that the Fourteenth Amendment had already accomplished the object of the new amendment, making it superfluous. But the Congress that considered the Blaine Amendment acted only eight years after the Fourteenth Amendment had been ratified. It included some twenty-three members of the Thirty-Ninth Congress, two of whom had been members of the Joint Committee on Reconstruction, which had drafted the Fourteenth Amendment. Thus, if the Blaine Amendment had been thought superfluous in light of the Fourteenth Amendment, at least some indication of this belief surely would appear in the legislative history of the Blaine Amendment. The historical record, however, contains no such evidence. To the contrary, the record suggests a congressional understanding that the proposed amendment would "prohibit the States, *for the first time*, from the establishment of religion [and] from prohibiting its free exercise."[5] The inference seems inescapable: the Fourteenth Amendment, as originally understood, did not incorporate the Establishment Clause for application to the states.

There is substantial historical evidence, then, that whatever their intentions with respect to the Bill of Rights generally, the framers and ratifiers of the Fourteenth Amendment did not intend to incorporate the Establishment Clause for application against the states. Although this conclusion is firmly supported by the evidence, some might choose to read the historical record differently. I turn next, therefore, to two additional—and even more basic—reasons for rejecting the historical validity of incorporation with respect to the Establishment Clause. These reasons depend more on an analysis of language and logic than on historical evidence that some may regard as controversial, and they independently compel a rejection of the incorporation argument.

First, there is the problem of language. By prohibiting laws "respecting an establishment of religion,"[6] the Establishment Clause states a limitation on the power of government. But unlike the other provisions of the Bill of Rights, this clause does not designate any obvious individual beneficiaries. Indeed, a prohibition on establishment might serve a variety of purposes beyond protecting the rights of particular individuals. Thus, it is not easy to see how the language of the Fourteenth Amendment, even if read broadly, can be said to incorporate this provision for application to the states.

The "incorporating" language of the Fourteenth Amendment provides that "[n]o State shall make or enforce any law which shall abridge the privileges or immunities of citizens of the United States; nor shall any State deprive any person of life, liberty, or property, without due process of law...."[7] Putting aside the question of whether these words fairly can be read to incorporate *any* of the Bill of Rights, note that the words at least would limit any such incorporation to the protection of "privileges" and "immunities" of "citizens," as well as the rights of "persons" to be free from unlawful "deprivations" of life, liberty, or property. These limitations would seem to exclude the Establishment Clause. Concededly, this problem could be resolved through a skillful manipulation of the pertinent constitutional language. But the very need for such manipulation undercuts a claim that the words were originally intended to have the ascribed meaning.

Second, an originalist incorporation of the Establishment Clause for application to the states creates logical difficulties. The originalist contention is that the framers and ratifiers of the Fourteenth Amendment intended to incorporate by reference the Bill of Rights, making its norms—as originally understood for application to the federal government—apply to the states in the same way. But recall the original understanding of the Bill of Rights, and especially the narrow, federalistic purpose that underlay the Establishment Clause. To the extent that a provision in the Bill of Rights, as originally understood, reflected a general principle concerning the proper role of government and the rights of individuals, the framers and ratifiers of the Fourteenth Amendment might logically have concluded that the federal constitution should be extended to protect that principle against state as well as federal infringement. But the Establishment Clause, as originally understood, did not embrace any such general principle; it embraced only a policy of *federalism* on the subject of church and state. To "incorporate" this policy of states' rights for application *against* the states would be utter nonsense, for there would be no norms to incorporate. It would be the incorporation of an empty set of values, akin to an incorporation of the Tenth Amendment for application against the states.

To be sure, the framers and ratifiers of the Establishment Clause intended to preclude the federal government from taking certain action. If we accept the *Everson* side of the *Everson*-Rehnquist historical debate, for example, the Establishment Clause denied to the federal government a broad range of power with respect to religious matters. Theoretically, the framers and ratifiers of the Fourteenth Amendment could have intended to "incorporate" this prohibition for application to the states, thereby precluding the states from exercising any power with respect to religion that was previously denied to the federal government. Even though the Establishment Clause was designed to further the end of federalism, its prohibitions against the federal government could be extended to the states for other reasons. This argument would provide a set of norms to be incorporated, thereby avoiding the problem of an empty set. The argument would require us to assume, however, that the framers and ratifiers of the Fourteenth Amendment meant to impose on the states, as a general principle concerning the proper role of government, a rule that had been formulated only as a means for allocating authority between the federal and state governments. This would have been a truly radical, if not mindless, act of incorporation, an act we should not readily impute to the officials who adopted the Fourteenth Amendment.

The language of the Fourteenth Amendment, coupled with the federalistic motivation for the Establishment Clause, make it exceedingly difficult to argue that the framers and ratifiers of the Fourteenth Amendment intended to incorporate the Establishment Clause for application against the states. At the very least, the problems of language and logic discussed above impose a heavy burden of persuasion on those who wish to advance such an historical argument. Given that the historical argument for incorporating *any* of the Bill of Rights is difficult, and given the circumstances surrounding the Blaine Amendment, I cannot imagine how that burden could be met.

NOTES

The note number from the original article is shown in the parenthesis at the end of each citation.

1. Jonathan Elliot, *The Debates in the Several State Conventions on the Adoption of the Federal Constitution*, 2nd ed., vol. 3 (Philadelphia: J. B. Lippincott, 1836), p. 330. (104)

2. Joseph Gales, *Annals of Congress*, vol. 1 (1789), pp. 431–32. (106)

3. *Wallace v. Jaffree*, 472 U.S. 38, 113 (1985) (Rehnquist, J., dissenting). (111)

4. HR J. Res. 1, 44th Cong., 1st sess., *Congressional Record* 4 (1875): 205 (emphasis added). (120)

5. *Congressional Record* 4 (1876): 5561. (124)

6. U.S. Constitution. amend. 1. (127)

7. U.S. Constitution. amend. 14, para. 1. (129)

THE INTELLECTUAL ORIGINS
OF THE ESTABLISHMENT CLAUSE

Noah Feldman

***

B. The Establishment Clause and Governmental Structure: The Neo-Federalist or Structuralist Objection

At least since the 1950s, some constitutional historians have argued that the language of the Establishment Clause as actually enacted was intended in part to prevent Congress from interfering with existing state establishments....

This view has received renewed attention and support in recent years within the context of what is sometimes called the neofederalist project. Neofederalism draws attention to the federal structure of the Bill of Rights and to the Framers' concern with limiting the powers of Congress....

The neofederalist view of the Establishment Clause...might be read to

---

New York University Law Review 77 (May 2002): 346, 405–12.

minimize the degree to which the Clause was concerned with liberty of conscience. If federalism animated the Clause, and if some meaningful element of this federalist impulse was to protect state establishments from congressional interference, then perhaps it is unfair to see the Clause primarily as a protector of individual liberty of conscience. Perhaps the Clause should be seen simply to make the question of establishment a local issue to be resolved within the domain of the states and kept from the federal government.

Several scholars have advanced a similar version of this view, but without the emphasis on the general structural concerns of the Bill of Rights. These scholars argue that because the Framers disagreed about whether government funding of religion was a good idea, they could not possibly have intended the Establishment Clause to embody an answer to this problem. The Clause must have been intended to "leav[e] the matter of church-state relations to the individual states."[1] On this view, the Establishment Clause represented a compromise between those who supported the elimination of nonpreferential support, as in Virginia, and New Englanders who supported continued nonpreferential arrangements. The consequence of this argument is that

> [i]f we ask, therefore, what principle or theory of religious liberty the framers and ratifiers of the religion clauses adopted, the most accurate answer is "None." They consciously chose not to answer the religion question.... This observation suggests that it is futile to try to extrapolate or reconstruct a principle or theory of religious liberty from the original meaning of the religion clauses.[2]

The appeal of the structuralist view of the Establishment Clause is understandable. It consists with a broader view of the structure of the Bill of Rights itself and it gives significant meaning to the otherwise awkward formulation "respecting an establishment of religion." What is more, there is something fashionably postmodern about the argument that no principle greater than compromise underlies the Establishment Clause.

The problem with the structuralist view, however, is that the historical evidence does not bear it out. To begin with, the argument that the language of the Clause was intended specifically to protect state establishments is implausible on several grounds. First, there is no evidence in the debates that the last-minute change of language to "respecting an establishment of religion" was intended to protect existing state establishments. Nearly every draft until the conference committee's final formulation said that "Congress shall make no law establishing religion or faith."

Furthermore, as Thomas J. Curry argues, the Framers were using the word "establishment" to refer to a frankly preferential religious arrangement. At the time of the framing of the Establishment Clause, only the New England states had arrangements that anyone could have called "establishments." The dominant Congregationalists, of whom the New England delegations in Congress were exclusively composed, generally did not consider their arrangements to constitute establishment at all. Baptist opponents of the New England Way did (pejoratively) call it an establishment, but there is no reason to think that the New Englanders would have sought protection for their mode of funding against Congress through language that required their system to be called an establishment.

Second, and more importantly, it is unlikely that anyone discussing the Clause believed Congress would have the power to interfere with state religious affairs through normal legislation. No part of the Constitution conferred such a power. There was never any hint that Congress could, on the basis of legislation alone, interfere with state religious affairs.

Consider next the argument that the Framers of the religion clauses "could not have agreed on a general principle governing the relationship of religion and government,"[3] so that the Clause must have been concerned primarily with local control, rather than liberty of conscience. There is little or no indication in the debates surrounding the Clause that the Framers even acknowledged that there was a difference between the New England arrangement and that of the other states. As Curry puts it, there existed

> almost total obliviousness on the part of the House to Church-State dissension in New England.... This lack of awareness extended even to the Representatives from New England itself. Although Baptists bitterly opposed the New England system of state support for churches, none of them sat in Congress. The Congregationalists dismissed out of hand assertions that their system could be unfair, and opposing views hardly registered on their consciousness. Further, few Americans outside of New England knew of the stinging Church-State disputes that took place there.[4]

In the brief House discussion of Madison's proposed amendment, there was one exchange that raised the issue of New England arrangements. On the table was draft language that "no religion shall be established by law, nor shall the equal rights of conscience be infringed."[5] Madison explained that "he apprehended the meaning of the words to be, that Congress should not establish a religion, and enforce the legal observation of it by law, nor compel men to worship God in any manner contrary to their conscience."[6] Benjamin Huntington of Connecticut objected:

> [Huntington] understood the amendment to mean what had been expressed by the gentleman from Virginia; but others might find it convenient to put another construction upon it. The ministers of their congregations to the Eastward were maintained by the contributions of those who belonged to their society; the expense of building meeting-houses was contributed in the same manner. These things were regulated by by-laws. If an action was brought before a Federal Court on any of these cases, the person who had neglected to perform his engagements could not be compelled to do it; for a support of ministers, or building of places of worship might be construed into a religious establishment. By the charter of Rhode Island, no religion could be established by law; he could give a history of the effects of such a regulation; indeed, the people were now enjoying the blessed fruits of it. He hoped, therefore, the amendment would be made in such a way as to secure the rights of conscience, and a free exercise of the rights of religion, but not to patronize those who professed no religion at all.[7]

Curry interprets this passage to mean that Huntington "feared the amendment might give Congress power to interfere with existing arrangements in the individual states."[8] If this were correct, then perhaps the final version of the Clause could be read to protect states from congressional interference. But on closer analysis, this interpretation is imprecise. Huntington wanted to avoid an interpretation of the Constitution that would bar the New England states' practices of collecting local taxes to support churches. His first statement about "congregations to the Eastward" expressed concern not that Congress might interfere with state establishments, but that the proposed constitutional language, stating that "no religion shall be established by law," might be construed to extend to states, not just to Congress. Huntington did not wish to say that the New England arrangements were an establishment—establishment was a potentially derogatory term—but he was prepared to say that the New England Way might be construed into an establishment. Huntington was not worried about whether Congress would actively bar or interfere with state establishments. He simply sought clarification that the proposed constitutional language would not encroach on New England practices.

Huntington's second statement, in which he referred ironically (if technically incorrectly) to the example of Rhode Island, followed from his concern that the Constitution not be read to prohibit state establishments. To draft the amendment in such a way as to bar state establishment (as he imagined the Rhode Island charter to read) might allow those bound by bylaws to escape paying church maintenance that they owed. Huntington was very clear, however, that he favored protection of "rights of conscience" and "free exercise of religion." He simply thought these could be protected by language that would not mention establishment and so would preclude the interpretation that worried him.

Huntington was not worried that language protecting liberty of conscience would interfere with New England arrangements. He was not worried that anyone would argue that paying what he owed under bylaws would violate his liberty of conscience. He naturally assumed that no one would be obligated to pay for a church not his own, because this would obviously violate liberty of conscience.

The two responses to Huntington confirm this interpretation. First, Madison proposed that "if the word national was inserted before religion, it would satisfy the minds of honorable gentlemen. He believed that the people feared one sect might obtain a pre-eminence, or two combine together, and establish a religion to which they would compel others to conform."[9] By clarifying that the amendment was intended to avoid a national establishment, Madison was reassuring Huntington that the Constitution would not interfere with nonpreferential state establishments. Dissatisfied with Madison's proposal, Samuel Livermore proposed without explanation that the draft language be amended to read: "Congress shall make no laws touching religion, or infringing the rights of conscience."[10] This proposal, which was shortly adopted, followed Madison's clarificatory explanation of the purpose of the amendment as restricted to what *Congress* could or could not do in the national sphere. It therefore clarified that the amendment would not infringe on what states could do regarding their own religious affairs. But this language did not suggest that Congress was being barred from interfering in state affairs—that issue was not even on the table.

It emerges from this analysis that the Framers could and did agree on a principle to justify the Establishment Clause: the protection of liberty of conscience at the federal level. Madison stated explicitly that the purpose was to avoid a national religion that would "compel others to conform." Huntington, the only person involved in the debate who so much as alluded to New England's nonpreferential arrangements, agreed with this principle and in fact insisted on his support for "rights of conscience." He believed, like most New Englanders, that the nonpreferential New England arrangements, whether considered establishments or not, did not violate liberty of conscience, and he wanted such arrangements to continue.

It is thus anachronistic to argue that real (if marginal) disagreement over whether nonpreferential funding violated liberty of conscience made it impossible for the Framers to agree on a principle underlying the Establishment Clause. The Framers agreed that liberty of conscience was to be respected, and they further agreed that a preferential establishment was always undesirable because it violated liberty of conscience. They did not express any specific view on whether the New England arrangements in practice violated liberty of conscience, because they decided to restrict themselves to federal matters. Thus, they abandoned Madison's proposed separate amendment, to the effect that "no State shall infringe the equal rights of conscience, nor the freedom of speech or of the press, nor of the right of trial by jury in criminal cases."[11] The sole recorded objection to this proposed amendment was that of Thomas Tucker, who said that "it goes only to the alteration of the constitutions of particular States. It will be much better, I apprehend, to leave the State Governments to themselves, and not to interfere with them more than we already do."[12] It would hardly be supposed that the Congress refrained from regulating states with respect to free speech and trial by jury because there was a lack of agreement on the principles underlying these matters. To the contrary, Congress refrained presumably because it thought that it was good housekeeping to leave such matters to the states.

The Establishment Clause as enacted was, obviously, concerned with federal establishment, not with the states. But the relevant question is why the Framers wanted formally to preclude a federal establishment. The answer can be gleaned easily from the contemporary discussions: Establishment was understood to be incompatible with liberty of conscience because it compelled support for a church with which dissenters disagreed.

***

NOTES

The note number from the original article is shown in the parenthesis at the end of each citation.

1. Daniel O. Conkle, "Toward a General Theory of the Establishment Clause," *Northwestern University Law Review* 82, no. 4 (1988): 1113. (330)

2. Steven D. Smith, *Foreordained Failure: The Quest for a Constitutional Principle of Religious Freedom* (New York: Oxford University Press, 1995), p. 21. (331)

3. Conkle, "Toward a General Theory of the Establishment Clause," p. 1133. (335)

4. Thomas J. Curry, *The First Freedoms: Church and State in American to the Passage of the First Amendment* (New York: Oxford University Press, 1986), p. 205. (336)

5. Joseph Gales, ed., *Annals of Congress*, vol. 1 (1789), p. 757. (337)

6. Ibid., p. 758. (338)

7. Ibid. (339)

8. Curry, *The First Freedoms*, p. 203. (340)

9. Gales, *Annals of Congress*, p. 758. (343)

10. Ibid. p. 759. (344)

11. Ibid. p. 783. (345)

12. Ibid. (346)

THE BILL OF RIGHTS:
CREATION AND RECONSTRUCTION

AKHIL REED AMAR

***

The Establishment Clause did more than prohibit Congress from establishing a national church. Its mandate that Congress shall make no law "*respecting* an establishment of religion" also prohibited the national legislature from interfering with, or trying to *dis*-establish, churches established by state and local governments. In 1789, at least six states had government-supported churches —Congregationalism held sway in New Hampshire, Massachusetts, and Connecticut under local-rule establishment schemes, while Maryland, South Carolina, and Georgia each featured a more general form of establishment in their respective state constitutions. Even in the arguably "nonestablishment" states, church and state were hardly separate; at least four of these states, for

Akhil Reed Amar, *The Bill of Rights: Creation and Reconstruction* (New Haven, CT: Yale University Press, 1998), pp. 32–35, 246–49, 251–54.

example—in their constitutions, no less—barred non-Christians or non-Protestants from holding government office. According to one tally, eleven of the thirteen states had religious qualifications for office holding. Interestingly, the federal Establishment Clause as finally worded most closely tracked the proposal from the ratifying convention of one of the staunchest establishment states, New Hampshire, that "Congress shall make no laws *touching* religion"; this proposal, if adopted, would obviously have immunized New Hampshire from any attempted federal disestablishment.[1] In the First Congress, Representative Samuel Livermore from New Hampshire initially won the assent of the House for this wording, only to lose in turn to another formulation. But when all the dust had settled, the final version of the clause returned to its states' rights roots. In the words of Joseph Story's celebrated *Commentaries on the Constitution,* "the whole power over the subject of religion is left exclusively to the state governments."[2]

The key point is not simply that, as with the rest of the First Amendment, the Establishment Clause limited only Congress and not the states; that point is obvious on the face of the amendment and is confirmed by its legislative history. ...Nor is the main point exhausted once we recognize that state governments are in part the special beneficiaries of, and rights holders under, the clause; indeed, the same thing could be said, to some degree, about the free-speech clause. The special pinprick of the point is this: the nature of the states' Establishment Clause right against federal disestablishment makes it quite awkward to mechanically "incorporate" the clause against the states via the Fourteenth Amendment. Incorporation of the free speech clause against states does not negate state legislators' own First Amendment rights to freedom of speech in the legislative assembly. But incorporation of the Establishment Clause has precisely this kind of paradoxical effect; to apply the clause against a state government is precisely to eliminate its right to choose whether to establish a religion—a right clearly confirmed by the Establishment Clause itself.

To put the point a slightly different way, the structural reasons that counsel caution in attempting to incorporate the Tenth Amendment against the states seem valid here, too. The original Establishment Clause, on a close reading, is not antiestablishment but pro-states' rights; it is agnostic on the substantive issue of establishment versus nonestablishment and simply calls for the issue to be decided locally. ... But how can such a local option clause be mechanically incorporated *against* localities, requiring them to pass no laws (either way) on the issue of—"respecting"—establishment?

***

Thomas Jefferson, often invoked today as a strong opponent of religious establishment, appears to have understood the states' rights aspects of the original Establishment Clause. Although he argued for an absolutist interpretation of the First Amendment—the federal government should have *nothing* to do with religion in the states, control of which was beyond Congress's limited delegated powers—he was more willing to flirt with governmental endorsements of religion at the state level, especially where no state coercion would impinge on dissenters' freedom of conscience. The two ideas were logically connected; it was especially easy to be an absolutist about the federal government's involvement in religion if one understood that the respective states had broad authority over their citizens' education and morals. Thus, President Jefferson in 1802 refused to proclaim a day of religious Thanksgiving, but Governor Jefferson had agreed to do so some twenty years before. . . .

***

FREEDOM OF RELIGION

***

Begin with the Establishment Clause text prohibiting Congress from making any law "respecting an establishment of religion." We have seen that these words, as originally written, stood as a pure federalism provision. Congress could make "no law respecting [state] establishment [policy]"—that is, no law either establishing a national church or disestablishing a state church. On this reading, the clause was utterly agnostic on the substantive issue of establishment; it simply mandated that the issue be decided state by state and that Congress keep its hands off, that Congress make no law "respecting" the vexed question. In short, the original Establishment Clause was a home rule–local option provision mandating imperial neutrality.

Agnosticism, home rule, and imperial neutrality made a good deal of political sense in 1789, when half the states gave specified sects privileged status and the other half didn't. Proestablishment New Hampshiremen and antiestablishment Virginians might sharply disagree on the substantive issue of church-state relations but could agree on the jurisdictional idea that Congress should keep out: this was the lowest common denominator.

The precise wording of the clause, though, gave rise to a critical ambiguity: what about federal territories? Public debates over the Constitution and Bill of Rights in the 1780s and 1790s paid remarkably little heed to the territories. These debates took place within existing states—ratification of the Constitution under Article VII and of the Bill of Rights under Article V occurred state by state, and Americans living outside a state had no formal role. Furthermore, these debates focused overwhelmingly on the ways in which an upstart Congress might displace the powers of existing state governments, governments that had century-deep roots.

***

On the very day it debated an early version of the Establishment Clause, the First Congress pushed forward an ordinance to govern the western territory by extending the Confederation Congress's Northwest Ordinance of 1787, a regime that one leading scholar has described as "suffused with aid, encouragement, and support for religion."[3] Over the next two decades, Congress applied this regime to other territories, and various territorial governments aided and sponsored religion in sundry ways. Some modern scholars have read all this as a record of sheer hypocrisy—"no law" apparently did not mean "no law." Others have claimed that early congressional practice shows that only strict and totalizing sectarian establishments were banned by the First Amendment, and that generalized support for religion was not covered by the clause. But a federalism-based reading can offer a third possibility: the clause merely barred Congress from interfering with *state* establishment policy. Putting the textual point functionally, perhaps Congress, when legislating in a plenary way for a territory, stood in the shoes of a state government and could adopt the same kinds of proreligion laws that states could.

***

As the nineteenth century wore on, the technically correct notion that the Establishment Clause applied to the territories began to mutate, giving way in some places to a different—substantive—interpretation. A territorial legislature derived all its powers from Congress; thus, what Congress could not do, its territorial agent could not do. When, say, Fourth Amendment rights were at stake, it made little difference whether its ban on general warrants—"no Warrants shall issue, but..."—was phrased as a limit on Congress or on its territorial agent. But to say that, for example, the Iowa territorial legislature "shall make no law respecting an establishment of religion" was rhetorically to say something rather different than that Congress should make no such law. Unlike Congress, the Iowa territorial legislature obviously had no power to legislate over other states; thus to say that *this* legislature should make no law obviously implied no law *in the territory*. The agnostic federalism reading—hard enough for some to see when the Establishment Clause addressed "Congress"—faded from view, replaced by a substantive antiestablishment interpretation.

As various territorial legislatures matured into state legislatures, it seemed only natural to bind them to the same (substantive) nonestablishment rule, using language borrowed from the federal template. When Iowa gained statehood in 1846, its first state constitution proclaimed in its Bill of Rights that "[t]he general assembly shall make no law respecting an establishment of religion or prohibiting the free exercise thereof," words repeated verbatim in its Constitution of 1857.[4] Virtually identical phrases appeared in the territorial Constitution of Deseret in 1849, and its successor Utah Territory draft constitution of 1860. Similarly, in the 1859 Constitution of the Jefferson Territory (today known as Colorado), we find the following clause: "The General Assembly shall make no laws respecting an establishment of religion, nor shall any religious test be required of any citizen."[5] In his influential constitutional treatise of 1868, the respected Michigan jurist Thomas Cooley likewise wrote that, under prevailing state constitutions, state legislatures were barred from creating "[a]ny law respecting an establishment of religion."[6]

***

In the 1780s half the states featured sectarian establishments; by the 1860s none did. Virtually all states in the mid-nineteenth century favored religion generally, and some privileged Christianity or Protestantism above other religions, but none singled out one Christian sect for special favor. The common denominator among states had thus shifted dramatically, and popular understandings of the Establishment Clause may have reflected this shift. What began as an agnostic but strict federalism rule—*no law* intermeddling with religion in the states—was gradually mutating into a soft substantive rule: religion in general could be promoted, but not one sect at the expense of others....

But even if by 1866 the Establishment Clause was no longer a state right, pure and simple, can we really say that it was a private right of discrete individuals, as opposed to a right of the public at large? To the extent a state created a coercive establishment, decreeing that individuals profess a state creed or attend a state service or pay money directly to a state church, such coercion would implicate bodily liberty and property of discrete individuals and would thus intrude upon paradigmatic privileges and immunities of citizens. (Put another way, all these examples also seem like textbook violations of religious "free exercise.") But what of a noncoercive establishment—say, a simple state declaration on a state seal proclaiming Utah "the Mormon State"?

***

The historical evidence from the 1860s and early 1870s is somewhat sparse and rather mixed. On the one hand, a variety of congressmen catalogued the "personal rights" protected by the First Amendment as encompassing speech, press, petition, and assembly, but not nonestablishment: rather, they spoke only of "free exercise" or of "freedom of conscience." On the other hand ... silence alone does not prove much, and even this seemingly selective silence went unelaborated.... Several Congressmen and commentators in the late 1860s and early 1870s did treat nonestablishment as an individual right, but here, too, we find little elaboration.

Perhaps the greatest elaboration came from Thomas Cooley's influential 1868 treatise. Under prevailing state constitutions, wrote Cooley, states generally could not enact "[a]ny law respecting an establishment of religion.... There is not religious *liberty* where any one sect is favored by the State.... It is not toleration which is established in our system, but religious *equality*."[7] Even a noncoercive establishment, Cooley suggested, violated principles of religious liberty and religious equality—violated norms of equal rights and privileges. And once we see this, it turns out that the question—should we incorporate the Establishment Clause?—may not matter all that much, because even if we did not, principles of religious liberty and equality could be vindicated via the Free Exercise clause (whose text, history, and logic make it a paradigmatic case for incorporation) and the equal-protection clause (which frowns on state laws that unjustifiably single out some folks for special privileges and relegate others to second-class status). Surely Alabama could not adopt a state motto proclaiming itself "the White Supremacy State"; such a motto would offend basic principles of equal citizenship and equal protection. And so a law that proclaimed Utah a Mormon state should be suspect whether we call this a violation of the establishment principles, free exercise principles, equal-protection principles, equal-citizenship principles, or religious-liberty principles. Once we remember that we are not incorporating clauses mechanically but reconstructing rights, we reach the unsurprising conclusion that our basic touchstones should be the animating Fourteenth Amendment ideals of liberty and equality.

***

NOTES

The note number from the original article is shown in the parenthesis at the end of each citation.

1. Jonathan Elliot, ed., *Debates on the Adoption of the Federal Constitution*, vol. 1 (1836; repr., Manchester, NH: Ayer, 1987), p. 326. (66)

2. Joseph Story, *Commentaries on the Constitution of the United States*, vol. 3 (Boston: Hilliard, Gray and Co., 1833), sec. 1873. (68)

3. See Gerard V. Bradley, *Church-State Relationships in America* (New York: Greenwood Press, 1987), p. 98 (describing the events of July 21, 1789); Joseph Gales, ed., *Annals of Congress*, vol. 1 (1834), p. 658; 1 Stat. 50, ch. 8. (75)

4. Iowa Constitution of 1846, art. 1, sec. 3; Iowa Constitution of 1857, art. 1, sec. 3. (81)

5. See William F. Swindler, ed., *Sources and Documents of United States Constitutions*, vol. 2 (Dobbs Ferry, NY: Oceana Publications, 1979), p. 18 (reprinting Constitution of Jefferson Territory, art. 1, sec. 3). (83)

6. Thomas M. Cooley, *A Treatise on the Constitutional Limitations Which Rest Upon the Legislative Power of the States of the American Union* (Boston: Little, Brown, 1868), p. 469. (84)

7. Ibid. (emphasis added). (94)

THE SECOND ADOPTION OF THE ESTABLISHMENT CLAUSE: THE RISE OF THE NONESTABLISHMENT PRINCIPLE

Kurt T. Lash

***

D. The "Put God in the Constitution" Movement

Those who continued to believe that Protestant Christianity was the state religion chafed against the drum roll of decisions to the contrary. Faced with the inexorable divorce of Christianity from the law of the land, religious Republican groups focused their attention on the federal Constitution and the rhetorical effect of its failure to acknowledge the providence of the Christian God. In 1864, a group calling itself the National Reform Association formally petitioned Congress to adopt the following amendment to the Constitution:

> We the people of the United States, humbly acknowledging Almighty God as the source of all authority and power in civil government, the Lord Jesus

Arizona State Law Journal 27 (Winter 1995): 1131–38, 1142–45.

Christ as the Ruler among the nations, and His revealed will as the supreme law of the land, in order to constitute a Christian government... do ordain and establish this Constitution for the United States of America.[1]

In 1874, the Congress referred the matter to the Committee on the Judiciary which recommended the petition be rejected:

[The Founders] in full realization of the dangers which the union between church and state had imposed upon so many nations of the Old World, [decided] with great unanimity that it was inexpedient to put anything into the Constitution or frame of government which might be construed to be a reference to any religious creed or doctrine.[2]

The Founders had been anything but unanimous about the dangers of a union between church and state and had not intended to express any such nonestablishment value. However, by Reconstruction, northern state courts had translated the prohibition of the original Establishment Clause to be an expression of fundamental religious liberty. So complete was the reinterpretation of the Establishment Clause that its language—*sui generis* at the Founding—now began to appear in the organic law of the states. For example, the Iowa Constitution of 1857 declared: "The General Assembly shall make no law respecting an establishment of religion, or prohibiting the free exercise thereof."[3]

As adopted by the states, formally or otherwise, the reinterpreted Establishment Clause retained its original "dual nature," if in modified form. Recall that the original Establishment Clause had both a prohibitive and a protective aspect; it was intended to both prohibit establishments at the *federal* level while at the same time protecting establishments at the *state* level. Similarly, the principle of nonestablishment, which was by Reconstruction generally thought to inform the Clause, also had a prohibitive and a protective aspect; no government could legitimately prefer (prohibit) one religion over another or attempt to suppress (protect) religious exercise on religious grounds....

... Today, we think of establishment as government *support* of religion. In the mid-nineteenth century, however, government suppression of "heretical beliefs," forced religious observance of the Lord's Day, interference with church decisions involving their own doctrine and government, or forced participation in public school religious exercises were all "establishment" issues. According to an 1853 Senate Committee Report on congressional chaplains:

> If Congress has passed, or should pass, any law which, fairly construed, has in any degree introduced, or should attempt to introduce, *in favor* of any church, or ecclesiastical association, or system of religious faith, all or any one of these obnoxious particulars—endowment at the public expense, peculiar privileges to its members, *or disadvantages or penalties* upon those who should reject its doctrines or belong to other communions—such law would be a '*law respecting an establishment of religion*,' *and therefore in violation of the constitution*.[4]

In this way, the Establishment Clause came to represent a personal freedom. Over time, popular interpretation of the Clause focused not on the principle of federalism, but on the principle of "nonestablishment." By Reconstruction, the common interpretation of the Establishment Clause and its "counterparts" in the states was that no government had any legitimate power over religion as religion: the state could neither establish a preferred religion, nor could it visit "disadvantages or penalties" upon disfavored religious beliefs. Citizens by right were immune from such religious-based persecutions.

E. Nonestablishment Implications for the Incorporation of the Establishment Clause

Recall that the main objection to the incorporation of the Establishment Clause is that the Clause was intended to express a principle of states' rights. Thus, it makes no more sense to incorporate this clause against the states than it does the Tenth Amendment. If, on the other hand, the Clause was understood to express a principle of personal freedom—the principle of nonestablishment—this is a freedom that can just as easily be applied against the states as the federal government: no government (state or federal) has any legitimate power over religion as religion. A "new" interpretation, however, does not in itself alter the fact that the original Clause stood for federalism, not personal freedom. If by Reconstruction most people interpreted the Establishment Clause to express the principle of nonestablishment, perhaps this merely illustrates how wrong people can be about the Constitution. As a matter of originalism, one might argue, that popular misunderstanding cannot change the original meaning of the Clause.

If the focus of the inquiry was the "original meaning of the First Amendment," the objection has some force.... However, we are not seeking the *original* meaning of the Establishment Clause. Instead the endeavor is to determine the meaning of the *incorporated* Establishment Clause. This shifts the focus from the Founding to Reconstruction and the original meaning of the Fourteenth Amendment. If the people intended *this* Amendment to embrace the principle of nonestablishment, then the fact that they were "wrong" about the original Establishment Clause is irrelevant. Put another way, nothing prevents the people from reinterpreting the principle underlying the words of the Establishment Clause and incorporating this principle—as expressed by those words—into the Fourteenth Amendment.

But what possible reason is there to believe the drafters of the Fourteenth Amendment gave a second thought to nonestablishment principles? Wasn't the immediate task at hand the protection of black civil rights in the South? What does this have to do with religion? As it turns out, quite a bit.

III. THE SOUTH AND THE FOURTEENTH AMENDMENT

***

... By 1860, the South had erected the most comprehensive religious establishment to exist on American soil since Massachusetts Bay.

1. Southern Regulation of Religion

> The slave master *may* withhold education and the Bible; he *may* forbid religious instruction, and access to public worship. He *may* enforce upon the slave and his family a religious worship and a religious teaching which he disapproves ... There is no other religious despotism on the face of the earth so absolute, so irresponsible, so soul-crushing as this.[5]

Fearing religiously inspired insurrection—particularly after the 1831 slave revolt led by the Reverend Nat Turner—southern states enacted a constellation of laws that strictly controlled religious exercise. Black religious assemblies were heavily regulated; slaves were not permitted their own ministers, nor could they worship without the presence of a white man.

Particularly threatening to the southern establishment of slavery was the *idea* that the peculiar institution might violate the doctrines of Christianity. All black religious assemblies were carefully monitored to assure the promulgation of only pro-slavery Christianity ... Throughout the South, preachers criticizing slavery as contrary to the will of God faced public outrage and legal prosecution.

***

1. Commentary on Southern Regulation of Religion by the Architects of the Fourteenth Amendment

Southern regulation of religion was acknowledged and condemned by a variety of members of the Thirty-ninth Congress. Lyman Trumbull introduced the 1866 Civil Rights Act by pointing out that, under slavery, blacks were prohibited from "exercising the functions of a minister of the Gospel,"[6] and that the Black Codes continued to violate these "privileges essential to freemen."[7] Congressman Cydnor B. Tompkins of Ohio noted that southern states would "condemn as a felon the man who dares proclaim the precepts of our holy religion."[8] Representative James M. Ashley pointed out that "[u]nder the plea of *Christianizing* [blacks], [the South]...has silenced every free pulpit within its control, and debauched thousands which ought to have been independent."[9]

Given this recognition of southern regulation of religion, it is not surprising to find the Establishment Clause, along with the Free Exercise Clause, mentioned as "privileges or immunities," which were to be protected under the Fourteenth Amendment. In 1871, John Bingham, the author of Section One of the Fourteenth Amendment, recited in their entirety the first eight amendments to the Constitution—including the Establishment Clause—and declared his belief that the Fourteenth Amendment was designed to protect all such "privileges and immunities."[10] In an 1864 speech on the floor of the Senate, Senator and future vice-president Henry Wilson read the entire First Amendment...and declared that the southern states had trampled on these "great rights," which were "essential to liberty."[11]

Some scholars have noted that the people involved in the framing of the Fourteenth Amendment spoke more often about southern violations of "free exercise" and "the rights of conscience" than they did the "establishment of religion." For example, in his 1864 speech, Henry Wilson noted how "... utterly slavery disregards the right to a *free exercise* of religion."[12] Likewise, although Henry Dawes in the Forty-Second Congress listed "free exercise of his religious belief, and freedom of speech and of the press" as protected under the Fourteenth Amendment, he did not mention the Establishment Clause.[13]...John Bingham, in a speech before the House in 1871, declared that the Fourteenth Amendment gave Congress the power to prevent the South from restricting "freedom of press," "freedom of speech," and "the rights of conscience."[14]...Bingham mentions other First Amendment freedoms as protected under the Fourteenth Amendment, but omits any explicit reference to the Establishment Clause. Scholars such as Akhil Amar have suggested that these "abbreviated lists" imply that nonestablishment was not considered a personal right on the same level as free exercise or free speech.[15]

Upon reflection, it appears that these lists were exactly that: *abbreviations.* For example, in his 1864 speech, Henry Wilson first reads the *entire* First Amendment—including the Establishment Clause—and then goes on to paraphrase the amendment as protecting "[f]reedom of religious opinion, freedom of speech and press, and the right of assemblage for the purpose of petition."[16] Notice how Wilson substitutes for the religion clauses the phrase "freedom of religious opinion." Again, to modern ears, "freedom of religious opinion" sounds more like a matter for the Free Exercise Clause. However, to the nineteenth-century mind, suppression of religious opinion was the quintessential example of a government-imposed religious establishment. Similarly, in 1871, Bingham first lists the *entire* First Amendment—including the Establishment Clause—as examples of the privileges or immunities protected under Section One of the Fourteenth Amendment. Only *later* does he refer to southern restriction of "the rights of conscience."[17]...

In fact, the various remarks made by Reconstruction Congressmen reveal that little effort was made to distinguish between "free exercise," "the rights of conscience," and the wording of both the Establishment and Free Exercise clauses. This is not surprising given the fact that the rights of conscience were interpreted to include freedom from government-imposed establishments—a freedom which was itself considered an aspect of free exercise. Thus, even when the framers of the Fourteenth Amendment focused on the free exercise of religion, there is no reason *a priori* to interpret this as elevating the Free Exercise Clause over the Establishment Clause as a candidate for incorporation. The framers would not have made such a distinction: the rights of conscience included both free exercise and nonestablishment components. As Democratic Senator Thomas Norwood conceded in 1874:

> Before [the adoption of the Fourteenth Amendment] any state might have established a particular religion, or restricted freedom of speech or of the press....A state could have deprived its citizens of any of the privileges and immunities contained in those eight articles, but the Federal Government could not. But can a State do so now? If not why?...The reason is, that the citizens of the States have the new guarantee under the Fourteenth Amend-

ment; and though new privileges were not thereby conferred, additional guarantees were.[18]

NOTES

The note number from the original article is shown in the parenthesis at the end of each citation.

1. Anson Phelps Stokes, *Church and State in the United States*, vol. 3 (New York: Harper, 1950), pp. 584–85 (emphasis in original). (222)

2. Ibid., p. 588. (223)

3. Iowa Constitution of 1857, art. 1, sec. 3, in Benjamin Perley Poore, ed., *The Federal and State Constitutions, Colonial Charters, and Other Organic Laws of the United States*, 2nd ed., vol. 1 (Washington: Government Printing Office, 1878), pp. 552–53. (224)

4. Senate report no. 376, 32d Cong., 2d sess. 1-2, 1853 (emphasis added). (226)

5. William Goodell, *The American Slave Code in Theory and Practice: Its Distinctive Features Shown by its Statutes, Judicial Decisions, and Illustrative Facts* (1853; repr., New York: Negro Universities Press, 1968), pp. 254–55. (231)

6. "Congressional Globe," 39th Cong., 1st sess., January 27 and 29, 1866, in Alfred Avins, comp., *The Reconstruction Amendment's Debates: The Legislative History and Contemporary Debates in Congress on the 13th, 14th, and 15th Amendments* (Richmond: Virginia Commission on Constitutional Government, 1967), p. 121. (248)

7. Ibid. (249)

8. "Congressional Globe," 36th Cong., 1st sess., 1857 (1860). (250)

9. Avins, *The Reconstruction Amendment's Debates*, p. 81 (emphasis added). (251)

10. "Congressional Globe," 42d Cong., 1st sess., March 31, 1871, in Avins, *The Reconstruction Amendment's Debates*, pp. 510–11. (252)

11. "Congressional Globe," 38th Cong., 1st sess. 1202, 1864. (253)

12. Ibid. (emphasis added). (254)

13. See Avins, *The Reconstruction Amendment's Debates*, pp. 475–76 (remarks of Henry Dawes). (255)

14. Ibid., p. 85. (256)

15. Akhil R. Amar, "The Bill of Rights as a Constitution," *Yale Law Journal* 100 (1992): 1158 n.132 (citations omitted). (257)

16. "Congressional Globe," 38th Cong., 1st sess. 1202, 1864, in Avins, *The Reconstruction Amendment's Debates*, p. 65. (258)

17. "Congressional Globe," 42d Cong., 1st sess. app. 84, 1864, in Avins, *The Reconstruction Amendment's Debates*, p. 85. (260)

18. "Congressional Globe," 43d Cong., 1st sess., 1874, in Avins, *The Reconstruction Amendment's Debates*, p. 676. (262)

CHAPTER 4

THE COMPLEX BACKGROUND OF THE ESTABLISHMENT CLAUSE

THE ESSENTIAL RIGHTS AND LIBERTIES OF RELIGION IN THE AMERICAN CONSTITUTIONAL EXPERIMENT

JOHN WITTE JR.

***

I. THE "GENESIS" OF THE AMERICAN CONSTITUTIONAL EXPERIMENT

The religion clauses of the state constitutions and of the First Amendment, forged between 1776 and 1791, express both theological and political sentiments. They reflect both the convictions of the religious believers of the young American republic and the calculations of their political leaders. They manifest both the certitude of leading eighteenth century theologians such as Isaac Backus and John Witherspoon, and the skepticism of such contemporaneous philosophers as Thomas Jefferson and Thomas Paine. A plurality of theological and political views helped to inform the early American constitutional experiment in religious rights and liberties, and to form the so-called original intent of the constitutional framers.

Notre Dame Law Review 71, no. 3 (1996): 376–77, 388–404.

The American experiment in religious rights and liberties cannot, in my view, be reduced to the First Amendment religion clauses alone, nor can the intent of the framers be determined simply by studying the cryptic record of the debates on these clauses in the First Session of Congress however valuable that source is still today. Not only are these Congressional records incomplete, but the First Amendment religion clauses, by design, reflect only a small part of the early constitutional experiment and experience. The religion clauses, on their face, define only the outer boundaries of appropriate government action respecting religion—government may not prescribe ("establish") religion nor proscribe ("prohibit") its exercise. Precisely what governmental conduct short of outright prescription or proscription of religion is constitutionally permissible is left open for debate and development. Moreover, the religion clauses on their face bind only the federal government ("Congress"), rendering prevailing state constitutional provisions, and the sentiments of their drafters, equally vital sources of original intent. Finally, the drafters of the religion clauses urged interpreters to look not to the drafters' intentions, but, in James Madison's words, "to the text itself [and] the sense attached to it by the people in their respective State Conventions, where it received all the authority which it possesses."[1] The understanding of the state conventional delegates was derived from their own state constitutional experiments and experiences, which are reflected in contemporaneous pamphlets, sermons, letters, and speeches. A wide range of eighteenth-century materials must thus be consulted to come to terms with the prevailing sentiments on religious rights and liberties in the young American republic.

A. Four Views of Religious Rights and Liberties in the Late Eighteenth Century

Within the eighteenth-century sources at hand, two pairs of theological perspectives on religious liberties and rights were critical to constitutional formation: those of congregational *Puritans* and of free church *evangelicals*. Two pairs of contemporaneous political perspectives were equally influential: those of *enlightenment* thinkers and *civic republicans*. Exponents of these four perspectives often found common cause and used common language, particularly during the Constitutional Convention and ratification debates. Yet each group cast its views in a distinctive ensemble, with its own emphases and its own applications.

***

B. The Essential Rights and Liberties of Religion

Despite the tensions among them, exponents of these four groups generally agreed upon, what New England Puritan jurist and theologian Elisha Williams called, "the essential rights and liberties of [religion]."[2] To be sure, these "essential rights and liberties" never won uniform articulation or universal assent in the young republic. But a number of enduring and interlocking principles found widespread support; many of which were included in state and federal constitutional discussions. These principles included liberty of conscience, free exercise of religion, pluralism, equality, separationism, and disestablishment of religion. Such principles remain at the heart of the American experiment today.

***

1. Liberty of Conscience

Liberty of conscience was the general solvent used in the early American experiment in religious liberty. It was universally embraced in the young republic—even by the most churlish of establishmentarians. The phrase "liberty of conscience" was often conflated with the phrase "free exercise of religion," "religious freedom," "religious liberty," "religious privileges," or "religious rights."...Such patterns of interwoven language appear regularly in later eighteenth-century writings; one term often implicated and connoted several others. To read the guarantee of liberty of conscience too dogmatically is to ignore the fluidity of the term in the eighteenth century.

Nonetheless, many eighteenth-century writers ascribed distinctive content to the phrase. First, liberty of conscience protected *voluntarism*—"the right of private judgment in matters of religion," the unencumbered ability to choose and to change one's religious beliefs and adherences. The Puritan jurist Elisha Williams put this matter very strongly for Christians in 1744....

> Every man has an equal right to follow the dictates of his own conscience in
> the affairs of religion. Every one is under an indispensable obligation to
> search the Scriptures for himself...and to make the best use of it he can for

his own information in the will of God, the nature and duties of Christianity....[3]

James Madison wrote more generically in 1785: "The Religion then of every man must be left to the conviction and conscience of every man; and it is the right of every man to exercise it as these may dictate." The evangelical leader John Leland echoed these sentiments in 1791:

> Every man must give an account of himself to God and therefore every man ought to be at liberty to serve God in that way that he can be reconcile it to his conscience....[4]

Puritan, enlightenment *philosophe*, and evangelical alike could agree on this core meaning of liberty of conscience.

Second, and closely related, liberty of conscience prohibited religiously based *discrimination* against individuals. Persons could not be penalized for the religious choices they made, nor swayed to make certain choices because of the civil advantages attached to them. Liberty of conscience, Ezra Stiles opined, permits "no bloody tribunals, no cardinals inquisitors-general, to bend the human mind, forceably to control the understanding, and put out the light of reason, the candle of the Lord in man."[5] Liberty of conscience also prohibits more subtle forms of discrimination, prejudice, and cajolery by state, church, or even other citizens. "[N]o part of the community shall be permitted to perplex or harass the other for any supposed heresy," wrote a Massachusetts pamphleteer, "...each individual shall be allowed to have and enjoy, profess and maintain his own system of religion."[6]

Third, in the view of some eighteenth-century writers, liberty of conscience guaranteed "a freedom and exemption from human impositions, and legal restraints, in matters of religion and conscience."[7] Persons of faith were to be "exempt from all those penal, sanguinary laws, that generate vice instead of virtue."[8] Such laws not only included the onerous criminal rules that traditionally encumbered and discriminated against religious nonconformists, and led to fines, whippings, banishments, and occasional executions of dissenting colonists. They also included more facially benign laws that worked injustice to certain religious believers—conscription laws that required religious pacificists to participate in the military, oath-swearing laws that ran afoul of the religious scruples of certain believers, tithing and taxing laws that forced believers to support churches, schools, and other causes that they found religiously odious. Liberty of conscience required that persons be exempt or immune from civil duties and restrictions that they could not, in good conscience, accept or obey....

It was commonly assumed in the eighteenth century that the laws of conscientious magistrates would not tread on the religious scruples of their subjects.... Where general laws and policies did intrude on the religious scruples of an individual or group, liberty of conscience demanded protection of religious minorities and exemption. Whether such exemptions should be accorded by the legislature or by the judiciary, and whether they were per se a constitutional right or simply a rule of equity—the principal bones of contention among recent commentators—the eighteenth-century sources at my disposal simply do not clearly say.

All the early state constitutions include a guarantee of liberty of conscience for all....

The principle of liberty of conscience also informed some of the federal constitutional debates on religion. Article VI of the Constitution explicitly provides: "[N]o religious Test [oath] shall ever be required as a Qualification" for public office, thereby, *inter alia*, protecting the religiously scrupulous against oath-swearing.[9] ... [Also, of course, the First Amendment provides that] "Congress shall make no law...prohibiting the free exercise [of religion]." ... Since Congress cannot "prohibit" the free exercise, the public manifestation, of religion, a fortiori Congress cannot "prohibit" a person's private liberty of conscience, and the precepts embraced therein.

Liberty of conscience was the cardinal principle for the new experiment in religious liberty. Several other "essential rights and liberties of religion" built directly on this core principle.

2. Free Exercise

Liberty of conscience was inextricably linked to free exercise of religion. Liberty of conscience was a guarantee to be left alone to choose, to entertain, and to change one's religious beliefs. Free exercise of religion was the right to act publicly on the choices of conscience once made, without intruding on or obstructing the rights of others or the general peace of the community.... Religion, Madison wrote, "must be left to the convictions and conscience of every man; and it is the right of every man to exercise it as these may dictate."[10] For most eighteenth-century writers, religious belief and religious action went hand-in-hand, and each deserved legal protection.

Though eighteenth-century writers, or dictionaries, offered no universal definition of "free exercise," the phrase generally connoted various forms of free public religious action—religious speech, religious worship, religious assembly, religious publication, religious education, among others. Free exercise of religion also embraced the right of the individual to join with like-minded believers in religious societies, which religious societies were free to devise their own modes of worship, articles of faith, standards of discipline, and patterns of ritual....

Virtually all of the early state constitutions guaranteed "free exercise" rights—adding the familiar caveat that such exercise not violate the public peace or the private rights of others. Most states limited their guarantee to "the free exercise of religious worship" or the "free exercise of religious profession"...A few states provided more generic free exercise guarantees. Virginia, for example, guaranteed "the free exercise of religion, according to the dictates of conscience"[11]...provided it was mandated by conscience. The Georgia constitution provided even more flatly: "All persons whatever shall have the free exercise of their religion; provided it be not repugnant to the peace and safety of the State."[12] The First Amendment drafters chose equally embracive language of "the free exercise" of religion. Rather than using the categorical language preferred by state drafters, however, the First Amendment drafters guaranteed protection only against Congressional laws "prohibiting" the free exercise of religion. Whether Congress could make laws "infringing" or "abridging" the free exercise of religion—as earlier drafts sought to outlaw—was left open to subsequent interpretation.

3. Pluralism

Eighteenth century writers regarded "multiplicity," "diversity," or "plurality," as an equally essential dimension of religious rights and liberties. Two kinds of pluralism were distinguished.

Evangelical and enlightenment writers urged the protection of *confessional pluralism*—the maintenance and accommodation of a plurality of forms of religious expression and organization in the community. Evangelical writers advanced a theological argument for this principle, emphasizing that it was for God, not the state, to decide which forms of religion should flourish and which should fade.... Confessional pluralism served to respect and reflect this divine prerogative. Enlightenment writers advanced a rational argument. "Difference of opinion is advantageous in religion," Thomas Jefferson wrote:

> The several sects perform the office of a *Censor morum* over each other. Is uniformity attainable? Millions of innocent men, women, and children, since the introduction of Christianity, have been burnt, tortured, fined, imprisoned; yet we have not advanced one inch towards uniformity.... Reason and persuasion are the only practicable instruments.[13]

Madison wrote similarly that "the utmost freedom... arises from that multiplicity of sects which pervades America,... for where there is such a variety of sects, there cannot be a majority of any one sect to oppress and persecute the rest."[14] Other writers added that the maintenance of multiple faiths is the best protection of the core guarantee of liberty of conscience.

Puritan and civic republican writers insisted as well on the protection of *social pluralism*—the maintenance and accommodation of a plurality of associations to foster religion. Churches and synagogues were not the only "religious societies" that deserved constitutional protection. Families, schools, charities, and other learned and civic societies were equally vital bastions of religion and equally deserving of the special protections of religious rights and liberties. These diverse social institutions had several redeeming qualities. They provided multiple forums for religious expressions and actions, important bulwarks against state encroachment on natural liberties, particularly religious liberties, and vital sources of theology, morality, charity, and discipline in the state and broader community....

Pluralism was thus not just a sociological fact for several eighteenth century writers; it was a constitutional condition for the guarantee of true religious rights and liberties. This was a species and application of Madison's argument about pluralism in *Federalist Paper No. 10*—that the best protection against political tyranny is the guarantee of a multiplicity of interests, each contending for public endorsement and political expression in a federalist republic.

4. Equality

The efficacy of liberty of conscience, free exercise of religion, and confessional pluralism depended on a guarantee of equality of all peaceable religions before the law. For the state to single out one pious person or one form of faith for either preferential benefits or discriminatory burdens would skew the choice of conscience, encumber the exercise of religion, and upset the natural plurality of faiths. Many eighteenth-century writers therefore inveighed against the state's unequal treatment of religion. Madison captured the prevailing sentiment: "A just Government...will be best supported by protecting every Citizen in the enjoyment of his Religion with the same equal hand which protects his person and property; by neither invading the equal rights of any Sect, nor suffering any Sect to invade those of another."[15]

This principle of equality of all peaceable religious persons and bodies before the law found its way into a number of early state constitutions....

The principle of equality also found its place in early drafts of the First Amendment religion clauses, yielding such phrases as: "nor shall the full and equal rights of conscience be in any manner, or on any pretext, infringed";[16] "Congress shall make no law establishing one religious sect or society in preference to others....";[17] and "Congress shall make no law establishing any particular denomination of religion in preference to another...."[18] Madison, in fact, regarded protection of the "equal rights of conscience" as the "most valuable" guarantee for religious liberty, and he argued that it should be universally guaranteed at both the federal and state levels.[19] These provisions and arguments were abandoned for the more generic guarantees of disestablishment and free exercise at the federal level—guarantees which presumably are to apply equally to all religions.

5. Separationism

The principle of separationism was designed primarily to protect religious bodies and religious believers in their inherent rights.

On the one hand, separationism guaranteed the independence and integrity of the internal processes of religious bodies. Elisha Williams spoke for many churchmen when he wrote: "[E]very church has [the] *Right* to *judge* in *what manner* God is to be *worshipped* by them, and *what Form of Discipline* ought to be observed by them, and the *Right* also of *electing their own Officers*."[20] In the mind of most eighteenth-century writers, the principle of separation of church and state mandated neither the separation of religion and politics nor the secularization of civil society. No eighteenth-century writer would countenance the preclusion of religion altogether from the public square or the political process. The principle of separationism was directed to the institutions of church and state, not to religion and culture.

On the other hand, the principle of separationism also protected the liberty of conscience of the religious believer. President Thomas Jefferson, for example, in his famous 1802 Letter to the Danbury Baptist Association, tied the principle of separationism directly to the principle of liberty of conscience:

> Believing with you *that religion is a matter which lies solely between man and his God*, that he owes account to none other for his faith or his worship, that the legislative powers of government reach actions only, and not opinions, I contemplate with sovereign reverence that act of the whole American people which declared that their legislature should "make no law respecting an establishment of religion, or prohibiting the free exercise thereof," *thus building a wall of separation between church and State....*[21]

Separatism thus assured individuals of their natural, inalienable right of conscience, which could be exercised freely and fully to the point of breaching the peace or shirking social duties. Jefferson is not talking here of separating politics and religion. Indeed, in the very next paragraph of his letter, President Jefferson performed an avowedly religious act of offering prayers on behalf of his Baptist correspondents: "I reciprocate your kind prayers for the protection and blessing of the common Father and Creator of man...."[22]

The principles of pluralism, equality, and separationism—separately and together—served to protect religious bodies, both from each other and from the state. It was an open question, however, whether such principles precluded governmental financial and other forms of support of religion altogether. Evangelical and enlightenment writers sometimes viewed such principles as a firm bar on state support, particularly financial support, of religious beliefs, believers, and bodies....

[Such] sentiments can be found in contemporaneous Baptist tracts, particularly those of Isaac Backus and John Leland. Puritan and republican writers often viewed such principles only as a prohibition against direct financial support for the religious worship or exercise of one particular religious group. General governmental support for religion—in the form of tax exemptions to religious properties, land grants and tax subsidies to religious schools and charities, tax appropriations for missionaries and military chaplains, and similar general causes—were considered not only licit, but necessary for good governance.

6. Disestablishment

For some eighteenth-century writers, particularly the New England Puritans who defended their "slender establishments," the roll of "essential rights and liberties" ended here. For other writers, however, the best protection of all these principles was through the explicit disestablishment of religion. The term "establishment of religion" was a decidedly ambiguous phrase—in the eighteenth century, as much as today. The phrase was variously used to describe compromises of the principles of separationism, pluralism, equality, free exercise, and/or liberty of conscience. The guarantee of "disestablishment of religion" could signify protection against any such compromise.

According to some eighteenth-century writers, the guarantee of disestablishment protected separationism. In Jefferson's words, it prohibited government

> from intermeddling with religious institutions, their doctrines, discipline, or exercises.... [and from] the power of effecting any uniformity of time or matter among them. Fasting and prayer are religious exercises; the enjoining them an act of discipline. Every religious society has a right to determine for itself the times for these exercises, and the objects proper for them, according to their own peculiar tenets....[23]

This view of disestablishment of religion was posed in the penultimate draft of the Establishment Clause: "Congress shall make no law establishing articles of faith or a mode of worship...."[24]—a provision rejected for a mere generic guarantee.

For other eighteenth-century writers, the guarantee of disestablishment protected the principles of equality and pluralism by preventing government from singling out certain religious beliefs and bodies for preferential treatment. This concept of disestablishment came through repeatedly in both state and federal constitutional debates....

For still others, disestablishment of religion meant foreclosing government from coercively prescribing mandatory forms of religious belief, doctrine, and practice—in violation of the core guarantee of liberty of conscience. Such coercion of religion inflates the competence of government. As Madison wrote:

[It] implies either that the Civil Magistrate is a competent Judge of Religious Truth; or that he may employ Religion as an engine of Civil policy. The first is an arrogant pretension falsified by the contradictory opinions of Rulers in all ages, and throughout the world: the second an unhallowed perversion of the means of salvation.[25]

Such coercion of religion also compromises the individual's liberty of conscience. As the Pennsylvania Constitution put it: "[N]o authority can or ought to be vested in, or assumed by any power whatever, that shall in any case interfere with, or in any manner controul [*sic*], the right of conscience in the free exercise of religious worship."[26]

The vague language of the First Amendment—"Congress shall make no law respecting an establishment"—could readily accommodate these separationist, equality, or noncoercion readings of "disestablishment." Congress may not "establish religion" outright. Nor may Congress make laws that "respect" an establishment of religion—that is anticipate, "look towards," or "regard with deference," such an establishment, to use common eighteenth-century definitions of "respecting."[27] The best way to assess whether a Congressional law violates this prohibition is to see whether it compromises any one of the cardinal principles of separationism, equality, and noncoercion protected by the disestablishment guarantee.

7. Interdependence and Incorporation of Principles

For all the diversity of opinion one finds in the Constitutional Convention debates, pamphlets, sermons, editorials, and broadsides of the eighteenth century, most influential writers embraced this roll of "essential rights and liberties of religion"—liberty of conscience, free exercise of religion, pluralism, equality, separationism, and disestablishment of religion. To be sure, many of these terms carried multiple meanings in the later eighteenth century. And to be sure, numerous other terms and norms were under discussion. But in the range of official and unofficial sources at my disposal, these principles were the most commonly discussed and embraced.

On the one hand, eighteenth-century writers designed these principles to provide an interwoven shield against repressive religious establishments. Liberty of conscience protected the individual from coercion and discriminatory treatment by church or state officials and guaranteed unencumbered, voluntary choices of faith. Free exercise of religion protected the individual's ability to discharge the duties of conscience through religious worship, speech, publication, assembly, and other actions without necessary reference to a prescribed creed, cult, or code of conduct. Pluralism protected multiple forms and forums of religious belief and action, in place of a uniformly mandated religious doctrine, liturgy, and polity. Equality protected religious individuals and bodies from special benefits and from special burdens administered by the state, or by other religious bodies. Separationism protected individual believers, as well as religious and political officials, from undue interference or intrusion on each other's processes and practices. Disestablishment precluded governmental prescriptions of the doctrine, liturgy, or morality of one faith, or compromises of the principles of liberty of conscience, free exercise, equality, pluralism, or separationism.

On the other hand, eighteenth-century writers designed these principles to be mutually supportive and mutually subservient to the highest goal of guaranteeing "the essential rights and liberties of religion" for all. No single principle could by itself guarantee such religious liberty. Simple protection of liberty of conscience provided no protection of religious actions or organizations. Pure pluralism could decay into religious relativism and render the government blind to the special place of religion in the community and in the Constitution. Simple guarantees of the equality of religion could render governments indifferent to the widely divergent needs of different forms of religion. Pure separationism could deprive the church of all meaningful forms and functions, and deprive states of an essential ally in government and social service. Pure nonestablishment could readily rob society of all common values and beliefs and the state of any effective religious role. Eighteenth-century writers, therefore, arranged these multiple principles into an interlocking and interdependent shield of religious liberties and rights for all. Religion was simply too vital and too valuable a source of individual flourishing and social cohesion to be left unguarded on any side.

NOTES

The note number from the original article is shown in the parenthesis at the end of each citation.

1. Letter from James Madison to Thomas Richie (September 15, 1821), in *Letters and Other Writings of James Madison*, vol. 3 (Philadelphia: J. B. Lippincott, 1821), p. 228. (23)

2. See Elisha Williams, *The Essential Rights and Liberties of Protestants: A Seasonable Plea for The Liberty of Conscience, and the Right of Private Judgment in Matters of Religion, Without any Control from Human Authority* (Boston: S. Kneeland and T. Green, 1744). (78)

3. See Elisha Williams, *The Essential Rights and Liberties of Protestants*, pp. 7–8. (91)

4. John Leland, *The Rights of Conscience Inalienable* (New London, CT: T. Green and Sons, 1791). (92)

5. Ezra Stiles, *The United States Elevated to Glory and Honor* (New Haven, CT: Thomas and Samuel Green, 1783), p. 56. (94)

6. *Worcestriensis*, no. 4 (1776), reprinted in Charles Hyneman and Donald S. Lutz, eds., *American Political Writing During the Founding Era, 1760–1805*, vol. 1 (Indianapolis: Liberty Press, 1983), p. 449. (95)

7. John Mellen, *The Great and Happy Doctrine of Liberty* (1795), p. 17. (96)

8. Ibid., p. 20. (97)

9. See, e.g., Joseph Story, *Commentaries on the Constitution of the United States*, vol. 3 (Boston: Hilliard, Gray, 1833), p. 703. (110)

10. James Madison, *Memorial and Remonstrance Against Religious Assessments* (1785). (116)

11. Virginia Constitution of 1776, sec. 16. (121)

12. Georgia Constitution of 1777, art. 56. (122)

13. Thomas Jefferson, *Notes on the State of Virginia, Query* 17, in Philip Kurland and Ralph Lerner, eds., *The Founders' Constitution*, vol. 5 (Chicago: University of Chicago Press, 1987), pp. 79, 80. (125)

14. James Madison, "Debates" (June 12, 1788), in Jonathan Elliot, *The Debates in the Several State Conventions on the Adoption of the Federal Constitution*, 2nd ed., vol. 3 (Philadelphia: J. B. Lippincott, 1836), p. 330. (126)

15. Madison, *Memorial and Remonstrance Against Religious Assessments*, in Robert A. Rutland and William M. E. Rachal, eds., *The Papers of James Madison*, vol. 8 (Charlottesville: University of Virginia Press, 1973), p. 298, para. 8. (131)

16. Joseph Gales, ed., *Annals of Congress*, vol. 1 (1834), p. 434. (138)

17. *Journal of the First Senate*, vol. 1 (1802), p. 70. (139)

18. Ibid. (140)

19. Gales, *Annals of Congress*, pp. 783–84. (141)

20. Elisha Williams, *The Essential Rights and Liberties of Protestants*, p. 46. (142)

21. Thomas Jefferson to Danbury Baptist Association (January 1, 1802), in H. A. Washington, ed., *The Writings of Thomas Jefferson*, vol. 8 (Washington: Tyler and Maury, 1853), p. 113. (143)

22. See Mark DeWolfe Howe, *The Garden and the Wilderness: Religion and the Gov-

ernment in American Constitutional History (Chicago: University of Chicago Press, 1965), pp. 1–3. (144)

23. Letter from Thomas Jefferson to Rev. Samuel Miller (1808), in Andrew A. Lipscomb and Albert Ellery Bergh, eds., *The Writings of Thomas Jefferson*, vol. 11 (Washington: 1904), pp. 428–29. (149)

24. *Journal of the First Session of the Senate*, vol. 1 (1802), p. 77. (150)

25. Madison, *Memorial and Remonstrance*, p. 298, para. 5. (155)

26. Pennsylvania Constitution of 1776, art. 2. (157)

27. For illustrative eighteenth-century texts, see *The Compact Edition of the Oxford English Dictionary*, vol. 2 (Oxford: Clarendon Press, 1971), p. 2512. (158)

THE SEPARATION OF THE RELIGIOUS AND THE SECULAR: A FOUNDATIONAL CHALLENGE TO FIRST AMENDMENT THEORY

Laura Underkuffler-Freund

E. The Meaning of the Second Great Principle: Freedom from Establishment of Religion by Government

The nature of colonial religious establishments and the state establishments ... [i]n the New England, middle-Atlantic, and southern areas... varied but were admixtures of the same basic characteristics: taxpayer assistance to religious institutions, state enforcement of favored religious observance and conformity, religious tests for public office or general civil capacity, and other preferential treatment on the basis of religious affiliation or belief. Although attempts to enforce or prohibit particular religious practices declined by the time of the Revolution, and systems designating single religious institutions

William and Mary Law Review 36, no. 3 (March 1995): 930–31, 933–39, 942–42, 945–54, 956–60.

as recipients of state financial assistance were largely replaced by systems implementing taxpayer choice, deeply institutionalized schemes of governmental religious preference existed throughout the colonies at the dawn of the Founding Era.

There has been much debate over whether the First Amendment to the Constitution was intended to prohibit all federal financial aid to religious institutions. Whatever the particular intentions of the framers of this document, it is clear that an "establishment," in the general understanding of the time, encompassed any tax monies given directly to a religious institution, whether designated by the state or by the taxpayer's choice. By the time of the Revolution, schemes of taxpayer choice had succeeded single payee plans in New England and elsewhere, and these programs clearly were understood to be "establishments" as well.

***

Although religious "establishments" were thought broadly to include religious tests for office and other religious preferences established by law, the simultaneous prohibition of religious establishments and the existence of religious tests and other religious privileges appeared to go unchallenged.... Many who rejected governmental financial aid to religion still supported test oaths, restriction of public office holding to Christians or to Protestants, and the enforcement of blasphemy laws. The most likely explanation for such contradictions lies not in a differing understanding of what an "establishment" was, but in the common (unquestioned) assumption that these were Protestant Christian states, where the only issue concerned the legal preference or "establishment" of particular Protestant groups.

The reasons for the growth and persistence of religious establishments were complex and undoubtedly ranged from the attempted consolidation of spiritual and political power to deep concerns about the nature of religious duty and its role in organized society. Of particularly lasting concern, both to those who advocated the maintenance of religious establishments and to those who advocated their abolition, were the common beliefs that religious establishments were necessary for the survival of both religion and the state. Both beliefs were brought to these shores from Europe, and both were heavily entrenched in all regions and in all social and religious classes—even among those who often dissented from the particular establishments chosen.

Although the belief that government establishment was necessary for the promotion (and even the survival) of religion was clearly not universal, it is found throughout the writings of this era.... Leo Pfeffer has written that in Virginia,

> [t]his was the crucial issue: was the support of religion the concern of the state, or was it a matter to "be left to voluntary contribution"? The lines were clear; to one group, liberty meant disestablishment and separation and vol-untariness, because man's relation to his Maker was not within the jurisdic-tion of civil government; to the other, establishment meant "order and internal tranquility, true piety and virtue... peace and happiness," and was therefore quite properly a state responsibility.[1]

***

Because religion was believed to be necessary for morality, and morality was necessary for the survival of society and its governmental institutions, sup-porters made attempts to justify the existence of state religious establishments on this ground as well.... Rufus King argued that Christianity was entitled to special state support and protection because its belief that the deeds of this world would be rewarded or punished was a necessary foundation for the force of moral law. Numerous state constitutions set forth special financial support or prerogatives for particular religious groups, citing the "duty" of citizens to worship God or the necessity of religion and religious institutions for the preservation of social order and government....

The general desire for protection of free religious exercise, together with a belief in the fundamental role of religion in society and government, led to complex, conflicting, and ambiguous views of religious institutions. The pos-itive role of religious institutions in fostering the moral restraints necessary for the maintenance of social bonds and republican government was widely believed and widely acknowledged....

The potential power of religious institutions was not, however, an unmit-igated blessing. It created fear as well as promise. Belief in the necessity of religiously based values for social and governmental cohesion, and belief in the importance of religious institutions in the propagation of those values, did not lead to the conclusion that religious institutions should be involved in governmental affairs. With the exception of early theocracies in the New

England colonies, the relationship between institutional church and state was viewed as a one-way street—government was free to aid religious institutions, but religious institutions were precluded from involvement in the affairs of government. Even New England Federalists, who gave actual or tacit approval to existing schemes of state support for religious institutions, distrusted the involvement of those institutions in governmental affairs. Although the inculcation of moral values was seen as a vital and legitimate function of religious institutions, the involvement of these institutions in the structures of political power was not....

***

Reformers attacked all three assumptions of those who favored religious establishments: that establishments were necessary for religion, that establishments were necessary for republican government, and that state aid could be given to religious institutions while maintaining their preclusion from the affairs of government. James Madison launched a most concerted attack upon the theoretical underpinnings of establishment theories. In his famous *Memorial and Remonstrance Against Religious Assessments*, he argued that state funding for teachers of Christianity must be opposed "[b]ecause the establishment proposed by the Bill is not requisite for the support of the Christian Religion," "[b]ecause experience witnesseth that ecclesiastical establishments, instead of maintaining the purity and efficacy of Religion, have had a contrary operation," and "[b]ecause the establishment in question is not necessary for the support of Civil Government."[2] Madison attacked the chain of reasoning of establishment proponents at its root, arguing that state support was, in fact, antithetical to religious freedom, and undermined the role that religious values might play in the maintenance of civil society and government....

***

Others launched similar attacks. Jefferson argued that Pennsylvania and New York "have long subsisted without any establishment at all. The experiment was new and doubtful when they made it. It has answered beyond conception. They flourish infinitely. Religion is well supported; of various kinds, indeed, but all good enough; all sufficient to preserve peace and order...."[3]

Reformers did not attack the foundational belief of traditional proponents of establishments—that religion was necessary to sustain the moral fiber of society and the governmental institutions founded by that society. Rather, they attacked the assumption that state support of religion was constructive, rather than destructive, of religious faith and flourishing. For them, religious faith was a matter of individual conviction, and governmental efforts to support or enforce religion would only work toward its destruction.

The existence of state aid to religious institutions raised, for reformers, the distinct and overwhelming danger of the aggregation of governmental and religious institutional power. This "establishment of religion by government" was, in their view, the inevitable historical product of governmental aid to religion and the consequent involvement of religious and governmental institutions in each other's affairs....

As President of the United States, Madison vetoed an attempt by Congress to incorporate the Episcopal Church in the District of Columbia. This bill, which prescribed the organization and governance of the church, was opposed by Madison on grounds that echo modern entanglement doctrine. The bill, Madison wrote, violated the Establishment Clause and the "essential distinction between civil and religious functions." "This particular church...would...be a religious establishment by law, a legal force and sanction being given to certain articles in its constitution and administration."[4] The provisions in the bill granting the church authority to provide for the support of the poor was likewise dangerous, because they "would be a precedent for giving to religious societies as such a legal agency in carrying into effect a public and civil duty."[5]...

In addition, reformers openly challenged the traditional belief that the state could give aid to religious institutions while simultaneously precluding their involvement in the structures of political power. Reformers viewed the traditionalists' belief that establishments could be a one-way street—with state aid to religious institutions; but no reciprocal involvement of religious institutions in the affairs of government—as a painful and dangerous naiveté. They ridiculed the expectation that religious institutions, whose financial welfare and, perhaps, very existence depended upon the beneficence of civil government and its laws, would remain separate and apart from the affairs of government....

Fear of church-state merger also proceeded on a more subtle basis: that the establishment of religion by government threatened the equality of all religious sects in the eyes of the law. Reformers vehemently believed that "no man or class of men, ought, on account of religion to be invested with peculiar emoluments or privileges, nor be subjected to any penalties or disabilities"[6] and that the involvement of government in the making of distinctions between citizens on this basis violated required neutrality. By clear implication, the existence of religious establishments also attempted to influence religious exercise and practice in violation of rights of conscience....

***

Reformers acknowledged the difficulties inherent in the concept of institutional separation of church and state...Even those who favored the general theory of church-state separation disagreed about the particulars of its implementation. The Northwest Ordinance, as originally drafted, reserved one section of land in each township for religious purposes. Such general support of religion by government was advocated by many moderates. Madison, on the other hand, applauded the ordinance's demise, remarking, "[h]ow a regulation, so unjust in itself, so foreign to the Authority of [Congress,] so hurtful to the sale of the public land, and smelling so strongly of an antiquated Bigotry, could have received the countenance of a [congressional committee] is truly [a] matter of astonishment."[7]

Particular disagreement erupted on issues of governmental involvement in recommendations, proclamations, and exercises that were (at least arguably) religious in nature. Evangelical Protestant groups and others exhibited extreme concern over public calls for religious services....

For government to *require* public religious activities would clearly have violated church/state separation in the view of reformers; on the question of government recommendation, or government example, the responses were mixed.... After the adoption of the Federal Constitution by the First Congress, a resolution was offered which requested that the President recommend to the people of the United States a day of thanksgiving and prayer. Objection was raised that "'it is a business with which Congress has nothing to do; it is a religious matter,...proscribed to us.'"[8] The resolution carried, and Washington issued the proclamation.

Jefferson, when President of the United States, refused to follow suit. He explained:

> I consider the government of the United States as interdicted by the Constitution from intermeddling with religious institutions, their doctrines, discipline, or exercises.[9] ...

The argument that such governmental edicts were merely recommendatory, without civil or criminal sanction, failed to persuade him. "It must be meant, too," he wrote, "that this recommendation is to carry some authority,...perhaps in public opinion."[10] This "change in the nature of the penalty [did not] make the recommendation less a *law* of conduct for those to whom it is directed."[11]...

In his Presidential years, Madison issued Thanksgiving Day proclamations, bowing to the power of tradition, the cultural expectations of the people, and the example of predecessors. He later wrote almost apologetically of his yielding on this issue, stressing that he was "always careful to make the Proclamations absolutely indiscriminate, and merely recommendatory;...a day, on which all who thought proper might *unite* in consecrating it to religious purposes, according to their own faith and forms."[12] He acknowledged that these proclamations deviated from his principles of separation of church and state, and "lost sight of the equality of *all* religious sects in the eye of the Constitution."[13]...

Similar conflicts surrounded the issue of the appointment of federal chaplains. Congressional chaplains were first established by Act of Congress on September 22, 1789...Madison signed an act reauthorizing the appointment of Congressional chaplains in 1816. In his later writing, Madison repudiated this practice:

> Is the appointment of Chaplains to the two Houses of Congress consistent with the Constitution, and with the pure principle of religious freedom? In strictness the answer on both points must be in the negative. The Constitution of the U.S. forbids everything like an establishment of a national religion. The law appointing Chaplains establishes a religious worship for the national representatives, to be performed by Ministers of religion, elected by a majority of them; and these are to be paid out of the national taxes. Does not this involve the principle of a national establishment...? The establishment of the chaplainship [in Congress] is a palpable violation of equal rights, as well as of Constitutional principles: The tenets of the chaplains elected [by the majority] shut the door of worship [against] the members whose creeds [and] consciences forbid a participation in that of the majority....[14]

These views were shared by Protestant religious leaders, such as John Leland; they apparently were not shared by many others of the age.

Objections to the use of religion by government were grounded in three powerful ideas: that religion must be, and is, wholly exempt from the cognizance of government; that governmental involvement in religious activities destroys the requirement of government neutrality among religious sects; and that any institutional merger of church and state must be avoided. Despite these concerns, routine governmental papers were replete with mention of "God," "Nature's God," "Providence," and other religious references. Religious references on the Great Seal of the United States were apparently deemed desirable by conservatives and reformers alike....

***

F. Summary and Conclusion

The historical record is far from unambiguous. Political spokesmen, traditional religionists, and the leaders of emerging dissident religious groups often had radically different world views and radically different images of the existing social and governmental order. Differences pervaded the goals, motivations, and understandings of language of the participants in the great dialogue.

Although these differences existed, various strains of congruence among reformers can be found. Religiously based truths, however understood, were widely believed to be the foundation of the ultimate moral principles on which civil society and republican governmental systems depended. Natural law, natural rights, and similar concepts were the articulations of what was believed to be man's apprehension of the transcendent truths of the universal natural order. Calls for "liberty," "justice," "truth," "equality," and so on had extraordinarily cohesive power, whatever differences their makers intended.

Even those who clearly fell within the Enlightenment tradition assumed the existence of a Provident natural order and the workings of transcendent or religious beliefs and ideals in private and public life. The explosion of scientific discovery and social scientific thinking in the eighteenth century led not to an abandonment of religion, but to attempts to harmonize religious concepts with scientific discoveries and emerging beliefs in a rational, self-sustaining natural order.... The task that the articulate spokesmen of this era set for themselves was not the eradication of the religious from public life, but the development of ways in which the avowedly religious nature of the people could be fostered while protecting religious and governmental institutions from destruction, each by the other.

The implementation of these ideas as part of a governmental plan was the subject of great conflict. As ideas of reform gained momentum, they crystallized around a core concept: the call for freedom of conscience. Freedom of conscience encompassed ideas of individual free inquiry and private judgment. It was used to describe the process by which many believed that religious belief and conviction were formed....

The protection of freedom of conscience lay at the base of two great and emerging principles: free exercise of religion and the destruction of religious establishments by government. Neither was a simple concept with simple acclaim and obvious application. The understandings of these principles, and how they should be implemented to protect the deeper goals that they represented, were the subjects of deep disagreements. The principles were not neat or exclusive, with clearly defined boundaries into which human activities could be sorted.

...There was nearly universal agreement that free religious exercise included freedom to pursue religious activities and worship, although the extension of these rights to disfavored religious groups often was denied in principle and in practice. Despite such inconsistencies, a consensus emerged that free religious worship must include the ability to erect houses of worship of the design desired; the freedom to attend, or not to attend, religious services; and the freedom of religious institutions to control their doctrines, disciplines, and exercises....

***

Similarly, indirect attempts by government to enforce or to promote particular beliefs—through the use of test oaths for public office, public taxation for religious organizations, and so on—increasingly were viewed in hostile terms. Such religious establishments by government were seen as potentially corrupting on various levels: to individuals, who would be forced to act in ways contrary to the dictates of conscience in order to obtain public power or benefits; to religious institutions, which would lose their spiritual and actual autonomy in the scramble for governmental largesse and political power; and to government, which would, through alliance or merger with religious institutions, lose its ability to respect and protect the needs of all citizens in accordance with fundamental concepts of equality.

The importance of religious belief to the moral foundations of society and government, which was asserted by those who supported religious establishments, was not denied by those who opposed them. Although religious institutions were seen as necessary expressions of religious freedom, and as valuable contributors to the inculcation of moral values, their merger with government was believed to hold the potential for intellectual tyranny and the destruction of the very freedom of conscience that their existence represented. The question was how to preserve the benevolent function of religious institutions without fostering an aggregation of governmental and religious institutional power. In early colonial days, many believed that this balance could be accomplished through state support of religious institutions in a myriad of ways. By the time of the Constitutional Convention of 1787, and the confrontation of these issues in the context of a national polity, a consensus was clearly emerging that it could not. Conditions of religious diversity, and persistent calls for the general sanctity of individual belief, rendered existing mergers of religious institutions with government increasingly untenable.

The implementation of these principles was uneven and fraught with inconsistency, even among the influential reformers of the age. Although schemes that forced individuals to pay toward the maintenance of others' religious institutions were widely condemned by the time of the Revolution, schemes that merely forced individuals to pay toward the maintenance of their own religious institutions were supported, at least lukewarmly, by many of the articulate spokesmen of this era. Only as time progressed, and such establishments were increasingly opposed on free conscience and free exercise grounds, were inroads against them made as well. Historical practices, political pressures, and unquestioned belief in the positive role of religion in society and in government led to many unusual configurations. Announcements of principles of equality coexisted with religious test oaths in state constitutions. Reformers, working from the same principles, both opposed and supported the issuance of Thanksgiving Day proclamations and the teaching of Christianity at a publicly financed university. Although general principles were clear, their implementation often was not.

Although inconsistencies can certainly be found, the thrust of the reformers' message was clear. Moreover, the difficulty in determining the proper implementation of principles of church state separation was rooted in a deeper reality: that the religious impulse and American culture were deeply intertwined. The prevailing view throughout this era, shared by traditionalists and reformers alike, was that religion was an accepted and necessary part of human expression and communal life. The question was how to end direct and indirect governmental compulsion in matters of conscience, while maintaining the social structures and the fabric of shared values believed to be necessary for social cohesion and free government.

NOTES

The note number from the original article is shown in the parenthesis at the end of each citation.

1. Leo Pfeffer, *Church, State, and Freedom* (Boston: Beacon Press, 1967), p. 108. (446)

2. James Madison, *Memorial and Remonstrance Against Religious Assessments* (1785). (471)

3. Thomas Jefferson, "Notes on the State of Virginia," in Merrill D. Peterson, ed., *The Portable Thomas Jefferson* (New York: Viking Press, 1975), p. 212. (477)

4. James Madison, "Veto Message" (February 21, 1811), in Saul K. Padover, ed., *The Complete Madison: His Basic Writings* (New York: Harper, 1953), p. 307. (484)

5. Ibid. (485)

6. James Madison, *Virginia Journal* (1776), in Norman Cousins, ed., introduction to *"In God We Trust": The Religious Beliefs and Ideas of the Founding Fathers* (New York: Harper, 1958), p. 301. (489)

7. Letter from James Madison to James Monroe (May 29, 1785), in William T. Hutchinson and William M. E. Rachal, eds., *The Papers of James Madison*, vol. 8 (Chicago: University of Chicago Press, 1962), pp. 285, 286. (498)

8. Anson P. Stokes, *Church and State in the United States*, vol. 1 (New York: Harper, 1950), p. 487. (505)

9. Letter from Thomas Jefferson to Rev. Samuel Miller (January 23, 1808), in Albert E. Bergh, ed., *The Writings of Thomas Jefferson, Containing His Autobiography, Notes on Virginia, Parliamentary Manual, Official Papers, Messages and Address, and Other Writings, Official and Private, Now Collected and Published in their Entirety for the First Time*, vol. 11 (Washington, 1907), p. 428. (507)

10. Ibid., pp. 428–29. (508)

11. Ibid., p. 429. (509)

12. Letter from James Madison to Edward Livingston (July 10, 1822), in *Letters and Other Writings of James Madison*, vol. 3 (Philadelphia: J. B. Lippincott, 1867), pp. 273, 275. (512)

13. Ibid., pp. 274–75. (513)

14. Elizabeth Fleet, "Madison's 'Detached Memoranda,'" *William and Mary Quarterly* 3 (1946): 534, 558–59. (516)

SECTION II

GOVERNMENT FUNDING OF RELIGIOUS INSTITUTIONS AND RELIGIOUS ACTIVITIES

EDITOR'S INTRODUCTION

SUPREME COURT CASES ADJUDICATING GOVERNMENT FUNDING OF RELIGIOUS INSTITUTIONS AND ACTIVITIES

The United States Supreme Court has decided numerous cases involving government funding of religious schools and other faith-based institutions over the last 50 years. The first modern case, *Everson v. Board of Education*, 330 U.S. 1 (1947), declared that taxpayer funds could not be used to support religious activities or institutions. The majority opinion (which is included in this anthology), however, upheld a law reimbursing families for the transportation costs they incurred in sending their children to religious schools in publicly operated busses. The next case, *Board of Education v. Allen*, 392 U.S. 236 (1968), upheld a state program providing secular textbooks to students at both public and private schools, including religious schools. In an important sense, the Court in *Allen* took a significant step beyond its earlier decision in *Everson*. Public transportation was an intrinsically secular function—administered by local government and entirely divorced from the education that students received at religious schools. As such it could be analogized to police and fire protection and other general public services. School textbooks, on the other hand, would be part of the educational program supervised by religious school authorities.

In *Lemon v. Kurtzman*, 403 U.S. 602 (1971), the Court struck down state grants supplementing the salaries of teachers of secular subjects at private schools and state contracts that reimbursed private schools for their actual expenditures for teachers salaries, textbooks, and instructional materials. In *Lemon*, the Court set out a test for evaluating state funding programs that included religious institutions as grantees. "First, the statute must have a secular legislative purpose; second, its principle or primary effect must be one that neither advances nor inhibits religion; finally, the statute must not foster 'an excessive government entanglement with religion.'" Ibid. at 612–13 (citations omitted). Commonly referred to as the "*Lemon* test," this standard was utilized by courts to adjudicate Establishment Clause disputes for the next three decades.

As originally conceived and applied, the *Lemon* test proved to be a formidable barrier against most forms of state aid to religious schools. Direct aid to "pervasively sectarian religious institutions," a class which included most primary and secondary religious schools, was generally recognized to violate the Constitution. As the Court stated in *Hunt v. McNair*, 413 U.S. 734, 743 (1973), "Aid normally may be thought to have a primary effect of advancing religion when it flows to an institution in which religion is so pervasive that a substantial portion of its functions are subsumed in the religious mission..." This presumption about advancing religion might be rebutted if funding programs included adequate provisions for the monitoring and supervision of the uses to which state aid would be put—in order to guarantee that public funds were not used for religious purposes. The implementation of such requirements, however, was held to constitute a prohibited entanglement of government with religion. Thus, state aid to religious schools either unconstitutionally advanced religion if it created a risk that the public funds would be used for religious purposes or it unconstitutionally entangled government with religion if it contained adequate monitoring mechanisms to preclude that result.

Even under the *Lemon* test, a few aid programs survived constitutional review, although the distinctions the Court drew between valid and invalid funding provisions were often criticized as arbitrary and inconsistent. A brief description of some representative cases during this period should illustrate the scope of the Court's approach. In *Committee for Public Education v. Nyquist*, 413 U.S. 756 (1973), for example, the Court struck down programs reimbursing families for religious school tuition, providing tax deductions to parents whose children attended private schools, and offering direct grants for the maintenance and repair of private school facilities. During the same term, in *Levitt v. Committee for Public Education*, 413 U.S. 472 (1973), the Court also ruled that it was unconstitutional for the state to reimburse private schools for the costs of various functions mandated by state law—including recordkeeping and the administration and grading of teacher-prepared exams.

Two years later in *Meek v. Pittenger*, 421 U.S. 349 (1975), the Court concluded that it violated the Establishment Clause for a state to loan instructional materials, including maps, charts, and laboratory equipment, to religious schools. The provision of remedial instruction, guidance counseling, and speech and hearing services by state employees to students attending religious schools on the school's premises was also struck down as unconstitutional. Relying on the earlier precedent of *Allen*, the Court in *Pittenger* did uphold a textbook loan program providing secular books to students attending any elementary or secondary school, private or public. In contrast to the *Levitt* and *Pittenger* decisions, however, in *Wolman v. Walter*, 433 U.S. 229 (1977), the Court accepted state programs funding the distribution and scoring of standardized tests for students at religious schools, providing speech and hearing diagnostic services to such students, and offering therapeutic, guidance and remedial services to students if the services did not occur on the premises of religious schools they attended.

In 1985, in *Grand Rapids School District. v. Ball*, 473 U.S. 373, the Court struck down a state program under which state teachers provided remedial instruction to religious school students after hours on the school's premises. In *Aguilar v. Felton*, 473 U.S. 402, decided the same term, a similar, federal remedial program was invalidated.

During this period, the Court's general opposition to the public funding of religious schools recognized certain limits to its Establishment Clause concerns. First, in cases such as *Tilton v. Richardson*, 403 U.S. 672 (1971), and *Roemer v. Board of Public Works*, 426 U.S. 736 (1976), the Court seemed more willing to permit public funding for secular activities at religious colleges than it had been with regard to grants to elementary and secondary schools. Second, in *Mueller v. Allen*, 463 U.S. 388 (1983), the Court upheld a law allowing the parents of children attending either public or private schools to deduct educational expenses for tuition, textbooks, and transportation from the gross income they reported on their income tax forms. The opinion in *Mueller* particularly emphasized that while some of the state funds at issue might ultimately be paid to religious schools, that result would only occur through the private choice of individual parents as to the schools their children would attend.

After 1985, the Court's approach to questions about the funding of religious schools and other religious institutions began to change in important respects. In part, this doctrinal shift built on the analytic distinction emphasized in *Mueller* between direct grants of aid and indirect support that would only reach religious schools and their students if channeled to them by the independent choices of private intermediaries. Thus, in *Witters v. Washington Deptartment of Services for the Blind*, 474 U.S. 481 (1986), the Court held that the Establishment Clause does not prohibit a state from providing financial assistance for vocational rehabilitation and training to a blind student who chose to study at a Christian college to prepare for a career as a pastor or a missionary. Following *Witters*, in *Zobrest v. Catalina Foothills School District*, 509 U.S. 1 (1993), the Court concluded that the government was not precluded from paying for a sign language interpreter for a deaf student attending religious school. Critical to the Court's conclusion in both cases was the fact that the government assistance was provided to a class of disabled students—some of whom independently decided to use the government's support to pursue their education in a religious school.

In *Zelman v. Simmons-Harris*, 536 U.S. 639 (2002), in the most far reaching indirect aid decision it has issued to date, the Court upheld voucher subsidies providing substantial tuition aid to students in Cleveland, Ohio—pursuant to a program in which the great majority of participating private schools were religious schools. Again, the Court emphasized that state funds were provided to a large class of citizens on the basis of neutral criteria, and that the decision of families to use their tuition grants at religious schools was the result "of their own genuine and independent private choice." (The *Zelman* case is discussed at length in Thomas Berg's article in this section of the anthology.)

In addition to these indirect aid decisions, the Court also demonstrated a new willingness to permit direct state support of pervasively sectarian organizations engaged in educational or social welfare services. In *Agostini v. Felton*, 521 U.S. 203 (1997), the Court overruled *Aguilar* and that part of its decision in *Ball* invalidating programs providing remedial services by public employees to religious school students on the school's premises. The Court saw little reason to believe that public school teachers would include religious content in their otherwise secular programs simply because their services were offered in a religious school's building. It also modified the entanglement prong of the *Lemon* test. Concerns about entangling government and religion would only be relevant to the constitutionality of direct aid programs if they had the effect of inhibiting or advancing religion.

In a more significant retreat from prior cases, in *Mitchell v. Helms*, 530 U.S. 793 (2000), the Court upheld a federal program providing aid for instructional and educational materials including computers, software, library materials and services, and reference works to religious schools. In doing so, the Court overruled prior cases and rejected the idea that the fact that aid to religious schools might be divertible to religious uses was relevant to the Establishment Clause inquiry. Indeed, four justices argued in a plurality opinion that as long as state aid to public and private schools (either direct or indirect) was allocated pursuant to neutral criteria and did not itself contain religious content, its use by schools for religious instruction and indoctrination would not violate constitutional guarantees.

In an additional line of cases, beginning with *Widmar v. Vincent*, 454 U.S. 263 (1981), and extending through *Good News Club v. Milford Central School*, 533 U.S. 98 (2001), the Court has repeatedly ruled that it violates the Free Speech Clause of the First Amendment for the state to deny access to public property to speakers or groups engaged in religious expressive activities when the same property is open to similarly situated speakers or groups expressing secular messages. While almost all of these cases involved access to publicly property made available to private citizens for expressive purposes, one case applied a similar free speech analysis to the allocation of public funds. In *Rosenberger v. Rector & Visitors of the University of Virginia*, 515 U.S. 819 (1995), the University awarded grants from students fees to a wide range of student organizations engaged in expressive activities, but refused to provide comparable support to a student group that wanted to publish a religious periodical. The Court ruled that in the context of a general funding program in which the University disavowed any educational interest in, or control over, the student activities it supported, such discrimination against religious viewpoints violated the Free Speech Clause.

CHAPTER 5

DIRECT AID

RELIGIOUS FREEDOM AT A CROSSROADS

MICHAEL W. MCCONNELL

III. A RELIGION CLAUSE JURISPRUDENCE FOR A PLURALISTIC NATION

A jurisprudence of the Religion Clauses must begin with a proper understanding of the ideals of the Clauses and the evils against which they are directed. We can then formulate legal doctrine. The great mistake of the Warren and Burger Courts was to embrace the ideal of the secular state, with its corresponding tendencies toward indifference or hostility to religion. The mistake of the emerging jurisprudence of the Rehnquist Court is to defer to majoritarian decision making. A better understanding of the ideal of the Religion Clauses, both normatively and historically, is that they guarantee a pluralistic republic in which citizens are free to exercise their religious differences without hindrance from the state (unless necessary to important purposes of civil government), whether that hindrance is for or against religion.

The great evil against which the Religion Clauses are directed is

University of Chicago Law Review 59 (Winter 1992): 168–69, 183–87.

government-induced homogeneity—the tendency of government action to discourage or suppress the expression of differences in matters of religion. As Madison explained to the First Congress, "the people feared one sect might obtain a preeminence, or two combine together, and establish a religion to which they would compel others to conform."[1] As such authorities of the day as Thomas Jefferson and Adam Smith argued, government-enforced uniformity in religion produced both "indolence" within the church and oppression outside the church.[2] Diversity allows each religion to "flourish according to the zeal of its adherents and the appeal of its dogma,"[3] without creating the danger that any particular religion will dominate the others. At some times in our history, and even in some isolated regions of the country today, the great threat to religious pluralism has been a triumphalist majority religion. The more serious threat to religious pluralism today is a combination of indifference to the plight of religious minorities and a preference for the secular in public affairs. This translates into an unwillingness to enforce the Free Exercise Clause when it matters, and a hypertrophic view of the Establishment Clause.

When scrutinizing a law or governmental practice under the Religion Clauses, the courts should ask the following question: is the purpose or probable effect to increase religious uniformity, either by inhibiting religious practice (a Free Exercise Clause violation) or by forcing or inducing a contrary religious practice (an Establishment Clause violation), without sufficient justification? The baseline for these judgments is the hypothetical world in which individuals make decisions about religion on the basis of their own religious conscience, without the influence of government. The underlying principle is that governmental action should have the minimum possible effect on religion, consistent with achievement of the government's legitimate purposes.

***

3. Equal Access to Public Resources

One of the most important eighteenth-century abuses against which the no-establishment principle was directed was mandatory support for churches and ministers. This system was support for religion qua religion; it singled out religion as such for financial benefit. Secular institutions, activities, and ideologies received no comparable form of assistance. Religious assessments were eliminated in Virginia, Maryland, and most of the southern states by

1789, and in New England by 1834. As the Supreme Court has noted, the struggle against religious assessments was a central event in the development of the philosophy of the Religion Clauses of the First Amendment.

In the ensuing 150 years, the government began to assist in a wide range of charitable and educational activities, formerly left to private (frequently religious) endeavor. Frequently, the government chose to enter these fields not by setting up its own agencies, but by making financial contributions to private institutions that supplied services to the public. Common examples included higher education, hospitals, and orphanages. An advantage of private administration over public was that it preserved diversity, since different institutions would bring a different perspective and approach to the activity. The ultimate beneficiaries thus had a degree of choice. A student interested in a Catholic education could go to a Catholic college; a patient needing to keep to a kosher diet could go to a Jewish hospital; a dying mother wanting her child to be raised as a Protestant could designate a Protestant orphanage. A citizen need not forfeit public benefits as a condition to exercising the religious option. In its only case involving government aid to a religious institution prior to 1947, *Bradfield v. Roberts*, the Court held that the religious affiliation of a Catholic hospital was "wholly immaterial" to its right to receive government funds.[4]

When government funding of religiously affiliated social and educational services became a constitutional issue in the late 1940s, the Court properly looked back at the religious assessment controversy. But it missed the point. The Court did not notice that the assessments against which the advocates of disestablishment inveighed were discriminatory in favor of religion. Instead, the Court concluded that taxpayers have a constitutionally protected immunity against the use of their tax dollars for religious purposes. This immunity necessitated discrimination against religion, thus turning the neutrality principle of the assessment controversy on its head.

The Court's analysis failed to recognize the effect of the change in governmental roles. When the government provides no financial support to the nonprofit sector except for churches, it aids religion. But when the government provides financial support to the entire nonprofit sector, religious and nonreligious institutions alike, on the basis of objective criteria, it does not aid religion. It aids higher education, health care, or child care; it is neutral to religion. Indeed, to deny equal support to a college, hospital, or orphanage on the ground that it conveys religious ideas is to penalize it for being religious. It is a penalty whether the government excludes the religious institution from the program altogether... or requires the institution to secularize a portion of its program....

The underlying issue is precisely the same as that in *Sherbert v. Verner*. The question in *Sherbert* was whether the state could deny benefits to an individual otherwise eligible for unemployment compensation on the ground that she refused to make herself available for work on her Sabbath day.[5] The Court recognized that the denial of a benefit, under such circumstances, is equivalent to a "fine" for adhering to her religious convictions.[6] ... The same point applies to nondiscriminatory support for hospitals, colleges, orphanages, and schools. The government supports them not as religious institutions but as colleges, hospitals, orphanages, and schools. To deny benefits to an otherwise eligible institution "forces [it] to choose between following the precepts of [its] religion and forfeiting benefits, on the one hand, and abandoning one of the precepts of [its] religion in order [to obtain support], on the other hand."[7] If the Court was correct to abandon the right-privilege distinction under the Free Exercise Clause, and I believe it was, the Court was illogical and inconsistent to hold to the right-privilege distinction under the Establishment Clause. Equal access to public resources is not a "privilege," and it does not violate the Establishment Clause.

This inconsistent application of the right-privilege distinction is the most fundamental cause of the contradiction between the *Lemon* test and the Free Exercise Clause. *Lemon* assumes an outmoded conception of government aid, which treats equal access as "aid." The Free Exercise Clause, at a minimum... prohibits discrimination against an institution solely on the ground that it is religious. The *Lemon* test outlaws nondiscriminatory treatment and the Free Exercise Clause requires it.

We must therefore reject the central animating idea of modern Establishment Clause analysis: that taxpayers have a constitutional right to insist that none of their taxes be used for religious purposes. Properly conceived, the taxpayer has a right to insist that the government not give tax dollars to religion qua religion, or in a way that favors religion over nonreligion, or one religion over another. But the taxpayer has no right to insist that the government discriminate against religion in the distribution of public funds. In this pluralistic country, taxpayers come in all varieties of belief and unbelief. To tax everyone, but to dispense money only to secular organizations, is to use government's coercive power to disadvantage religion.

Moreover, it follows that if religious organizations have a constitutional right to equal access to public programs, the government may not condition their access on rules which burden their practice of religion, unless the rules are closely related to the purposes of the program. For example, if the government made grants to organizations providing vocational training, the government could not, in effect, exclude Jewish organizations by requiring all recipients to remain open on Saturday, unless Saturday operations could be persuasively shown to be necessary to the successful conduct of the program. Similarly, if the government provided vouchers for education, the government could not exclude Catholic schools by requiring that recipient schools distribute birth control devices to the students, unless birth control distribution is necessary to education. The test is the same as in any other free exercise case. The threat of loss of funding is an "indirect" burden on the exercise of religion, and cannot be allowed unless there is an overriding governmental purpose. Conditions on spending are indistinguishable in principle from direct regulation.

This does not mean that all participants in government programs have an unlimited constitutional right to engage in religious speech in the context of the program. The test is whether participants have the right to engage in political or other controversial secular speech. Religious speech rights are not superior; nor are they inferior. Thus, in government programs in which grantees are paid to convey a particular message to the public (and no other), religious speech restrictions are permissible and may even be required. In *Bowen v Kendrick*,[8] for example, the federal government made grants to various public and private organizations, including some affiliated with religion, for the purpose of conducting programs to promote responsible attitudes toward sex among adolescents. The government forbade grantees to "teach or promote religion" in the course of the funded programs, and the Supreme Court held that this restriction is mandated by the Establishment Clause. Since this was not a program that permitted free speech about controversial topics of the grantees' choice, but instead one based on structured curricula approved in advance by the federal agency, any claim of free speech rights was properly rejected.

By contrast, it would not be permissible to restrict the rights of artists receiving grants under the National Endowment for the Arts to produce art on religious themes. If artists can convey controversial messages about politics and culture without censorship, it would be unconstitutional to deny them a similar right when they convey messages about religion....

NOTES

The note number from the original article is shown in the parenthesis at the end of each citation.

1. "Speech of James Madison" (August 5, 1787), in Joseph Gales, ed., *Annals of Congress*, vol. 1 (1834), p. 758. (238)

2. See Thomas Jefferson, *Notes on the State of Virginia* (Trenton: 1784), pp. 214–20, query 17; Adam Smith, *The Wealth of Nations* (Ward, Lock and Co., 1838), pp. 622–44. (239)

3. *Zorach v. Clausen*, 343 U.S. 306, 313 (1952). (240)

4. *Bradford v. Roberts*, 175 U.S. 291, 298 (1899). (299)

5. *Sherbert v. Verner*, 374 U.S. 398, 403 (1963). (307)

6. Ibid., p. 404. (308)

7. Ibid. (310)

8. *Bowen v. Kendrick*, 487 U.S. 589 (1988). (314)

FEDERAL FUNDS FOR PAROCHIAL SCHOOLS? NO.

LEO PFEFFER

1. Church-State Separation

***

The struggle for religious liberty and the separation of church and state in America is largely a history of the struggle against compulsory taxation for religious purposes....

Perhaps the most dramatic and critical battle took place in Virginia in 1786, the year before our federal constitution was written. A bill was introduced in the legislature of that state whose purpose it was to provide tax funds for the teaching of religion. The bill provided that every taxpayer could designate the sect or denomination that would be the beneficiary of his payment. After a bitter struggle the bill was defeated, largely as a result of the efforts of James Madison, the father of our Constitution, and the author of our Bill of Rights.

Notre Dame Law Review 37 (1962): 310–22.

The major factor in the defeat of the measure was Madison's monumental *Memorial and Remonstrance,* one of the great documents in the history of American freedom. In it, Madison set forth 15 arguments against government support of religion, arguments that are as valid today as they were in 1786. Basically they fall into two classes; those predicated on the concept of voluntariness in matters of conscience, and those predicated on the concept that religion is outside the jurisdiction of political government—the two aspects of what five years later were to become the opening words of the Bill of Rights, "Congress shall make no law respecting an establishment of religion or prohibiting the free exercise thereof." It is for this reason that the Supreme Court has held that Madison's struggle against the Virginia bill is an important part of the legislative history of the First Amendment.

The defeat of the Virginia bill in 1786 was followed by the enactment of Jefferson's great Virginia Statute Establishing Religious Freedom. This law, too, reflected the dual aspect of what was later to be the religion clause of the First Amendment—voluntariness and separation. The Act forbade the use of tax funds for religious purposes, and prohibited such use even if a taxpayer's money were to be paid exclusively to the religion of his own choice.

***

The First Amendment was added to the Constitution in 1791, but it was not until 1947 that the Supreme Court found it necessary to provide a definitive interpretation of the amendment's ban on laws respecting an establishment of religion. In that year, in the case of *Everson v. Board of Education*[1] the Court specifically interpreted the amendment as barring all government aid to religion and as erecting a wall of separation between church and state....

[Critics of this analysis argued] that the Court had misread history and distorted the intent of the framers of the amendment. It was not, the critics contended, the purpose of the First Amendment to divorce religion from government or to impose neutrality between believers and nonbelievers, but only to meet in a practical way the problems raised by the existence of a multiplicity of sects. This was done by requiring the government to be neutral as among these competing sects and forbidding it to favor one at the expense of the others. The amendment was not intended to bar the government from aiding or supporting religion and religious institutions so long as the aid and support are granted equally and without preference to some faiths or discrimination against others....

***

It is…clear today [however] that the First Amendment bars federal aid to churches and church schools whether such aid is preferential or not. This bar is not motivated by hostility to religion, but on the contrary by a recognition that government helps religion best by leaving it strictly alone.…

Our Constitution and Bill of Rights were adopted before the development of our public school system, and the application of the First Amendment to public education was therefore not clear. But by 1875 our public school system had become firmly established, and the application to it of the principle of separation of church and state was eloquently stated by President Grant in his address that year to the Grand Army of the Tennessee:

> Encourage free schools and resolve that not one dollar appropriated for their support shall be appropriated for the support of any sectarian schools.… Leave the matter of religion to the family altar, the church, and the private school, supported entirely by private contributions. Keep the church and state forever separated.[2]

These words are as relevant today as they were when they were uttered… That they reflected the universal feeling of the American people is evidenced by the fact that in the century and three quarters that have passed since our Constitution was adopted, Congress has never enacted a single measure for the support of church schools. It is evidenced further by the fact that although there are 50 state constitutions and 50 state legislatures, each completely independent of the others, in every one of the states without exception it is unlawful to grant tax-raised funds for the support of church or parochial schools.…

***

2. Religious Liberty

Perhaps because of the United States Supreme Court's [decisions in *Everson* and subsequent cases], the emphasis on the part of the proponents of federal aid to parochial schools has shifted from the Establishment Clause to the Free Exercise Clause. The claim is that the exclusion of parochial schools from a program of federal aid to public schools infringes upon religious liberty. The argument in support of this claim runs something like the following.

In 1925, in the case of *Pierce v. Society of Sisters*,[3] the Supreme Court ruled that it would be an infringement upon the religious liberty of Catholic parents to compel them to send their children to public schools in violation of their conscience. However, many Catholic parents cannot afford to pay the tuition required to keep their children in parochial schools in addition to the taxes they pay to maintain the public schools. Hence, unless the government, by granting financial aid to the parochial schools, makes it economically feasible for the parents to send their children to such schools, the guaranty of religious liberty declared in the *Pierce* case becomes a vain and empty promise. Exercise of religion which is financially prohibitive, it is asserted, cannot be called the free exercise of religion.

***

Of course, the *Pierce* case has not been overruled or superseded and remains today sound constitutional law. But the reason for this is simply that it is not inconsistent with the ... [Establishment Clause] principle that the government may not finance church schools. It is one thing to say that religious liberty forbids the government from closing down church schools, as the Oregon legislature sought to do in the *Pierce* case; it is something entirely different to say that religious liberty also requires the government to finance these schools.

***

... During the past decade there has been a growing movement to fluoridate the water supply in order to protect the teeth of our children. Many municipalities have engaged in the program. But drinking fluoridated water violates the conscience of Christian Scientists. A number of suits have been brought to stop the program, but all have proved unsuccessful and the Supreme Court has refused to interfere with these decisions. It would undoubtedly be a great expense for Christian Scientists living in communities with a fluoridated water supply to purchase unfluoridated water as required by their conscience and the demands of life. Compulsion of life is at least as potent as compulsion of law, yet I have not come across a single report of a demand by Christian Scientists that the government give them money so that they can buy such water and thus be economically able to exercise their freedom of religion. I doubt very much that, if such a demand were made, serious consideration would be given to it by the courts.

***

There is a religious liberty issue in the question of federal aid for parochial schools, but it is one very much different from that asserted by the proponents of such aid. Rather than religious liberty being infringed upon by the exclusion of parochial schools from federal aid, the reverse is closer to the truth. The most serious infringement upon religious liberty before our Bill of Rights was adopted was the use of tax-raised funds for religious purposes. In the great Virginia Statute Establishing Religious Freedom,[4] it was eloquently stated that "to compel a man to furnish contributions of money for the propagation of opinions which he disbelieves is sinful and tyrannical." Is it not a violation of the religious liberty of Catholics to compel them to pay for the propagation of the faith of Jehovah's Witnesses, or for Jehovah's Witnesses to compel them to pay for the propagation of the Catholic faith? And is this not exactly what happens when tax-raised funds are used to finance church schools?

[State courts have recognized that the separation of church and state protects religious liberty.] In *Swart v. South Burlington Town School District*, the Vermont court said:[5]

***

> Considerations of equity and fairness have exerted a strong appeal to temper the severity of this mandate. The price it demands frequently imposes heavy burdens on the faithful parent. He shares the expense of maintaining the public school system, yet in loyalty to his child and his belief seeks religious training for the child elsewhere. But the same fundamental law which protects the liberty of a parent to reject the public system in the interests of his child's spiritual welfare, enjoins the state from participating in the religious education he has selected.

In *Dickman v. School District*, the Oregon Court stated:[6]

> ... [There is a] danger that the acceptance of state aid might result in state control over religious instruction. Some religious leaders, including leaders

in the Catholic Church, have opposed the acceptance of public funds on this ground....

The danger of government control is a real one. Indeed, it may well be questioned whether the government can constitutionally grant tax-raised funds to private institutions without exercising some control on how those funds are to be used...[S]ome government control there must be if governmental funds are granted to schools.

This, in any event, has been the uniform lesson of history. Wherever and whenever governmental funds have been used for religious education there has always been some measure of governmental control. This is true even in those communist states, such as Poland and Hungary, whose governments are committed to the Marxian principle that religion is an evil which must be eradicated as quickly as possible. It is also true in those countries in which there is a close relationship between church and state. The measure of control may vary from state to state and from time to time, but nowhere has there been a complete divorcement of state control from state financing.

3. Discrimination

It is also argued that exclusion of parochial schools from a program of federal aid constitutes discrimination against Catholic parents and children.

There was a time in American history when the demand by Catholics for equality and non-discrimination was valid. In many states, particularly east of the Mississippi, the earliest public schools were little more than continuations of existing Protestant church schools. When the general community took over these schools, their Protestant bias and their Protestant practices often continued.... [I]n Boston an eleven-year-old Catholic boy named Tom Wail was beaten almost to a pulp by his public school teacher because of his refusal to read from the Protestant Bible.

Similar incidents occurred in countless public schools; and these were a major factor in inducing the Catholic community in the United States to establish its own school system, where Catholic children would not be discriminated against because of their religion.

All this, however, is past history. Today the public school welcomes the Catholic child as a full and equal companion of all children. No religious doctrines contrary to his faith are taught in the public schools, and no religious practices unacceptable to him are carried on there. The anti-Catholic bias in the textbooks has long been eliminated, and the entire atmosphere of the public school is such as to assure the Catholic child a feeling and actuality of full equality.

Where, then, is the discrimination? Would it not be more accurate to suggest that here too the converse is more accurate? Public schools are supported by all taxpayers regardless of race or religion and are open to all children regardless of race or religion. But, for the most part, church schools are open only to children of the faith that maintains the schools. Does it not constitute discrimination to tax a Protestant parent to support a Catholic school which his child may not enter, or to tax a Catholic parent to support a Jewish school which is closed to his child? Is not this truly discrimination?

***

4. Double Taxation

Along with the arguments that failure to grant tax-raised funds to parochial schools constitutes an infringement of religious liberty and is discriminatory, the most frequently asserted argument in favor of such grants is that to deny them would subject parents of parochial school children to double taxation. According to this argument the parent is taxed to support the public school which, by reason of conscience, his children cannot attend, and then he is taxed again to support the parochial school that his children do attend.

This assertion, however, is itself predicated upon the fallacy that the education of a child is a matter which concerns only the parents of that child and that they alone are benefited by the fact that their child is educated. Hence, according to this assumption, they should be free to decide whether to buy the education for their child in a public or a parochial school, and if they decide in favor of the latter, they should not be required to pay for the former...

This is a fallacy because it ignores the basic premise of America's educational system; that it is the whole community which is benefited when children are educated and that the whole community is concerned not only with the fact of children's education but also with the type of education the children shall receive.

***

It is for these reasons that education in the United States is compulsory, and that a parent is not permitted to decide that he wants no education for his child. For the same reasons public education is universal and free, and its cost is borne by the entire community, even those who have no children at all or whose children attend non-public schools. And it is for the same reasons that control of the public school is in the hands not of the parents alone but of the entire community. School board members are elected by the vote of all citizens of a school district, not only those who have children in the public schools, and those elected to be members of the school board need not be parents of children in the public schools.

It is in this vital respect that public schools differ from private and parochial schools. The cost of public education is borne by all citizens because all citizens govern and control it. If the citizens of a community are dissatisfied with the way their schools are operated it is within their power to vote in a new school board whose policies will more closely reflect the community's will. No such power exists in respect to private or parochial schools. No matter how deep the dissatisfaction of the general community with a non-public school's policies and methods may be, there is nothing the community can do about it. For the public to be taxed to support an institution over which it has no control and in which it is not represented, is truly taxation without representation.

Those who wrote into our national charter the mandate that church and state must be kept separate and independent of each other were not motivated by any hostility to religion. On the basis of a long and tragic history of the commingling of church and state they reached the conclusion that the cause of religion is best served by separation and independence. Similarly, opposition to public funds for private education is not motivated (at least on the part of this writer, whose children received their elementary education in a private, religious day school) by hostility to private schools. America has room for both public and private schools. But schools can remain private only if they are privately financed. Once compulsory taxation replaces voluntary contributions as the source of support the schools have no moral right to call themselves private. Perhaps more important, the public will sooner or later refuse to consider them private, and will impose upon them the same regulation and control to which other publicly financed agencies are and must be subject in a democratic society.

The premise upon which the First Amendment rests is as valid today as it was in 1791. The absolute separation of church and state is best for the church and best for the state and secures freedom for both.

NOTES

The note number from the original article is shown in the parenthesis at the end of each citation.

1. *Everson v. Board of Education of the Township of Ewing, et al.*, 330 U.S. 1, 15–16 (1947). (11)

2. Quoted in *McCollum v. Board of Education*, 333 U.S. 203, 218 (1948). (18)

3. *Pierce v. Society of Sisters*, 268 U.S. 510 (1925). (22)

4. William Waller Hening, *Statutes at Large*, vol. 12 (1823), p. 80. (31)

5. 122 Vt. 177; 167 A. 2d 514 *cert. denied*, 366 U.S. 925 (1961). (32)

6. 366 P.2d 533 (Oregon, 1961). (33)

PUBLIC AID TO PAROCHIAL SCHOOLS

Paul A. Freund

...[A] discussion of state aid to parochial schools can profitably start with the Supreme Court decision...in *Board of Education v. Allen.*[1] The case was brought by members of a local school board to enjoin the [enforcement of a law]...that requires them to lend textbooks, under stated conditions, to students enrolled in grades seven to twelve of parochial and private, as well as public schools. The statutory conditions are that the book be required for use as a text for a semester or more in the particular school and that it be approved by a board of education or similar body, whether or not designated for use in any public school....

***

The decision [by the United States Supreme Court to uphold the challenged statute]...purported to rest on the principle of *Everson v. Board of Education,*[2] a 1947 decision upholding state reimbursement of bus fares for school chil-

---

Harvard Law Review 82 (June 1969): 1680, 1682–87, 1689–91.

dren regardless of the school they attend. Everson was a five-to-four decision, which Justice Black, writing the majority opinion, was at pains to say went to "the verge."[3] It in turn rested on the analogy of police and fire protection for church buildings: a general safety measure could be applied for the benefit of the community—indeed might have to be so applied—irrespective of the religious or non-religious character of the beneficiaries. Thus it could be said that an ordinance permitting schoolchildren to ride for half fare might (or must) encompass all, whatever school they attend. The same principle would, in my view, support free medical examinations or hot lunches for all school-children, wherever they might be found....

Now buses and nurses and lunches are not ideological; they are atmos-pherically indifferent on the score of religion. Can the same be said of text-books chosen by a parochial school for compulsory use, interpreted with the authority of teachers selected by that school, and employed in an atmosphere deliberately designed through sacred symbol to maintain a religiously rev-erent attitude? ...

In the realm of books, the apt analogy to bus fares would be the public library, accessible to every schoolchild, aiding the pupils and no doubt the schools themselves, but managed by public authorities not delegating respon-sibility for selection of books or personnel or symbolic decor to any religious group, and certainly not engaged in the business of supplying instructional materials, the staple requirements of denominational schools. It is hardly sur-prising that Justice Black, the author of the bus decision, was a fierce dissenter in the textbook case....

***

[W]hy does observance of the ancient religious guarantees of the First Amendment continue to be important? Beyond ancestral voices, are there now any grounds of policy or polity that are threatened? Three such grounds need to be considered: voluntarism in matters of religion, mutual abstention of the political and the religious caretakers, and governmental neutrality toward reli-gions and between religion and non-religion. In a large sense, both of the guar-antees of the First Amendment—the Free Exercise and the non-Establishment Clauses—are directed harmoniously toward these purposes, though in the context of specific governmental measures the two guarantees may point in different directions and the purposes themselves may be discordant.

The policy of voluntarism generates least tension between the Free Exercise and non-Establishment Clauses. Religion must not be coerced or dominated by the state, and individuals must not be coerced into or away from the exercise or support of religion. The school-prayer decisions reflected the principle of voluntarism on both counts: taxpaying families could not be required to support a concededly religious activity; nor could pupils, by the psychological coercion of the schoolroom, be compelled to participate in devotional exercises. When the state provides textbooks, taxpayers are forced to finance books selected by sectarian authorities for instruction in denominational schools maintained at considerable expense to preserve and strengthen the faith [as well as to serve the public purpose of providing instruction in secular subjects]....

It will be argued that if the general taxpayer is coerced for an improper purpose where public funds buy parochial school books, the parochial school families are similarly coerced into paying taxes to support public schools, which, to be sure, their children are legally free to attend but which they regard either as an enemy of all religion, or, if "secularism" itself be deemed a form of religion, then as a friend of a repellent kind of religion. Note that this argument does not deny that the principle of voluntarism is violated by aid to parochial schools; the argument... [rather relies] on an argument of reciprocity or fairness or neutrality. Note too that if it is indeed the case that public schools are an enemy of religion, or a fountainhead of an obnoxious kind of religion, then the argument, it seems, should call for the abolition of the public schools as being themselves in violation of the First Amendment....

If textbooks were selected by the public school authorities to be used in public and parochial schools alike, the problem of voluntariness for the taxpayer might be mitigated somewhat, but by no means removed. It was this aspect of the New York case—the selection of books by the parochial schools—that particularly troubled Justice Fortas, who, like Justices Black and Douglas, dissented. But consider the position if the selections were in fact to be made by the public authorities. The parochial schools might well consider their own autonomy—their voluntarism—compromised. In certain school districts the reverse might obtain: for the sake of uniformity the school authorities would be pressured into selecting books for the public schools that were particularly desired by the parochial schools. In that event there would be a double loss of voluntariness by the general taxpayer.

This risk of intrusion from one side or the other points up a second policy embodied in the religious guarantees—mutual abstention—keeping politics out of religion and religion out of politics. The choice of textbooks in any school is apt to be a thorny subject.... For the identity and integrity of religion, separateness stands as an ultimate safeguard. And on the secular side, to link responsibility for parochial and public school texts is greatly to intensify sectarian influences in local politics at one of its most sensitive points.

The third policy—in addition to voluntarism and mutual abstention—is governmental neutrality, among religions and between religion and non-religion. It is this policy that is chiefly relied on by proponents of public aid. The concept of neutrality is an extremely elusive one... Let me illustrate one difficulty of definition. One might suppose that "neutrality" requires the law to deal evenhandedly with Jehovah's Witnesses and Unitarians. Yet in the school prayer cases Unitarians (speaking generally) succeeded in eliminating all ceremonial prayers from the public schools, while in the flag-salute case Jehovah's Witnesses succeeded only in getting themselves excused from a ceremony that to them was at least as unacceptable and religious in nature as the prayers were to the Unitarians. In fact, the Witnesses regard the flag-salute as the profanation of a religious gesture, a bowing before idols, a Black Mass in the schoolroom. And yet their claim was recognized only to the extent of excusal, exposing them to the repugnant ceremony. Why? Because the prevailing, dominant view of religion classifies the flag salute as secular, in contravention of the heterodox definition devoutly held by the Witnesses. Neutrality, that is, does not assure equal weight to differing denominational views as to what constitutes a religious practice.

Nor is there any general principle that requires the state to compensate those who out of religious conviction incur a handicap under law. Pupils in public schools may (perhaps must) be excused on their religious holidays; but it scarcely follows that those pupils are not responsible for the work they miss, even if they must resort to the expense of private tutoring. Businesses that close on Saturday as a religious observance and must close on Sunday under the law are disadvantaged materially because of religious faith; but exemption from the Sunday laws is not required. The state requires a certain formal ceremony to render a marriage valid in law, and provides magistrates at public expense who are available to satisfy this requirement. For those couples, however, whose religious faith compels them to hold an ecclesiastical ceremony, additional expense is involved, either to the couple or to their church or both. Must the state therefore compensate the minister or the bridegroom and

bride? Would it help their case to insist that no true marriage can be celebrated without churchly blessing and that a ceremony before a judge is anti-
religious, a profanation subsidized with public money? Would not the answer
be: If your religion prevents you from availing yourself of the public facility
and impels you to make a financial sacrifice for the sake of your faith, surely
the spirit of religion is the better served by your act.

***

We turn, then, to this alternative thesis of public aid: that there is a religious
element in education that is pervasive, inescapable, and inseparable....

***

... [C]onsider the ... view of inseparability—that public school education is
itself necessarily religious, but in a perverse sense, as so-called secularism is
itself a form of religion, however degraded a form. If a state school worships
the Anti-Christ, equal support is due to a school that worships Christ. But we
must be careful not to construct a syllogism out of a metaphor of this kind,
any more than out of the countervailing metaphor, "wall of separation." ... To
say that the absence of Crucifixes or Torahs in a public school is itself a religious statement is either a play on words or an idiosyncratic characterization,
like the Jehovah's Witnesses' view of the flag salute, which is not controlling
as a definition of religion. To say that moral training cannot be separated from
religious training in a constitutional sense is to contradict the judgment
underlying the one reference to religion in the constitutional text prior to the
Bill of Rights—that no religious test "shall ever be required" for "any Office
or public Trust under the United States."[4] For if good moral character is relevant to holding a position of public trust, and if religious training is essential
to sound morality, it would have been reasonable to allow a religious test as at
least a presumptive assurance of moral qualification.

Actually the confrontation between so-called secularism and the religion
of parochial schools is not as stark as I have here assumed in order to meet the
proponents of public aid on their own ground. In point of fact most parents
who avail themselves of the public schools are anxious that their children
shall receive religious training, but outside the community of the school, in
the home and the church or in an after-hours church school or a Sunday

school. Taking this into account, the idea of reciprocity or neutrality becomes more complex. Public aid to parochial schools maintained by Catholics or Lutherans or Orthodox Jews would in some measure benefit the religious mission of these faiths, because religion, on our present hypothesis, permeates all their instruction. As a counterpart, the Baptists and other separationists could fairly insist that equalization would require some contribution by the state to their own churches or Sunday schools which perform the same mission that would be subsidized in the parochial schools of other denominations. It would be ironic if the Baptist separationists, who triumphed over the Anglican theocrats in the historic struggle against establishment in Virginia, should find themselves disadvantaged in the name of a Constitution that repudiated establishment.

NOTES

The note number from the original article is shown in the parenthesis at the end of each citation.

1. *Board of Education of Central School District No. 1 v. Allen*, 392 U.S. 236 (1968). (1)
2. *Everson v. Board of Education of the Township of Ewing, et al.*, 330 U.S. 1 (1947). (9)
3. Ibid., p. 16. (10)
4. U.S. Constitution, art. 6. (21)

THE ESTABLISHMENT CLAUSE
AND AID TO PAROCHIAL SCHOOLS

Jesse H. Choper

***

... [M]y proposal is that governmental financial aid may be extended directly or indirectly to support parochial schools without violation of the Establishment Clause so long as such aid does not exceed the value of the secular educational service rendered by the school....

II. An Establishment Clause Rationale

A proposal permitting governmental financial assistance to parochial schools not exceeding the value of secular services they render comports with a general rationale for the Establishment Clause that reflects both contemporary and historical aims.

California Law Review 56, no. 2 (April 1968): 265–69, 277–79, 283–84, 287–91, 295–98, 300–303.

157

A. Historical Support

Although the indistinctness of the precise historical designs of the Establishment Clause has already been noted, several aims emerge quite lucidly. Its paramount purpose then, like its major concern today, was to safeguard freedom of worship and conscience—in a word, to protect religious liberty. And it is equally clear that this purpose comprehended the intention that "the conscience of individuals should not be coerced by forcing them to pay taxes in support of a religious establishment or religious activities."[1] In other words, as part of the general attempt to safeguard religious belief, the Establishment Clause sought to protect taxpayers from being forced by the federal government to support religion.... Whatever other historical bases for the establishment ban, it is beyond reasonable dispute that it purported to secure religious liberty, in particular by prohibiting taxation for religious purposes. That historical intent conforms with the contemporary American view that "it is a violation of religious liberty to compel people to pay taxes to support religious activities or institutions."[2]

B. The Scope of the Establishment Clause

Given this background, the broad philosophy of church-state relations reflected in the nonestablishment precept becomes manifest: Governmental action for *religious* purposes is highly suspect; it is constitutionally objectionable when it impinges on religious liberty either...by compromising the individual's religious beliefs, or...by directly coercing the individual to support religion by allocating tax funds for sectarian use. On the other hand, governmental action for *secular* purposes does not fall within the core of the Establishment Clause's concern—the "nonestablishment guarantee is directed at public aid to the *religious* activities of religious groups."[3]

***

III. DEFINITION OF SECULAR PURPOSE

The broad Establishment Clause rationale described above would generally forbid government expenditures for strictly religious purposes and would bar governmental action for these purposes if infringements of religious liberty followed. On the other hand, it would generally permit the state to act for secular purposes. Thus, it is analytically critical to decide what constitutes a secular purpose and how it should be determined. This is frequently a perplexing inquiry because a law may be enacted for a multiplicity of purposes and may produce a multiplicity of effects. A Sunday closing law, for example, may have the secular purpose of promoting the general welfare by creating a day of respite or the religious purpose of forbidding work to enhance church attendance.

Certain aspects of the problem are quite clear. The fact that religious groups sponsored a law—or even were its sole sponsors—does not make its purpose nonsecular; the Civil Rights Act of 1964 might not have passed without the support of churchmen. Nor...should existence of a secular purpose turn on judicial examination of legislative motives—a long, forbidden psychoanalytic attempt to find the "*real* reason," articulated or unspoken, for passing a law. Rather, whether government action is secular or religious should generally be determined by the nature of its *independent* or *primary* effect....If the primary effect is to accomplish a nonreligious public purpose, the action should generally be held immune from Establishment Clause attack. But if the primary effect is to serve a religious end, the action's purpose should not be characterized as secular even though an *ultimate* or *derivative* public benefit may be produced.

A. Illustrations

Specific instances are necessary to illustrate the point. It has been maintained that public school prayer recitation and Bible reading serve the secular purpose of producing profound convictions in children, thus making them better citizens. But if such are the effects, they come about only if the primary goal of these practices—the implanting of spiritual and religious beliefs—is achieved; the purported secular ends are derivative from the primary religious effect. Thus, under the analysis suggested above, the purpose of the governmental action is religious.

Sunday closing laws also serve an undeniably religious end by encouraging church attendance in removing the obstacle of having to report for work. But they also produce an independent secular effect—"a Sunday atmosphere of recreation, cheerfulness, repose, and enjoyment."[4] And this secular effect is in no way dependent on or derived from the religious impact of the statute.

Governmental actions whose secular benefits flow from the achievement of a primary religious effect must be suspect under the Establishment Clause. Such actions "employ Religion as an engine of Civil policy."[5] Allowing such actions would literally read the clause out of the First Amendment; it would justify government subsidization of that church that the government found best inculcates its members with the deep convictions that make for better citizenship. But governmental action that produces independent secular efforts should generally be unassailable even if an equally necessary or inevitable effect is the benefitting of religion. If not, the fire department could not protect burning churches.

***

IV. Aid to Parochial Schools

A. Secular Purpose

At least some governmental aid to support parochial education serves a primary or independent secular purpose. No one can deny the state's legitimate interest in improving the educational quality of all schools, or the benefits to society in general from education, or even the national defense interest in an enlightened citizenry....

***

Parochial schools perform a dual function, providing some religious education and some secular education. Government may finance the latter, but the Establishment Clause forbids it to finance the former. That government money may be used for partial support of church schools does not mean that "it can also be used for the support of our churches, and that we are moving toward a union of church and state in America."[6]...

It must be perceived that by using tax funds to support the secular aspects of parochial education, the state expends no more than would be required either to support parochial school pupils if they attended existing public schools, or to establish additional public schools at various sites for all pupils presently attending parochial schools, neither of which alternatives raises colorable constitutional objection. This point is not made to prove that either the

Free Exercise Clause or political fairness demands government aid for parochial schools. Rather, it demonstrates that, where the state affords public money to finance the secular aspects of education in church-related schools, it imposes a tax burden essentially identical with that which it could constitutionally impose for separate secular facilities. To do so in no way violates the historical and contemporary policy underlying the Establishment Clause against infringing religious liberty through taxation for religious purposes.

***

C. The Compensable Amount

The constitutional principle proposed herein speaks of the secular educational services rendered by the church-affiliated school. Assuming that these services may be isolated, little difficulty arises where their cost is the same to the parochial school as to the public school system. Because government may properly finance the secular education of all children, whatever their religious faith, payment to a parochial school under these circumstances of the same amount that such education costs in the public schools should be immune from Establishment Clause protest: No tax funds are being expended for strictly religious purposes; no more tax funds are being used than would be if the pupils were in public schools; the church obtains no financial benefit except compensation for the cost of secular services rendered. A fortiori, there is no difficulty if the cost of providing this service in the parochial school is less than it is in the public school system, as is not unlikely, and government pays the parochial school only this lesser amount.

But suppose that the cost of providing secular educational services in the parochial school is less than is the cost in the public school system and government pays the parochial school the latter amount. Although here also no more tax funds are being expended than would be if the pupils were in public schools, the church obtains a net financial benefit. Nevertheless, this should not violate the Establishment Clause.... If any organization—profit or nonprofit, religious or nonsectarian—provides a secular service to government at the "going rate," and is able to profit thereby because of low labor costs, efficiency, or any other reason, the Constitution should not be held to prohibit it....

It must be recalled that government assistance to religion which neither infringes religious liberty nor expends tax funds for strictly religious purposes should not be considered violative of the establishment bar. Thus, in the context of the immediate discussion, it is the "cost" to the public and not the "aid" to religion that is determinative. As long as the government receives in full the secular services purchased, the relative cost or profit to religion of supplying those services should have no relevance to the Establishment Clause. Its prohibition should be satisfied by a showing that the government is getting the secular services it paid for. . . .

***

Finally, suppose that the cost of providing secular educational services in the parochial school exceeds the cost in the public school system and government pays the parochial school the former amount. Although the church here does not obtain funds that may be used for strictly religious purposes, more tax funds are being expended than would be if the children were in public schools. There should, nonetheless, be no violation of the Establishment Clause. So long as the state expenditure is in fact for a primary secular goal, no tax funds are being used for strictly religious purposes.

D. The Permeation Issue

1. The Facts

Probably the most complex matter concerning public financial assistance to parochial education is the permeation (or integration) issue. It is frequently contended that [religious teaching permeates the educational experience at religious schools, even in ostensibly secular subjects]. . . .

***

2. Extent of Permissible Aid

Under the rationale proposed in this article, public financial assistance to parochial education may not exceed the value of the secular educational service rendered. One relatively effortless way of avoiding the whole problem of permeation in this connection is simply to ignore it by taking the position that "the secular character of secular subjects is not changed by a moral or religious permeation"; "that it is impossible to study and interpret man and his activities apart from his moral and religious values"; and that "the National Merit Scholarship competition...is clear evidence that students who attend church-related schools receive a secular education as good as that received by students in our public schools."[7] On this reasoning, there would be no prohibition to financing accredited parochial schools on a lump-sum parity with public schools without further investigation.

But this may be too simple. Competitive examinations and sociological studies are not so exact as to determine conclusively that the educational services rendered in parochial schools are as complete and effective and have the same impact from a nonreligious perspective on the overall development of the student as does public school education. Viewed from the basis of per-hour input, it is reasonable to assume that this is not the case, given the parochial school time spent on religious instruction. And it is clear that the state may not subsidize religious instruction or indoctrination, no matter where undertaken.

The Establishment Clause prohibition against using tax funds for strictly religious purposes appears to require a more careful scrutiny to assure that only the secular aspects of parochial school education will be publicly financed. But to admit "an admixture of religious with secular teaching"[8] is the beginning, not the end, of the inquiry. To concede that "commingling the religious with the secular teaching does not divest the whole [course or activity] of its religious permeation and emphasis,"[9] is not to conclude that no part of the course or activity may be aided with public money.

A secular subject parochial school course or activity may concurrently serve independent, dual purposes—that is, full secular value may be obtained for the time and resources expended, and religious interests may also be served. If such is the case, the entire course or activity serves a primary secular purpose—and may therefore be fully financed—the aid to religion notwithstanding. On the other hand, a secular subject parochial school course or activity may partially serve both religious and secular ends. Here, an allocation must be made; only the secular product may be publicly financed. Of course, if a "secular subject" parochial school course or activity is in reality religious instruction, it cannot be publicly funded at all; and if it is exclusively secular in purpose, it may be totally funded.

(a) The Relevance of "Atmosphere."... That the general atmosphere of parochial schools –as created by religious symbols, teachers in religious attire,

and compulsory religious exercises and courses—is oriented toward religious goals should not affect the constitutional judgment as to whether the particular course or activity may be publicly funded. The clearly sectarian purpose of these accouterments produces no infringement of religious liberty, since students attend the parochial schools of their own volition. And since public funds are not used to subsidize these items, but only for the proven secular aspects of the educational experience, no expenditure of tax money for religious purposes results.

(b) *Judicial Definition of "Religion."*—Under the analysis proposed...the question whether a particular course or activity serves a primary secular purpose, a primary religious purpose, or mixed purposes must ultimately be for the Court....

***

Pragmatically, the issue should rarely arise, at least in the foreseeable future, for it is highly unlikely, as a matter of political reality, that the total amount of governmental assistance to parochial education will even approach the conceded value of the secular educational services it renders.

(c) *Illustrations....* The second grade arithmetic text assigned in a Catholic parochial school may use sectarian characters, illustrations or examples, phrasing arithmetic problems in terms of rosary beads instead of apples, and using pictures of parochial schools instead of public schools.... Trumpet instruction may involve an unusual amount of religiously oriented music, and French language instruction may include a high concentration of religiously significant words or reading.

Considerations of religious liberty, not present in voluntarily attended parochial schools, might prevent all or some of this in public schools. But in the examples above, full secular value seems to have been obtained for the time and resources expended, despite the fact that religious interests may also have been served.

(1) *Burden of Justification.*—Some educators might urge that the above uses of sectarian material did not afford the parochial pupils a secular educational experience completely analogous to that offered in the public schools. If such a case is made, the state or federal financing agency and the recipient parochial school should have the burden of justifying allocation of the full cost of the course to the secular side of the ledger....

***

(2) Examples.—In a parochial school biology text or course, after a full explanation of the theory of evolution, the church's perspective on the matter may also be fully articulated. Or, in the civics course, the concept of racial equal protection may be amplified by presenting both the relevant secular and theological values. Since there would seem to be no constitutional objection to such an objective presentation in the public schools there should likewise be none here, despite the concurrent religious educational value, and despite the fact that these matters may never be mentioned in the average public school class. They still have significant secular educational value. Even a parochial school course in "religion" itself may so qualify if properly handled.

There is a very fine line, however, between objective presentation and subtle commitment and this truth is not confined to parochial schools. Some texts used in public schools—and, undoubtedly, some teachers—unintentionally emphasize Humanistic or antireligious values. Undoubtedly, the opposite is also true. Such emphasis will vary from public school to public school, dependent in part on the cultural, religious, and racial composition of the students and teachers. To the extent that this is constitutionally permissible, effectively unavoidable, or de minimis in the public schools, it should be similarly unobjectionable in the parochial schools for the purpose of public funding—subject always to the burden of justification discussed above.

A parochial school history course or text may teach that all major events are related to or produced by one of the basic truths of the religion, or may emphasize the contribution of one religion over all others.... An advanced biology text or course may omit all references to birth control, sterilization, and euthanasia, or specifically reject most parts of evolutionary theory and shift scientific concepts so that they appear to be based on religious tenets. A parochial school geography text may describe only Catholic families in various cultures, or the teacher may ask the students to map all Catholic churches in the state of Nebraska.

Clearly, some or all of these parochial school activities... cannot be fully supported with public funds. Either the quantity of religious perspective has deprived the course of full secular educational value, or the quality of sectarian permeation has so slanted the material as to have partially undermined or even fully destroyed its secular content. The very description of these courses and texts appears to state a sufficient case to shift the burden of justifying any quantum of secular value to those defending governmental support.

***

NOTES

The note number from the original article is shown in the parenthesis at the end of each citation.

1. Paul Kauper, *Religion and the Constitution* (Baton Rouge: Louisiana State University Press, 1964), p. 9. (43)

2. Ibid., p. 14. (50)

3. P. Freund, *Religion and the Public Schools* (Cambridge: Harvard University Press, 1965), p. 11 (emphasis added). (55)

4. *McGowan v. Maryland*, 366 U.S. 420, 448 (1961). (108)

5. James Madison, "Memorial and Remonstrance Against Religious Assessments," set forth in *Everson v. Board of Education of the Township of Ewing, et al.*, 330 U.S. 1, 67 (1947) (appendix). (110)

6. Alvin W. Johnson and Frank H. Yost, *Separation of Church and State in the United States* (Minneapolis: University of Minnesota Press, 1948), p. 112. (153)

7. Blum, "Our Federal Constitution and Equal Justice in Education," in Daniel D. McGarry and Leo Ward, eds., *Educational Freedom and the Case of Government Aid to Students in Independent Schools* (Milwaukee, WI: Bruce Publishing, 1966), pp. 138–43, 153. (222)

8. *Everson v. Board of Education*, 330 U.S. 1, 47 (1947) (dissenting opinion of Rutledge, J.). (225)

9. Ibid. (226)

CHAPTER 6

INDIRECT AID OR VOUCHERS

THE INCREASINGLY ANACHRONISTIC CASE
AGAINST SCHOOL VOUCHERS

IRA C. LUPU

My father spent the last ten weeks of his life in St. Peter's Hospital in Albany, New York. Neither he nor his family had directly selected this hospital; rather, he was there as a result of his physician's admitting privileges. A small Crucifix hung on the wall of every room in which he received treatment. Catholic priests, as well as clergy from other denominations, frequently dropped into rooms at St. Peter's to see if patients needed prayers or other words of comfort. My father was Jewish, and he had not led a religiously observant life, but his childhood experience had brought him close to Catholic clergy. In my presence (and, to my knowledge, throughout his stay), he welcomed the prayers of the priests he encountered at St. Peter's. My father was Medicare-eligible, and the United States eventually paid a very substantial sum to the hospital for the medical care he received in the concluding period of his life.

No Religion Clause scholar or advocate of whom I am aware would argue

Notre Dame Journal of Law, Ethics, and Public Policy 13 (1999): 375–76, 385–92.

that government payment to St. Peter's Hospital for the cost of medical service for my father's benefit violated the Establishment Clause. Yet, this expenditure obviously contributed to the financial well-being of a sectarian institution. My father's Medicare eligibility permitted him to utilize, without charge to him, the services of that institution, and those services were rendered in a sectarian religious environment. Indeed, his vulnerability at that moment made him unusually susceptible to the religious influences in that setting, although he was in no way compelled to respond to those stimuli.

Why are these arrangements uncontroversially accepted in the community of Religion Clause scholars, while comparable arrangements involving elementary and secondary school students produce so much controversy? Why do many of our citizens think that school vouchers and medical vouchers are so different in their constitutional significance?

Impressionability alone cannot sustain the distinction; at the end of life, and in all times of grave illness, hospital patients may be quite as impressionable as young students. Either medical vouchers are constitutionally questionable when they may be used at sectarian hospitals, or the constitutional case against school vouchers cannot effectively be sustained. After years of wrestling with the question, I have come to the conclusion that the constitutional case against school vouchers is extremely weak; indeed, in this article, I question the force of the constitutional case against direct state aid to sectarian elementary and secondary schools. The arguments against vouchers— usually characterized as indirect aid to sectarian schools because families are an intervening force between the state and these schools—and the arguments against direct aid rest on precedents and policies whose contemporary relevance has dwindled dramatically.

***

III. The Crumbling Argument From Precedent— *Everson, Lemon,* and Their Progeny

All of the doctrinal machinery... [and all of the Supreme Court's cases restricting aid to religious institutions and attempting to distinguish direct and indirect aid except *Everson*] involve direct aid to elementary and secondary schools, [and] reflect state attempts to aid an overwhelmingly Catholic set of private schools. Justice Jackson's dissenting opinion in *Everson,* and Chief

Justice Burger's opinion for the Court in *Lemon*, are open and conspicuous tracts about the pervasive religious indoctrination thought to accompany the system of Catholic education. The principles generated by these two cases rest entirely upon judicial perceptions of the utter inseparability of religion from education in the settings of such schools.... These are inquiries into the sociology of a particular faith, and arguably prejudiced ones at that, masquerading as an inquiry into the meaning of the Constitution.

The Protestant paranoia fueled by waves of Catholic immigration to the U.S., beginning in the mid-nineteenth century, cannot form the basis of a stable constitutional principle, and the stability of the principle has been undermined by the amelioration of those concerns. From the advent of publicly supported, compulsory education until very recently, aid to sectarian schools primarily meant aid to Catholic schools as an enterprise to rival publicly supported, essentially Protestant schools. But the anti-Catholic prejudice that drove this aspect of separationism has been progressively undermined in the last forty years. The election of John Kennedy was among the key ingredients of the change, as was the increased consciousness of prejudice that the civil rights movement provoked. The pronouncement of the church itself, in Vatican II's Declaration of Religious Freedom, in favor of religious liberty for all and church-state separation in the modern world, helped reassure non-Catholics that the church was no longer engaged in a campaign to dominate secular institutions.

The suburbanization and upward mobility of American Catholics has also been a major contributing force; as Catholics have left inner cities, the bastions of parish schools, they have become less inclined toward traditional participation in the Church, including educating their children in the prescribed sectarian way. As a result of this migration, Catholic schools in the inner cities have been forced to become more ecumenical in their approach in order to attract enough students, a significant number of whom are non-Catholic, to survive. When *Lemon* was decided in 1971, less than three percent of the students in Catholic elementary and secondary schools were not of the Roman Catholic faith; by the late 1990s, that percentage had quadrupled.

Simultaneously, the rise of evangelical Protestant movements in America, the tendency among many American Jews to choose sectarian education, and the inclination among various immigrant groups to emphasize parochial education all have stimulated the creation of non-Catholic sectarian schools and a corresponding demand among non-Catholics for government policies supportive of religious education. At the time of *Lemon*, 65 percent of all private schools and 75 percent of all sectarian schools in the United States were Roman Catholic schools, and these schools contained 90 percent of all the pupils then enrolled in sectarian schools....

By sharp contrast, in 1995–96, Catholic schools represented only 29.8 percent of the private elementary and secondary schools in the United States, and their enrollment represented 50.1 percent of the students enrolled at such schools. Because many students now enrolled at Catholic schools are non-Catholic, non-Catholics probably now represent the majority of students enrolled in sectarian schools in the United States.

If the line of decisions from *Everson* to *Lemon* was driven substantially by the then-demographics of public and private education, coupled with anti-Catholic animus, what remains to justify principles forbidding direct aid to sectarian elementary and secondary schools? For me, the key to this inquiry lies in the Virginia history upon which Justices Black and Rutledge so famously and heavily relied in *Everson*. The historical episode that, according to the *Everson* justices, crystallized the constitutional no-aid principle now embodied in the Establishment Clause, involved the 1784 proposal in Virginia for a "Bill Establishing a Provision for Teachers of the Christian Religion" (hereinafter "the Bill")....Madison's famous Memorial and Remonstrance[1] vigorously advocated against the enactment of the Bill, and it was soon defeated. A key element in the Bill's failure, not apparent from its text or from the Memorial and Remonstrance, was its significance in the Virginia struggle to disestablish the Anglican Church. Viewed only on its face, however, the Bill had certain critical features which should be recalled in any attempt to generate first principles from the Virginia history.

First, and most obviously, the Bill was limited to support of the Christian religion. Even Chief Justice Rehnquist, writing in support of jettisoning the "wall of separation" metaphor, recognized that this feature of the Virginia history should be viewed as forever settling the proposition that the state may not enact sectarian preferences.[2]

Second, the tax proposed by the Bill was not designed to augment general revenues. Rather, the Bill included a tax earmarked for this particular purpose. Whether one was supporting a sect in which one was active or not, one's tax contribution was being segregated to particular sectarian use. This is a symbolically and psychologically important feature of the arrangement. If one were subject to the tax, one could not say (as modern taxpayers do) that one is supporting the government generally without necessarily approving of all of the government's programs. Rather, under an earmarked tax scheme, the feel of the arrangements is involuntary support of a religious sect, even if the taxpayer gets to designate which one. This aspect of the Virginia tax highlighted its establishmentarian character and clashed with theological presuppositions, shared by Madison and others, that support for religion (not government) must be voluntary.

Third, the Virginia scheme against which Madison protested was not aimed at supporting existing schools and their instructional personnel. Rather, the monies were to be spent by those in charge of religious communities for "provision of a Minister or Teacher of the Gospel of their denomination, or to providing places of divine worship."[3] The funds could thus be used to build churches, without any provision whatsoever for education of the young. To be sure, the scheme permitted taxpayers to designate their payments for "the encouragement of seminaries of learning within [their respective] Counties,"[4] but, despite this nod to Jeffersonian sentiment, no such institutions existed at the time. Taxpayers thus could devote their payments to religious sects or to a set of future institutions which might never come into being. As a consequence of the taxpayer choices for which there were the greatest and most immediate incentives, the Virginia assessment scheme would have directly and immediately aided sects and their clergy in their religious mission.

Fourth, the education expected in the arrangements that would have been subsidized by the Virginia Bill was rudimentary at best. The Bible would have been the text of central importance, and the educational emphasis would have been primarily on religious virtue, and secondarily on basic reading, writing and arithmetic. Put in today's terminology, the "secular value" of such an education would have been fairly small, and the religious value large by comparison.

Our educational and legal circumstances in the twentieth century are dramatically different, in ways that cast enormous doubt on any principle barring direct financial assistance, for secular educational purposes, to state-accredited sectarian schools. First, . . . the role of education in the twentieth century is vastly different from what it was in the eighteenth. Education is the road to individual mobility and society-wide progress on every front. . . .

Second, as described above, the mix of sectarian schools in America bears absolutely no resemblance to the world of colonial Virginia, in which nothing resembling an elementary or secondary educational institution of today ever appeared. According to the most recent survey by the U.S. Department of

Education, sectarian schools now represent a wonderfully pluralistic assortment of religious affiliations. Although Catholic schools still represent a plurality, at slightly under 30 percent, that percentage has dropped dramatically since the time of *Lemon*, when Catholic schools represented 75 percent of religiously affiliated schools. Sectarian schools are now operated in substantial numbers by a wide variety of Protestant Christians, by Greek Orthodox, Islamic, and Jewish communities, and by many others. This mix suggests that government aid to sectarian schools will not produce the Protestant versus Catholic political divisions that so worried prior generations.

Third, no contemporary proposal for school vouchers or direct subsidies to private schools would be likely to rely on earmarked taxes. Rather, the state would inevitably rely upon a portion of some more generally available source of revenue. As a consequence, taxpayers would not have the experience proposed for eighteenth-century Virginians of designating tax payments to a particular sect. Instead, today's taxpayers would make their payments and understand, as is always and everywhere the case, that some appropriated monies would be spent on purposes and projects with which some do not agree.

Fourth, contemporary regimes of education are inevitably characterized by processes and standards of government accreditation. Unlike the situation in early America, all states have compulsory education laws, and accreditation is the key to school survival; attendance at unaccredited schools will not satisfy those laws. Accordingly, government will retain control over the activities of sectarian schools. Voucher programs and any direct state financing will only serve to increase the demand for, and the likelihood of, such regulation.

The battle over state support for religion in late eighteenth-century Virginia makes a great story, but it has little to do with education in the United States in the next millennium. If a state were once again to expend monies for the support of the clergy and places of divine worship, such a measure would be clearly prohibited by the Establishment Clause. But the maintenance of such a prohibition on contemporary attempts at widening the choices available to parents of schoolchildren, through mechanisms of public finance, cannot be sustained for much longer.

NOTES

The note number from the original article is shown in the parenthesis at the end of each citation.

1. The *Memorial and Remonstrance* is printed in the appendix to the dissent of Justice Rutledge in *Everson v. Board of Education of the Township of Ewing, et al.*, 330 U.S. 1, 63–72 (1947) and is included in this collection. [Hereafter 330 U.S.]. (61)

2. *Wallace v. Jaffree*, 472 U.S. 38, 106 (1985). (62)

3. 330 U.S. 73. (64)

4. Ibid., p. 74. (65)

THE PRICE OF VOUCHERS FOR RELIGIOUS FREEDOM

Laura S. Underkuffler

I. Introduction

In *Pierce v. Society of Sisters*,[1] the Supreme Court held that a state's role in the education of its citizens must yield to the right of parents to provide an equivalent education for their children in a privately operated school—including a religious school—of the parents' choice.... [In this essay, I] address how the principles of individual volition or individual choice, which *Pierce* represents, intersect—as a constitutional matter—with proposals to establish or extend public voucher programs to religiously affiliated elementary and secondary schools.

The importance of this question, in human terms, is something that I have personally experienced. While in college, I had the opportunity to teach a class of fifteen sixth-grade girls attending Presentation Elementary School, a Roman Catholic institution located in the near west side of Chicago. The experience was one that will stay with me for the rest of my life. The sheer

University of Detroit Mercy Law Review 78 (Spring 2001): 463–64, 466–68, 470–77.

ebullience and creative power of those girls, and their willingness to welcome me—a stranger from another world—into their midst, taught me more about the indomitability of the human spirit than any other single experience.

I also knew then, as I know now, that the availability of that school for those students was a life-altering and life-giving experience for them. All of the students whom I taught had failed in the public schools. It is therefore with a divided heart that I write of what I see as dangers in the use of public vouchers in religiously affiliated schools. I know that there are real children whose opportunities depend upon the resolution of this issue. However, I have concluded that the serious constitutional concerns that voucher programs raise are too important to be ignored, even if there is a difficult cost involved in the defense of those principles.

The availability of public moneys through voucher programs for religiously sponsored education seems, on the surface, to be a victory for freedom of conscience and individual choice. I have concluded, however, that the enactment of such programs—and their necessary approval by courts—would require that important constitutional principles regarding religious freedom be jeopardized. The upholding of voucher plans would be, one might say, a Pyrrhic victory for those who value freedom of conscience—if it is a victory at all. For in winning the right to channel public money in this way to religious schools, religious communities will, in the long run, serve forces that will undermine religious tolerance and the constitutionally protected place of freedom of conscience in our constitutional scheme.

Our country has a long history of political and legal opposition to the payment of public tax monies to religious institutions....

***

[While the Court has permitted the state to contribute limited secular equipment and material to students attending religious schools,] [t]he giving of cash grants of state money to religious schools has been traditionally viewed ... as an entirely different matter. It is fair to say that the giving of *unrestricted* cash grants to religious elementary and secondary schools has been assumed by the Court for more than five decades to be an unconstitutional advancement of religion by government. If a religiously affiliated elementary or secondary school is a "pervasively sectarian" institution—if the school's secular educational function and its religious mission are "inextricably intertwined"[2]

—then the use of public money for that school's general support has been viewed as the use of public money for religious purposes in violation of the Establishment Clause...

The core of the Court's objection to the giving of unrestricted cash grants to religious schools apparently has been the view that since such schools are religious institutions—since the education that they offer is "subsumed in the religious mission,"[3] with religious practices and the propagation of faith as integral parts of their programs and curricula—there is no functional way to distinguish the giving of cash grants to these schools and the giving of cash grants to churches, synagogues, and mosques. The fact that education in secular subjects goes on while the schools conduct religious activities and fulfill their religious missions has not, in the Court's view, sufficiently distinguished these religious institutions.

Vouchers are clearly unrestricted cash grants of state funds and—if given directly to religious schools—they would, without doubt, violate traditional Establishment Clause prohibitions. In an attempt to avoid this problem, advocates of vouchers have made two different but related arguments. First, they argue that the prohibition on unrestricted cash grants to religious institutions is inapplicable to voucher programs, because the decision to use voucher money for religious-school education is made by students or their parents, not by state authorities. Second, they argue, *even if* the money that reaches religious schools is deemed to be the result of state action, the substance of the Establishment Clause does not prohibit these payments. In their view, the Establishment Clause does not prohibit the "substantial" funding of religious institutions and activities, as the Supreme Court has traditionally held; rather, it only prohibits state favoritism for or against particular religious sects, or for or against religion generally. Since voucher programs give public money to religious and secular institutions on an evenhanded or "neutral" basis, they present no violation of the Establishment Clause.

The first theory—that independent, individual decision making may be the "causative agent" for Establishment Clause jurisprudence—has its roots in a series of cases decided by the Supreme Court from the mid-1980s to the present.... The theory of these cases was that "public funds become available to sectarian schools 'only as a result of numerous private choices of individual[s]...,' thus distinguishing [these programs from those]...involving 'the direct transmission of assistance from the State to the schools themselves.'"[4] As a result, any advancement of religion that resulted from these programs "cannot be attributed [in a constitutional sense] to state decision making."[5]

***

What is important is what is missing from this approach. In particular, absent is any mention of the traditional requirement that the state aid provide only "incidental" benefit to religious schools. Under [this] approach, aid that is "neutral" and distributed in accordance with "private choice" would presumably be constitutional, even if it provided all, or nearly all, of a religious school's funding.

***

III. PRIVATE CHOICE AND NEUTRALITY: HIDDEN DANGERS FOR RELIGIOUS FREEDOM

A. The Dispositive Power of Private Choice

... Voucher plans, it is argued, are not school-aid programs in the traditional sense, but rather general welfare programs for students and their parents. If, as Justice Thomas observed, a state can issue a paycheck to one of its employees, knowing that the employee may direct the funds to a religious institution, there seems to be little obvious reason why a state cannot give vouchers to parents or students, who can, in turn, use that money for religious education. In both cases, state funds are given to individuals who may direct those funds to religious activities and religious institutions. If individual decision making eliminates Establishment Clause issues in the first context, it is argued, it should do so equally in the latter.

This theory—which I have called the "theory of the individual as causative agent"[6]—assumes that intervening individual decision-making breaks any constitutionally cognizable connection between the state action and the religious use. Under this theory, one simply looks to see if there is a private individual or entity whose actions or choices are responsible—in a causal sense—for the religious result. If there is, any constitutionally cognizable connection between the state's action and the religious result is eliminated.

***

In my view, [however,] there is no convincing basis on which to distinguish voucher plans [from direct aid programs]. The key in such cases is whether the individual choices that are made are *anticipated* and *authorized* by the state funding scheme. We must ask, in each case, whether the state retains an interest in the use of state funds beyond the individual decisional act. And, if it does, we must determine whether the individual decision making in question is something that furthers that interest in an anticipated and authorized way.

Voucher plans are established because of the vital public function—the education of children—which private schools perform. The use of public money in private religious schools is anticipated and authorized *because* of the schools' discharge of this function. The individual parental decisions made under voucher plans are not unrelated and unanticipated actions that break the connection between state payment and ultimate recipient; they are not cases in which an individual—such as a state employee, spending a paycheck—uses the money for something in which the state retains no interest. Rather, the individual parental decisions made pursuant to these plans are anticipated and authorized actions which *accomplish the goal*—the public funding of (private and public) education—*which the government has previously identified.*

If, therefore, the direct payment of tax moneys to religious elementary and secondary schools is something which the Constitution forbids, the fact that money is laundered through "private choice" under a state voucher plan does not, and should not, alter that unconstitutional result. We cannot, through this mechanism, avoid the more fundamental question that voucher plans present: whether such state funding—*in itself*—violates Establishment Clause guarantees.

B. The Principle of Neutrality

The idea of government neutrality as an important part of Establishment Clause analysis is well established in Supreme Court jurisprudence. State neutrality—in the sense of equal treatment of all persons before the law, regardless of religious affiliation or identity—was one of the cardinal principles of reformers during the American Founding Era and is a bedrock principle today....

The critical issue is whether neutrality, in this sense, is *all* that the Establishment Clause requires. This is actually an old debate, which has gained momentum with the question of the use of voucher money in religious schools. If our only concern is state neutrality—if our only concern is that government not endorse, reward, or otherwise favor institutions or citizens on the basis of religious (or nonreligious) identity or belief—then, it is argued, the Establishment Clause presents no obstacle to voucher plans. The core idea of vouchers is that money will be available to all students and to all schools. This fact, and the mechanism of parental choice, guarantee that vouchers will not involve endorsement or favoritism of any kind.

***

The idea of government neutrality (in this sense) as the sole and dispositive content for Establishment Clause guarantees seems, at first glance, to be a favorable outcome for religious freedom. Under this understanding, religious individuals and institutions suffer no disability as the result of their religious status; they are, in particular, the potentially equal beneficiaries of government tax-funded largesse. But is this really the positive development for religious freedom that is imagined?

This neutrality—or, more accurately, this *parity*—paradigm is, unfortunately, a two-edged sword. For what it gives to freedom of conscience and individual choice through eligibility of religious institutions for government largesse, it takes from these very same values in critical ways.

First, the Establishment Clause prohibition on the payment of tax money to religious institutions for religious activities has been grounded in the belief that forcing individuals to support the religious beliefs of others—through the power of taxation—involves a particularly difficult violation of conscience. The enmeshing of government and religious institutions in this way was one of the practices to which reformers in the American Founding Era most bitterly objected. We can ignore this objection, and the prohibitions it involves, only if we believe that the particular violation of conscience that government funding presents is—for some reason—no longer true.

The idea that compelled taxpayer support of the religion of others presents no particular violation of conscience—that such compulsion inflames no particularly dangerous or divisive passions—might be plausible if the plan were to involve only the funding of mainstream religious groups....

However, voucher plans that are premised upon the principle of neutrality *cannot*, by their very nature, be limited to such schools. If neutrality is to govern the operation of these programs, then *all* religious institutions, no matter how unfamiliar or even abhorrent their views, must be the equal recipients of such funds. If we publicly fund parochial schools, Quaker schools, Jewish schools, and other mainstream institutions... then we must also fund the private religious schools that preach religious hatred, racial bigotry, the oppression of women, and other views. It is one thing to tolerate intolerance; it is another thing to fund it....

In addition, the idea that compelled financial support of the religions of others involves no particular violations of conscience for those who must pay endangers religious freedom in another way. If one believes that religious issues pose no particular difficulties for freedom of conscience—if one believes that coerced funding of religion is no different from the coerced funding of social programs, or foreign policy, or other uses with which one disagrees—then the traditional disabilities under which religious institutions have labored are eliminated. But this advantage comes, for them, at a cost. For with the triumph of the neutrality or "parity" paradigm in Establishment Clause jurisprudence comes, inevitably, the triumph of the neutrality or "parity" paradigm in the Free Exercise context, as well.

The fundamental reason for the different treatment of religious and secular institutions, as reflected in traditional understandings of the Establishment Clause, is the belief that *religion is different*, and that religious institutions reflect that difference. We worry about the merger of religion and government—we worry about the endorsement of religion by government—we worry about the funding of religion by government—because of the *particular* value and resultant power that religion has in individual lives. The movement to a neutrality or "parity" paradigm in Establishment Clause jurisprudence is possible only if we shed this idea. To decide that religious institutions can be funded on a par with secular ones, we must decide, as an implicit matter, that religious institutions are no different from secular ones. To do this, we must first conclude that religion as a specially powerful—and a specially valuable—force in human lives is one to which we no longer subscribe.

If we take this step—if we reject the idea that religion or freedom of conscience has any special power or value which justifies the imposition of particular legal *prohibitions*—then we must also reject the idea that religion or freedom of conscience has any special power or value which justifies the extension of particular legal *protections*. The same special characteristics that justify special treatment in one context drive special treatment in the other. If religion claims no special value or power, requiring its institutional separation from the processes of government, then it can likewise claim no special value or power, requiring its protection from ordinary political processes and ordinary laws. Indeed, we find that—with the advance of the neutrality or "parity" paradigm in Establishment Clause cases—has come its advance in the Free Exercise context, as well. In a recent doctrinal shift, the Supreme Court held that free exercise claims (as a class) will generally lose to public interests expressed as a part of "religiously neutral" state laws.[7]... The rise of neutrality or "parity" as the operative paradigm in this context was a marked departure from the Supreme Court's traditional approach, under which religious beliefs and practices were protected, absent a compelling state interest, from the operation of "otherwise neutral" state laws. This development should not, however, be an unanticipated one: if religion is not special in one context, there is no obvious reason why it should be in the other.

The issue of vouchers has, unfortunately and paradoxically, raised an issue that has tremendous implications for our understanding of First Amendment guarantees. We must grapple with whether, as a fundamental matter, religion or freedom of conscience is a uniquely powerful force in human life and law.... Does religion have unique power, such that compelled taxpayer funding of religious activities and religious institutions is somehow more opprobrious, and more dangerous, than the funding of other activities and institutions? Does religion have unique power, such that protection of its practice, and its institutions, is uniquely justified? These are the questions that the neutrality or "parity" paradigm, in all of its facets, presents. And so—for all of the gains that this idea might yield for choice and freedom of conscience, in some ways—we must ask whether it is worth the cost.

NOTES

The note number from the original article is shown in the parenthesis at the end of each citation.

1. 268 U.S. 510 (1925). (1)
2. *Lemon v. Kurtzman,* 403 U.S. 602, 657 (1971). (13)
3. *Hunt v. McNair,* 413 U.S. 734, 743 (1973). (17)
4. *Zobrest v. Catalina Foothills School District,* 509 U.S. 1, 9 (1993). (22)

5. Ibid., p. 10. (23)

6. Laura S. Underkuffler, "Vouchers and Beyond: The Individual as Causative Agent in Establishment Clause Jurisprudence," *Indiana Law Journal* 75 (2000): 167. (44)

7. *Lyng v. Northwest Indian Cemetery Protective Association*, 485 U.S. 439 (1988); and *Employment Div. v. Smith*, 494 U.S. 872 (1990). (55)

SCHOOL VOUCHERS AND RELIGIOUS LIBERTY: SEVEN QUESTIONS FROM MADISON'S *MEMORIAL AND REMONSTRANCE*

VINCENT BLASI

***

A close reading of the *Memorial and Remonstrance* yields, in my judgment, seven questions pertinent to the voucher issue. They are:

First, is the formal inclusion of church-operated schools in a public funding scheme, including the transfer of public funds directly to such religious institutions, a violation of the principle that religion must be wholly exempt from the cognizance of the state? In colloquial terms, does the degree of institutional interaction and recognition entailed in a voucher scheme violate the principle of separation that Madison held dear?

Second, can a voucher system that neither prefers nor excludes any religion ever amount to the type of establishment that Madison opposed?

Cornell Law Review 87 (March 2002): 787–89, 792, 795–96, 800–808, 810–11.

183

Third, is a voucher system an effort to, in Madison's words, "employ Religion as an engine of Civil policy," a strategy he termed an "unhallowed perversion of the means of salvation"?[1] What is wrong with civil authorities drawing upon the resources, material and otherwise, of religions in the pursuit of a civic good such as quality or diverse education?

Fourth, would a voucher system lead participating religions to become too dependent on the state over time, to the detriment of their religious purity and vitality?

Fifth, would the fact that certain religions receive a substantial state subsidy and may come to depend on it lead them to be less willing to criticize public officials or mobilize resistance to public policies, thereby diminishing what has historically been one of the major checks on governmental injustice and neglect?

Sixth, would the ongoing implementation of a voucher system, with all the fiscal and regulatory decisions that would be entailed, generate contests and resentment along religious lines that might, in Madison's words, "destroy that moderation and harmony which the forbearance of our laws to intermeddle with Religion has produced among its several sects"?[2] Or would the decision to include religious schools in the public financing of education actually reduce the "animosities" and "jealousies" that Madison considered an enduring threat to the republic?

Seventh, would a voucher system deny to any citizens "equal title to the free exercise of [r]eligion" by subjecting some to peculiar burdens and others to peculiar benefits so far as the capacity to practice their religions is concerned; or conversely, can the move to a voucher system be defended as equality *enhancing* in this regard?[3]

These are the pertinent Madisonian questions for the voucher controversy, and except for the first two, they are not easy to answer.

... Taken together, the last five questions reflect Madison's penchant for thinking about issues of liberty and legitimacy in structural terms. He had little faith in legalistic guarantees—"parchment barriers" he dismissively called them.[4] Instead, he focused on such matters as institutional incentives, checks and balances, object lessons from the past, and scenarios of decay and abuse. His assumptions regarding how power would be exercised were pessimistic. His deepest concern was with the tyranny of the majority. He considered the abuse of power by majorities to be more likely to occur the smaller the political community. He sought to forestall and contain abuses of power by means of perspicacious institutional design. His approach to the subject of church and state was in this spirit.

If we are to be guided by Madison in grappling with the voucher issue, we need to consider, under pessimistic assumptions, what would be the institutional consequences for religion and for governance of that proposed restructuring of educational financing....

***

The second question about vouchers that derives from the *Memorial and Remonstrance* concerns the role of exclusivity and favoritism in Madison's conception of establishment. Can an arrangement that employs no religious criteria for eligibility, and in other respects exhibits no preference among religious beliefs, ever be an establishment of religion as Madison used the term? The General Assessment provided only for allotments authorized by individual taxpayers to *Christian* denominations. No provision allowed the Jews, Muslims, and atheists of the Commonwealth to direct their taxes to the teachers of their beliefs. The best they could do was to specify that their taxes go to a common school fund. In the *Memorial and Remonstrance,* Madison describes the General Assessment as an establishment of Christianity and warns that it could lead to a narrower establishment of particular Christian Sects. Would a more inclusive scheme such as the prototypical voucher plan fall outside his conception of establishment?

The answer is: not necessarily. We ought not to assume that Madison considered the General Assessment's denial of access to public funding to non-Christian denominations to be the fatal defect. Most of the arguments he mounted against the proposal take the form of claims relating to undesirable incentives and consequences. Many of those arguments, which I will canvass shortly, would impeach a subsidy that supported all religions without limitation. At no juncture in his sustained campaign against the General Assessment did he so much as imply that the proper remedy might be a broadening of the class of beneficiaries. Indeed, at one stage of the legislative process the bill actually included non-Christian religions in its coverage, and Madison worked tirelessly to defeat it at every stage.... A school voucher program may not amount to an establishment of religion in Madisonian terms, but the fact that such a program is not confined to religious schools and is administered without religious favoritism by no means proves the point.

***

[Are] vouchers...problematic because they threaten to compromise the purity and efficacy of religion by placing religious institutions in a position of financial dependency on the state, or on the state-created market? This is the fourth question on my list of seven.

Madison's discussion of the General Assessment is explicit, in fact strident, about how the experience of financial establishment corrupts religious institutions.... We might be tempted to confine Madison's dependency critique to the historical practice of establishing a single religion and supporting it without regard to the wishes of the populace. But remember that he offered these observations about corruption while challenging a funding proposal that permitted each taxpayer to specify which denomination would receive his coerced contribution and allowed him to direct his tax payment away from all religions to the common school fund. Madison's concern in this passage is not preference, but rather corrupting dependency.

It is not difficult to imagine scenarios whereby the availability of vouchers could corrupt religious education. Participation in a voucher scheme might be conditioned on the willingness of participating schools to admit students without regard to their religious beliefs, to eschew religious tests in faculty hiring, and to refrain from requiring students to attend religious ceremonies or profess religious beliefs. Any of these restrictions could change the character of the religious education offered.... [Also] market pressures introduced by a voucher scheme could create incentives for a religious school to modify its curriculum and general character in a more ecumenical direction so as to appeal to a broader range of voucher-wielding consumers....

***

...Notions of corruption, distortion, enervation, even compromise are meaningless in the absence of a baseline. We can say with some confidence that a school voucher program will affect religious priorities and practices. Not so obvious, however, is whether those effects overall will be detrimental to the particular religions that participate. Dependency on public resources is a dangerous condition for religion, to be sure, but so is the condition of competing in the educational marketplace with the well-financed institutions—and some would say the religiously subversive orthodoxies—of the modern welfare state. Even in the absence of vouchers, sectarian schools that are supported wholly out of tuition payments and voluntary contributions have financial incentives to recast their offerings to recruit students....

There is much more to be said on this point, but for now I conclude with some misgiving that although the possible corrupting effects on religion of a voucher system are serious, they are not so clear or pronounced that Madison's warnings about the dangers of dependency should be considered telling against the arrangement. Nevertheless, an observer who would learn from Madison ought to place far more emphasis on these risks of dependency than has occurred to date in the voucher debate.

**

[The] prospect of the waning of the common school, which may or may not occur under a voucher system, suggests the importance of the sixth question on my list, relating to political strife.

Madison objected to the General Assessment in significant part because he thought such public funding of religion would "destroy that moderation and harmony which the forbearance of our laws to intermeddle with Religion has produced among its several sects."[5] The very appearance of the proposal, he asserted, "has transformed that Christian forbearance, love and charity, which of late mutually prevailed, into animosities and jealousies, which may not soon be appeased."[6]...Would the publicly funded balkanization of primary and secondary education have this result?

I can think of three major sources of political discord that a voucher program might introduce. First, some taxpayers will resent seeing even a symbolic portion of their tax contribution go to the teaching of religious tenets they reject. Second, some religions, for example those that already heavily invest in education, inevitably will benefit more from a voucher system than others. The jealousies to which Madison alluded in the *Memorial and Remonstrance* were due largely to the fact that the smaller, proselytizing religions saw the General Assessment, which provided that public funds could be spent only on salaries for clergy and church buildings, as a bailout of the Episcopal Church, with its peculiar problems of clergy recruitment and building damage and its lack of emphasis on proselytizing. One can imagine similar suspicions of favoritism attending decisions regarding the specific design and implementation of a voucher system. Third, a population increasingly educated in enclaves of religious homogeneity *may*, by virtue of reduced exposure to persons who think differently, exhibit more of the inbred animosities that so concerned Madison. Even if a high degree of civic common ground is now beyond our reach and perhaps undesirable in any event, some capacity in the populace to compromise and to accept political defeats is indispensable. Too much religious parochialism may reduce that capacity, at least when it is not leavened by sustained experiences of personal interaction beyond the confines of the faith.

Each of these threats to moderation and harmony strikes me as real even if difficult to estimate. Much would seem to turn on what kind of voucher plan is implemented.... In deciding upon the amount of the voucher payment and the regulatory strings that go with it, we must take great care to minimize the risk of differential denominational impact. This priority counsels against restrictions on religious criteria for student admissions and faculty hiring. Voucher schools should also be permitted, if they so choose, to require all students to participate in worship services.

Intelligent design can counteract some of the sources of discord that vouchers might introduce, but can do little, I am afraid, to mitigate the religious enclave problem. Educational enclaves are not good for the democratic process, but I fear that as a society we have already traveled rather far down that path. Nevertheless, a voucher system would almost certainly exacerbate the phenomenon of religious clustering.

In evaluating the probable impact of vouchers on political good will, we must not assume that all is rosy with the status quo. Parents who pay both school taxes and private tuition feel imposed upon. Bitter struggles over what is taught in the public schools often divide parents along religious lines. The mushrooming phenomenon of homeschooling constitutes, for most parents who undertake it, a species of civic alienation. Vouchers cannot eliminate these tensions and antipathies, but they might reduce some of the pressure.

My bottom line on this point is tentative and tortured. The stakes here, at least to a Madisonian, are high indeed. That may counsel risk aversion, but I think we run risks by leaving undisturbed the current pre-voucher pattern of escalating, self-righteous, and often ill-tempered sectarian involvement in the politics of public education, followed by bigoted and paranoid reaction to that phenomenon. On balance, the priority Madison attached to preserving a spirit of moderation and harmony in political life does not, I conclude, provide a sufficient reason to consider a voucher system an imprudent or un-constitutional mixing of religious and civil institutions.

The seventh and final Madisonian question concerns the principle of equality. There can be no dispute that considerations of equal treatment lay at the core of Madison's conception of religious liberty, both his aversion to any form of religious establishment and his emphasis on the notion of "free exercise."...No fewer than five of the fifteen paragraphs of the *Memorial and Remonstrance* make explicit appeals to equality.[7] Several others invoke notions of natural right and the rule of law that for Madison and his intellectual milieu were bound up with egalitarian premises: equally the creatures of God, entering civil society on equal terms, equality before the law, and the like. Madison objected to the General Assessment in no small part because he did not believe it treated the citizens of Virginia equally in the free exercise of their religion. Undoubtedly, moreover, these considerations of unequal treatment were a dominant factor in the resounding political defeat of the General Assessment that he engineered.

Given the relative inclusiveness of the proposed scheme for funding churches and clergy, not to mention the opt-out provision permitting tax-payers to direct their payments to the general education fund, one wonders exactly why Madison objected to the General Assessment so fiercely on grounds of equality. What demanding conception of "equal title" or "equal rank of Citizens" did he employ?[8]

The narrowest answer to this question is [that Madison believed the General Assessment denied] the equal right to free exercise because it would have excluded non-Christian religions from the funding program. Although the General Assessment would not have required the small number of professed Jews, Muslims (mostly Turks), Deists, agnostics, and atheists of the Commonwealth to support religions in which they did not believe—they could have directed their taxes to the school fund—they could not have advanced the teachings of their creeds with the aid of the tax collector's coercive authority. In that regard, the proposal disadvantaged them in comparison to their Christian counterparts.

As explained above, this interpretation of Madison's objection to the General Assessment fails to account for the fact that he never urged a broad-ening of the coverage scheme and maintained his opposition even when the bill before the Assembly for a time did provide for the inclusion of non-Christian religions.... [T]he better interpretation is that he perceived the General Assessment to deny citizens the "equal title to the free exercise of

Religion"[9] because of its unequal treatment of and impact upon various Christian denominations.

On its face, the bill provided for special treatment of the Quakers and Menonists by exempting them from the restriction applied to all other denominations that funds provided by the government be used only for buildings and salaries for the clergy. This exemption was perfectly logical because as a matter of theology the Quakers and Menonists did not erect edifices for worship and did not have clergy. Nevertheless, the exemption did permit them to use public funds to finance proselytizing efforts, an activity other denominations such as the Baptists and Presbyterians had emphasized in late-eighteenth-century Virginia. In the *Memorial and Remonstrance*, Madison alluded specifically to this favorable treatment of Quakers and Menonists: "Ought their Religions to be endowed above all others with extraordinary privileges by which proselytes may be enticed from all others?"[10]

He also asserted that the General Assessment would subject some sects to "peculiar burdens."[11] He did not specify what those peculiar burdens might be or which sects would suffer them, but a good surmise is that he was referring to the burdens that would be borne by Christians who believed that only voluntary contributions engendered inspired preaching and manifested the proper devotion....

***

Are any of these various equality concerns present in the case of educational vouchers? There can be little doubt that some religions would benefit far more than others from the availability of public money to cover the general operating expenses of private education. One religion especially, the Roman Catholic Church, has developed over the years an extensive infrastructure for providing religious education and a culture that encourages members of its faith to seek such schooling. Other religions have an educational infrastructure up and running, if on a smaller scale. During the last two decades there has been an upsurge in the number and variety of religions operating schools, but there remain many faiths in many locales that do not do so. One would hope and expect that some religions previously unable to provide sectarian education would be financially empowered by a voucher system to undertake that ambitious project. Even so, under no imaginable scenario would an educational voucher program benefit religions equally, or in proportion to their memberships, or according to any other principle of equitable distribution. How much should this bother a Madisonian?

To answer that question, one needs to distinguish the problem of unequal material benefits and burdens from that of unequal civic status. On the dimension of material impact, it is wildly unrealistic, at least in the modern welfare state, to require all laws to distribute burdens and benefits equitably among religious faiths. Laws exempting conscientious objectors from military service, subsidizing hospitals and nursing homes, prohibiting the use of hallucinogenic drugs, restricting the alteration or destruction of architectural landmarks, offering tax deductions for charitable contributions, and exempting buildings used for religious purposes from property taxes all benefit or burden some faiths and their adherents much more than others. . . .

One way to narrow Madison's equality principle is to link it more closely with the concept of "free exercise." Today we tend to look upon "equal protection" and "free exercise" as wholly separate notions, both fundamental to our constitutional structure but not conceptually integrated. That is not how Madison viewed the matter. He objected to the General Assessment in large part because he considered the inequality built into the arrangement to be not simply unfair but a threat to the capacity of the disfavored sects to practice their religion "according to the dictates of Conscience."[12] A crucial source of his concern was the claim by some denominations, especially the more evangelical Christian sects such as the Baptists, that *compulsory* support of their clergy impaired the fundamental relationship that must obtain between preachers and their congregations. That the unequal denominational impact in this respect was not due to a differential inscribed on the face of the statute, and could not be proved to be intended by the legislature—although the more evangelical sects had their suspicions—did not forestall Madison's objection. . . .

Should we consider the differential denominational impact of educational vouchers to be a threat to the capacity of adherents of the disfavored faiths to engage in the free exercise of their religion? As discussed above, some religions might experience pressure to get into the education business, if only to retain adherents tempted by the high-quality schools run by rival sects. Such a reluctant move would alter the priorities of a religion, but should we consider it an impairment of free exercise comparable to the practical inability to keep clergy dependent on voluntary contributions? Even without vouchers, religions that operate good schools exert competitive pressure on rival faiths, particularly in areas where the public schools are mediocre.

To my mind, the consideration that looms the largest in grappling with this difficult question of differential impact on the free exercise of religion is the effect already exerted by the massive public investment in elementary and secondary education. Unlike the situation when Madison opposed the General Assessment, today there is no such thing as the exercise of religion free from the distorting impact of state policy, certainly not as concerns education. Thousands, perhaps millions, of parents who otherwise would send their children to religious schools do not do so because they cannot afford the tuition on top of the school millage assessments they pay, or because the alternative of a secular education is so much more economical. Moreover, the expense of operating religious schools is made greater by the intervention of the state, both by regulations that can impose significant costs and by competitive pressure to invest in expensive facilities and extracurricular activities. This pattern of educational choice has consequences for the free exercise of religion.... If today financial incentives generated by civil policy induce large numbers of citizens to decouple education from religion, their free exercise of religion is impaired, more so than is the case with the other examples listed above of laws and public expenditures that have a differential denominational impact

This argument proves too much....

***

One must be careful not to inflate the argument just sketched beyond its equality-driven bounds. Were it not for the pressures on the free exercise of religion created by the system of public education, any effort by the state to make religious education financially feasible would be deeply antithetical to Madison's conception of church-state relations. For as much as he respected the need of persons and groups to be free to practice their religion according to the dictates of conscience, he did not believe it is the role of civil authorities and institutions to encourage or facilitate that practice. The role of the state, in his conception, is to stay out of the way.... A voucher system that facilitates religious education can be justified in Madisonian terms only to the degree that it neutralizes the distorting pressure previously created by the intervention of the state in education.

***

I realize that I have not been able to answer these last five Madisonian questions relating to incentives and consequences in anything like a definitive fashion. Another person as steeped in Madison's ideas as I have been recently could well decide, contrary to my judgments, that a voucher system that included parochial schools would cheapen religious authority, create a corrupting dependency, silence potential critics of government, introduce new sources of civic discord, and violate fundamental equality norms relating to the free exercise of religion....

Perhaps, the difficulty of these questions proves that we—and Madison—cannot have it both ways: a multiplicity of politically mobilized but nevertheless distinctive and uncorrupted religious sects that serve as a check on government, combined with politics of civility, moderation, mutual respect, equal civic status, and significant common ground.... But [Madison's] *Memorial and Remonstrance* at least should convince us that we cannot resolve this momentous issue in peremptory fashion by giving controlling weight to the features of inclusiveness and parental choice (to uphold a voucher scheme) or the direct subsidization of purely sectarian teaching (to strike it down)....

NOTES

The note number from the original article is shown in the parenthesis at the end of each citation.

1. James Madison, "Memorial and Remonstrance Against Religious Assessments," in Jack N. Rakove, ed., *James Madison: Writings* (New York: Library of America, 1999), p. 32, para. 5. (17)
2. Ibid., p. 34, para. 11. (18)
3. Ibid., p. 31, para. 4 (emphasis omitted). (19)
4. Letter from James Madison to Thomas Jefferson (October 17, 1788), in Rakove, ed., *James Madison: Writings*, pp. 418, 420. (20)
5. Madison, "Memorial and Remonstrance," p. 34, para. 11. (55)
6. Ibid. (internal quotation marks omitted). (56)
7. Ibid., pp. 31–36, paras. 4, 8–9, 14–15. (61)
8. Ibid., pp. 31–32, 33–34, paras. 4, 9. (64)
9. Ibid., p. 31, para. 4 (emphasis omitted). (70)
10. Ibid., p. 32, para. 4. (74)
11. Ibid., p. 31, para. 4. (75)
12. Ibid. (83)

EVALUATING SCHOOL VOUCHER PROGRAMS THROUGH A LIBERTY, EQUALITY, AND FREE SPEECH MATRIX

ALAN E. BROWNSTEIN

II. AN ALTERNATIVE FRAMEWORK FOR EVALUATING THE CONSTITUTIONALITY OF SCHOOL VOUCHER PROGRAMS

... Conventional separation of church and state arguments [in judicial opinions often lack coherence and seem arbitrary and unpersuasive]....

***

These weaknesses in historically accepted justifications for a no aid principle would not be as problematic as they are if there were not substantial arguments on the opposing side of this debate. But there are concrete, legitimate arguments that support the funding of religious educational institutions....

Connecticut Law Review 31 (Spring 1999): 885–87, 889–92, 894–98, 902–903, 909, 911–12, 916–21, 923–24, 926–27.

Clearly, the decision to have one's children attend a religious school is a constitutionally protected one. And it is also clear under current law that as a result of making that decision, religious parents will be denied the state support for the non-religious aspects of their children's education that is provided to parents electing to send their children to public, and sometimes private, secular schools.

There is a real cost here, a real burden that results from the application of the no aid principle. It makes no sense to ignore the reality of this cost in evaluating the constitutionality of voucher programs. The arguments in favor of interpreting the Establishment Clause to bar aid to religious schools have to be persuasive enough to justify this result. In my judgment, it is a close case. Affirming the tradition barring aid to religious schools requires more attention to a range of constitutional concerns and real world consequences than conventional separation of church-state arguments provide.

A. Interpreting the Establishment Clause in Terms of Religious Liberty, Religious Equality, and Freedom of Speech

... The problem [with developing coherent religion clause doctrine is that] religion is an inordinately complicated aspect of life and law that implicates several important constitutional values. Religion for constitutional purposes involves personal and institutional liberty and autonomy (in my view the right of the individual and congregations, rather than the state, to make self-defining decisions). It involves equality among groups; a form of equality that is analogous to, but in some ways distinct from, the equality mandated by the Equal Protection Clause that protects certain classes against discrimination. It also involves speech and belief. Government should avoid distorting the marketplace of ideas through state action that empowers or silences religious expression.

These values will often be in conflict with each other. Maximizing religious liberty in some circumstances, for example, undermines religious equality among the diverse faiths in a community and it may distort the marketplace of ideas in favor of religious messages.... Working out the interplay of these various interests and values will, of necessity, be difficult and it must involve some room for judicial discretion.

***

B. The Doctrinal Significance of Upholding Voucher Programs

The problem with vouchers is the problem with funding sectarian religious organizations to provide public services... that have value independent of any religious content. Vouchers avoid certain problems and concerns with direct funding. They make it more difficult, for example, for the government to manipulate the allocation of funds to politically favored faiths or from politically disfavored faiths. Vouchers also limit the inferences that might be drawn from funding. When parents use a voucher to provide educational services for their children, there is less of a suggestion that the government itself is approving or supporting the institution receiving the funds. Nonetheless, the funding of religious institutions even through vouchers still raises serious liberty, equality, and speech concerns.

***

1. The Nature and Potential Scope of Constitutionally Unrestricted Voucher Programs

Let us assume for the moment that in order for school voucher programs to be constitutional all voucher programs of any kind must be upheld notwithstanding the fact that state funds will be used to subsidize pervasively sectarian religious organizations and that a very high percentage of the funds distributed through vouchers will be allocated to religious institutions. According to this supposition, the only requirement imposed by the religion clauses on voucher programs is the mandate that the funding scheme must be formally neutral between religious and secular programs and among the programs sponsored by different religions....

It would seem that under this doctrinal model, voucher programs would be constitutionally available in any context in which religious groups desire public services to be offered through private religious conduits. Religious schools, parks, recreational facilities, libraries, drug treatment centers, job training centers, hospitals, and clinics might all be supported. Whenever religious or other groups convince the legislature to contract out services currently provided by government to private conduits, the legislature may adopt a voucher program that can be used to fund whatever secular benefit the program provides under either religious or non-religious auspices.... The fact that the overwhelming majority of individuals and institutions that made use of a voucher alternative were religious in nature would have no bearing on the constitutionality of the program.

***

Institutions receiving vouchers under this model would be free to discriminate on the basis of religion in hiring staff to provide whatever services the vouchers are intended to support. They would also be free to discriminate on the basis of religion in accepting students, clients, or patients. Indeed, if the constitutional logic of vouchers suggests that by conveying funds through the independent decisions of individuals and families, the state is not involved in the operational choices of the service providing institutions where the vouchers are spent, these institutions would be free, at least for constitutional purposes, to discriminate on the basis of race, gender, and ethnic background as well....

Finally, under this permissive interpretation of the religion clauses, the legislature would be entitled to employ whatever formally neutral criteria it considers appropriate in determining which institutions may receive vouchers without regard to the disproportionate impact of its requirements on the allocation of state funds among the religious groups and institutions in a community. The legislature could not refuse to allow vouchers to be spent at the schools of a particular religion, such as Catholic schools, of course. It could, however, refuse to allow vouchers to be used at schools that do not teach evolution or that do not offer remedial tutorials on Saturday. [Under current free speech and free exercise case law,] it seems difficult to argue that such formally neutral requirements constitute unconstitutional conditions or otherwise violate the Free Exercise Clause.

Moreover, the allocation of funds among religious groups could be substantially skewed by voucher criteria that do not implicate specific beliefs or practices. A state, for example, might be concerned that small, new fly-by-night schools would open up and take advantage of uninformed parents with vouchers to spend—while providing their children an inferior education masked by misleading marketing. To avoid this problem, without incurring the intrusive burden of carefully monitoring the quality of the schools claiming to be eligible to receive vouchers, the state might decide that only schools with over three hundred students that have been in existence at least five years will be certified as acceptable voucher recipients. The result of such a restriction, of course, would be to deny the religious schools of many faiths, particularly minority faiths in a community where there are not enough children of a particular religion to justify a large school, meaningful access to the voucher program. That consequence, however, would not be of constitutional significance.

***

2. The Impact of Constitutionally Unrestricted Voucher Programs on Religious Liberty, Religious Equality, and the Marketplace of Ideas

The expanded use of vouchers under the doctrinal framework I have described creates the potential of fragmenting what is currently understood as the public life of society along religious lines. Jobs, resources, programs, and services would be allocated among religious faiths to the extent that the choices of individuals and families reflected such preferences. Moreover, it is at least arguable that if voucher programs proliferate, religious and secular groups which would not ordinarily choose to participate in the religious fragmentation of public services may become motivated to do so in a defensive reaction to the choices of other groups.

***

A. The Impact of Vouchers on Religious Liberty

Vouchers promote religious liberty in three important ways. They assist parents who want to send their children to religious schools by increasing their ability to afford to do so. They make more funds available and more job opportunities available for teachers and other staff who want to be able to work in a religious environment that fully accommodates the beliefs and practices of their faith. Finally, they enable religious institutions to maintain their religious identity without losing access to state support which would otherwise be available to them.

Voucher programs will also undermine religious liberty in significant ways. Perhaps the most direct impact will result from the incentives that are created by allowing religious institutions to reserve public resources for the employment of individuals of their own faith. The control of public funds creates power, and the ability to restrict the spending of those funds along religious lines allows that power to be used to burden religious choices in a very concrete way. When employment opportunities are granted or denied on the basis of religious beliefs and practices, there is a coercive effect on religious liberty. When the government funds the employment opportunities that are religiously restricted, the state is implicated in the coercion. To the extent that the criteria used in determining which institutions are eligible to receive vouchers skews the allocation of resources among religious faiths, the coercion becomes even more pronounced.

***

A voucher program may also lead to abridgements of religious liberty by increasing state regulation of religious schools and other institutions which elect to receive vouchers and by increasing the dependency of religious individuals and organizations on government support and approval. Dependency concerns are unavoidable. There is no constitutional mechanism or doctrine that can guarantee continued financial support for a program. Nor can any rule of law prevent legislators from indirectly punishing political opposition by withdrawing support from particular programs.

    ...If regulatory conditions are attached to vouchers, the burden they impose on religious liberty is obvious. Religious institutions will confront the difficult choice of turning down state subsidies or altering their programs in ways that may conflict with the tenets of their faith. The impact on minority faiths will be particularly acute. Larger religions may have sufficient political influence to prevent the adoption of voucher criteria that is inconsistent with their beliefs and practices. Smaller religions lack that ability and will be more dependent on the good will and sensitivity of the administrators of the voucher program.

***

[It is not clear that the Constitution protects religious schools from direct regulations. Moreover,] [t]he state may have far greater discretion to impose conditions on the receipt of funds than it could impose by virtue of its regulatory authority alone. While parents and schools may argue that some of the regulations imposed on schools receiving vouchers constitute unconstitutional conditions, the utility of this contention under recent authority is limited at best. Within the confines of a funded program, government appears to have substantial discretion to control the activities of the project receiving a subsidy. It is not clear why vouchers should operate any differently than direct grants in this regard.

Moreover, unconstitutional condition arguments against the regulation of voucher recipient schools create a particularly complex problem. If the challenge to a substantive curriculum requirement, for example, is predicated on free exercise doctrine, a question arises whether a similar challenge is available to all private schools on free speech grounds. If the answer is in the affirmative, government's power to determine the nature and quality of the educational product it is subsidizing is sharply restricted. If unconstitutional condition arguments are only available to religious schools, the allegedly evenhanded and neutral nature of the voucher program itself is undermined....

***

B. The Impact of Vouchers on Religious Equality

1. The Contours of Religious Equality

I have argued elsewhere...that the Establishment Clause provides a constitutional guarantee of religious equality that is analogous to, but in important respects distinct from, the equality mandate that applies to racial, ethnic, and gender groups and classifications. My focus here is on equality among religious groups, not equality between secular and religious belief systems. Even from a group or class perspective, however, the belief and behavioral dimensions of religion distinguish it from these other subjects of constitutional equality principles. Religion is simply more complicated than the attributes that define these other protected classes. Notwithstanding these differences, however, there is a group and status dimension to the protection that religion receives under the Constitution that cannot be avoided. Thus, the Establishment Clause implicates constitutional values promoting respect, integration, and equal opportunity and constitutional concerns relating to stigma, isolation, and discrimination in addition to its function in preserving religious liberty.

To the extent that constitutionally unrestricted voucher programs fragment public services and resources along religious lines, they risk undermining religious equality in significant ways. I want to focus on four specific concerns... Religious fragmentation of public life deprives religious minorities of valuable job opportunities. It denies religious minorities equal access to government-subsidized benefits. It indirectly coerces the communal isolation of minority groups. It reduces opportunities for public interaction that promote empathy, tolerance, and mutual respect.

***

2. Religious Equality and Discrimination in Hiring on the Basis of Religion

The equality implications of subsidizing religious schools... [that are permitted to] discriminate on the basis of religion in hiring staff with the public funds that they receive are serious. Substantial resources currently available for the hiring of individuals of diverse faiths will be allocated to religious institutions that may reserve them for individuals who subscribe to particular religious beliefs and practices. Otherwise capable job applicants of other faiths can be excluded from access to these resources at the religious institution's discretion. If we assume that a substantial majority of the private schools that will be eligible for vouchers are religious schools, teachers of a minority faith comprising one percent of the population of the United States that operates one percent or less of America's religious schools may be denied access to over 90 percent of these state-funded teaching jobs.

There are a variety of responses to this equality concern. Religious exclusivity is not always considered to be burdensome to people of other faiths. That is true enough. People of one faith experience neither stigma nor the loss of valued opportunities if religious conditions limit their access to a house of worship or their employment as clergy of another faith. The burden of exclusivity changes substantially, however, if religious discrimination is extended to limit access to the secular component of job functions and the public resources that subsidize them. Proponents of such discrimination may argue that the harm resulting from such discrimination is necessary to protect the religious liberty of the hiring institution, but that does not alter the fact or magnitude of harm to the excluded job applicant.

***

... [Even if religious discrimination in hiring is not invidious or based on prejudice, it] can dramatically limit the opportunities of religious minorities. Benign racial discrimination pursuant to affirmative action programs may not be intended to disparage or harm white applicants who do not obtain jobs that are offered to minority candidates. Surely, however, the lack of invidious intent alone does not suggest that such programs should be entirely immune from constitutional scrutiny or that the magnitude of a program and the extent to which it limits the employment opportunities of those racial groups that are burdened by it are irrelevant to a program's constitutionality.

Perhaps the most thoughtful and conceptually sophisticated response to the equality concerns I have described challenges the basic foundation on which my analysis is predicated. Religious discrimination in hiring, it is argued, cannot be meaningfully analogized to the racial, ethnic, or gender discrimination that the Constitution and many federal and state civil rights statutes prohibit. Rather, religious discrimination is a form of belief discrimination. This distinguishes it from the various kinds of status discrimination that the Equal Protection Clause and many civil rights laws prohibit. Belief discrimination by private institutions is generally tolerated in our society. Further, pervasively ideological secular organizations receiving public funds, such as environmental organizations, would be permitted to discriminate on the basis of secular and political beliefs in hiring employees to perform state-funded functions. Religious discrimination by religious organizations should not be understood to offend equality principles any more or less than belief discrimination by state-funded secular organizations.

I think this argument seriously mischaracterizes the nature of religion. Religion involves beliefs, obviously enough, but religion is more than a set of ethical, social, political, and even spiritual beliefs.... One of the intrinsic attributes of religion is that in many ways it is a status, a statement of who a person is as much as it is a statement of what a person believes. That is why religious equality is more properly analogized to gender or ethnic equality than to belief equality and why discrimination on the basis of religion is more problematic than discrimination on the basis of secular beliefs.

For many religious individuals, religion is not only a set of beliefs to which they subscribe, it is a description of the group and community to which they belong. Like groups defined by ethnic identity and nationality, religious groups are often tied together directly or indirectly by family and homeland and other cultural and physical connections that reinforce commonality of beliefs. Indeed, in a very real sense, religion can be a form of ethnic identity....

***

... [R]eligious identity is [also] part of our familial identity.... [M]ost religious individuals are born into a faith in a way that has no direct correspondence to other beliefs. Surely a child born to a Catholic family is born Catholic in some meaningful sense. If both parents were also Republicans, environmentalists, or vegetarians, we would be unlikely to say that the child was born a Republican or an environmentalist. Religion involves the interpersonal relationships that define who we are in a special way. It determines who we marry as well as the significance of that union, whether we have children and how they should be raised and educated, our understanding of death and the way we memorialize deceased relatives and ancestors. There simply is no sense in which discrimination based on a person's beliefs about air pollution, for example, can be understood to be directed at the identity, personal and communal relationships, and place in the world of an individual. Religious discrimination is directed at all of these core attributes of the individual.

***

There is a final reason why religious discrimination is more appropriately analogized to discrimination based on race, ethnicity, and gender rather than discrimination based on belief. Society's decision to protect certain groups from discrimination is based to a large extent on history and power relationships....

There is ... no history that suggests that the accumulated power of people with various secular beliefs cannot be trusted in making housing, employment, and educational decisions regarding people of opposing or different secular beliefs. We have no history that indicates that people who seriously oppose many forms of air pollution, for example, and people who are willing to tolerate air pollution to a greater extent will discriminate against individuals who hold one belief or the other to an unacceptable extent.... This has not been a problem that required a legislative, much less a constitutional, solution.

Religion is different.... Power is exercised on the basis of religious identity in our society and that power has been used abusively to limit substantially the places where people of various faiths could live, work, or study. Religious discrimination in America must be understood in historical context. Here, there is a history of invidious discrimination. Civil rights statutes prohibit religious discrimination while ignoring discrimination based on secular beliefs, in part, because there was a perceived problem to resolve in one case but not the other.

***

3. Religious Equality and Equal Access to Government Benefits of Equal Value

Religious institutions receiving vouchers provide a variety of unique benefits to their patrons.... Religious schools offer a spiritually meaningful and supportive environment for the education of children. Even non-religious courses may reflect a religious perspective on issues relating to theology and morality. Being a part of a community of co-religionists nurtures and reinforces an individual's commitment to specific beliefs and rituals.... For religious families, sending children to a religious school provides distinct and special benefits to the students themselves and it promotes the strength and continuity of the religion in which they believe.

Voucher programs will make these special benefits available to some parents and children who could not afford to attend a religious school without state support. The open question is whether the Constitution requires that the increased access to these religiously grounded benefits that vouchers provide must be made equally available to families of different faiths. Obviously, the state may not facially discriminate against particular religious persuasions, but formally neutral criteria restricting the availability of vouchers may result in significant substantive inequality among religions. Depending on the conditions attached to vouchers, access to religious schools and the resulting benefits such access provides may be far more available to certain religions than others.

In part, this problem is the flip side of the burden on religious liberty that vouchers may create, but here the impact is on religious equality rather than religious liberty. In the most stark and obvious situation, certain neutral rules restricting the use of vouchers may limit their availability to persons of particular religious faiths because the criteria used to determine eligibility directly conflicts with the tenets of a group's religion. Even if the criteria used to determine eligibility does not directly conflict with the tenets of a particular faith, however, restrictions on the use of vouchers may substantially skew their availability among religions as an indirect consequence of the beliefs and practices of certain faiths. A state might decide, for example, that it will only allow vouchers to be spent at schools that achieve a certain level of cost efficiency in the provision of educational services. But the religious beliefs and practices of some faiths may increase the cost of their educational programs relative to the programs of other faiths.

The size of a religious community may also be an important factor in determining the utility of vouchers and the availability of religious institutions at which they may be used. If efficiency criteria is utilized in identifying eligible schools, economies of scale may enable larger faiths to offer educational services at a lower cost per student. If conditions for eligibility are based on the scope of the educational program or the equipment available to support it, smaller faiths will also experience greater difficulty in satisfying the state's requirements....

***

4. Religious Equality and Religious Integration

The Constitution's equality provisions reflect an integrative ideal....

***

Religious integration serves many of the same equality functions as racial integration. There is a macro and a micro dimension to this constitutional value. From the more abstract perspective, integration creates the possibility of the kind of fluid democratic pluralism that reduces some of the negative influence of factions. In particular, it serves to dissolve the barriers between groups that permit the abuse of discrete and insular minorities.

In theory, democracy works for minorities as well as majorities because our political status is multi-faceted. We may be minorities in some aspects of our lives, but members of the majority with regard to other roles and interests. In many contexts, there may be no majority because there are too many diverse and competing interests in a political community for any one group to dominate on a particular issue. In this kind of a sociopolitical environment, we may be allies with certain individuals because we are members of the same union or trade association while we may be opponents of these same individuals because we live in different parts of town and each of our neighborhoods wants the new elementary school that is being planned to be located in their area.

This kind of an analysis presupposes a political, economic, and social environment in which people from diverse groups live and work together and share the public life of a community with each other. If all, or most, Hispanics or African-Americans, or all, or most, Jews or Catholics lived in separate communities and worked in ethnically or religiously homogeneous work environments, the fluidity, mix of relationships, and mutuality of interests described above would be far more restricted. Ethnic or religious minorities would become minorities in all aspects of life. Their needs and interests would be easily isolated from those of others and could be safely ignored without the majority incurring any costs or burdens itself. In this fundamental sense, discrete and insular minorities are not defined by physical characteristics. They are created by political, economic, and social decisions that isolate them from the rest of society.

From a micro perspective, ethnic or religious exclusivity in housing and work isolates individuals and groups from each other in the many contexts where their common humanity, abilities, and interests would be forming bonds of empathy and mutual respect. Interpersonal interactions allow for the kind of direct communication that messages transmitted through third parties can never convey as effectively....

***

If unrestricted vouchers fragment the public life of communities along religious lines, the religious demographics of a community will become a much more important factor in determining people's decisions as to where they will live. Resources previously allocated to non-religious institutions and services will now be distributed through religious organizations. The activities and services subsidized may be offered by and for people of different religious persuasions. Public institutions, in addition to losing substantial resources, lose the time, energy, and effort of families that will have transferred their commitments to private, religious institutions.

For a family of a minority religion, the cost of living in a community where there are relatively few members of one's faith increases substantially under this system. Until community members of their faith comprise a population of sufficient size to take advantage of vouchers and create religious institutions that provide whatever services the voucher programs encompass, their opportunities will be limited to whatever services the public sector, the non-religious private sector, and the religious institutions of other faiths provide. In some communities, that may be a sufficiently strong and varied range of public or non-religious, private services and there will be little change from a pre-voucher environment. In other cases, the allocation will be very different. The public sector may diminish in size significantly. The scope, availability, and quality of public services may all decline.

Not only may fewer satisfactory opportunities be available to religious minorities in a post-voucher world, but their locations will be more limited. For most people, having primary and secondary schools and other institutional services in the neighborhood or as close to the neighborhood as possible, is of special importance. In communities where schools and other services are fragmented along religious lines, the most effective way to further that objective is for people of the same faith to live in the same general area. Then the religious school will be a neighborhood school. To the extent that a family's housing choices track the schools its children will attend, religious integration in neighborhoods may decline as housing patterns become more homogeneous....

**

Religious exclusivity in employment can create similar results. If government-subsidized jobs are going to be allocated according to the religious demographics of a community because voucher funds are spent at institutions that choose to discriminate on the basis of religion in hiring, certain employment opportunities for members of minority faiths may depend in part on enough families of the same religion living in a community to justify the development of religious institutions that hire people of their faith. The economics of vouchers reward religiously homogeneous communities of a substantial size by providing them resources they can control and jobs for co-religionists. The more dispersed the people of a particular faith may be, the less likely it will be that they can utilize effectively the power to control resources that vouchers provide.

**

VOUCHERS AND RELIGIOUS SCHOOLS: THE NEW CONSTITUTIONAL QUESTIONS

THOMAS C. BERG

In *Zelman v. Simmons-Harris*,[1] the Supreme Court held that it is constitutional to include religious schools in programs of vouchers given to families for elementary and secondary education. The decision...indicates that most carefully designed voucher programs that include religious schools will survive challenge under the First Amendment's Establishment Clause....

***

A. The Holding

The program involved in *Zelman* was enacted by the Ohio legislature as a response to the failure of Cleveland's public schools, which have ranked "among the worst performing...in the Nation"...Under the program, a stu-

---

University of Cincinnati Law Review 72 (Fall 2003): 153–63.

dent in the Cleveland public schools could remain in the public schools and receive a grant to pay for extra tutorial sessions; alternatively, the student could attend a private school or certain other public schools and receive a grant (a "scholarship") to pay for tuition, up to a maximum of $2,250 and 90 percent of tuition costs.... The eligible schools included not only any private school in Cleveland, but also any public school district adjacent to Cleveland that decided to participate in the program....

***

[F]or almost twenty years before *Zelman*, the Court had increasingly switched [from a traditional "no aid to sectarian schools" approach] to a very different analysis: one that asks not whether a religious school in fact receives aid, but rather whether the government has skewed aid toward the choice of a religious school. Put differently, in the Court's terms, the question now is whether the program is one of "true private choice," under which aid flows to a religious school not because of any favoritism for religion in the terms of the program, but because the individual beneficiaries of the aid choose to use it at the religious school.[2]

***

The Court emphasized three features in finding Cleveland's program to be one of "true private choice." First, the program's terms were "neutral in all respects toward religion:" families were eligible to receive vouchers, and schools to participate, "without reference to" whether they were religious.[3] The provisions for aid to religious schools were no more favorable than those for other schools: indeed they offered less than half of the assistance given to community (*i.e.*, charter) schools and magnet schools in the Cleveland district, and less than half of the assistance to a participating suburban public school, which ... would receive a voucher on top of the state's regular contribution to the per-pupil cost. Neutrality of terms, the Court says, promotes parental choice, because when the terms are neutral they create "no 'financial incentive [s]' that 'ske[w]' the program toward religious schools."[4] Neutrality in this sense is fairly simple for a voucher program to satisfy. The state should simply make aid usable at religious schools on the same terms as it does for non-religious schools.

Second, the Court emphasized that the Cleveland program provided aid not "directly to religious schools," but only to individual beneficiaries— parents and families—"who, in turn, direct the aid to religious schools... of their own choosing."[5]... [Importantly, the] restriction [of aid] to secular uses does not apply to a program that aids individuals and lets them choose where to spend the aid. Thus, even a "pervasively sectarian" school may benefit from such aid, and the state need not do the monitoring (to limit the aid to secular classes) that the Court previously had found objectionable.

Finally, the Court emphasized that the program offered "genuine opportunities for Cleveland parents to select secular educational options" as alternatives to religious schools.[6] The reasoning implicit in this factor is that if there are actually no secular alternatives to religious schools, then even under formally neutral program terms, families have no "genuine choice" and the effect of the program is to "coerc[e]" them into choosing religious schools.[7] But the Court was relatively flexible in determining whether sufficient secular options existed, finding a number in Cleveland that qualified, including secular private schools, magnet and charter schools in the Cleveland public system, and even the extra tutoring in the regular public schools.

In particular, the majority refused to infer a lack of genuine options from the high percentage of religious choices in the program. In one year, 96 percent of those who chose vouchers used them at religious schools, which made up 82 percent of the participating private schools. The Court noted that the 82 percent figure was virtually identical to the percentage of religious schools among Ohio private schools generally and thus could not plausibly be attributed to any features of the program. More importantly, the Court said that the percentage of vouchers in fact used at religious schools was irrelevant, for two reasons. First, "[t]he constitutionality of a neutral [aid] program" should not turn on how recipients actually choose to use the aid.[8] Second, the question of genuine alternatives "must be answered by evaluating *all* options Ohio provides Cleveland schoolchildren," including the many "nontraditional" options in the public school system, which, if included, would have dropped the percentage of students enrolled in religious schools down to twenty percent.[9]...

B. Zelman's Key Ideas. A Brief Defense

The first of *Zelman's* key premises is that when an individual receives a voucher provided on a neutral basis and then uses it at a religious school, the "advancement of a religious mission [is] attributable to the individual recipient, not to the government."[10] The government merely provides the aid to citizens and, given the neutrality of the terms, creates no incentives for families to choose religious schools over others.... In [earlier decisions, the Court used the analogy]... that a "true private choice" program of benefits was like "the government issuing a paycheck to an employee who, in turn, donates a portion of that check to a religious institution."[11] This rationale amounts to a holding of "no state action" advancing religion.... With *Zelman*, the private choice rationale now fully governs cases involving state aid to individuals.

The private-choice rationale leads logically to the Court's conclusion that the amount of aid actually used at religious schools is irrelevant. The religious schools are already operating, for reasons independent of the state, and families choose to use their grants at those schools for reasons that are likewise independent of the state: the family's religious ideology, the school's educational performance, or its disciplinary policies.

The Court's dismissal of the actual results of voucher choices has drawn fire from commentators. Ira Lupu and Robert Tuttle, for example, argue that the state was responsible for the Cleveland results because the high preexisting percentage of religious schools made them a dominant option, especially in the light of the poor quality of the unreformed Cleveland public schools. Thus, although Lupu and Tuttle support the constitutionality of some school choice arrangements, they argue that the Cleveland program "steered families toward religious experience," and that the state should have "an affirmative duty... to take steps to improve the mix," by, for example, requiring suburban public schools to participate.[12] Along the same lines, Steven Green and, (before *Zelman*) Alan Brownstein have both argued that voucher programs "lead to greater religious inequality" because small faiths find it more difficult than larger faiths to set up schools and to satisfy the typical eligibility criteria for receiving voucher students.[13] Both Green and Brownstein criticize the "private choice" rationale for emphasizing form over substance—for overlooking the disparate impact that choice programs have in favor of certain faiths that operate K-12 schools.[14]

Such arguments, however, typically fail to confront the fact that absent a voucher program, the state's funding arrangement likely has as much or more of a disparate impact on choices concerning religious education. Absent vouchers, the state funds only one, secular category of schools: public schools, including variations such as charter schools and magnet schools. Because these various public options must be secular in nature—the Establishment Clause forbids religious teaching or exercises as part of their program—they are unacceptable or at least deeply unattractive to many devout religious families of varying faiths. Other families, again of varying faiths, may find religious schools attractive because of the moral atmosphere and discipline they provide. Thus, as Eugene Volokh has put it, the fact that "[r]ight now, all standard K-12 spending goes to secular education" is "itsel[f] a powerful 'disparate impact' favoring secular uses and disfavoring religious uses."[15] To argue that voucher aid in practice "steers" students toward religious schools requires overlooking or minimizing the extent to which, in practice, a world without religious-school vouchers "steers" students away from religious and toward secular schools.... Even if the choice enactment fails, as the Cleveland program did, to bring in the whole range of secular private schools, it nevertheless adds significantly to the number of schooling options, which *prima facie* should mean that parents' choices are steered less than they were before.

For this reason, I think that Professors Lupu and Tuttle are too demanding when they dismiss out of hand the state's argument that it was not politically feasible to mandate the participation of suburban public schools in the Cleveland voucher program. To set a standard that is, in political terms, unrealistically high is to ensure that voucher programs will not be enacted or survive, thus perpetuating the monopoly of public schools, with their own strong effect of pushing many parents away from religious schools....

Likewise, to argue that school choice worsens the unequal position of minority faiths, one has to assume that the existing public schools are satisfactory to those faiths. If a small religious group cannot afford to open its own schools with a voucher program, then it certainly cannot do so without a voucher program. In other words, in the absence of such a program, its members would surely be limited to public schools. The arguments of several Orthodox Jewish groups in *Zelman* confirm that public schools are unacceptable for families of some minority faiths, and that school choice increases their ability to follow their conscience in choosing their children's education. Indeed, for low-income families, vouchers may be essential to satisfying their conscience....

The primary rejoinder to this argument is that many members of minority faiths greatly prefer a public school to a school that would instruct their children in another faith. But it is unlikely that school choice will come close to eliminating the public school option in any locality. Moreover, as Professor Volokh has argued, the way to deal with this remote possibility is to mandate the continuation of a public school in districts where school choice operates, not to take the extreme step of invalidating vouchers altogether. In short, although differential effects from a formally neutral voucher program may be a matter of concern, they scarcely justify having a constitutional rule that requires flat-out, facial discrimination against religion. Including religious schools on equal terms in a school choice program is not a mere matter of form. It does good things for religious liberty and equality as a matter of substance.

Zelman implicitly recognizes the above points in its second key premise. The Court said that to assess whether families have genuine secular alternatives, one must take into account "*all* options Ohio provides Cleveland schoolchildren," including the various public alternatives to the regular public schools: community (charter) schools, magnet schools, and supplemental tutoring in the regular schools.[16] To state this proposition explicitly was important. In its 1970s decisions striking down programs of aid to private schools, the Court often had focused on the aid program in isolation and then objected that the vast majority of eligible schools were religious. This, of course, ignored the fact that the state already provided a complete subsidy in the form of a free education to children attending public schools. The no-aid decisions explicitly or implicitly assumed that public schools were the neutral baseline and aid to private schools, therefore, a departure in favor of religion. ... That argument obviously, begs the question: it assumes that the public schools are the neutral baseline for education in funding, when in fact they may be better seen as simply a secular competitor to religious schools....

***

C. Zelman and Future Establishment Clause Challenges to School Choice

Zelman's analysis suggests that it will be relatively easy for a voucher program that includes religious schools to satisfy the Establishment Clause. Consider the two common contexts for such programs.

First, consider the situation of vouchers for low-income families in failing public schools, as in Cleveland. This is the most likely situation for the enactment of a voucher program, in political terms, because there is an appealing moral argument for giving low-income families some power to choose better performing schools, a power their higher income counterparts already exercise.

Most of the notable failing public school systems are large urban systems; and these school systems almost always have charter or magnet schools, which *Zelman* treats as genuine options (indeed, under *Zelman* even extra tutoring in public schools counts). To be sure, there is a strong argument that the entirely *unreformed* public schools of a failing system cannot count as a genuine alternative to religious schools; the very premise of choice legislation in such a context is that the public schools are inadequate. I agree with Professors Lupu and Tuttle that a commitment to true parental choice in matters of religion and education entails some scrutiny of the quality and desirability of secular alternatives. But when public-school reforms are among the available options, *Zelman* correctly signals a less than rigid attitude toward assessing their quantity and their quality. … This flexibility is appropriate. A strict attitude toward the adequacy of secular alternatives might mandate the exclusion of religious schools from many neutral voucher programs.… A voucher program with religious schools included generally works an increase in families' choice, even if the program has some imperfections, and courts should not block such incremental improvements by demanding that the secular alternatives be sparkling in quality.

Turning to the second context, imagine that a state goes beyond addressing a failing system and offers vouchers for any family in the state as an alternative to public school. Such a program is very unlikely to be enacted, in part because it is not limited to the most morally compelling case of low-income students in failing public schools. Still, the program would likely be upheld under the reasoning of *Zelman*, at least as to most schools in the state. Most public schools would be educationally adequate and thus, unlike the failing system, would count as a genuine alternative to religious schools. And if the regular public schools count, they will almost always dwarf private-school enrollment.

NOTES

The note number from the original article is shown in the parenthesis at the end of each citation.

1. *Zelman v. Simmons-Harris*, 536 U.S. 639 (2000). (1)
2. *Mueller v. Allen*, 463 U.S. 388, 399–400 (1983); *Witters v. Wash. Department of Services for Blind*, 474 U.S. 481, 487 (1986); *Zobrest v. Catalina Foothills District*, 509 U.S. 1, 10–11 (1993). (15)

3. 536 U.S. 653. (17)

4. Ibid. (19)

5. Ibid., p. 649. (20)

6. Ibid., p. 619. (23)

7. Ibid., p. 655. (24)

8. Ibid., p. 658. (27)

9. Ibid., pp. 656, 659–60. (28)

10. Ibid., p. 652. (29)

11. *Mitchell v. Helms*, 530 U.S. 793, 842 (2000). (32)

12. Ira C. Lupu and Robert W. Tuttle, "*Zelman's* Future: Vouchers, Sectarian Providers, and the Next Round of Constitutional Battles," *Notre Dame Law Review* 78 (2003): 947; Lupu and Tuttle, "Sites of Redemption: A Wide-Angle Look at Government Vouchers and Sectarian-Service Providers," *Journal of Law and Politics* 18 (2002): 599–600. (37)

13. Steven K. Green, "The Illusionary Aspect of 'Private Choice' for Constitutional Analysis," *Willamette Law Review* 38 (2002): 559; Alan Brownstein, "Evaluating School Voucher Programs Through a Liberty, Equality, and Free Speech Matrix," *Connecticut Law Review* 31 (1999): 920–23. (38)

14. Green, "The Illusionary Aspect of 'Private Choice' for Constitutional Analysis," p. 573; Brownstein, "Evaluating School Voucher Programs Through a Liberty, Equality, and Free Speech Matrix," p. 922. (39)

15. Eugene Volokh, "Equal Treatment Is Not Establishment," *Notre Dame Journal of Law, Ethics and Public Policy* 13 (1999): 348. (42)

16. 536 U.S. 656. (50)

CHAPTER 7

CHARITABLE AND SOCIAL WELFARE SERVICES BY FAITH-BASED PROVIDERS

A CONSTITUTIONAL CASE FOR GOVERNMENTAL COOPERATION WITH FAITH-BASED SOCIAL SERVICE PROVIDERS

CARL H. ESBECK

***

I. OLDER ASSUMPTIONS: SEPARATIONISM AND A
TRADITIONAL ANALYSIS OF CASE LAW

***

... [W]hen it comes to direct assistance—that is, a government's general program of assistance flows directly to all organizations, including faith-based providers of services—then separationism is the Court's beginning frame of reference. Separationism makes three assumptions. First, it assumes that a sacred/secular dichotomy accurately describes the world of religion and the

Emory Law Journal 46, no. 1 (Winter 1997): 9–11, 17–27, 34–40.

work of faith-based providers called to minister among the poor and needy. That is to say, the activities of faith-based providers can be separated into the temporal and the spiritual. This assumption, of course, is vigorously challenged by neutrality theorists. Second, separatists assume that religion is private and that it should not involve itself with public matters, with "public" often equated to "political" or "governmental" affairs. The neutrality principle rejects this private/ public dichotomy as well, insisting that personal faith has public consequences and that the practice of religious faith can lead to cooperation with the government in achieving laudable public purposes. Third, separatists assume that a government's welfare assistance equates to aid for the service provider. Neutrality theories contest this characterization as well, describing the situation as one of cooperation between government and independent sector providers, with the joint aim being society's betterment through the delivery of aid to the ultimate beneficiaries.

As a general proposition, the Supreme Court has said that direct forms of reimbursement can be provided for the "secular" services offered by a religious organization but not for those services comprising the group's "religious" practices. Thus, if an organization's secular and religious functions are reliably separable, direct assistance can be provided for the secular functions alone. But if they are not separable, then the Court disallows the assistance altogether, with the explanation that the Establishment Clause will not allow the risk of governmental aid furthering the transmission of religious beliefs or practices.

The juridical category the Court utilizes to determine whether a general program of direct assistance risks advancing religion is whether the provider is "pervasively sectarian." Should the provider fit the profile of a pervasively sectarian organization, then separationist theory prohibits any direct aid to the provider. The one small exception is aid that, due to its form or nature, cannot be converted to a religious use. For example, the Court has allowed independent religious schools to receive government-provided secular textbooks and bus transportation between a student's home and school.

**

In laying down its rules concerning programs of direct assistance, the Supreme Court has adopted a funds-tracing analysis rather than a freed-funds analysis. That is, the Court interprets the Establishment Clause as forbidding the direct flow of taxpayer funds, as such, to pay for inherently religious activities....

The harm that separationists fear is not that privately raised dollars are freed as a consequence of the government's program so that they may be reallocated to a religious use. Rather, the feared harm is that governmental monies (collected as taxes, user fees, fines, sale of government property, etc.) may be used to pay for such inherently religious activities as worship, prayer, proselytizing, doctrinal teaching, and devotional scriptural reading. Indeed, separationists on the Court have been most insistent that the Establishment Clause "absolutely prohibit[s] government-financed or government-sponsored indoctrination into the beliefs of a particular religious faith."[1]

Although it will scandalize separationists, the rest of us are led to probe below the bluff and bluster and ask the following: "Is the harm resulting from government-collected monies going to religion so self-evident and severe?" As citizens we are taxed to support all manner of policies and programs with which we disagree. Tax dollars pay for weapons of mass destruction that some believe are evil. Taxes pay for abortions and the execution of capital offenders, that some believe are acts of murder. Taxes pay the salaries of public officials whose policies we despise and oppose at every opportunity. Why is religion different? ... Accordingly, with reference to the Court's interpretation of the Establishment Clause, it must again be asked, "Is the harm that separationists would have us avoid at all cost so self-evident and severe?"

... [T]he answer separationists give is that there are two such harms which the Establishment Clause is designed to safeguard against, and history demonstrates that they can be quite severe: first, divisiveness within the body politic along sectarian lines; and, second, the damage to religion itself by the undermining of religious voluntarism and the weakening of church autonomy. Separationism has yet to give a convincing argument that these two harms will befall the nation as a result of the equal involvement of faith-based providers in social service programs. The harm of sectarian divisiveness within the body politic is not altogether different in kind or more threatening than tax funding for other ideologies and programs that citizens find disagreeable. And the harm to religion itself when too closely allied with government, while real and threatening, can be adequately protected by writing into the welfare legislation safeguards for protecting the religious character and expression of faith-based providers.

II. New Assumptions: A Paradigm Shift to Governmental Neutrality

Neutrality theory approaches the debate over the Establishment Clause from an altogether different point of entry. According to this theory, when government provides benefits to enable activities that serve the public good, such as education, health care, or social services, there should be neither discrimination in eligibility based on religion, nor exclusionary criteria requiring these charities to engage in self-censorship or otherwise water down their religious identity as a condition for program participation. The neutrality model allows individuals and religious groups to participate fully and equally with their fellow citizens in America's public life, without being forced either to shed or disguise their religious convictions or character. The theory is not a call for preferential treatment for religion in the administration of publicly funded programs. Rather, when it comes to participation in programs of aid, neutrality merely lays claim to the same access to benefits, without regard to religion, enjoyed by others. Finally... the neutrality principle rejects the three assumptions made by separationist theory: that the activities of faith-based charities are severable into "sacred" and "secular" aspects, that religion is "private" whereas government monopolizes "public" matters, and that governmental assistance paid to service providers is aid to the providers as well as aid to the ultimate beneficiaries.

Should separationism eventually be dislodged from its place as the controlling paradigm, it will be said that this change began in 1981 with the Supreme Court's decision in *Widmar v. Vincent.*[2] [*Widmar* held that it violates the free speech clause of the First Amendment to deny religious speakers and groups the same equal access to public property for expressive purposes the state provides to secular organizations, and that it does not violate the Establishment Clause for the state to permit such equal access. The free speech analysis of *Widmar* has been affirmed in a long line of cases culminating with *Rosenberger v. Rector* and *Visitors of the University of Virginia.*[3] ...

Following [these decisions]... equal treatment has... become the normative rule of law concerning private speech of religious content or view-point. ... [T]his equality-based rule is instrumental to neutrality theory.

***

Before continuing with the argument for neutrality theory...a digression is necessary to address the rationale for grounding the major competitor to separationism in the juridical concept of governmental neutrality rather than equality. As it turns out, a rule of equality works quite well when the church/state dispute is over access to benefits. However, when the Establishment Clause challenge is to legislation that exempts religious organizations from regulatory burdens, the normative rule of law continues to follow a separationist model. Accordingly, when the issue is relief from government-imposed burdens, religious groups want to be viewed not as equal to others, but as separate and unique.

As a juridical concept, neutrality integrates into a single coherent theory both (1) allowing religious providers equal access to benefits, and (2) allowing them separate relief from regulatory burdens. The rationale entails distinguishing between burdens and benefits.

The Supreme Court has repeatedly held that the Establishment Clause is not violated when government refrains from imposing a burden on religion, even though that same burden is imposed on the nonreligious who are otherwise similarly situated. *Corporation of Presiding Bishop v. Amos*[4] is the leading case. *Amos* upheld an exemption for religious organizations in federal civil rights legislation. The exemption permitted religious organizations to discriminate on a religious basis in matters concerning employment. Finding that the exemption did not violate the Establishment Clause, the Court explained that "it is a permissible legislative purpose to alleviate significant governmental interference with the ability of religious organizations to define and carry out their missions."[5] When the Court permits a legislature to exempt religion from regulatory burdens, it enables private religious choice.

The Court's rationale is twofold. First, to establish a religion connotes that a government must take some affirmative step to achieve the prohibited result. Conversely, for government to passively "leave religion where it found it" logically cannot be an act establishing a religion. Referencing the First Amendment's text, the words "shall make no law"[6] imply the performance of some affirmative act by government, not maintenance of the status quo. Stating the practical sense of the matter, Professor Laycock observed that "[t]he state does not support or establish religion by leaving it alone."[7] Second, unlike benefit programs, religious exemptions reduce civic/religious tensions and minimize church/state interactions, both matters that enhance the nonentanglement so desired by the Establishment Clause.

Should the Court in the future permit a legislature to design welfare programs that confer direct assistance without regard to religion, it would be following a rule of equal treatment as to religion. However, exemptions from burdens and equal treatment as to benefits have a common thread that ties the two together. In following an equality-based rule as to benefits, equality is not an end in itself but a means to a higher goal. That goal is the minimization of the government's influence over personal choices concerning religious beliefs and practices. The goal is realized when government is neutral as to the religious choices of its citizens. Thus, whether pondering the constitutionality of exemptions from regulatory burdens or of equal treatment as to benefit programs, in both situations the integrating principle is neutralizing the impact of governmental action on personal religious choices. From that common axis, it makes sense to agree with the Court's holding, in cases such as *Amos*, that religious exemptions from legislative burdens are consistent with the Establishment Clause, and, on the other hand, to insist that the Establishment Clause permits the equal treatment of religion when it comes to financial benefits.

It would be rhetorical, but still a fair comment, to say that in neutrality theory religion gets the best of both worlds: religion is free of burdens borne by others but shares equally in the benefits. However, this observation is not an argument against the neutrality principle but a commendation of it. No one need apologize for a model of church/state relations that maximizes religious liberty (subject, of course, to the reasonable demands of organized society) and limits the power of the modern regulatory state. This combination of liberty and limits is what the First Amendment is about. It was the First Amendment, after all, that expressly singled out religion as an attribute of human nature that called for special treatment.

***

As we look at the progression from *Widmar* to *Rosenberger* in terms of the Court's attitude toward enabling personal religious choice, there is a logical continuum. The Court has moved toward neutralizing government's impact on religious belief and practice. In *Widmar*, the Establishment Clause was not violated when the government provided a direct benefit in the form of reserved meeting space (classrooms, heat, and light) because of the larger public purpose at issue—enriching the marketplace of ideas. In *Rosenberger*, the Establishment Clause was not violated when the government provided a direct benefit in the form of funding (paid printing costs) for the same reason as in *Widmar*—the larger public purpose of enriching the marketplace of ideas. Both the classroom space and payment of printing costs were valuable benefits to which a sum certain could be assigned. Free access to other forms of valuable direct benefits easily come to mind: bulletin boards, photocopy machines, computers for word processing and e-mail, facsimile machines, organizational mailboxes, organizational office space, and even something as common as use of a telephone. All of these direct benefits when provided to a wide variety of student organizations, including organizations that are either religious or have religious viewpoints, would be permitted by the *Widmar/Rosenberger* interpretation of the Establishment Clause.

Indeed, there is no logical stopping place as the circumstance evolves from funding private expression without regard to religion to funding a social program without regard to religion. The essential requisite, as far as the Establishment Clause is concerned, is that in the case of expression, the creation of the public forum have a public purpose. In the case of a social service program, its enactment must have a public purpose as well.

The general principle of law that emerges is that the Establishment Clause is not violated when, for a public purpose, a program of direct aid is made available to an array of providers selected without regard to religion. In recently enacting the Church Arson Prevention Act,[8] Congress made use of this principle. Section 4(a) of the Act enables nonprofit organizations exempt under § 501(c)(3) of the Internal Revenue Code, which are victims of arson or terrorism as a result of racial or religious animus, to obtain federally guaranteed loans through private lending institutions. This of course means churches can obtain the necessary credit to repair or rebuild their houses of worship at reduced rates. The Act, quite sensibly, treats churches the same as all similarly situated exempt nonprofit organizations. The public purpose is to assist the victims of crime. The federal guarantee represents a form of direct aid to religion, but because the aid is neutrally available to all 501(c)(3) organizations, it does not violate the Establishment Clause.

In the context of welfare legislation, the public purpose is for government and the independent sector to engage in a cooperative program that addresses the temporal needs of the ultimate beneficiaries, and to do so in a manner that enhances the quality or quantity of the services to those beneficiaries. If some of the providers happen (indeed, are known) to be religious, and in the course of administering their programs they integrate therein religious beliefs and practices, that is of no concern to the government. As long as the beneficiaries have a choice as to where they can obtain services, thereby preventing any religious coercion of beneficiaries, and as long as the public purpose of the program is met, the government's interest is at an end.

For a welfare program to have a public purpose, more is required than that the program merely be facially neutral as to religion. The legislation must have as its genuine object the pursuit of the good of civil society. Permissible public purposes encompass health (including freedom from addictions), safety, morals, or meeting temporal needs, such as shelter, food, clothing, and employment.

Unlike separationism, in neutrality theory it makes no difference whether a provider is "pervasively sectarian" or whether the nature of the direct aid is such that it can be diverted to a religious use. Most importantly, the courts no longer need to ensure that governmental funds are used exclusively for "secular, neutral, and nonideological purposes"[9] as opposed to worship or religious instruction. Neutrality theory eliminates the need for the judiciary to engage in such alchemy.

For faith-based providers to retain their religious character, programs of aid must be written to specially exempt them from regulatory burdens that would frustrate or compromise their religious character. Not only is this essential to attracting their participation, but it is in the government's interest for these providers to retain the spiritual character so central to their success in rehabilitating the poor and needy....

In neutrality theory it might be asked, "Just what is left of the Establishment Clause?" The answer is "Quite a lot!"...[T]he Establishment Clause continues to prohibit the government from adopting or administering a welfare program out of a purpose that is inherently religious. For example, the no-establishment principle does not permit as the object of legislation the pursuit of worship, religious teaching, prayer, proselytizing, or devotional Bible reading. Characterizing the purpose of a program of aid as "nonsectarian" or "secular" should be avoided, for that just clouds the issue. Mere overlap between a statutory purpose and religious belief or practice does not, without more, make the legislation unconstitutional. Finally, although the Establishment Clause does require a public purpose, the neutrality principle is not concerned with unintended effects among religions. Accordingly, the Establishment Clause is not offended should a general program of aid affect, for good or ill, some religious providers more than others, as long as any disparate effect is unintentional.

***

CONCLUSION

As one facet of the nation's overall effort to reform welfare, it is imperative to increase the involvement of the independent sector in the delivery of government-assisted social services. A significant part of the voluntary sector presently engaged in social work consists of faith-based nonprofit organizations. Indeed, these religious charities are some of the most efficient social service providers, as well as among the most successful, measured in terms of lives permanently changed for the better. Although some faith-based providers have been willing to participate in government-assisted programs, many are wary about involvement with the government because they rightly fear the debasing of their religious character and expression. Consequently, what is needed is legislation that invites the equal participation of faith-based organizations as social service providers, while safeguarding their religious character, which is the very source of their genius and success.

Achieving this goal will require change in how Americans conceive of the role of modern government, which fortunately is already underway. For starters, the activity of government must not be thought of as monopolizing the "public." Rather, civil society is comprised of many intermediate institutions and communities that also serve public purposes, including the independent sector of nonprofit faith-based providers.

Further, independent sector providers that opt to participate in a government welfare program are not in any primary sense to be regarded as "beneficiaries" of the government's assistance. Rather, it is those who are the ultimate object of the social service program—the hungry, the homeless, the alcoholic, the teenage mother—who are the beneficiaries of taxpayer funds. As they deliver services to those in need with such remarkable efficiency and effectiveness, faith-based providers, along with others in the voluntary sector, give far more in value, measured in societal betterment, than they could possibly receive as an incident of their expanded responsibilities. This is not a case of tax dollars funding religion.

Rightly interpreted, the Establishment Clause does not require that faith-based providers censor their religious expression and secularize their identity as conditions of participation in a governmental program. So long as the welfare program has as its object the public purpose of society's betterment—that is, help for the poor and needy—and so long as the program is equally open to all providers, religious and secular, then the First Amendment requirement that the law be neutral as to religion is fully satisfied.

NOTES

The note number from the original article is shown in the parenthesis at the end of each citation.

1. *Grand Rapids School District v. Ball*, 473 U.S. 373, 385 (1985). (70)
2. *Widmar v. Vincent*, 454 U.S. 263 (1981). (81)
3. 115 S. Ct. 2510 (1995). (86)
4. *Corporation of Presiding Bishop v. Amos*, 483 U.S. 327 (1987). (92)
5. Ibid., p. 335. (93)
6. U.S. Constitution, amend. 1. (95)
7. Douglas Laycock, "Towards a General Theory of the Religion Clauses," *Columbia Law Review* 81 (1981): 1416. (96)
8. Public Law 104–155, 104th Cong. (1996). (136)
9. *Committee for Public Education v. Nyquist*, 413 U.S. 756, 780 (1973). (143)

INTERPRETING THE RELIGION CLAUSES IN TERMS OF LIBERTY, EQUALITY, AND FREE SPEECH VALUES— A CRITICAL ANALYSIS OF "NEUTRALITY THEORY" AND CHARITABLE CHOICE

ALAN E. BROWNSTEIN

II. A CRITIQUE OF "NEUTRALITY THEORY"

***

A. The Lack of Neutrality in Neutrality Theory

Perhaps the most glaring defect of [using] neutrality theory [as a basis for upholding charitable choice legislation] is its lack of commitment to neutrality itself. In theory and practice, neutrality theory does not live up to its own ideals, whether we are talking about neutrality between secular and religious belief systems or neutrality among religious faiths.

Notre Dame Journal Law, Ethics and Public Policy 13 (1999): 246–51, 253–56, 270–71, 273–76, 278.

Neutrality theory claims that its goal is "the minimization of government's influence over personal choices concerning religious beliefs and practices."[1] One would presume that this objective precludes government actions that create incentives for or against engaging in religious practices or adopting religious beliefs. The theory does not explain, however, how granting exemptions for religiously motivated conduct, but not acts of secular conscience, promotes such a neutral result.

A system of free exercise exemptions or statutory accommodations of only religiously motivated conduct promotes religious beliefs and practices in a variety of respects. As a general matter such a legal regime creates the impression that religious moral principles are more worthy of respect than secular beliefs. Further, religious moral convictions provide a more useful value system to the individual under this framework because they free the individual from the risks and burdens associated with being subject to inconsistent requirements. If a person influenced by both secular and religious values is told that the government will only respect the individual's acts of conscience if they are derived from religious sources, an incentive is created to look to one's religious beliefs to justify moral conduct.

No one suggests that these general incentives will draw secular individuals irresistibly to spiritual life. They operate incrementally on the margin and cumulatively. If the situation were reversed and only secular acts of conscience were exempted from general laws, however, I would be hard pressed to deny that such a framework created incentives favoring secular beliefs.

Recognizing that the provision of regulatory exemptions for religiously motivated conduct creates incentives that favor religion does not establish that such exemptions are constitutionally impermissible. Indeed, in many cases I believe religious exemptions are constitutionally justified if not required. Evaluated in isolation, there is often a persuasive argument that granting an exemption for a religious practice distorts incentives in favor of religion far less substantially than the incentives against religious practice that are created if the exemption is denied.

This does not mean, however, that the incentives in favor of religion that the granting of exemptions creates are constitutionally irrelevant and never need to be taken into account. On the contrary, ... the development of constitutional standards to further the goal of incentive neutrality requires a wider and more holistic perspective. If regulatory exemptions result in incentives favoring religion, the granting of exemptions creates an imbalance in the constitutional ledger that may help to justify other decisions, creating counter-vailing incentives, that move the system closer to equilibrium. It is this lack of attention to the consequences of granting religious exemptions that calls the commitment of neutrality theory to true incentive neutrality into question.

***

Neutrality theory is even more deficient in its approach to government spending and the disproportionate impact of facially neutral spending pro-grams among various religious faiths. Surely, all the criticism of the Supreme Court's decision in *Employment Division v. Smith*[2] and the battles over the fed-eral Religious Freedom Restoration Act ("RFRA")[3] established one important principle of religion clause jurisprudence. Formal neutrality in government decision making does not adequately protect or promote religious liberty or equality. This principle is as true for government spending decisions as it is for regulatory laws.

It is true that formally neutral laws and spending decisions do not distin-guish between secular and religious beliefs or among different religious faiths on their face. In a superficial sense these laws require that everyone must be treated the same way. In that formal sense, such government decisions are neutral and evenhanded. But we know that this kind of neutrality is a sham. Because different religious groups and individuals are not similarly situated, these formally neutral laws undermine religious liberty and promote inequality. For religious liberty and equality to be meaningfully protected, we have to look behind the formal neutrality of the law and examine its real world effects and consequences.

Yet [proponents of charitable choice]...ignore this important lesson when government spending is at issue. Far from incorporating the doctrinal structure of pre-*Smith* Free Exercise law and RFRA into the review of gov-ernment spending programs, neutrality theory seems to track the analysis of *Employment Division v. Smith* quite comfortably. As long as state grants are dis-tributed according to some neutral criteria that on its face allows both reli-gious and secular organizations to compete for funding, Free Exercise and Establishment Clause requirements are satisfied.

It is difficult to understand the justification for this doctrinal bifurcation between regulation and spending. When the government denies unemploy-ment compensation to a Seventh Day Adventist or a Jewish person because they will not accept work on Saturday, the incentives created by this decision and the burden it imposes on religious liberty seem obvious. Surely, similar incentives are created when the criteria the government uses in deciding whether to fund particular religious organizations for the provision of welfare services requires the grantee to operate its program on Saturday. Both decisions are formally neutral. Both decisions are substantively unequal and unfair to religious faiths that recognize Saturday as the Sabbath. Yet neutrality theory apparently condemns the former and upholds the latter.

***

An additional hypothetical concerning the funding of religious and secular schools should help to illustrate the problem here. Assume that the government in addition to funding the public schools, allows different private groups, including religious groups, to bid for community-wide contracts to provide secular educational services to children. Tracking the charitable choice provisions, the law providing such funding allows any religious group receiving a contract to promote its faith at school through private funding and to discriminate on the basis of religion in hiring teachers and staff. There are several religious schools in the community already, but, not surprisingly, the largest school, let us say it is Methodist, is able to underbid its competitors and receives the contract. Now there will be two state-funded schools in the community. One is a secular public school and the other is a pervasively sectarian Methodist school that teaches religion along with secular subjects (although the former instruction is privately funded).

... [S]urely a constitutional theory that identifies its primary goal as minimizing government incentives that influence religious decisions should consider this result to be problematic. Neutrality theory, however, appears to be "neutral" between this kind of a funding decision and more egalitarian arrangements. If the goal of neutrality theory is to try to recreate as closely as possible the religious decisions that would be reached by private parties acting individually or through private agreement if the government was not involved, these "neutral" arrangements for funding secular social or educational services through religious institutions seem starkly inconsistent with that objective.

Neutrality theory also ignores the incentives created by allowing a religious organization to discriminate on the basis of religion in hiring employees to perform public functions it has contracted with the state to provide. Assume the public functions at issue had previously been provided by the state itself or by secular organizations prohibited by law from discriminating on the basis of religion and that individuals of diverse faiths were employed in the delivery of those services. Then the state substantially reduces the funding available to government or secular providers and uses the funds it has saved to subsidize religious organizations that have demonstrated their ability to successfully administer similar services. Those individuals previously employed by the state or secular organizations, who lost their jobs when the state's funding was redirected, are told that jobs requiring their expertise and background are now available from the newly subsidized religious organizations—however, applicants must pass a religious test governing both their beliefs and behavior to be eligible to be hired. Where their previous employers had some obligation to reasonably accommodate the religious needs of employees on the job and no authority to discriminate against employees on the basis of their religious activities off the job, now these employees must comply with the religious mandates of a different faith on and off the job. Apparently, from the perspective of neutrality theory, this change in job opportunities and working conditions does not create incentives that influence religious decisions.

The charitable choice provisions of the recent welfare reform act implicate virtually all of the incentives ignored by neutrality theory that are discussed above. The statute permits funds to be allocated according to facially neutral criteria without regard to the allocation of resources among different faiths. There are no constraints on programmatic requirements that have the effect of precluding particular religions from participating. No attention is paid to the possibility that religious beliefs and practices may increase the cost or impair the efficiency of certain religious providers making it highly unlikely that those faiths will receive contracts from the state. The incentives created by any disparity of allocation among faiths are not taken into account in any way. Similarly, charitable choice allows publicly funded job opportunities to be offered or withheld on the basis of religious beliefs or practices without regard to the coercive effect of such inducements on the religious decisions of employees. Thus, the same criticisms that apply to neutrality theory are equally applicable to the charitable choice framework which serves as a concrete manifestation of this constitutional model in action....

B. Moving Beyond Liberty—The Role of Equality and Instrumental Speech Values in Interpreting the Religion Clauses

***

... [P]roponents of neutrality theory see *Rosenberger* [*v. Rector & Visitors of the University of Virginia*],[4] and a line of free speech cases preceding it as establishing a principle of evenhanded treatment when government subsidizes secular and religious private activities. Even if government support for secular, but not religious, charities providing services to the poor did not formally violate freedom of speech requirements, they argue, constitutional antipathy to viewpoint discrimination informs our understanding of the religion clauses and undermines the legitimacy of such funding arrangements. Religious and secular beliefs are in competition across a broad spectrum of American culture and the Constitution should not be interpreted in a way that distorts the marketplace of ideas by favoring one worldview or the other. At a minimum, this principle should permit government to make financial support available to religious and secular institutions on a non-discriminatory basis.

Grounding a constitutional commitment to neutral funding requirements on a freedom of speech foundation, however, raises serious questions that neutrality theory does not adequately address. The recognition that religious and secular perspectives constitute competing viewpoints creates a disturbing tension between neutrality theory's two central principles: the exemption of religiously motivated conduct from neutral laws of general applicability (and the protection of religious institutions from regulatory intrusions), and the insistence that religious and secular individuals and organizations must be provided equal access to government benefits and subsidies. The problem, of course, is that providing special regulatory exemptions and institutional autonomy for the proponents of one viewpoint but not the other raises constitutional concerns about the distortion of the marketplace of ideas that are as serious as those that result from one-sided funding arrangements.

Freedom from regulatory burdens empowers institutions. It reduces their costs and increases their ability to exercise control over their members, attract new adherents, fulfill their normative mission, and, perhaps most importantly, maintain their sense of continuous and distinct identity. The ability to engage in conduct that satisfies moral requirements and to perform rituals that demonstrate allegiance to a belief system or deity without state interference reinforces viewpoints and demonstrates their force and authority. These rights have substantial utility for speakers in competition with conflicting viewpoints.

Because in so many contexts religious individuals and institutions are speakers with a distinct message to communicate not only to believers, but to the public, it is not easy to isolate the religious practices of individuals and the institutional autonomy of religious organizations from the messages that they both express. Religion and speech are too closely connected and intertwined to ignore the effect of protecting religious liberty on freedom of speech concerns. I take it as self-evident that a law providing adherents of left-wing beliefs regulatory exemptions and a degree of regulatory autonomy not available to adherents of right-wing beliefs would be struck down as blatant viewpoint discrimination. Similarly, if a statute such as RFRA applied only to Protestants and was unavailable to protect the religiously motivated practices and rituals of Catholics, Jews, and Muslims, the law would violate the Free Speech Clause of the First Amendment as well as other constitutional provisions.

How then can Free Exercise exemptions or a statute such as RFRA be justified under either the Free Speech Clause or the Establishment Clause of the First Amendment? As a formal, doctrinal matter, the special religious autonomy endorsed by neutrality theory arguably challenges the most basic proscriptions of free speech doctrine. Indeed, if free speech doctrine prohibits viewpoint-discriminatory restrictions on the state's subsidizing of private religious organizations despite the Establishment Clause prohibition against direct state support for religious activities, as the *Rosenberger* decision suggests according to some neutrality proponents, it is difficult to understand why free speech doctrine does not also prohibit viewpoint-discriminatory regulatory exemptions for religious institutions and individuals notwithstanding whatever Free Exercise or legislative accommodations of religion are asserted to justify different treatment. Similarly, if free speech principles compel an interpretation of the religion clauses which allows, but does not require, government to subsidize (or refuse to subsidize) religious and secular institutions on an evenhanded basis, it is difficult to understand why these same principles do not justify similar discretion and evenhandedness when regulatory exemptions are at issue. Under this latter analysis, the Constitution would not prevent government from funding religious organizations once it elected to fund secular ones, and it would not prevent government from denying religious exemptions once it concluded that exemptions should not be available for secular acts of conscience....

It is not clear that neutrality theory even recognizes this issue, much less that it provides an adequate response. Certainly, the proposition that religious practices and institutions should be treated as the exact equivalents of their secular counterparts when government spending decisions are reviewed, while religion receives a uniquely favored status when it is burdened by regulatory legislation, does nothing to achieve the kind of neutrality between viewpoints and speakers that we associate with free speech values....

The charitable choice provisions magnify this contradiction. On the one hand, according to the statute, funding for public welfare services must be made available to secular or religious organizations on a non-discriminatory basis. On the other hand, religious organizations and religious speech alone receive special immunity from speech regulations imposed by government as a condition for the receipt of funds, and religious organizations alone are permitted to discriminate on the basis of religion in hiring employees to perform publicly funded functions. If religious and secular beliefs and institutions are competing for the hearts and minds of citizens, it is difficult to understand how this system can be characterized as non-discriminatory, evenhanded treatment of these two conflicting perspectives....

CONCLUSION

Neutrality theory and the charitable choice provisions of welfare reform are directed at real problems in constitutional doctrine and in American society. But... [n]eutrality theory simplifies religion clause jurisprudence by ignoring important constitutional values. Indeed, it does not even fairly and adequately protect religious liberty. State funding of religious organizations is problematic and controversial because of legitimate concerns about the fairness of allocation arrangements and the fear that politically powerful groups will aggrandize state resources... Given the diversity of religious faiths in the United States, a constitutional guarantee that only requires that subsidies must be distributed according to formally neutral criteria does not come close to adequately addressing this problem.

Neutrality theory ignores equality concerns entirely. Fragmenting public services along religious lines raises serious equality concerns for minority faiths. Neutrality theory ignores this issue. Discrimination in hiring on the basis of religion that denies qualified persons valuable job opportunities solely because they are of the wrong religious faith goes to the core of constitutional equality principles. Yet under neutrality theory, government may authorize private religious organizations that contract with the state to perform secular public functions to use the state funds they receive to hire only those employees who satisfy sectarian religious standards.... [T]here is nothing in neutrality theory that suggests that the potential exclusionary effect of such policies is of constitutional significance. The burden on people of minority faiths of a system that allows majoritarian religious organizations to exercise their liberty by reserving jobs funded by state resources for persons of their own faith is not recognized in any way.

NOTES

The note number from the original article is shown in the parenthesis at the end of each citation.

1. Carl H. Esbeck, "A Constitutional Case for Governmental Cooperation with Faith-Based Social Service Providers," *Emory Law Journal* 46, no. 1 (1997): 26. (14)
2. *Employment Division v. Smith*, 494 U.S. 872 (1990). (21)
3. 42 U.S.C. (1994), paras. 2000bb to bb-4. (22)
4. *Rosenberger v. Rector and Visitors of the University of Virginia*, 515 U.S. 819 (1995).

REMEMBERING THE VALUES OF SEPARATISM AND STATE FUNDING OF RELIGIOUS ORGANIZATIONS (CHARITABLE CHOICE): TO AID IS NOT NECESSARILY TO PROTECT

WILLIAM P. MARSHALL

INTRODUCTION

Establishment Clause limitations on government aid to religion are softening....

***

Before grieving too hard over separatism's passing, however, it is worth placing its demise in context. The American experience is such that there never has been an absolute boundary between church and state in the United States. Church and state have overlapping spheres, overlapping constituen-

Journal of Law and Politics 18 (Spring 2002): 479–88, 493–98.

cies, and overlapping responsibilities. Constitutional law reflects, rather than denies, this reality. It never has demanded an absolute separation between church and state.

What is true, however, is that even if the ideal of separatism itself never has been actualized, its rhetoric and its underlying policies have had force in framing the constitutional and legislative debates over church/state relations in America. Even when there have been no legal impediments to state aid to religion, separationist arguments have been raised in opposition to aid programs, and those arguments frequently have carried the day....

Does the current turn in constitutional law towards a more deferential approach to aid to religion programs mean that the policy arguments against such programs also should be discounted? Or should we "remember" the values of separatism in making legislative choices? This essay concludes the values of separatism should continue to inform legislative judgment. To aid religion is not always to protect it, and the protection of religion and religious freedom fostered by separatism should not be forgotten even as the constitutional barriers to state aid to religion continue to subside....

I. CHARITABLE CHOICE AND THE VALUES OF SEPARATISM

Charitable choice allows religiously based organizations to compete for government funds in the provision of various social services, including substance abuse treatment, job training, child care, and housing assistance. Its purpose, as described in its implementing legislation, is as follows:

> to allow States to contract with religious organizations, or to allow religious organizations to accept certificates, vouchers, or other forms of disbursement [under a relevant government program], on the same basis as any other nongovernmental provider without impairing the religious character of such organizations, and without diminishing the religious freedom of beneficiaries of assistance funded under such program.[1]

Although the term was coined in 1996 as part of welfare reform, charitable choice had its antecedents. Religiously affiliated organizations always were eligible to compete for grant awards, and many, such as Catholic Charities and Lutheran Social Services, often did. Charitable choice, however, was an attempt to allow participating religiously based organizations to retain more of their sectarian character than had been allowed previously. Thus, for example, the charitable choice legislation provides that religious organizations receiving state funds need not remove "religious art, icons, scripture, or other symbols" from the locations in which they dispense social services.[2] A participating religious organization also may attempt to retain its identity by discriminating along religious lines in employment (under the Title VII statutory exemption allowing for religious discrimination by religious employers), as long as it is eligible for the Title VII exemption prior to participating in the charitable choice program.

Charitable choice does, however, impose some limits on an organization's religious activity. Recipient organizations may not discriminate against program beneficiaries on the basis of religious belief and may not use government funds to engage in "sectarian worship, instruction, or proselytization."[3] States also must assure that non-religious provider alternatives are available to program beneficiaries.

The challenges that such programs raise to separatism's values are considerable. Four are worth noting here: undermining religious integrity, church-state entanglement, government evaluation of religion, and sectarian divisiveness. Each will be discussed in turn.

A. Undermining Religious Integrity

Integral to separationist theory is that government sponsorship of religion can be harmful to religion. The initial American evangelical position, after all, was that the separation of church and state was necessary to preserve religion's purity and integrity. As advanced by Roger Williams and others, this position held that state affirmation and endorsement of religion weakened religion by fostering its dependence upon the state.

Charitable choice threatens this concern in a number of ways. First, an organization dependent on government monies increasingly is beholden more to government and less to its own members for its existence. The strength of its internal bonds is weakened accordingly.

Second, receipt of government funds threatens a religious organization's internal structure. Private organizations receiving government monies experience significant pressure to become more like the government bureaucracies they replace because government money is linked closely to government regulation and expectations. In order to be able to continue to receive funds, the recipient organization must conform itself to the government standards. The culmination of this is both a loss of the private organization's unique character and a private sector that increasingly looks like the state.

Third, an organization dependent upon the government may lose its moral authority in speaking out against government actions with which it disagrees. How, for example, will a church be able to criticize a government program fighting homelessness when that church receives funds as part of the government effort fighting this problem?

B. Church-State Entanglement

A second separatism policy is to prevent excessive church-state entanglement. Limiting entanglement serves to protect both church and state by preserving separate spheres of authority. Similar to the concern underlying limiting government sponsorship of religion, the non-entanglement principle works to limit government's influence over a religious institution in order to preserve the religion's autonomy and integrity. The non-entanglement policy also seeks to prevent church-state conflict. Thus, in *Walz v. Tax Commission*,[4] the Court upheld a church property tax exemption based in part on the policy of eliminating potential church-state confrontations in the form of tax evaluations, tax liens, and tax foreclosures.

Charitable choice poses numerous entanglement problems. First, because charitable choice programs involve granting taxpayer funds to religious organizations, they require some government monitoring of the organizations to assure financial accountability. Second, the limitation on the use of government funds for proselytization, instruction, and worship necessitates some governmental oversight to assure that this prohibition is followed—a matter that inevitably will engender dispute because the line between these activities and faith-based efforts to combat such social ills likely is quite gray. Where, for example, in a faith-based program designed to combat substance abuse does secular treatment begin and religious instruction end? Third, the competitive grant process itself inevitably requires government review of the potential recipient organization. How can the granting agency determine the merits of a particular program if it does not investigate it?

Some have maintained that these entanglement concerns are not inevitable and may be mitigated by certain measures. Professor Esbeck, for example, has argued that monitoring could be accomplished through self-audits with the requirement that "[a]ny discrepancies uncovered by a self-audit must be promptly reported to the government along with a plan to correct the deficiency."[5] Indeed, he suggests that such concerns may justify exempting religious organizations from some of the regulatory measures accompanying charitable choice programs altogether. But this cure may be even worse than the disease.

First, some quality control is necessary to assure a program is working. Establishment issues aside, basic principles of good government demand that public monies be dispensed wisely and in accord with their intended purposes. And while it may be true that religious organizations generally should be trusted to act in compliance with the law, every group has outliers. Second, providing religious organizations with what amounts to special privilege in the competitive process may raise constitutional concern.... [T]he lessening of judicial resistance to aid to religious organizations has been based in large part on the perception that the programs in question were neutral between religion and nonreligion.... Third, government oversight cannot be avoided. Competitive grants require competitive assessments. To exclude religious organizations from having to submit to an evaluation is to undercut the "choice" in the charitable choice.

C. Government Evaluation of Religious Organization

... [A] principle that is at the heart of separatism [is that] ... [t]he government is incompetent to judge religion.

Charitable choice may not necessarily place the government in the position of evaluating a religious organization's religion, but it does place the government in the position of evaluating the religious organization's approach to social issues and its efficacy in curing social ills. This is risky business.

The determination in a competitive process of which group can better solve a social problem is, in the best of circumstances, an inexact science. The problem, however, is exacerbated when religion enters the picture. After all, success in fighting a particular problem is likely to mean one thing to a government bureaucrat and quite another to a religious leader. Has an organization "succeeded" in its drug abuse program if a client is still using drugs but has developed a deep and abiding belief in God? Has the organization failed if that is the result? Whose definition of success or of failure should prevail?

D. Sect Preference

Finally, separatism also implicates the principle that church and state should be kept apart in order to prevent real or perceived sect preference by the government. Again, charitable choice undercuts this policy. First, through competitive grant programs, charitable choice can, and will, pit religious groups against each other in the pursuit of government monies. This will almost certainly lead to the perception of sectarian preference when one religious group is chosen for government funding over other religious applicants. This perception, in many cases, also is likely to be accurate. Under charitable choice, local officials award social services grants. Consider then an instance where the largest denomination in town is competing for a substance abuse grant with a sect that many in the community view as a cult. Is it likely that the choice of providers will be made on purely objective grounds?

There may be an even greater problem when the competing applicants are both prominent within the community. How should a local official choose between the local Lutheran agency and the local Catholic organization in awarding a grant dealing with child welfare without creating an impression of improper preference? How can the official avoid giving the impression that he believes one religion is better able to handle this problem than another?

***

III. THE POLITICAL IMPETUS BEHIND AID TO RELIGION

***

There are a number of reasons behind the current popularity of aid to religion programs. The first, and least controversial from a church-state perspective, is pragmatic. The sad truth is that many government attempts to solve social problems have failed; and supporting religiously affiliated programs may more effectively further social policy than does the status quo (although the record on this is far from clear). The case of public education is directly on point. In some localities, for example, the public school system is in such terrible shape that alternative schooling may provide the only chance for a child to receive a competent education. And in many cases, the best alternative schooling available is found in the parochial schools....

Similar arguments have been put forward in favor of government support of religiously based service agencies. Epidemic drug use, teen pregnancy, domestic violence, and other social ills have cried out for new solutions. Charitable choice has been advanced as an alternative that at least has the potential to succeed when little else seems to work.

Second, support for funding religious institutions on the same plane as non-religious institutions also may be explicable, on a more theoretical level, on grounds that the distinction between religion and non-religion has waned in contemporary society. Moral beliefs often are based upon both secular and religious concerns, and their derivation often is not even clear in the mind of the believer, much less apparent to the outside observer. Religion and non-religion also, arguably, serve similar functions. They are integral in the formation of an individual's self-identity, they inform political choices, they foster the development of pluralistic communities, and they frame matters of conscience....

This functional equivalency argument...might work in the Establishment Clause context. Why should a secular organization that is dedicated by secular moral principle to provide shelter for the homeless be eligible for government assistance, while an organization whose similar mission is based on religious belief is denied similar status?

Third, and of principle concern for our purposes, the push for state aid to religion in part can be explained as part of a reaction by some to what is perceived as an over-secularization of the culture. Religion, it has been perceived by some, has been inappropriately marginalized in the society and placed in a second-best status vis-a-vis secular norms and practices. Fortifying religion by both the imprimatur and the tangible benefit of state financial support is seen as a way to combat this dominant secularism.

Whether the marginalization claim is accurate is beyond the scope of this essay. Suffice it to say that there are powerful arguments on both sides....

***

But whatever the merits of the marginalization claim, it has cast the debate over aid to religion programs with an unfortunate gloss. Support of aid to religion is considered to be pro-religion; opposition is seen as flowing from an anti-religious secularism. The previous sections hopefully establish that this is not so. The interest in fostering and protecting religion is on both sides of the charitable choice debate. Charitable choice, in short, is a complex matter with no easy solutions.

Hopefully, however, there is a broader lesson to be learned from this discussion. Although separatism may not be the law of the land, its values have had powerful force in the American religious experience. We have suffered minimal sectarian division and few instances of church-state conflict—all while maintaining a religious freedom and a religious vitality that is unique in the world. If we are then moving even further "Beyond Separatism,"... we may want to think twice about how far down this path we intend to journey. The notable fact about the role of separatism in protecting and fostering both the state and religion is straightforward. It works.

NOTES

The note number from the original article is shown in the parenthesis at the end of each citation.

1. 42 U.S.C. (Supp. 2002), para. 604a(b). (20)
2. Ibid., para. 604a(d)(2). (21)
3. 42 U.S.C (Supp. 2002), para. 604a(j). (26)
4. *Walz v. Tax Commission*, 397 U.S. 664 (1970). (33)
5. See Carl H. Esbeck, "Charitable Choice and the Critics," *New York University Annual Survey American Law* 57 (2000): 30–31. (35)

SECTION III

GOVERNMENT PROMOTION OR EXPRESSION OF RELIGIOUS BELIEFS

EDITOR'S INTRODUCTION

SUPREME COURT CASES EVALUATING GOVERNMENT PROMOTION OR EXPRESSION OF RELIGIOUS BELIEFS

The earliest cases relating to government promotion of religious beliefs involved the public schools and were somewhat uncertain in their analysis. In *McCollum v. Board of Education*, 333 U.S. 203 (1948), the Court struck down a "release time" program which permitted students, with their parents permission, to receive instruction in their faith from religious teachers in public school classrooms during the last hour of the school day. In 1952, however, a release time program providing a similar opportunity for religious instruction near the end of the school day—but this time in local denominational facilities located off of the school's grounds—was upheld in *Zorach v. Clauson*, 343 U.S. 306, 313 with the Court affirming that "We are a religious people whose institutions presuppose a Supreme Being."

Ten years later, the Court reviewed religious exercises offered in the public schools under the sponsorship and supervision of school authorities. In *Engel v. Vitale*, 370 U.S. 421 (1962), the Court held that it violated the Establishment Clause for teachers to direct their students to recite a brief, nondenominational prayer composed by the State. Following the reasoning of *Engel*, state laws requiring the reading of verses of the Holy Bible to students each morning, without comment, were struck down in *Abington School District v. Schemp*, 374 U.S. 203 (1963). In both cases, the Court concluded that the religious exercises were coercive, although students had the formal right to be excused from participating in them. But the Court also made it clear that the coercive nature of the religious exercises was not essential to its holding in either case. State-sponsored prayer and Bible readings violated the Establishment Clause even if they were free from direct or indirect compulsion because the Constitution prohibited government from allying itself with a particular tradition of prayer or religious belief.

In addition to prohibiting state sponsored prayers in the public schools, the Court interpreted the Establishment Clause to limit the posting of religious displays and restrict religious influence on the school curriculum. In 1968, in *Epperson v. Arkansas*, 393 U.S. 97 (1968), a law prohibiting the teaching of evolution in the public schools was struck down on the grounds that government could not restrict what was taught in schools to only those ideas that were consistent with particular religious beliefs. In *Stone v. Graham*, 449 U.S. 39 (1980), the Court invalidated a law requiring the display of the Ten Commandments in every public school classroom in the state. Applying the *Lemon* test [see *Lemon v. Kurtzman*, 403 U.S. 602 (1971)], the Court concluded the law was unconstitutional because it lacked any secular purpose.

Disputes about government sponsored prayers and religious displays were not limited to public school settings—although religion in schools remained a continuing area of controversy. In *Marsh v. Chambers*, 463 U.S. 783 (1983), the Court upheld the long standing practice of the Nebraska legislature of opening legislative sessions with a prayer offered by a chaplain paid by the state. Noting the inconsistency between this state-supported religious exercise and prior case law, the Court explained that opening a legislative session with a prayer is so "deeply embedded" in American tradition that it could not violate the Establishment Clause. In a much more controversial decision, *Lynch v. Donnelly*, 465 U.S. 668 (1984), the Court upheld a city's purchase and display of a Christmas crèche, or Nativity scene, as part of its annual Christmas display. In her concurring opinion in *Lynch*, Justice O'Connor suggested a new standard for adjudicating Establishment Clause cases, an "Endorsement" Test that required the Court to determine whether the challenged state action endorsed or disapproved of religion or a specific faith. O'Connor explained that government action that endorsed religion was unconstitutional because it "sends a message to non-adherents that they are outsiders, not full members of the political community, and an accompanying message to adherents that they are insiders, favored members of the political community."

The Court applied the Endorsement Test in 1989 in *Allegheny County v. ACLU*, 492 U.S. 573, to invalidate a privately donated crèche display located, during the Christmas season, on the Grand Staircase of the Allegheny County Courthouse. In the same case, it upheld a display of a large Chanukah menorah and Christmas tree located outside the City-County building and described by an accompanying sign as a "salute to liberty." Four justices challenged the majority's adoption of the Endorsement Test in *Allegheny County* and argued that state action must be at least implicitly coercive to violate the Establishment Clause.

During this same period and for the following decade, the Court's attention remained directed at religion in the public schools. In *Wallace v. Jaffree*, 472 U.S. 38 (1985), the Court struck down a state statute authorizing a moment of silence for meditation or prayer in public school classrooms. Closely reviewing the language of the statute and its legislative history, the Court concluded that it lacked a secular purpose and was an attempt to endorse prayer in the public schools. Two years later, the Court focused again on the lack of a secular purpose in *Edwards v. Aguillard*, 482 U.S. 578 (1987), in holding that a law requiring the "Balanced Treatment for Creation-Science and Evolution-Science in Public School Instruction" failed to serve any goal other than the advancement of a specific religious account of the creation of the world.

The Court's continued commitment to the principle that state sponsored religious exercises in public schools violated the Establishment Clause was tempered by an equally strong commitment to the principle that private, student initiated religious expression in the public schools did not do so. Thus, in *Board of Education v. Mergens*, 496 U.S. 226 (1990), the Court upheld a federal law prohibiting school districts receiving federal funds from discriminating against student clubs on the basis of the political, religious, or philosophical content of their activities. In rejecting a school district's contention that the "Equal Access Act" violated the Establishment Clause to the extent that it required the District to grant recognition to a student Christian club, the Court emphasized that "[T[here is a crucial difference between *government* speech endorsing religion, which the Establishment Clause forbids, and *private* speech endorsing religion, which the Free Speech and Free Exercise Clauses protect."

In *Lee v. Weisman*, 505 U.S. 577 (1992), however, the Court was equally clear that constitutional restrictions on *state-sponsored* prayer and religious exercises extended to all school programs—including those that occurred outside of the classroom or regular instructional periods. Using language that emphasized coercion rather than endorsement as the controlling principle, the Court held that it violated the Establishment Clause for a school to invite a member of the clergy to deliver an invocation or benediction at public school graduation ceremonies.

Building on the distinction the Court recognized in *Mergens* between government and private speech, many school districts sought to circumvent the Court's holding in *Lee v. Weisman* by attempting to structure the delivery of prayers at school events in a way that appeared to avoid state sponsorship or approval of religious expression. One common approach was for the school authorities to delegate the decision whether or not to have a prayer, and who would be chosen to deliver it, to the student body by holding an election among students to resolve these questions. In *Santa Fe Independent School District. v. Doe*, 530 U.S. 290 (2000), a case involving prayers delivered over the public address system before school football games, the Court made it clear that such attempts were unconstitutional. Government cannot escape constitutional requirements by substituting majority determinations through referendums for state decision making.

More recently, the Court confronted a constitutional challenge to the inclusion of the words "under God" in the Pledge of Allegiance, the well known affirmation of national loyalty that school children are directed to recite in many public school classrooms each morning. In *Newdow v. U.S. Congress*, 328 F. 3d 466 (2003), a panel of the Ninth Circuit Court of Appeals held that asking students to profess the religious belief that the United States is a nation "under God" in the context of reciting a loyalty oath both coerces participation in a religious exercise and endorses monotheistic religious beliefs in violation of the Establishment Clause. When the case reached the Supreme Court, three justices would have rejected the Court of Appeals' analysis on the merits. The majority, however, in *Elk Grove Unified School District. v. Newdow*, 542 U.S. 1 (2004) reversed the Ninth Circuit's decision on the grounds that Mr. Newdow, the plaintiff in the case, lacked standing to bring a claim based on his daughter's classroom experience since he was not her custodial parent.

In 2005, the Court decided two separate cases involving government sponsored displays or monuments depicting the Ten Commandments by a 5-

4 vote. *McCreary County v. American Civil Liberties Union*, 125 S. Ct. 2722 (2005), held that the hanging of copies of the Ten Commandments on the walls of two County Courthouses violated the Establishment Clause because the displays lacked a secular purpose. The Counties' attempt to expand the display after litigation commenced by adding additional documents of historical value did not alter the Court's conclusion about their original and continuing religious purpose. In *Van Orden v. Perry*, 125 S. Ct. 2854 (2005), however, the Court held that the placement of a privately donated monument portraying the Ten Commandments on the Texas State Capitol grounds, among many other monuments and historical markers, did not violate the Establishment Clause. Justice Breyer voted with the majority in both cases. He distinguished the display he voted to uphold in *Van Orden* from the display he found unconstitutional in *McCreary* on the grounds that the former monument was placed among multiple historic displays around the State Capitol, it had not created any controversy for over forty years after its initial placement, and there were no religious objectives surrounding its origin—all of which suggested that its continued display did not offend Establishment Clause principles.

CHAPTER 8

GOVERNMENT, RELIGION, AND CULTURE
AN OVERVIEW

RELIGIOUS FREEDOM AT A CROSSROADS

MICHAEL W. MCCONNELL

***

B. A Pluralist Approach to the Establishment Clause

***

4. Government Influence over Education and Culture

A final threat to religious autonomy arises from governmental control over many of the institutions of education and culture. In an earlier era, when these were under private control, the government's voice was far less prominent in the marketplace of ideas. The influence of government is likely to foster homogeneity with respect to religion, since it is likely to reflect a broadly acceptable, majoritarian view of religion—in short, to support a civil religion.

University of Chicago Law Review 59 (Winter 1992): 175, 188–95.

If it were possible to insist that government be "neutral" in its speech about religion, this would be highly desirable. Unfortunately, in the context of government speech—unlike regulation and spending—"neutrality" is an unattainable ideal. Whenever the government communicates to the people, it will favor some ideas and oppose others. The only truly effective way to reduce government influence on our religious lives through its speech would be to reduce the governmental presence in our cultural and educational institutions. Requirements of accommodation and equal treatment can solve (or at least greatly mitigate) the problems created by the regulatory and spending powers, but there are no perfect solutions to the problems created by the government's vastly increased role in the culture.

There are three baselines from which the neutrality of government speech might theoretically be evaluated. The first is complete secularization of the public sphere. If the "neutral" position were one in which religion is completely relegated to the private sphere of family and the institutions of private choice, any reference to religion in the public sphere would be a departure from neutrality....

Serious enforcement of this position would bring about a radical change in the cultural fabric of the nation. Initial litigation has focused on what have been called "distinctively religious elements," such as crèches, crosses, and menorahs. But multitudes of other symbols, deeply engrained in our public culture, are no less distinctively religious. Christmas trees are symbols of Christmas, too, and many non-Christians (not to mention some Christians) consider them inappropriate for secular institutions. Certainly the star on top of the tree is a religious symbol. And if the star is a religious symbol, so are the pretty lights along the sidewalks of Michigan Avenue in downtown Chicago. Although most of us do not recognize the symbolism, these lights signify the advent of what the gospel of John calls the "true light that enlightens every man."[1] Thanksgiving conveys a religious message, as do the speeches of Abraham Lincoln and the Reverend Martin Luther King Jr.— which would have to be censored before they could be made a part of public celebrations. Many of our cities have religious names; many of our historic sites reflect religious aspects of the culture. To strip public property of all religious elements (when public property is used to convey secular messages of every kind and description) would have a profoundly secularizing effect on the culture.

The problem with the secularization baseline is that it is not neutral in any realistic sense. A small government could be entirely secular, and would have little impact on culture. But when the government owns the street and parks, which are the principal sites for public communication and community celebrations, the schools, which are a principal means for transmitting ideas and values to future generations, and many of the principal institutions of culture, exclusion of religious ideas, symbols, and voices marginalizes religion in much the same way that the neglect of the contributions of African American and other minority citizens, or of the viewpoints and contributions of women, once marginalized those segments of the society. Silence about a subject can convey a powerful message. When the public sphere is open to ideas and symbols representing nonreligious viewpoints, cultures, and ideological commitments, to exclude all those whose basis is "religious" would profoundly distort public culture.

A useful thought experiment is to imagine what a "neutral" policy toward religion would look like in a socialist state, where the government owned all the land and all the means of mass communication. In such a world, the government would be constitutionally required to erect and maintain churches, synagogues, temples, mosques; to hire priests, ministers, imams, and rabbis; to disseminate religious tracts and transmit religious programming; and to display religious symbols on public land at appropriate occasions. If it did not, there would be no opportunity for the practice of religion as traditionally understood. Indeed, a "neutral" state would attempt to replicate the mix of religious elements that one would expect to find if the institutions of culture were decentralized and private—much as the government must do today in the prisons and the military. No one would contend, in a socialist context, that a policy of total secularization would be neutral.

To be sure, we do not live in a socialist state. But we have socialized many of the important avenues for public interchange and the transmission of culture. Within that sphere, total secularization is not a "neutral" answer, either. Even Justice Brennan has warned that too zealous an elimination of religious symbols might appear as "a stilted indifference to the religious life of our people."[2] Thus, there is a growing consensus that the public schools have erred in eliminating from the curriculum virtually all discussion of how religion has influenced history, culture, philosophy, and ordinary life. For the most part, this decision by the schools has reflected a cowardly tendency to avoid anything controversial, but the effect is to create a distorted impression about the place of religion in public and private life....

Some argue for a totally secular public sphere not on the spurious ground that this would be "neutral," but on the ground that the First Amendment committed the United States to a certain public philosophy: a liberal, democratic, secular "civil religion," which is entitled to a preferred status—even a monopoly status—in our public culture. As an historical assertion about the meaning of the First Amendment, however, this position is plainly false. Virtually the entire spectrum of opinion at the time of the adoption of the First Amendment expected the citizens to draw upon religion as a principal source of moral guidance for both their private and their public lives. The Establishment Clause prevented the federal government from interfering with the process of opinion formation by privileging a particular institution or set of religious opinions, but it left the citizens free to seek guidance about contentious questions from whatever sources they might find persuasive, religious as well as secular. As a normative proposition, the secularization position must depend on an argument that secular ideologies are superior to religious. But some secular ideologies are divisive, exclusionary, and evil; just as some religious ideologies are tolerant, open-minded, and beneficent (and vice-versa). The republican solution is to leave the choice of public philosophy to the people. There is a great irony in the claim that liberal, democratic, nonsectarian positions have a superior constitutional status to religious positions. Such a position is illiberal (since it denies the people's right to determine what will bring about the good life), undemocratic (since it conflicts with the democratic choices of the people), and sectarian (since it is based on a narrow point of view on religious issues).

A second possible baseline is the degree of religious expression that an "objective observer" would deem appropriate in the public sphere—Justice O'Connor's Endorsement Test. But this actually states no baseline at all; it is merely a restatement of the question. These issues are passionately contested within our culture. For example, to some (heavily represented in legal academia), inclusion of a nativity scene in a Christmas display on government property is an act of blatant intolerance. With equal sincerity, others (less well represented in legal academia), maintain that deliberate exclusion of a nativity scene from a Christmas display places the prestige and influence of the government in favor of materialism and against religion. The "Endorsement Test" is justified on the ground that it will ensure that no class of citizens defined by religious perspective is made to feel like an "outsider" to the political community. If so, it is necessary to pay serious attention to both points of view. Both sides are sincere, and both consider themselves in danger of being marginalized. Unfortunately, it is not possible for both to prevail, and there is no objective standpoint for choosing one over the other (that is, no standpoint that both could, in principle, accept). The "objective observer" does not, therefore, offer even a theoretically possible baseline for the evaluation of neutrality.

The indeterminacy of this approach might not, in itself, be a sufficient basis for rejecting it. Other constitutional doctrines are almost equally indeterminate. The special problem of this approach is that it exacerbates religious division and discord by heightening the sense of grievance over symbolic injuries. When religious symbols are upheld, the judicial imprimatur adds to the injury (especially when the standard applied is that of the putative "objective observer" [implying that the losers are not "objective"]). When religious symbols are driven from the public square, this alienates a different but equally sincere segment of the population. Does anyone believe that the annual outbreak of lawsuits over the symbols of the December holidays advances the cause of civic harmony or religious understanding? When a constitutional doctrine aggravates the very problem it is supposed to solve, without offering hope for resolution, it should be replaced.

The third possible baseline is the state of public culture in the non-government-controlled sector. If the aspects of culture controlled by the government (public spaces, public institutions) exactly mirrored the culture as a whole, then the influence and effect of government involvement would be nil: the religious life of the people would be precisely the way it would be if the government were absent from the cultural sphere. In a pluralistic culture, this is the best of the possible understandings of "neutrality," since it will lead to a broadly inclusive public sphere, in which the public is presented a wide variety of perspectives, religious ones included. If a city displays many different cultural symbols during the course of the year, a nativity scene at Christmas or a menorah at Hannukah is likely to be perceived as an expression of pluralism rather than as an exercise in Christian or Jewish triumphalism. If the curriculum is genuinely diverse, exposing children to religious ideas will not have the effect of indoctrination. Individuals should be permitted to opt out of participating in those religious (or anti-religious) aspects of the program that are objectionable to them on grounds of conscience, but there is no reason to extirpate all religious elements from the entire curriculum. The same is true of the public culture: opt-out rights should be freely accorded, but the general norm should be one of openness, diversity, and pluralism.

If members of minority religions (or other cultural groups) feel excluded by government symbols or speech, the best solution is to request fair treatment of alternative traditions, rather than censorship of more mainstream symbols. If a government refuses to cooperate with minority religious (and other cultural) groups within the community, there may be a basis for inferring that the choice of symbols was a deliberate attempt to use government influence to promote a particular religious position.

Courts should not encourage the proliferation of litigation by offering the false hope that perfect neutrality can be achieved through judicial fine-tuning. Judicial scrutiny should be reserved for cases in which a particular religious position is given such public prominence that the overall message becomes one of conformity rather than pluralism. Certainly they should not allow official acts that declare one religion, or group of religions, superior to the rest, or give official sponsorship to symbols or ceremonies that are inherently exclusionary. Particular care should be taken where impressionable children are involved. But courts should be cautious about responding to particular contestable issues in isolation. It is impossible to tell whether a particular event, symbol, statement, or item is an indication of diversity or of favoritism if it is viewed without regard to wider context.

**

NOTES

The note number from the original article is shown in the parenthesis at the end of each citation.

1. John 1:9 (Revised Standard Version). (323)
2. *Lynch v. Donnelly,* 465 U.S. 668, 714 (1984). (325)

RELIGIOUS LIBERTY AS LIBERTY

Douglas Laycock

I. The Fundamentals

Religious liberty is first and foremost a guarantee of liberty. To be sure, the guarantee is of liberty within a specified domain; it is liberty with respect to religious choices and commitments. But religion is not guaranteed, and neither is secularism—only liberty is guaranteed. Within the liberty guaranteed by the Religion Clauses, the free human beings who make up the sovereign People may experience a Great Awakening of Christianity, a mass conversion to Islam or New Age mysticism or any other faith, or an overwhelming swing to atheism. In the Supreme Court's inelegant but accurate phrase, the state should neither advance nor inhibit religion.

Religious liberty does not presuppose that religion is a good thing, nor that faith is bad or subordinate to reason. These are equal and opposite errors.

Journal of Contemporary Legal Issues 7 (Fall 1996): 313–14, 316–22, 339–40, 347–48, 351–52.

Religious liberty guarantees instead that each citizen in a free country may believe as he will about the existence and characteristics of God and about the role of faith.

Religious liberty does not constitute America as a Christian nation, nor does it establish a "secular public moral order."[1] These too are equal and opposite errors. Each assumes that on the most fundamental religious questions, the Constitution has taken a position. But the core point of religious liberty is that the government does not take positions on religious questions—not in its daily administration, not in its laws, and not in its Constitution either.

Religious liberty does not view religion as a good thing to be promoted, nor as a dangerous force to be contained. But people who view religion in each of these ways struggle to capture the Religion Clauses for their side. Each side claims that it won the late twentieth century culture wars and took over the government—two hundred years ago. These too are equal and opposite errors. What happened two hundred years ago is that conflict over theology, liturgy, and church governance was confined to the private sector, the federal government was declared a permanent neutral, and all factions were given equal political rights and a guarantee of religious liberty no matter what faction took over the government. In 1868, those guarantees were extended to the states.

***

B. The Religion-Neutral Case for Religious Liberty

An acceptable explanation of the Religion Clauses must make sense of the ratified text... [T]he strongest such explanation would make sense of the ratified text without entailing commitments to any proposition about religious belief. On what theory would the Founders single out the domain of religious choice and commitment for a special guarantee of liberty? The answer seems to me obvious, and while it is not at all illogical, it depends far more on history than on logic. Three secular propositions are sufficient to justify a strong commitment to religious liberty.

First, in history that was recent to the American Founders, governmental attempts to suppress disapproved religious views had caused vast human suffering in Europe and in England and similar suffering on a smaller scale in the colonies that became the United States. The conflict had continued for centuries without producing a victor capable of restoring peace by suppressing all opposition. This is prima facie reason to forever ban all such governmental efforts. Madison argued:

> Torrents of blood have been spilt in the old world, by vain attempts of the secular arm to extinguish Religious discord, by proscribing all difference in Religious opinions. . . .[2]

The negative goal is to minimize this conflict; the affirmative goal is to create a regime in which people of fundamentally different views about religion can live together in a peaceful and self-governing society.

Second, beliefs about religion are often of extraordinary importance to the individual—important enough to die for, to suffer for, to rebel for, to emigrate for, to fight to control the government for. This is why governmental efforts to impose religious uniformity had been such bloody failures. But this is also an independent reason to leave religion to the people who care about it most, which is to say, to each individual and to the groups that individuals voluntarily form or join.

Third, beliefs at the heart of religion—beliefs about theology, liturgy, and church governance—are of little importance to the civil government. Failure to achieve religious uniformity had not led to failure of the state. By the time of the American founding, experience had revealed that people of quite different religious beliefs could be loyal citizens or subjects. The claim here is not that religious beliefs are *wholly* irrelevant to the government; it may be that some religious beliefs are more conducive than others to behaviors the government legitimately seeks to encourage or require. But this indirect and always debatable government interest in religious beliefs will never make religious beliefs as important to the government as to the individual (the second proposition), and experience showed that government could not impose the religious beliefs it wanted anyway (the first proposition).

This third proposition was the most controversial of the three, and some in the founding generation were not sure it applied to Catholics, or to the hypothetical atheists that occasionally appeared in their rhetoric. Some citizens today continue to believe that atheists are unreliable citizens and that decent government cannot survive without a critical mass of believers. But with increasing religious pluralism, longer experience, and the universalizing logic of legal principle, the law at least has made the point general. It is enough for the state to regulate behavior, not belief, to regulate conduct, not theology or liturgy or church governance. The state could enforce the murder laws in 1791 without agreeing on the proper mode of worship or the proper form of church governance; it can enforce the murder laws today without agreeing on the Ten Commandments, the Sermon on the Mount, the Kantian imperative, or the utilitarian calculus as the best explanation for those laws. It is a sufficient explanation that the People have enacted such a law through constitutional processes and that it violates no limitation on governmental authority enacted by the People through a more authoritative process.

These three propositions are readily inferable from the history of failed governmental attempts to achieve religious uniformity. They are in no sense religious claims; they are testable against the facts of history and the experience of governments and citizens. They are equally accessible to believers and nonbelievers; they are consistent with the most profound belief and with the most profound skepticism.

These three propositions are entirely neutral about the truth or value of any religious belief save one: the third proposition necessarily rejects any belief that the State should or must support religion. But that belief is rejected in the Establishment Clause itself, so it must necessarily be rejected in any justification for the Establishment Clause. Those who believe that religious exercise requires the instruments of government, or that state support is essential or important to continued religious belief, are really arguing for repeal of the Establishment Clause or for its minimalist interpretation.

These three propositions are entirely adequate to explain a special guarantee of religious liberty, in which religion is to be left as wholly to private choice and private commitment as anything can be. Once it is understood that government efforts to control religious belief create conflict and suffering, and that they cannot succeed without the most extraordinary tyranny (and often not even then), any government will abandon such attempts if it is committed to liberty or even if it is committed only to utilitarian avoidance of human suffering. Once it is understood that religion is far more important to individuals than to the government, the same considerations of liberty and utility argue for leaving religion entirely to individuals and their voluntary groups.

C. Some Implications of These Reasons

Most obviously and most powerfully, these three propositions argue for separating the coercive power of government from all questions of religion, so that no religion can invoke government's coercive power and no government can coerce any religious act or belief.

***

The case for extending this guarantee of neutrality to the noncoercive powers of government—for separating those powers too from all questions of religion—is weaker than the case for separating the coercive powers, but I think the case is easily strong enough. Government should be entirely neutral in matters of religion even when it coerces no one. That is, government should not sponsor or endorse a church or any set of beliefs about religious questions, and it should not resolve or seek to influence disputes about religion.

My three propositions suggest several reasons for this commitment to neutrality even where there is no coercing. First, because beliefs about religion are so much more important to individuals than to the government, individuals and their voluntary groups should be free to develop their own beliefs about religion without the distorting influence of government. Government influence interferes with a matter important to individuals, a matter that many individuals believe is sacred and to be ordered by God, with little gain to government if religious choices and commitments are generally unimportant to government.

Second, because religious choices and commitments are so important to so many individuals, and because of the history of government efforts to suppress disapproved religions, many citizens will be highly sensitive to any hint that government disapproves of their religious beliefs or even that it prefers some other set of religious beliefs. This sensitivity is illustrated by fights over crèches, public prayers, and conscientious objection today, and by Baptist and Presbyterian complaints about remnants of recognition for the formally disestablished Episcopal Church in eighteenth-century Virginia. Individuals and groups will fear that what starts with mere preference or disapproval will escalate to discrimination, suppression, or coerced participation in observances of the dominant religion. These fears gain substance from history, and also because the line between coercion and mere influence is easily crossed and hard to monitor or even define, as illustrated by Justice Kennedy's unsuccessful struggle to articulate a coherent coercion standard. Government attempts to influence religious choices and commitments cause some of the harms of government coercion and threaten the rest.

Third, these direct harms of noncoercive government influence have a corollary. If government is permitted to attempt to influence religious beliefs and commitments, each religious faction must necessarily seek to control or at least influence the government so that the faction's members will be more benefited than harmed. Even if government is permitted only to express views about religion, religious factions will seek to control or influence the government so that they can control or influence the religious views that it expresses. Individuals and groups will compete over which religions are respected and which are disrespected, and over which religions can feel safe and which must fear more serious government hostility in the future. Even if this conflict is confined to peaceful political processes, it is an unnecessary source of conflict over a matter of little legitimate importance to government; it diverts politics into unproductive issues and perpetuates religious conflict. Justice O'Connor captures a small part of this explanation with her recognition that government endorsements of religious beliefs make citizens of other faiths feel like outsiders or second-class citizens.

It is a plausible response that the dominant religious faction will so strongly demand government endorsement and practice of that faction's religion that the pursuit of neutrality will cause even more religious conflict than letting the dominant faction have its way. This necessarily entails the proposition that religious minorities should suffer in silence and hope things get no worse; it comes close to arguing that "the vitality of these constitutional principles [must] yield simply because of disagreement with them."[3] Which interpretation will minimize religious conflict is unanswerable empirically; all we can say is that a regime of religious liberty has dramatically reduced but not wholly eliminated religious conflict, and there is little reason to expect that to change.

But there is an answer in principle; only one of these interpretations has at least the potential to minimize religious conflict. If we could all agree on the principle of government neutrality toward religion, we could all abandon our efforts to influence government on religious matters, and devote all that energy to religious practice and proselytizing in the private sector. Conflict over the government's role in religion could, in theory, end. But if we interpret the Religion Clauses to mean that government may promote the religious views of the dominant religious faction so long as it refrains from coercion, we ensure perpetual battles for dominance, perpetual battles to control or influence the government's religious message. That interpretation abandons in principle the goal of eliminating conflict over the government's role in religion.

***

V. CONSTITUTIONAL TEXT AND HISTORY

***

Coercing citizens to support a religion in which they do not believe will often, and arguably always, violate the Free Exercise clause. If the Establishment Clause were also confined to coercion, it would be redundant. This redundancy in the coercion interpretation is textual support for the belief that the Establishment Clause goes beyond coercion, and therefore that noncoercive support of religion is an establishment. This reading is consistent with the fact that endorsements of the established church were part of the package of support that government gave to the established church, and in some cases in the period just before the First Amendment, endorsements were all or nearly all that the established church got.

This prohibition on endorsements makes Religion Clause neutrality an extraordinary kind of neutrality. Unlike political matters, government is forbidden to influence opinion even by persuasion. Religion is to be as free of government influence as anything can be in a society with a large government.

In general terms, the Free Exercise Clause prohibits government suppression of religion; the Establishment Clause forbids government support of religion. This balance between the clauses is further evidence for believing that government must be neutral toward religion, although the text is not specific enough to define neutrality without further inquiry. It is at least clear that each clause must be construed in light of the other, and in light of the rest of the First Amendment.

I reject... [the] view that this contrast between the clauses renders them inconsistent. That would be a last resort interpretation, after exhausting all attempts to reconcile the clauses. In fact, the reconciliation is not difficult, especially in the light of history. Both disestablishment and free exercise protect the liberty of individuals and their voluntary groups with respect to choices and commitments about religion. Government support of established churches had harmed the religious liberty of persons who did not believe in the teachings of the established church; in different ways, government support had harmed the religious liberty of the established church and its members. The two clauses together are complementary guarantees of religious liberty for both the majority (if any) and the various minorities, including nontheists.

***

VI. THE PRINCIPAL CONTEMPORARY ISSUES

***

B. Religious Speech

There have been vast amounts of litigation over religious speech, where I think the rules should be quite simple. Private speakers have freedom of speech; religious speech is high value speech (a reasonable textual inference from the Free Exercise Clause); private religious speakers should be as fully protected as though they were discussing politics. With qualifications confined to dictum, that is what the Supreme Court has held. Religious speakers are free to use public forums and to speak in places where they have a right to be. They are free to make religious arguments in political debates; any other rule would be transparent viewpoint discrimination.

By contrast, government speech about religion is tightly circumscribed by the Establishment Clause. Government should not conduct religious observances, and it should not take a position on religious questions. Usually the best course is for government to remain silent and provide ample public forums.

Sometimes government must speak about religion, most obviously in public school curricula. It must teach about the role of religion in history and in contemporary society. It must teach about society's moral expectations, and it cannot do that honestly without noting that for many citizens, morality has a religious base. In such situations, government must be scrupulously even handed, treating the range of religious and nonreligious views as neutrally as possible....

With respect to government speech, neutrality requires treating religion differently [than other subjects of speech]. Certainly religion must be treated differently from the myriad of political issues on which government takes positions and tries to lead opinion. More fundamentally, in many contexts government silence is more neutral than attempts at evenhanded speech. It is very hard to discuss religion in a way that is neutral and fair to the myriad of competing views. When government prays, it models a particular form of prayer. It puts its influence behind that form as opposed to all others, and behind prayer as opposed to no prayer at all. When government celebrates

Christmas, it puts its influence behind a particular version of how to celebrate Christmas—usually a secularized version, sometimes a devout version, always a public version—but a particular version, whatever it chooses. Government influence on religion is generally minimized by government silence and a public forum that is wide open to the broad range of views about religion that compete in the private sector.

Michael McConnell has argued that when government is large, government silence on matters of religion is itself a distortion of public discourse and a departure from neutrality. He has proposed a different measure of neutrality with respect to government speech:

> If the aspects of culture controlled by the government (public spaces, public institutions) exactly mirrored the culture as a whole, then the influence and effect of government involvement would be nil; the religious life of the people would be precisely the way it would be if the government were absent from the cultural sphere.[4]

This is logically perfect and practically disastrous. Government has no way to "exactly mirror the culture as a whole," or even to get in the ballpark. It has only the vaguest notion of how many Christians, Jews, Muslims, atheists, etc., are in the population, and no idea whatever of the distribution of views over how to celebrate Christmas, whether and how to take public note of Hanukkah, Passover, or Purim, or what are the means of salvation. In practice, Professor McConnell's approach would lead to predominant government expression of majoritarian religious views, diluted to appeal to the largest possible coalition, with occasional nods to influential minorities. In short, government statements on religion would be indistinguishable from those of a relatively tolerant government with an established church.

A far better way to make the public sphere mirror the culture is to open public forums to religious speech and to clearly provide that the responsibility for religious speech in those forums lies exclusively with the private sector. Religion is vibrant in the private sector; in such a regime, the public square would not remain naked for a single season. Those people who cared enough to say anything would say what they wanted, and we would get some sense of the distribution of views in the culture. Thus, with respect to government speech, I adhere to the view that the most nearly neutral course is for government to be quiet and let the private sector do it.

NOTES

The note number from the original article is shown in the parenthesis at the end of each citation.

1. Kathleen M. Sullivan, "Religion and Liberal Democracy," *University Chicago Law Review* 59 (1992): 198. (5)

2. James Madison, *Memorial and Remonstrance Against Religious Establishments* (1785), para. 11. (21)

3. *Brown v. Board of Education*, 349 U.S. 294, 300 (1955). (36)

4. Michael W. McConnell, "Religious Freedom at a Crossroads," *University Chicago Law Review* 59 (1992): 193. (174)

CHAPTER 9

RELIGIOUS EQUALITY AND RELIGIOUS ENDORSEMENTS

FROM LIBERTY TO EQUALITY: THE TRANSFORMATION OF THE ESTABLISHMENT CLAUSE

NOAH FELDMAN

INTRODUCTION

***

This Article shows... how the Supreme Court transformed the Establishment Clause by gradually developing a new justification for the separation of church and state: guaranteeing the political equality of religious minorities. According to this new justification, if church and state were entwined, religious minorities would feel excluded from the polity. This feeling of exclusion would create political inequality by impeding religious minorities' equal participation in the political life of the United States. The Establishment Clause would police the symbolic content of government action, keeping church and state separate in order to ensure political equality for religious

California Law Review 90, no. 3 (May 2002): 676–77, 694–98, 701–702, 706–18.

minorities. Instead of protecting religious dissenters from physical violence and coercion of conscience, the Clause would be understood to ease the potential psychological burdens of religious minority status in order to ensure political equality.

***

...If we are to have a clause in our Constitution that prohibits government from allying itself with only one intellectual, social, or cultural phenomenon, why should that phenomenon be religion? For the Framers, the Clause was understood to protect religious conscience, and so the answer was straightforward: religion deserved special protection from alliance with government because, more than other forms of action or belief, religion required free choice to be meaningful. But if, as the Court now maintains, the Clause guarantees the political equality of religious minorities, the answer is less obvious. Why should religious minorities, as opposed to other minorities, be singled out for special guarantees of political equality? Surely all citizens, not only religious minorities, deserve to be guaranteed political equality.

There exist several possible answers to the question "what is so special about religion," but none suffices to explain why the Establishment Clause should be read to protect religious minorities' political equality. Religious minorities are not uniquely vulnerable to political inequality, and religious discrimination in the United States has not been noticeably worse than discrimination on the basis of political ideology, immigrant status, or language, let alone race. Nor does the nature of religious belief or identity render religious affiliation uniquely in need of protection from second class status. In fact...there is no better reason to protect the political equality of religious minorities than the political equality of anyone else.

***

II. EQUALITY TRIUMPHANT: THE ENDORSEMENT TEST AND ITS MOTIVATIONS

***

B. Endorsement and the Post-War Development of the Clause's Purposes

Justice O'Connor's [use of an Endorsement Test to adjudicate Establishment Clause cases] belongs in the context of post-War developments in the theory of the Clause in three senses. First, the endorsement view of the Clause disconnected the Clause from the idea of liberty of conscience more than any other view of the Clause that had emerged since *Everson* [*v. Board of Education of Ewing Township*][1] ....

Second, the endorsement theory built upon a shift in focus in the post-War cases from the religious aspect of the dissenter's conscience to the political aspect of the minority's experience. While the eighteenth-century liberty of conscience theory of the Establishment Clause looked to the effect of establishment on the freedom of the dissenter to maintain his religious beliefs, under the Endorsement Test the Clause prevented the religious beliefs of religious minorities from affecting their equal political standing. The primary concern of the endorsement theory was therefore not the religious content of the dissenters' experience, but rather the political content of minorities' experience.

***

Third, and most importantly, the endorsement theory completed a sea change from a liberty-based view of the Establishment Clause to an equality-based view....

Although Justice O'Connor did not directly use the word "equality" in formulating the Endorsement Test, the ideal of equality fundamentally underlies her view that the Clause bars the state from making religion "relevant to political standing." Sending a message of favoritism or preference is wrong precisely because it detracts from the experience of equal political participation by minority and majority alike. Insider and outsider status are wrong because they are differentially distributed. In a good political society, everyone feels equally like an insider. Thus to the question, why separate church and state, the Endorsement Test offered an equality-based answer: Alliances between church and state create different, unequal classes of political citizenship, favored insider and disfavored outsider.

***

D. Why Endorsement?

If the endorsement theory in fact supplanted the liberty of conscience theory, it would be worthwhile to know why....

***

The first and most basic factor in the rise of political equality in the Establishment Clause context must surely be the emergence of equality as a dominant constitutional value in the post-War years. The core reason for the rise of equality over liberty is certainly the prominence of racial inequality as the single most important challenge to the American constitutional order since World War II. In the endorsement theory, concern with the particular position and experience of minorities transferred from the context of race to that of religion. Endorsement of religion, on this analogy, resembles government endorsement of whiteness.

One central theme of *Brown v. Board of Education*[2] was that governmentally imposed segregation violated equal protection because it conveyed a message of White superiority and Black inferiority. The Court in *Brown* even suggested, in a much-discussed footnote, that this message had affected the self-perception of African American children. The core of this theme was, then, that equal protection was violated not only by practical distinctions between treatment of Whites and Blacks, but by the symbolic content of discrimination in conveying a message of political inequality. Segregation, in this view, conveyed the message to African Americans that they were not full and equal members of American society. *Brown* could be reread to mean that the state must not tell Blacks that they are "outsiders, not full members of the political community, and an accompanying message to...[Whites] that they are insiders, favored members of the political community."[3]

There can be little doubt that this argument about why the Constitution prohibited segregation influenced the development of the endorsement theory by providing a paradigm of the kind of exclusionary messages that had negative effects in the political sphere. If it was unconstitutional for the state to endorse, in a sense, the majority race, it was plausible to argue that the state also violated the Constitution when it endorsed the majority religion....

III. Does Political Equality Work for the Establishment Clause?

***

A. Actual Political-Equality Harm and the Feeling of Exclusion

The first step in assessing the usefulness of political equality as a touchstone of analysis is to discern the harm suffered by members of religious minorities when the state "endorses" religion.... I argue that the harm must be not simply a feeling of exclusion, but rather an actual reduction in political equality. [But] ...the harm, it would appear, has something to do with citizens' perceptions and subjective experiences. The trouble with endorsement is that it "sends a message"[4] to the favored and the disfavored groups alike.... Once the citizens have interpreted the state's message, the endorsement theory assumes that their interpretation will affect their perceptions of their relationship to the polity. They will feel like "favored insiders"[5] or disfavored "outsiders."[6] They will feel, that is, like first-class citizens or second-class citizens.

To specify the content of feeling like a first-class or second-class citizen, imagine a case where government intentionally endorses the majority religion. Suppose the California legislature votes to hang a permanent and opulently expensive sign on the state-house door declaring that "All Good Californians are Christians." If this is not endorsement, nothing is. What is the harm to, say, Californian Muslims?

To begin with, Californian Muslims themselves almost certainly reject the idea that they cannot be both good Californians and Muslims. If the sign causes them harm, it must be because the state is telling them otherwise. Why should it matter that the state is telling Muslims that they cannot be good Californians?... [T]he core of the harm... [seems to be] that the state is creating conditions under which people seeking to realize their lives as Muslims and as Californians will face messages saying that it cannot be done.

Notice that the message, taken alone, has no effect; the sign itself does not directly stop anyone from being both a Muslim and a good Californian. The sign will disturb us only if we think it has some actual effect in the world. That effect could be direct. For example, the sign might make the Muslim feel that there are serious attitudinal obstacles that he must overcome to be a full Californian. The effect could also be indirect. The Muslim might laugh at the sign, but if Californian Christians see the sign and get the message that they are favored insiders, they may ignore Muslims in political debate or mistreat them in other ways that have political effects.

The crucial point is that the harm associated with the sign is its contribution to or creation of background conditions that impede Muslims' equal capacity to realize political lives as Muslims and Californians. To say that the Establishment Clause prohibits this harm is to say that the Clause aims to stop the state from creating conditions that would impede the equal ability of religious dissenters to realize their political lives.

Inequality, on this model, is more than just feeling. The sign causes harm precisely because it creates a hierarchy of political citizenship where none existed before. This newly created political hierarchy places new obstacles in the way of the Californian Muslim. The harm is not that the Muslim is made to feel bad about being a member of a religious minority. Rather, the experience of political exclusion on the basis of one's religious identity constitutes a real harm because it has practical consequences for democratic participation.

The ultimate goal of preventing endorsement, then, must be to permit minorities to act freely in the political sphere, without facing the burden of feeling specially excluded. Minorities should be able to realize their political membership without facing the barrier of feeling excluded from the political process. The feeling of political exclusion is real and powerful even if there are no formal legal barriers to political participation in place, because it makes the minorities feel like nominal members of a governmental regime to which they do not fully belong. By eliminating endorsement, the Establishment Clause facilitates minorities' participation as active subjects of democratic action.

B. Substantive Exclusion and Identity Exclusion

***

There are at least two types of exclusion that one might feel when government endorses someone else's religion. The first type goes to the substance of the religious minority's views. If I am a Catholic and the state endorses evangelical Protestantism, I may, for example, feel marginalized because I suspect that my Catholic belief that capital punishment is wrong will lose to some general evangelical Protestant preference for capital punishment.... The religious minority, in this model, feels excluded because the endorsement of religion signals a judgment that, in general, government will likely favor the substantive views of the religious majority. Call this type of exclusion "substantive exclusion."

The second type of exclusion that a member of a religious minority might feel goes not to the substance of his religious views, but to his identity. The Catholic in a Protestant town may feel excluded because endorsement sends him the message that Protestants are the "insiders": they will be elected to office, their voices will count for more in public debate, and they will generally do what they can to dominate the power structure.... This may have the incidental effect of leading to a greater implementation of Catholics' views, but this is a secondary effect of their domination, and not what primarily excludes the minority. Call this type of exclusion "identity exclusion."

The endorsement theory is only concerned with preventing identity exclusion, not substantive exclusion. It provides no protection against a feeling of marginalization associated with the likelihood of substantive political defeat. To see why this is so, compare the first sort of marginalization, related to substantive beliefs, with the experience of anyone who holds strong views on a range of subjects and discovers that he is in the minority with regard to those subjects. The civil libertarian living in a law-and-order town may see the sign over city hall announcing "A law-and order kind of place"; this will lead him to conclude that he is going to lose many battles over the scope of civil liberties there. His voice will be marginalized along the lines of the substance of his views. But this substantive exclusion, we recognize immediately, is part of the inevitable structure of democratic politics. The state sometimes expresses substantive views by endorsing them, and this tells dissenters they are at the margins politically. Yet this is not the sort of exclusion with which we are generally concerned. To be a regular loser in the political sphere is different from being a second-class citizen.

The civil libertarian's exclusion in the law-and-order town differs, however from identity exclusion. The civil libertarian knows he is a citizen, just like the law-and-order folks. He will not feel excluded as a member of a group in the same way as the Catholic in the Protestant town... Their exclusion is based on their membership in a particular religious group, or more precisely, their nonmembership in the religious group that has been endorsed. This exclusion has a different character than the common run of political exclusion of those whose views differ from the majority. The reason inheres in the structure of democracy, which the endorsement theory presumably does not mean to disturb: substantive minorities lose elections and do not get special protections. Identity minorities, on the other hand, may be legally or constitutionally protected against group-based exclusion. It is to this second, group-based exclusion that the endorsement theory must mean to direct itself.

***

C. What Is So Special About Religion?

Once we have seen that the Endorsement Test protects political equality against identity exclusion, we can ask the most basic question in evaluating the political-equality approach to the Clause: What is so special about religion? Why bother to protect religious dissenters in particular against political inequality? We can safely assume that violations of political equality are always undesirable—we do not wish to have first class and second-class citizens—but we have an Equal Protection Clause that guarantees equal protection of the laws. Why do we also need the Establishment Clause to prohibit the state from endorsing religion in ways that may create political inequality?

***

The background assumption here is that in general, the state may constitutionally choose to endorse or ally itself with all sorts of political or cultural or ideological positions. Federal, state, and local governments constantly take substantive positions on issues, and thus promulgate certain values. These forms of endorsement inevitably send messages of exclusion to some citizens whose deepest beliefs and identities are implicitly devalued. Government endorsement operates both on the level of symbolism and on the level of practical alliance. Is Veterans' Day to be celebrated? This may send a message of identity exclusion to pacifists. Labor Day? Exclusion of homemakers (or perhaps capitalists). Columbus Day? Native peoples. Many governments require the teaching of evolution in biology courses, an alliance with secularist ideology that excludes those who adhere to biblical literalism in matters of creation. All these forms of endorsement go to identity exclusion, not just substantive exclusion. If government may endorse all these diverse ideologies, regardless of the potential costs to political equality, why should government be prohibited from endorsing religion?

One possible answer to this question is that religion is, in fact, not special at all. This answer seems very implausible, however, because it amounts to a call for government neutrality with respect to any substantive value choices that might lead to feelings of identity exclusion. If the state must always maintain substantive value neutrality, then it cannot, for example, teach its children either to forgive those who harm them or to avenge wrongs. Each of these is a value choice.... It is, in short, difficult to imagine a government that avoids endorsing or embracing certain values. At a minimum, public monuments and holidays would have to go.... Since many government actions might be said to exclude some persons or groups, the result would be a government essentially paralyzed by the requirement that it exclude no one....

A second possible answer to the question is that religious minorities require protection more than other potentially excluded groups because religious minorities are peculiarly vulnerable to manifestations of political inequality. At first blush, the contingent facts of history would seem to form the strongest basis for this argument. After all, the Supreme Court itself has said both that we in the United States are "a Christian people"[7] and that we are "a religious people whose institutions presuppose a Supreme Being."[8] Such declarations might seem to constitute precisely the types of endorsement against which the Clause aims to protect dissenters. Surely these statements convey a message of political inequality to non-Christians and to non-religious persons, who are also among the religious minorities protected by the Establishment Clause under the Endorsement Test. But on closer examination, these statements...do not look much different than any other endorsement of substantive values by the judicial, executive, or legislative branches. This is not to say that these statements do not have the effect of endorsement; they surely do. It is only to question whether such statements have any greater effect than does, say, the federally sanctioned Thanksgiving holiday (taken in its contemporary cultural context) in conveying the message that Americans are the spiritual descendants of Pilgrims, not of those people who were already here when the Pilgrims arrived at Plymouth.

Nor does the history of religious discrimination in America render religious minorities uniquely in need of protection from political exclusion. There has been, for example, significant anti-Catholic discrimination in American history, but there has also been significant anti-Communist discrimination, some of it enacted into statute. Anti-immigrant discrimination, independent of religion, has been one of the most powerful forces in American political history, and remains powerful today. It, too, has taken the form of statutory law. Linguistic discrimination also has played a major part in our history, and still does. And of course, race remains the archetypal American axis of discrimination and political exclusion.

As a general matter, however, there is no constitutional provision outside the Equal Protection Clause that would protect Communists or immigrants or linguistic minorities from the kind of political inequality that results from symbolic government endorsement of anti-Communism or nativism or English-only aspirations. Unless the Equal Protection Clause were held to be violated by such symbolic provisions—always a possibility, but far from a legal certainty—these groups would have no constitutional protection from symbolic harms that create political inequality. If Communists or immigrants or non-English speakers are made to feel like second-class citizens by government endorsement of identities that exclude them, we tend to perceive this as part of the political process. Yet under the endorsement-test view of the Establishment Clause, the Constitution guarantees religious minorities that their political equality will not be impaired by government endorsement that might lead them to feel like second-class citizens.

In light of the various forms of discrimination in American history, it becomes difficult to argue convincingly that religious minorities are uniquely vulnerable to political harms associated with identity exclusion. It follows that the endorsement-test approach to the Establishment Clause suffers from a serious problem of either underinclusiveness or overinclusiveness. If one believes that other minorities should be protected from symbolic harms associated with political inequality, then the Clause does not do enough, and unjustifiably protects only religious minorities. If, on the other hand, one believes that the Constitution need not protect every potentially vulnerable American from the subjective experience of identity exclusion, then there is no reason to extend such protection to religious minorities. Either way, political equality does not serve as a satisfactory explanation for the Establishment Clause. In short, when it comes to political equality, there is nothing very special about religion.

D. Is Religious Exclusion Unique?

Although religious minorities are not uniquely vulnerable to harms against their political equality, there still might be other lines of argument that justify the view that the Establishment Clause protects religious minorities against symbolic harms to this equality. Perhaps the subjective experience of feeling excluded on the basis of religion differs in its consequences from other types of identity exclusion.

One might begin by claiming that religion is more basic and essential to selfhood than are many other forms of identity, because it goes to one's deepest beliefs. From here one could proceed in either of two divergent directions. One could claim that, by virtue of the profundity and foundational character of religion, religious identity is more difficult to change than most other types of identity. As a result, if one were to experience political exclusion on the basis of religion, one would feel fundamentally unable to do anything about this excluded status. The non-English speaker can learn English; the immigrant can become naturalized (unless barred by law). But the religious leopard cannot change his spots any more than the person of color can change his skin. Consequently, it might be said, political exclusion on the basis of religious identity is the worst sort of exclusion, comparable to race and perhaps sexual identity but to little else.

Alternatively, one might argue that because a person in fact has some control over his religious beliefs, the danger exists that one who suffers identity exclusion because of religion will change his religion and assimilate his identity into that of the religious majority. On this view, political exclusion based on religion is particularly pernicious not because it will render the religious minority helpless, but because it may induce him to change or abandon his most deeply held convictions. One who cannot change his race or national origin needs less protection, because he could not easily abandon his position even if he wanted to do so. Religious minorities, on the other hand, need special protection because their identities are simultaneously important and structurally vulnerable.

Neither of these two approaches successfully differentiates religion from some other very basic, yet simultaneously changeable phenomena. A person's culture, for example, has been described as basic to her experience of encountering the world, and so fundamental as to give shape to personhood itself. If this is so, then why not stop the state from endorsing any one culture, lest adherents of other cultures experience themselves as disfavored outsiders? The answer seems obvious enough: government implicitly endorses certain cultures all the time, and could hardly do otherwise.... Once again, one is left with the conclusion that the Endorsement Test approach to the Establishment Clause is either overinclusive or underinclusive.

***

E. The Upshot: Failings of Political Equality

The political-equality approach to the Clause cannot provide a compelling answer to the question "what is special about religion?" As a result, the political-equality explanation of the Clause can justify neither special protection for the political equality of religious minorities, nor a prohibition on government endorsement of religious ideas and teachings.

This conclusion about political equality may prove disquieting to some readers who have themselves experienced identity exclusion on the axis of religion.... But the argument advanced [here] does not mean to minimize the harm associated with such exclusion. [The argument is] rather, that such harms are no worse than harms associated with other sorts of second-class citizenship and identity exclusion. It may well be that all such harms should somehow be protected; or it may be that such symbolic, experiential harms should be resolved through the political process. This Article takes no position on that question. But this Article argues that the political-equality justification of the Clause should be subjected to critical scrutiny for its failure to explain why the Clause protects only religious minorities from political exclusion, and not others.

Does this failing of the political-equality theory mean that the political-equality approach to the Establishment Clause ought to be abandoned? The answer is a qualified yes. A constitutional theory ought to be able to explain its purpose in defensible terms; so long as it cannot, the theory cannot produce coherent constitutional doctrine.... [In fact,] the political-equality theory has produced distorted, counterintuitive outcomes in the Establishment Clause context.

NOTES

The note number from the original article is shown in the parenthesis at the end of each citation.

1. *Everson v. Board of Education of the Township of Ewing, et al.*, 330 U.S. 1 (1947). (21)
2. *Brown v. Board of Education*, 347 U.S. 483 (1954). (147)
3. *Lynch v. Donnelly*, 465 U.S. 668, 688 (1984) (O'Connor, J., concurring). (151)

4. Ibid. (170)
5. Ibid. (172)
6. Ibid. (173)
7. *Church of the Holy Trinity v. United States*, 143 U.S. 457, 471 (1892). (188)
8. *Zorach v. Clauson*, 343 U.S. 306, 313 (1952). (189)

HARMONIZING THE HEAVENLY AND EARTHLY SPHERES: THE FRAGMENTATION AND SYNTHESIS OF RELIGION, EQUALITY, AND SPEECH IN THE CONSTITUTION

ALAN E. BROWNSTEIN

III. RELIGION AS AN EQUAL PROTECTION INTEREST: THE PRIMA FACIE CASE FOR THE EQUAL PROTECTION OF RELIGIOUS MINORITIES

Identifying the Establishment Clause with the equal protection clause has produced protests...that this is "doctrinal imperialism" by which "the 'equal protection mode of analysis has come to dominate the interpretation of many other clauses of the Constitution.'"[1] In one sense, this is a curious argument in that in literal terms the reverse phenomenon has actually occurred. The *Lemon* test of the Establishment Clause is applied to most instances of allegedly disparate treatment of religious groups, while there is very little constitutional case law directly applying the equal protection clause to religious minorities. Since the Establishment Clause has become a de facto sub-

---

Ohio State Law Journal 51 (1990): 102–12, 134–37, 145–53.

stitute for an independent equal protection analysis of the treatment of religious minorities by the state, it is essential that whatever equal protection dimension of the Establishment Clause exists be recognized and respected.

***

To begin with, it should be emphasized that this discussion refers to the original core concern of the equal protection clause—the disparate treatment of the distinct and insular minority or disfavored class. Equal protection doctrine has also been extended to cover the exercise of fundamental rights including travel, voting, and speech.... [However,] [t]he subject here involves groups, not rights....

The criteria for identifying a suspect class for constitutional purposes includes several variables. Foremost is the presence of historical disadvantagement and victimization. The Court repeatedly refers to this factor in explaining its decisions. Moreover, it is the most convincing common denominator among those groups which the Court has identified to date as suspect: blacks, hispanics, asians, women, aliens, and illegitimates. It is also, of course, the central fact of the black historical experience which led to the ratification of the Fourteenth Amendment. Political powerlessness is also important. This is presumed for numerical minorities, but it can also be the product of the extended disadvantagement of a very large group, as with women. Distinct attributes of the suspect group and an insular group identity are relevant factors, but they are not necessary ones. Illegitimates are not easily identified and women are not insular in the conventional sense.

Immutability of the defining characteristics of a group is another frequently cited factor. It is clearly not a sufficient basis for creating a suspect class. Whether it is a necessary one remains unclear. Some illegitimates and aliens have the ability to change their status, but other members of these groups do not.

***

While all of the above criteria may be imprecise, they can be clarified by concentrating on a primary reason these factors are considered. The focus of the courts is to identify situations in which majoritarian decision making cannot be trusted to operate with some minimum level of fairness and efficiency.

This central concern gives special meaning and direction to these otherwise abstract and ambiguous factors.

Given all of these considerations, are religious groups suspect classes? There is little difficulty in identifying various religious groups as disfavored minorities in historical terms. Jews, Catholics, Mormons, and Quakers are obvious examples, although this list is hardly intended to be exclusive. Abuses against these and other faiths have included lynching; physical assaults; and discrimination in housing, employment, and education. Not every religious denomination may have experienced significant mistreatment, but that certainly is beside the point.... National ancestry constitutes a suspect class for every nationality even if some northern European groups may have had a more benign reception in the United States than did persons from other regions.

Political powerlessness also applies, although that requires some explanation. The power of religious groups is uneven. Some religions have been disproportionately successful in the political arena, while others have not. Current power relationships, however, can change quickly. As with race and nationality, temporary political success in particular areas does not undermine the necessity for long-term constitutional vigilance. As a prophylactic rule, the fact of numerical minority status is a virtually irrebuttable presumption of powerlessness for any faith with relatively few members.

While determining the "minority" status of different religions is not without difficulty, here again, an analogy to race and nationality can clarify the problem. Distinct nationalities, such as Poles or Italians, may be minorities in terms of ancestry, but, being white, comprise a racial majority. Similarly, while most specific sectarian denominations, such as Methodists or Mormons, are a minority in the United States, the general religious orientation of Protestant or Christian constitutes a majority and would hardly qualify as a class needing protection under conventional criteria.

The distinct and insular nature of religious groups varies among religions and over time. Some sects such as the Amish or Hasidic Jews blatantly meet this criterion. While religions cross racial lines, there are physical characteristics popularly associated with different religions, and prejudice toward religious minorities has often focused on physical characteristics as well as those relating to language and accent. Religious paraphernalia on one's person or home (often religiously required) can easily identify members of a minority faith. Also, the behavior of adherents of several faiths identifies and separates them from others as well. Dietary restrictions, the choice of Sabbaths or holy days, and the act of prayer itself, may make membership in many religions an identifiable characteristic of individuals. Co-religionists are also often insular in the sense that they live and work together. In all, a strong case can be made that conventional equal protection criteria apply here at least as strongly as they do with regard to women, aliens, illegitimates, and many nationalities. Certainly there is as much reason to mistrust the polity in its treatment of religious minorities as there is for other suspect classes.

***

Finally, there is the factor of immutability. If it is essential to the definition of a suspect class, [many] religious groups will arguably receive no special constitutional attention under the equal protection clause.... [I]n many circumstances a person can change their religion and by doing so will substantially alter the attitudes of others toward them....

A strong argument, however, can be raised against excluding religious groups from the coverage of the equal protection clause because the status of group members is a mutable condition. In conventional terms, immutable characteristics are relevant to a group's suspect class status for two reasons: 1) by definition, a burden directed toward an immutable attribute of an individual cannot be escaped, *i.e.*, the victim is trapped, and 2) the motives behind a burden directed at an immutable condition are intrinsically suspect; the state cannot explain its classification as an attempt to change or discourage the offending attribute.

Both of these explanations are seriously flawed as suspect class criteria. Whether one is trapped into suffering a burden imposed by government cannot be measured exclusively in absolute terms; it is an equally real condition whenever the value of the burdened attribute to the victim exceeds the cost of the burden....

As for the ostensibly more legitimate motives for burdening a mutable characteristic, there are many legitimate reasons for burdening immutable characteristics.... More importantly, there are an almost unlimited number of illegitimate reasons for burdening mutable characteristics....

Both of these immutability criteria weaknesses come into play when religious groups are considered as a potential suspect class. Many religious persons place an enormously high value on their adherence to their faith, even including a willingness to die to maintain it. For these individuals it is unrealistic to view this characteristic as mutable except perhaps for the most egregious of burdens. Similarly, one can hardly point to the mutability of religious faith as implying the legitimacy of laws that burden particular religious denominations....

Moreover...the Free Exercise Clause condemns as invidious the penalizing of religious beliefs. Thus, from an equality as well as a liberty perspective, the state's desire to stamp out benign belief systems on which individuals ground their identity and values is illicit and irrational. The equal protection clause can be understood to command a respect for diversity by choice as well as by birth.

An even more aggressive position may be taken on the issue. Not only is the mutability of religious affiliation not a bar to equal protection review of the treatment of religious minorities, but the mutability of religious beliefs makes the treatment of religious minorities particularly deserving of stringent equal protection review. The nature of religion is such that religious minorities are particularly vulnerable to unequal and injurious treatment by the state. Because suspect classifications such as race and national origin are immutable and cannot change, they are not intrinsically threatening to each other. They may compete for scarce resources, but the passive existence of each group does not undermine the viability of its peers. Religious beliefs, on the other hand, are intrinsically competitive and conflicting. Each seriously undermines the validity of the other. Even if many religions did not aggressively proselytize their faiths, as they do, this basic dissonance cannot be avoided.

As a consequence of the competitive tension among religious belief systems, religious groups have an incentive to discriminate against adherents of opposing faiths which is not inherent in other suspect classifications. The very fact of each group's mutability makes them less trustworthy as the majority and more vulnerable as a minority than may be true in other circumstances. In terms of the basic concern that legitimates heightened scrutiny under the equal protection clause, that of rigorously reviewing laws when the results of the political process cannot be trusted, laws discriminating against religious groups require the same level of scrutiny directed at laws discriminating against racial and ethnic groups.

This does not mean that the interpretation of the religion clauses must precisely parallel equal protection doctrine. It does demonstrate, however, that the same kinds of concerns which support the application of antidiscrimination and equality principles to laws involving racial, gender, and nationality groups arise in religion cases as well. History, vulnerability, bias, and mistrust provide important grounds for protecting the civil status of religious groups. No interpretive model of the religion clauses can be complete if it ignores or disregards this constitutional dimension.

C. The Uncharted Area—Reconciling Free Exercise Accommodations or Exemptions with the Prohibition Against Religious Preferences Required by the Establishment Clause

1. The Core Distinction between Equality among Religious Groups and Religious Freedom

***

... If religion is essentially a liberty interest [for constitutional purposes] and that is primarily what the Free Exercise Clause and the Establishment Clause protect, one can understand the argument of judges and commentators who insist that to violate the Constitution the state must act coercively to prohibit or compel worship. It should be clear, however, that much is sacrificed under such an analysis. Equal protection of a group's status involves a much broader mandate than protecting the right to worship... [L]iteral coercion is not essential to a finding of unconstitutional state action under equal protection review. The black victim discriminated against in education, housing, and employment is not being coerced as to his racial status. He cannot change that condition. He is being injured or burdened in a different way than coercion, but one which is recognized, nonetheless, to be a constitutional violation. Thus, acknowledging both the liberty and equality interests of religious groups recognizes the importance of having the right to practice the religion of one's choice protected *and* having one's status as a member of a minority faith affirmed as being of equal worth as the status of members of a majority religion.

Perhaps the most significant conclusion that results from acknowledging that religious groups have equal protection as well as liberty interests is that the seminal breakthrough in equal protection doctrine, the overruling of *Plessy v. Ferguson*'s[2] separate but equal rationale by *Brown v. Board of Education*[3] and its progeny, applies with rigor to religious groups. Presumably, few people would argue to the contrary. State segregation of public schools according to one's religious faith is surely unconstitutional. The striking down of a state miscegenation statute in *Loving v. Virginia*[4] is also directly on point. Religious miscegenation laws prohibiting Moslems from marrying Catholics, for example, are invalid. The list could be extended without raising serious debate.

If these analogies are accepted, however, one can see how far away the law has moved from a liberty oriented understanding of the religion clauses. For most people, the freedom to exercise their religion does not *require* attending school with people of different faiths, much less marrying them. Indeed, the latter act is regularly denounced by many religions. Accordingly, these decisions cannot be derived from religious liberty and autonomy rights alone. The protection of religious groups in equal protection terms must be assumed.

That understanding has important ramifications. The new and demanding message of *Brown* is that...[u]nacceptable inequality can arise from the impact of ostensibly equal conditions on the "hearts and minds" of the excluded group. And the impact of the conditions must be understood from the out group's perspective. The inability to understand this point was the most glaring weakness of the *Plessy* [Court's analysis]. You cannot ask the majority if their sensibilities are offended by being separated from the minority and act as if their responses are objectively applicable to everyone. That is how the negative black response to segregation could be viewed as minority hypersensitivity in *Plessy* rather than the authentic misery that results from pejorative isolation.

Moreover, it is important to remember the breadth of the *Brown* holding as it was applied to segregation outside of the classroom context. All segregation is unconstitutional—water fountains, park benches, bathrooms, and swimming pools. The message here could not be more insistent.... State recognition of individual preferences and associational liberties that have the effect of extolling one race as "superior" over and above other "inferior" races are invalid under this overriding constitutional command.

If the Establishment Clause subsumes basic equal protection principles, that same imperative should apply to religious groups as well as racial groups. The government cannot promote one religion over another, nor can it operate in a way that effectively segregates minority religious groups from majority faiths. The "hearts and minds" of the children of minority religious faiths are as vulnerable to enforced ostracism and being assigned a subordinate status as are the "hearts and minds" of the children of racial minorities.

Perhaps the language in recent Establishment Clause cases which seems to reflect this core understanding the closest is that of Justice O'Connor in her concurrences in *Lynch v. Donnelly*[5] and *Wallace v. Jaffree*.[6] "Direct government action endorsing religion or a particular religious practice is invalid," O'Connor writes, because "it sends a message to nonadherents that they are outsiders, not full members of the political community, and an accompanying message to adherents that they are insiders, favored members of the political community."[7]

Unfortunately, Justice O'Connor's statement is of little help to us in explaining why the Establishment Clause should be given this meaning and what the consequences of such an analysis would be. She never fully explains the origin of her "endorsement" approach. Even more problematic, O'Connor suggests that the Court is supposed to determine when the endorsement of religion occurs by virtue of what an objective observer, cognizant of both the Free Exercise Clause and the Establishment Clause, determines. Her theory thus stated lacks both a foundation and an analytic framework. It seems to identify the parameters of the Establishment Clause with the scope of O'Connor's personal empathy for the sensibilities of religious minorities.

Ultimately the validity and utility of O'Connor's basic insight depends on its being predicated on a firm equal protection footing.... The result may not coincide with all of O'Connor's views in recent Establishment Clause cases. It will, however, insure that her central concern about insiders and outsiders is implemented.

***

VI. THE PRACTICAL CONSEQUENCES OF AN EQUAL PROTECTION— AUTONOMY RIGHT ORIENTATION TO THE RELIGIOUS CLAUSES

A. State Endorsement of a Religious Faith

This problem involves the direct promotion by the state of a religious faith. It may include the conducting of religious worship by state officials, as in teacher sponsored prayer in the public schools, or the adoption and display of religious symbols by the state, as in the display of a crèche and cross in front of city hall to commemorate Christmas and Easter....

***

... The argument in favor of invalidating teacher directed school prayer or the display of religious symbols in public facilities [under an Endorsement Test] seems to track an orthodox equal protection analysis. Members of the religion whose prayer is adopted are given a benefit not provided to children of other faiths. Alternatively, and more seriously, the message of inclusion to some students, which the authorities communicate by their choice of prayers to recite, constitutes a message of exclusion to other children of different faiths. The exact same analysis applies with regard to the display of religious symbols such as the cross or the Star of David....

Arguments against invalidation of either teacher directed school prayer or state-sponsored religious displays may take one of several tacks. The most extreme position simply accepts blatant religious favoritism and suggests that religious minorities should just develop thick skins and learn to live with the fact of their outsider status. A modestly more moderate position, but one which is generally accepting of religious endorsements by the state [has been expressed by Justices Burger and Kennedy].... [T]hey insist that religious promotions consistent with historical practices and traditions must be upheld ... up to the point that they actually constitute an "establishment" of religion. [Under Kennedy's analysis, only] [s]tate action that carries endorsement to the point of proselytizing or other forms of indirect coercion, such as organized school prayer, would be unconstitutional... State sponsorship of a display celebrating the birth of Christ as the son of God would be acceptable to both Justices.

The[se] ... positions are, of course, completely inconsistent with [an] equal protection oriented analysis.... Neither Justice explains why equal protection principles do not require a more evenhanded approach to the issue of state religious endorsements. The justifications for an equal protection oriented analysis of religion clause issues... are never discussed.

There are alternative arguments to those of Burger and Kennedy, however, which may be raised against the invalidation of state sponsored religious displays... [w]ithin an equal protection framework.... The first relates to the nature and extent of the state's actions being subjected to constitutional review. Is government speech so directly constrained by the Establishment Clause that it cannot even mildly recognize or acknowledge the dominant religious propensities of the American people? Does even limited state affirmation of religious beliefs cause a sufficient injury to plaintiffs to warrant constitutional review? After all, no one is being physically excluded from public institutions. National origin constitutes a suspect classification, for example, yet the government may promote a variety of ethnic celebrations without violating the Constitution. If the state can support Cinco de Mayo Day and paint a green line down the center of the street on St. Patrick's Day, why does the sponsorship of religious symbols or prayer in the public schools cause so much controversy?

The answer to this challenge must begin by reiterating the unique nature of religious affiliation with regard to its impact on a person's sense of identity. Religion is a core part of one's sense of self. Other mutable attributes, such as political affiliation, are generally viewed as more tangential and ephemeral. For an opinion poll to list the percentage of Catholics who voted for Reagan in '84 and Dukakis in '88 seems rational. To ask how many Dukakis supporters converted to Catholicism this year sounds absurd on its face.

Indeed, a person's religion is often a more central aspect of their identity than their national origin. This is particularly true because in the United States the prior national ancestry of citizens has been superceded by a new national allegiance. Where our ancestors come from is a fading part of our identity often generations in the past and sometimes so commingled among various nationalities that it is too diffuse to be meaningful. Thus, the importance of religion to an individual may transcend questions of origin and ancestry because the former is an attribute of continuing vitality and reaffirmation, while the latter progressively becomes more attenuated as it is replaced by the individual's new nationality of being American.

Our religious commitments, on the other hand, in many instances are a contemporary ongoing part of who we are. They influence directly how we live. When members of different religious faiths intermarry, for example, they typically confront the immediate problem of one or the other converting to the religion of their spouse or, alternatively, they must negotiate a range of decisions with regard to how their divergent religious beliefs can be reconciled in a single family. Thus, religion is not only part of our personal history, it is a determining factor of our future behavior. For these reasons, when a religious person participates in his own form of worship, he often experiences a special feeling of acceptance and community. Any benefit a person receives by having his ethnic ancestry recognized or honored is often less substantial. Thus, the public celebration of different nationalities and different religious faiths may both constitute an unequal allocation of psychological benefits among citizens, but the latter is of much more substantial weight.

Religion differs from other important personal characteristics such as one's ethnic origin in another critical respect. There is no other facet of our existence which is at the same time so foundational *and* so vulnerable. National ancestry, being an immutable characteristic, differs from religious faith in that it is fixed and it cannot change, and its value or worth is not relational. Recognizing the virtues of the Irish says nothing about Italians who may well be equally praise worthy. Ethnic self-esteem is not a zero sum game, religious truth is. Nor are two individuals' respective ancestry in competition for the control of their identity and self-esteem. The celebrations of citizens of Polish ancestry are not intrinsically a threat to people of German ancestry. There is no danger that through a mixture of burdens, benefits, and influence the state may convince German-Americans to become Polish-Americans.

Conversely, the promotion of one religious belief is often a direct repudiation of another faith, a statement differentiating unavoidably between we and they. This distinction is critical. Religions represent communities as well as individual identities. They are a bridge to collective intimacy. Government support for the symbol of one faith will inevitably be construed to be a conclusion as to the respective place in society of those who identify with the belief system represented and, necessarily, the lesser status of those whose faith is contradicted by that message. Indeed, it is difficult to imagine how a different interpretation of the state's promotion of one faith's symbols and not another's can be defended.... The symbols selected to be promoted reflect the religious beliefs of political constituents and are controlled by the religious demographics of the community. As such, and given the dissonance of many faiths, what occurs is the public affirmation of one group with greater power over other groups with less power. Thus, the endorsement of religion by government is inherently self-congratulating to the majority and deprecating and threatening to the minority.

When it is clear that the source of religious promotion is government and not private, a violation of the Establishment Clause must occur. It does not matter that the message of favoritism is minor or avoidable. The communication of that message is offensive to the sensibilities of minority religionists in much the same way that segregated drinking fountains and bathrooms burdened the participation of black people in the public life of the Jim Crow South. These restrictions were constitutionally invalid because of their symbolic content alone.

... If all the benefits of a public school were equally available to all the students except that one water fountain out of fifty was reserved for whites alone and one fountain, to be equal, was reserved for blacks alone, that single act of segregation would be unconstitutional. But surely in this example it trivializes reality to argue that the burden of finding a different water fountain is what makes those two segregated water fountains unconstitutional. It is the message of exclusion and alienation that any act of segregation communicates that is unacceptable. The impropriety of that message does not change if it is conveyed by words or symbols instead of action or if it is only expressed some of the time....

The second challenge to Establishment Clause invalidation of state-sponsored religious exercises or messages raises a different but related issue. In cases such as ... *Lynch* [*v. Donelly*][8] and *Allegheny County* [*v. ACLU*],[9] the question before the Court was not only whether the state endorsement of sectarian beliefs was constitutional, but also whether the particular state action in question, ... the public sponsorship of a Christmas crèche or Chanukah menorah, did in fact constitute a prohibited endorsement.

***

The *Lynch* decision is the most problematic. It is difficult to understand the suggestion in Justice Burger's majority opinion that a Christmas crèche replete with angels and kings is somehow a nonreligious secular statement by the state. In every circumstance other than their promotion by the state, intrinsically and originally religious beliefs such as the biblical creation of the world, the granting of the Ten Commandments by God to Moses, and the birth of Christ as the Son of God would be recognized as having substantial and sectarian religious significance. While the argument can plausibly be made that some holiday related paraphernalia are so attenuated from the religious foundations of celebrations as to be neutral in meaning, that exception cannot encompass the whole. There is a difference between the Easter cross and the Easter bunny.

Once the religious nature of the display or symbol is acknowledged, a presumption of endorsement necessarily follows. It is a rebuttable presumption. Religious events, symbols, and images may be included in state promotions of art, literature, and history without conveying a message of endorsement.... The state easily will be able to make such a showing when there is a clear secular common denominator that explains and justifies its conduct (as in the hypothetical case where the government is challenged for displaying the Pieta in a national museum which also displays sculptures of Zeus and other non-Christian deities). In cases such as *Lynch*... and the crèche component of *Allegheny County*, however, where isolated promotions of beliefs consistent with only certain religious faiths are challenged so that no evenhanded explanation can justify the narrowness of the state's choices, this type of rebuttal would be unavailing and rightly so.

NOTES

The note number from the original article is shown in the parenthesis at the end of each citation.

1. Michael McConnell, "Neutrality Under the Religion Clauses," *Northwestern University Law Review* 81 (1986): 146. (54)

2. *Plessy v. Ferguson*, 163 U.S. 537, 548 (1896). (212)

3. *Brown v. Board of Education*, 347 U.S. 483, 495 (1954). (213)

4. *Loving v. Virginia*, 388 U.S. 1, 11 (1967). (214)

5. *Lynch v. Donnelly*, 465 U.S. 668, 687 (1984) (O'Connor, J., concurring). (224)

6. *Wallace v. Jaffree*, 472 U.S. 38, 67 (1985) (O'Connor, J., concurring). (225)

7. Ibid., p. 69. (226)

8. *Lynch v. Donnelly*, 465 U.S. 668 (1984). (282)

9. *Allegheny County v. American Civil Liberties Union*, 109 S. Ct. 3086 (1989). (283)

SYMBOLS, PERCEPTIONS, AND DOCTRINAL ILLUSIONS: ESTABLISHMENT NEUTRALITY AND THE "NO ENDORSEMENT" TEST

STEVEN D. SMITH

Among the proliferating array of proposals for reforming the doctrine of the Establishment Clause, the "no endorsement" test advocated by Justice O'Connor may seem the most promising.... To many observers, this would evidently be a welcome development; O'Connor's proposal has received the praise of numerous scholars who believe that a "no endorsement" test could provide doctrinal clarity and consistency, or that the test captures, at least in important part, the essential meaning of the Establishment Clause.

This article will argue that the "no endorsement" proposal does indeed represent a significant development—but for a less auspicious reason. Far from eliminating the inconsistencies and defects that have plagued establishment analysis, the "no endorsement" test would introduce further ambiguities and analytical deficiencies into the doctrine. Moreover, the theoretical justifi-

Michigan Law Review 86 (November 1987): 267, 276–79, 302–13.

cations offered for the test are unpersuasive. Despite these drawbacks, the "no endorsement" test appeals to scholars and jurists because it expresses the direction in which the establishment doctrine and analysis seems to be drifting; the test represents a culmination of the venerable quest to define a position of government neutrality—and, recently, of "symbolic" neutrality—towards religion....

***

A. Endorsement

Although the central concept in Justice O'Connor's test—"endorsement"—may at first glance seem straightforward, this appearance is misleading. Endorsement connotes approval; but approval may take various forms, and it is far from certain that O'Connor's test is intended, or can sensibly be understood, to prohibit all forms of governmental approval of religion. Upon examination, therefore, the concept of endorsement seems both elusive and elastic.

1. The Varieties of Religious Endorsement

Consider, for instance, the following varieties of approval or endorsement.

(1) Historically, proponents of different faiths have often assumed that since religions differ in their doctrines, practices, and claims to divine authority, not all of them could be correct; among diverse religions, rather, only one could fully enjoy God's favor and approval. Thus, disputes have raged over the issue of which religion is true or divinely preferred. If government took a position in a sectarian dispute by indicating that it accepted a particular religion as *the* true or divinely sanctioned faith, it would thereby endorse or approve that religion....

(2) Government might express a judgment that important doctrines of a religion are *true* without indicating that it believes the religion is *exclusively* true or divinely preferred....

(3) Without indicating any view on the truthfulness of religious doctrine, government might express a judgment that a religion, or religion generally, is *valuable* or *good* by suggesting, perhaps, that religion instills qualities of good citizenship or helps to maintain civil peace.

(4) Without indicating any view either as to religion's truthfulness or as to

its value to society generally, government might acknowledge that many individual citizens care deeply about religion and that the religious concerns of such citizens merit respect and accommodation by government....

Though not exhaustive, this list shows that the concept of "endorsement" may be understood in various senses....Except for her suggestion that some accommodations of religion should be permitted, however, O'Connor has failed to specify which senses of endorsement fall within her test's prohibition. As currently formulated, therefore, the test threatens to aggravate existing doctrinal confusion.

2. Can the Concept Be Clarified?

The foregoing criticism seemingly might be deflected by a refinement of the test; proponents might simply specify more precisely which forms of endorsement are included in the test's prohibition and which, if any, are not. But an examination of alternative constructions that might seek to refine the test shows that an attempt to specify the meaning of endorsement would create further difficulties.

a. A blanket prohibition. On the surface, the simplest way to achieve clarity would be to insist that *all* forms of endorsement are prohibited. Thus, even governmental actions or messages which recognize that religion has value, or which attempt to respect and accommodate the religious concerns of citizens, would be forbidden. But a sweeping prohibition applicable even to governmental accommodation of religion would force government to ignore religion and to disregard religion's distinctive interests and needs. The only permissible attitude for government to take with respect to religion, in other words, would be one of studied indifference... [But] in a polity in which government regularly acknowledges and accommodates citizen interests of various sorts, deliberate indifference toward one class of interests may easily shade into, and become indistinguishable from, disapproval—which Justice O'Connor's test would also forbid.

If not all kinds of endorsement are to be prohibited, however, then proponents of a "no endorsement" test must explain how to distinguish between particular forms of endorsement which are permissible and other forms which are not. Such a distinction, moreover, should not be merely arbitrary; it should be supported by an explanation that tells *why* some but not other kinds of endorsement amount to a constitutional evil...Even if a distinction between permissible and impermissible forms of endorsement were articulated and justified on a conceptual level, [however,] application problems of the most vexing sort would nonetheless remain.

***

A. Is the "No Endorsement" Principle Self-Evident?

The analysis in this section asks whether the central proposition contained in Justice O'Connor's proposal, *i.e.*, the proposition that government should be constitutionally precluded from endorsing or disapproving of religion, can be justified. To some, however, that central proposition may seem axiomatic or self-evident—and thus neither in need of nor susceptible of further justification. But this position is unpersuasive. Governmental endorsement of religion has a long history in this country. From the Continental Congress through the framing of the Bill of Rights and on down to the present day, government and government officials—including Presidents George Washington, Abraham Lincoln, and, of course, Ronald Reagan, not to mention the Supreme Court itself—have frequently expressed approval of religion and religious ideas. Such history may not prove that governmental approval of religion is constitutionally proper. But the history at least demonstrates that many Americans, including some of our early eminent statesmen, have *believed* such approval was proper. That fact alone is sufficient to show that the "no endorsement" principle is controversial, not easily self-evident.

Indeed, far from being self-evident, the "no endorsement" principle when viewed in context seems positively counterintuitive. Despite occasional calls for "strict separation" or "strict neutrality," virtually everyone concedes that some beneficial interactions between government and religion are allowable; even the self-professed absolutists who dissented in *Everson v. Board of Education* agreed that the state should at least extend police and fire protection to churches.[1] Thus, the critical question asks what criteria should be used to distinguish between those beneficial interactions that are permissible and those that are impermissible. Many establishment decisions have focused on the kind or extent of *actual material benefit* conferred on religion: Does the law at issue "have as a principal or primary effect the advancement or inhibition of religion?"[2] By contrast, Justice O'Connor's test discards actual material benefit as the governing criterion and instead looks primarily to the *message* that a law conveys. It is natural, and only partially misleading, to conclude that "O'Connor seems to be saying that appearance supercedes reality."[3]

Viewed in this way, however, the "no endorsement" principle is not axiomatic. On the contrary, it would hardly seem implausible to suggest that O'Connor has things exactly backwards: Government should not bestow *actual benefits* upon religion, it might be argued, but "mere" endorsement of religion is thoroughly in keeping with our traditions. Thus, proponents of a "no endorsement" approach to the Establishment Clause cannot rest on the assumption that their position is self-evident; they must be prepared to argue for it.

B. The Divisiveness Argument

A second theoretical justification might assert that a "no endorsement" principle serves to prevent division along religious lines. Justices and scholars have divided over whether prevention of religious division should be a governing policy in establishment analysis. Even if potential divisiveness is a proper and substantial constitutional concern, however, the connection between that concern and a "no endorsement" principle is tenuous at best. To be sure, governmental endorsement of religion may be divisive. By the same token, however, governmental *refusal to endorse* religion may be divisive. Indeed, if more than a few citizens believe that government *should* approve or support religion in some way, then a refusal by government to provide such approval or support may engender more contention than the approval itself would provoke. *Lynch* [*v. Donnelly*] is a case in point. Although Pawtucket's sponsorship of the crèche manifestly offended some of the city's citizens, *i.e.*, the plaintiffs, the attempt to remove the crèche generated an even greater wave of opposition and hostility; the mayor testified that he had "never seen people as mad as they are over this issue."[4] Nor is the Pawtucket experience atypical.

Thus, adoption of a "no endorsement" principle would not end division along religious lines. In the aggregate, moreover, it seems likely that adoption of such a principle would create incentives that would intensify religious conflicts. If the principle calls for invalidation of laws that are *perceived* as endorsing or disapproving of religion, as in Justice O'Connor's formulation, then opponents of a particular measure have every incentive to wield the equivalent of a "heckler's veto" by manifesting their disapproving reaction in demonstrative ways. Moreover, the same incentive may operate on both sides of a controversy; proponents of a measure may seek to demonstrate that its rejection or elimination would be perceived by many people as expressing *disapproval* of a religious value or belief. A test creating such incentives to demonstrative opposition is difficult to defend as a method of reducing religious division.

C. Endorsement and Political Standing

Cognizant of these difficulties, Justice O'Connor... purports to derive the "no endorsement" test from a more fundamental theoretical argument. Her starting premise is that "[t]he Establishment Clause prohibits government from making adherence to a religion relevant in any way to a person's standing in the political community."[5] This premise... is at least an appealing proposition, and the following analysis will assume that it is, in some sense, correct. O'Connor then asserts that governmental endorsement of religion "sends a message to nonadherents that they are outsiders, not full members of the political community."[6] Although this proposition may be debatable, the present discussion will accept the proposition as provisionally true.

Even if both propositions are accepted, however, O'Connor's argument nonetheless fails because she provides no plausible link between them. Her attempt to tie endorsement of religion to the political standing of citizens is unpersuasive. To be sure, a law diminishing or elevating the political standing of citizens on religious grounds *might* also endorse or disapprove of religion, and vice versa. But those consequences of such a law are practically and analytically distinct. Thus, a doctrine forbidding endorsement of religion would operate haphazardly at best in preventing diminution or elevation of citizens' political status on the basis of their religion.

At one time, for instance, many states had laws which excluded clergy from serving in the legislature; Tennessee's exclusionary provision survived until 1978, when it was struck down by the Supreme Court.[7] These laws plainly affected some persons' political standing on the basis of religion; the exclusionary laws made those persons ineligible for legislative office simply because they had chosen a religious vocation. On the other hand, whether the laws communicated approval or disapproval of religion is debatable; and the question conceivably might be answered differently in different jurisdictions. Such a law *might* reflect disapproval of religion, implying that ministers are unfit for public office. Conversely, the law might suggest *approval* of religion;

it might evince a belief that ministers are too virtuous, or are engaged in too important a calling, to be sullied and distracted by mundane political pursuits. Or the law might reflect neither approval nor disapproval of religion, but merely a belief that both religion and politics are better off when kept apart. Whether a given exclusionary law endorses or disapproves of religion thus remains an open question that cannot be answered without further factual investigation. By contrast, no similar factual investigation is needed in order to decide that the law affects political standing on religious grounds; it plainly does. The critical point is that a law barring clergy from the legislature affects political status on the basis of religion *whether or not* the law also endorses or disapproves of religion.

If laws can alter political status without endorsing or disapproving religion, the reverse is also true; a law or governmental practice can endorse religion without altering political standing. Ceremonial uses of prayer, such as the invocation given before a legislative session, or public religious allusions such as the motto on coins confessing "In God We Trust," may communicate support or approval for religious beliefs. But such endorsements do not appear to alter anyone's actual political standing in any realistic sense; no one loses the right to vote, the freedom to speak, or any other state or federal right if he or she does not happen to share the religious ideas that such practices appear to approve.

Of course, a message suggesting that minorities are not regarded and treated as full members of the political community might be *true*, minorities might actually be discriminated against in their political and civil rights. That possibility, however, hardly lends support to a test which specifies *endorsement* as the constitutional evil. Let us suppose that endorsements send messages telling minorities that they are not full members of the political community, and that they will be discriminated against in their political and civil rights. Such messages are either false or true. If the messages are false, and no discrimination is in fact occurring, then government is not in fact violating Justice O'Connor's basic premise that political standing should be independent of religion. If the messages are true, then government *is* violating that premise; but it is violating the premise by making religion relevant to political standing, *not* by sending messages which accurately acknowledge that fact. In this context, a doctrinal test or principle which focuses upon the *message*, rather than upon the underlying evil reflected in that message, seems positively perverse.

***

D. Alienation and Messages of Exclusion

Even if Justice O'Connor has failed to link messages of endorsement to a diminution of actual political standing, one might still agree with her contention that such messages are undesirable. It seems both humane and politically expedient, after all, that government should refrain from acting in ways that alienate some of its constituents by making them feel like "outsiders," even if the political and civil rights of such persons are not thereby diminished. Thus, a more sympathetic response to Justice O'Connor's argument might suggest that the "no endorsement" principle can be justified on the basis of a "nonalienation" policy, quite apart from any dubious linkage to "political standing."

In evaluating this suggestion, a broader reference to more general constitutional protections for belief and expression is helpful. The Supreme Court has ruled that the freedom of belief is absolute; and the freedom of speech, though not absolute, has received rigorous doctrinal protection. At the same time, the Constitution does not prevent government from adopting views and expressing judgments on a vast range of subjects. In making and expressing such judgments, government inevitably endorses some beliefs, disapproves others, and acts in ways that may cause some adherents of disfavored beliefs to feel like "outsiders"; but that consequence hardly precludes government from making judgments. Indeed, because governmental disapproval of the beliefs of particular citizens does not prevent such citizens from voting, running for office, advocating their own positions, serving on juries, or claiming the full panoply of rights extended by state and federal law, those citizens are considered to be fully protected in their freedoms of belief and expression.

Of course, some people may feel inhibited in matters of belief and expression by the knowledge that particular positions have been endorsed or rejected by government; and someone conceivably might propose that this inhibition be eliminated, and that the freedoms of belief and expression be given even greater protection, through the adoption of a prohibition forbidding governmental messages which disapprove of the beliefs of some citizens and cause them to feel like "outsiders." But such a proposal would be ill-conceived. Government cannot act without making judgments; and such judgments will inevitably conflict with, and thereby imply disapproval of, the beliefs of some citizens. Unless we are attracted to governmental paralysis, therefore, we must reject any generalized nonalienation requirement.

Justice O'Connor's argument for forbidding messages that make some people feel like "outsiders" on religious grounds, though directed at a narrower category of messages, is vulnerable to a similar objection. Religious diversity in this country is rich enough to ensure that *any* governmental policy in an area that potentially concerns religion will probably alienate some people. If public institutions employ religious symbols, persons who do not adhere to the predominant religion may feel like "outsiders." But if religious symbols are banned from such contexts, some religious people will feel that their most central values and concerns—and thus, in an important sense, they themselves—have been excluded from a public culture devoted purely to secular concerns. Once again, *Lynch* is illustrative: Whether the crèche was included in or removed from the Christmas display, the sincere religious sensibilities of some citizens would be offended. Cogent or not, the polemics of what may be called the "religious right" provide powerful evidence of the alienation and frustration generated by Supreme Court decisions that have excluded religious practices from some areas of public life, such as the schools, and that have established, in the view of some believers, an antireligious "secular humanism."

Indeed, alienation produced by Supreme Court decisions may be even more severe than alienation provoked by actions of legislatures or lower government officials. Legislative or municipal action, after all, represents temporary and possibly correctable policy—often of only a particular state or municipality. Offensive constitutional decisions, on the other hand, send a message telling the disfavored that their central beliefs and values are incompatible with the fundamental and enduring principles upon which the Republic rests.

***

In sum, the fact that citizens may sometimes feel like "outsiders," however unfortunate, does not provide a secure doctrinal foundation for the protection either of belief and expression generally or of religious belief in particular. Ultimately, a degree of alienation must be acknowledged as an inevitable cost of maintaining government in a pluralistic culture. In such a culture, some beliefs must, but not all beliefs can, achieve recognition and ratification in the nation's laws and public policies; and those whose positions are not so favored will sometimes feel like "outsiders." Because the phenomenon is inherent in a pluralistic culture, the aspiration to abolish that phenomenon, or to develop a conception of "political standing" that includes a right not to feel like an "outsider," constitutes a utopian vision rather than a realistic basis for formulating constitutional doctrine.

NOTES

The note number from the original article is shown in the parenthesis at the end of each citation.

1. *Everson v. Board of Education of the Township of Ewing, et al.*, in "Cases Adjudged in the Supreme Court of the United States at October Term, 1946," 330 U.S. 1, 60–61 (1947). (144)

2. This inquiry constitutes the second prong of the *Lemon* test and has thus been used in hundreds of decisions. (145)

3. Mark Gibney, "State Aid to Religious-Affiliated Schools: A Political Analysis," *William and Mary Law Review* 28 (1986): 144, n.164. (146)

4. *Donnelly v. Lynch*, 525 F. Supp. 1150, 1162 (D.R.I. 1981). (151)

5. *Lynch v. Donnelly*, 465 U.S. 668, 687; see also *Wallace v. Jaffree*, 472 U.S. 38, 69 (1985) (O'Connor, J., concurring). (157)

6. *Lynch*, 465 U.S. 668, 688 (O'Connor, J., concurring). (159)

7. *McDaniel v. Paty*, 435 U.S. 618 (1978). (161)

SECULAR PURPOSE

Andrew Koppelman

Introduction

Does the Constitution's prohibition of an "establishment of religion" bar the government from enacting laws whose only justification is based on the tenets of some religion? For decades the Supreme Court has thought so, holding that, to be constitutional, a law must "have a secular legislative purpose." But that may soon change. A growing faction of the Court, including the Chief Justice, may be ready to scrap the secular purpose requirement.

The doctrine cannot be discarded, however, without effectively reading the Establishment Clause out of the Constitution altogether. The result would be heightened civil strife, corruption of religion, and oppression of religious minorities. . . . And this terrible price will have been paid for nothing. Present doctrine already allows for what the doctrine's critics most value: state recognition of the distinctive value of religion. The state is already free to recog-

---

Virginia Law Review 88 (March 2002): 88–90, 95–98, 108–12, 140, 146–55.

nize the uniqueness of religion as a human concern, and the law does so by treating religion as something special in a broad range of legislative and judicial actions. What the state may not do—what the doctrine properly forbids it to do—is declare any particular religious doctrine to be the true one, or enact laws that clearly imply such a declaration of religious truth.

Critics of the doctrine raise four principal objections. First, the *rubber stamp objection* holds that nearly anything can satisfy the secular purpose requirement, because a secular rationale can be imagined for almost any law. Second, the *evanescence objection* claims that the "purpose" that the rule seeks either does not exist or is not knowable by judges. Who can know for certain what lawmakers had in mind when they enacted a statute? Third, the *participation objection* argues that the rule makes religious people into second-class citizens by denying them the right to participate in the legislative process. Should a law to shelter the homeless be deemed unconstitutional, this objection asks, if religious people supported it for religious reasons? Fourth, the *callous indifference objection* holds that the secular purpose requirement, if taken seriously, would forbid the humane accommodation of religious dissenters, such as the exemption of Quakers from military service.

The secular purpose doctrine can, if properly interpreted, handle all of these objections....

The secular purpose requirement follows directly from a principle at the core of the Establishment Clause: that government may not declare religious truth. Some laws plainly signify government endorsement of a particular religion's beliefs. These are the paradigmatic violations of the secular purpose requirement. An easy example is a statute that required public schools to post the Ten Commandments in every classroom, and thereby instructed students in "the religious duties of believers: worshipping the Lord God alone, avoiding idolatry, not using the Lord's name in vain, and observing the Sabbath Day."[1] The purpose of the law, plain on its face, was to proclaim a certain idea of religious truth. That purpose was religious, not secular. The law could not have been upheld without permitting government to declare religious truth.

If the doctrine is defended in this way, all four objections fail. The first three objections may be disposed of easily. The answer to the rubber stamp objection is that it is sometimes clear what a law is saying, and what is being said may be a claim about religious truth. The evanescence objection also fails, because the secular purpose requirement looks to the end toward which the statute is plainly directed, rather than to the hard-to-discern subjective legislative intent. The answer to the participation objection is that the secular purpose requirement looks at legislative outcomes rather than political inputs, so that a statute's constitutionality is not impugned by the mere fact that some people supported it for religious reasons.

The answer to the callous indifference objection is more complex, and it provides a window into the meaning of the Establishment Clause. A correct formulation of the secular purpose requirement helps to resolve a problem that has plagued First Amendment theory for decades: the apparent conflict between the Establishment Clause and the Free Exercise Clause of the First Amendment.

The root of the callous indifference objection is the claim that the secular purpose requirement flatly contradicts the Free Exercise Clause, which singles out religion as such for special protection. If the secular purpose requirement is understood to mean that government may never extend special favor to religion as such, then this criticism is sound. It is not logically possible for the Constitution both to be neutral between religion and nonreligion and to give religion special protection.

The proper response to this objection is to clarify the meaning of "secular purpose." If the logical objection is not to be fatal, then there must be some way of interpreting "secular purpose" so that it is at least possible for the government to give certain kinds of special treatment to religion. The answer, I will argue, is to understand "secular purpose" as forbidding any preference more specific than support for religion in general. Moreover, "religion-in-general" should in this context be understood to refer to the activity of pursuing ultimate questions about the meaning of human existence, rather than as any particular answer or set of answers to those questions. Thus understood, "religion" includes nontheistic religions such as Buddhism as well as nonreligions like atheism and agnosticism. If religion is understood at this abstract level, then government can favor religion, as religion, without declaring religious truth.

***

I. The Doctrine and Its Difficulties

A. The Secular Purpose Doctrine

The secular purpose doctrine is part of the Supreme Court's test for violations of the Establishment Clause of the First Amendment [set out in]...
Lemon v. Kurtzman.[2] ...

The Supreme Court has relied on the secular purpose [requirement] four times to invalidate a state statute. In *Epperson v. Arkansas,*[3] the Court struck down an Arkansas statute that prohibited the teaching of evolution in public schools and universities.... The absence of a secular purpose was fatal to the law:

> The overriding fact is that Arkansas' law selects from the body of knowledge a particular segment which it proscribes for the sole reason that it is deemed to conflict with a particular religious doctrine; that is, with a particular interpretation of the Book of Genesis by a particular religious group.[4]

In *Stone v. Graham,*[5] the Court invalidated a Kentucky statute that required public schools to post in each classroom a copy of the Ten Commandments, paid for by private contributions.... The Court... found that... the Commandments were a sacred text that included unquestionably religious edicts (for example, avoiding idolatry) [and that] the principal purpose of the law was "plainly religious."[6]

In *Wallace v. Jaffree,*[7] the Court declared unconstitutional an Alabama law which mandated a period of silence in public schools "for meditation or voluntary prayer."[8] The Court held that the law "was not motivated by any clearly secular purpose—indeed, the statute had *no* secular purpose."[9] The statute's principal sponsor had said that the bill's only purpose was religious, and no evidence to the contrary had been offered by the state. Moreover, Alabama law already mandated a moment of silence for "meditation." The only conceivable purpose of the new law, therefore, was to endorse religion. "The addition of 'or voluntary prayer' indicates that the State intended to characterize prayer as a favored practice."[10]

Edwards v. Aguillard[11] invalidated a Louisiana statute that mandated equal treatment for evolution and "creation science" in public schools. Neither theory was required to be taught, but if a teacher presented one theory, he was required to give equal attention to the other theory. The [Court determined] the state had failed to identify a "clear secular purpose" for the law[12] ... [Further] the legislative history revealed a purpose "to change the science curriculum of public schools in order to provide persuasive advantage to particular religious doctrine that rejects the factual basis of evolution in its entirety."[13] The Court concluded that "because the primary purpose of the Creationism Act is to endorse a particular religious doctrine,"[14] it was unconstitutional.

These four cases are far from typical. [In most cases, challenged statutes easily survive the secular purpose requirement under deferential review] ... [For example] [w]hen Sunday closing laws were challenged in *McGowan v. Maryland*,[15] the Court acknowledged that these laws originally had a religious purpose and that Sunday remains a day of religious significance to many citizens. But the Court held that "[t]he present purpose and effect of most of [these laws] is to provide a uniform day of rest for all citizens; the fact that this day is Sunday, a day of particular significance for the dominant Christian sects, does not bar the State from achieving its secular goals."[16] ...

* * *

II. The Need for a Secular Purpose Requirement

A. An Establishment Clause Axiom

Why should there be a secular purpose requirement at all? I would start with the following axiom: The Establishment Clause forbids the state from declaring religious truth. This proposition has been well settled for decades. ...

[T]he First Amendment's prohibition of "establishment of religion" is, among other things, a restriction on government speech. It means that the state may not declare articles of faith. The state may not express an opinion about religious matters. It may not encourage citizens to hold certain religious beliefs.

The axiom that the state may not declare religious truth is rooted in the underlying purposes of the Establishment Clause. Three reasons are typically given for disestablishment of religion; all of them support the restriction on government speech just described. One reason is civil peace: In a pluralistic society, we cannot possibly agree on which religious propositions the state should endorse. The argument for government agnosticism is that, unlike government endorsement of any particular religious proposition, it is not in principle impossible for everyone to agree to it.

A second reason for disestablishment is futility: Religion is not helped and may even be harmed by government support. Professor John Garvey notes that this principle has roots in the theological idea that "God's revelation is progressive," so that free inquiry will bring us closer to God.[17] The futility argument can also take the form of a sociological claim that state sponsorship tends to diminish respect for religion or a skeptical claim that the state does not know enough to justify preferring any particular religious view.

Finally, there is an argument based on respect for individual conscience. This argument states that the individual's search for religious truth is hindered by state interference.

The axiom that government may not declare religious truth entails restrictions on government conduct. It is a familiar point in free speech law that conduct which is not itself speech may nonetheless communicate a message and so be appropriately treated as speech. This means that the Establishment Clause's restriction on government speech is also a restriction on symbolic conduct. If government cannot declare religious truth, then it cannot engage in conduct the meaning of which is a declaration of religious truth. It would be illegitimate, for instance, for a state to erect a crucifix in front of the state capitol. It would also be illegitimate for the state to carve, over the entrance of the capitol, an inscription reading "JESUS IS LORD" or "THE POPE IS THE ANTICHRIST." The state simply is not permitted to take an official position on matters of religion.

Government, however, does more than just erect symbols. The most obvious way in which the government expresses an opinion is through the passage of legislation. In this arena, the government has available to it a particularly powerful type of symbolic conduct that is unavailable to other actors. Through legislation, the government can, and often does, express a point of view.

Suppose a statute is passed that makes it a crime for anyone to break the commandment to obey the Sabbath, as that commandment is understood by Orthodox Jews. That is, the law makes it a felony to operate machinery on the Sabbath, to drive a car, to turn on an electric appliance, or to make a telephone call... The problem with this law lies in the message it contains: It implicitly asserts the correctness of the commandment to keep the Sabbath holy... It declares religious truth. Thus, the secular purpose requirement works as a corollary to the axiom with which I began. If government cannot declare religious truth, then it cannot use its coercive powers to enforce religious truth.

The argument that I have just set forth is obviously a close cousin of Justice O'Connor's Endorsement Test. Its focus, however, is different. [Critics claim] that Justice O'Connor's Endorsement Test transforms the Establishment Clause from a prescription about institutional arrangements into a kind of individual right, a right not to feel like an "outsider."[18] In my view...[t]he question is not how outsiders feel about what the government is doing, but rather how the government itself is acting. Some government actions are tantamount to speech acts. They communicate. As Professor William Marshall has argued, "[i]t is the government's message that is critical, not the effects of that message."[19] The question is what is being said.

...The secular purpose requirement, as I understand it, follows from the axiom that government may not declare religious truth. Forbidden endorsement, endorsement that violates the secular purpose requirement, is government action that declares religious truth.

***

IV. DOES THE THEORY FIT THE CASES?

***

B. The Boundaries of Establishment: Back to the Secular Purpose Cases

If we look again at the secular purpose cases in light of the Endorsement Test as I have reformulated it, we end up not very far from the law as the Court has declared it....

The anti-Darwinism statute at issue in *Epperson v. Arkansas*[20] was properly invalidated, because it reflected state endorsement of the Christian fundamentalist view that the book of Genesis is literally true. So understood, *Epperson* is a remarkably easy case. Justice Hugo Lafayette Black...thought that the law might not be an endorsement of Christianity:

> It may be instead that the people's motive was merely...to withdraw from its curriculum any subject deemed too emotional and controversial for its public schools.[21]

But if the secular purpose requirement can be satisfied by legislators' secular desire to mollify their constituents' religious sensibilities, then this exception could easily swallow the rule. Even a bill establishing a church might in some circumstances be enacted by agnostic legislators hoping to avoid being voted out of office. Once more, the question is not whether the legislators had secular motives, but whether the law itself endorses a religious proposition.

The secular purpose that then-Justice Rehnquist thought validated the law in *Stone v. Graham*[22] was education: "[T]he Ten Commandments have had a significant impact on the development of secular legal codes of the Western World," and "[c]ertainly the State was permitted to conclude that a document with such secular significance should be placed before its students, with an appropriate statement of the document's secular import."[23] The trouble with this argument is its understatement. The Ten Commandments were not merely "placed before" the students; they were posted in every classroom in every grade, from kindergarten through high school. Probably no other document was so ubiquitous. Any religious text could be presented as merely being integrated into the curriculum in light of its secular significance. Mandatory Bible reading was once successfully defended on that basis. This argument could not have been accepted in *Stone* without willful blindness. *Stone* is another easy case.

The plausibility of the state's proffered secular justification is context-dependent.... The context in which the law was enacted is an objective fact about it, and one that the court may properly take into account in discerning the law's purpose. Thus, Professor Frederick Gedicks observes that the states' actions in *Epperson* and *Stone* were so contextually strange that they cannot plausibly be justified in terms of ordinary curricular decision making.

Wallace v. Jaffree[24] is the least defensible of the secular purpose decisions. This is the secular purpose opinion that relied most heavily upon the legislative history of the law in question. I have argued that it is never appropriate to rely on such history to find a lack of secular purpose, but the history that the Court relied on in *Wallace*—prominently, the post-enactment statements of a single legislator—was barely relevant. The Court also relied on objective evidence, such as the addition of the word "prayer" to the statute. There was, however, a persuasive secular reason for this addition: "clarifying that silent, voluntary prayer is not *forbidden* in the public school building."[25] There had been considerable confusion about the meaning of the Court's decisions with respect to school prayer, leading to horror stories that had become familiar by the time the law was enacted.... The statute can easily be understood as making it clear that students are not acting improperly if they use the moment of silence in order to pray.

Edwards v. Aguillard[6] is another evolution case, but it is harder to decide than *Epperson* because, while a benign explanation is possible, it is uncertain whether that explanation is credible. Any legal distinction will have hard cases at the boundaries, and the secular purpose prong is no exception.... [I]t was disputed in this case whether the legislature's purpose was to promote Christianity or to offer what it regarded as the most persuasive scientific information.... This debate is not resolvable in abstraction from the facts. Since the purpose of the legislative regime is difficult to discern from the face of the statute, the Court should have allowed evidence to be taken on the secular plausibility of the statute, rather than allowing the matter to be disposed of by a motion for summary judgment before trial.

***

Christmas nativity displays present the hardest case of all. Would a government that favored religion as such, while remaining scrupulously neutral with respect to any contested religious proposition, sponsor such displays? [Michael] McConnell has argued that the answer is yes. If government really wants to avoid interference with private religious ordering, then the public cultural sphere should mirror not secularism, but "the state of public culture in the nongovernment-controlled sector."[27] ...

In many parts of the United States, however, government speech that mirrors "the state of public culture in the non-government-controlled sector" will be overwhelmingly Christian. McConnell wants to permit inclusiveness and prohibit triumphalism, but given his criteria for inclusiveness, the two categories of governmental conduct will sometimes collapse into one another.

***

McConnell worries that if the public sphere were stripped of religious symbols, this "would have a profoundly secularizing effect on the culture."[28] And it is true that a completely secularized public sphere would look very different from the world we have now; to begin with, Los Angeles and San Francisco would have to change their names. This consequence is politically unthinkable, and little would be gained by such a revolution.

The better answer is to acknowledge the bland "*de facto* establishment of religion"[29] that prevails in the United States....

The "de facto establishment" should be understood as an exception to the Establishment Clause, confined to public rituals of long standing whose religious content is sufficiently bland. Some aspects of the de facto establishment, such as the names of cities and the placement of "In God We Trust" on the currency, have become drained of religious significance in the minds of many Americans. Professor Richard Fallon also notes the anger and resentment that judicial rejection of these practices would arouse, and argues that institutional self-interest probably plays a role in insulating these practices from Establishment Clause challenge.[30]

Have I just given away the store? I do not think so. The exception is one that in its nature cannot allow the creation of new instances. In addition, it has never been held to apply to the public schools, where the dangers of religious imposition are generally agreed to be the strongest (and where the secular purpose requirement has had the greatest impact).

Religious holiday displays are more problematic. The Court has not regarded them as part of the de facto establishment, and they are by now anything but innocuous in their impact. Is it possible for such displays to avoid preferences among religions? McConnell derides the Court's "three-plastic animals rule" which, he thinks, suggests that religious displays are only permissible if they are surrounded by dreadful holiday kitsch.[31] He draws this inference from the last two crèche cases decided by the Court. In *Lynch v. Donnelly*,[32] a majority of the Court permitted a nativity scene that was surrounded by a Santa Claus house, reindeer, candy-striped poles, a Christmas tree, carolers, figures of a clown, an elephant, a teddy bear, hundreds of colored lights, a banner stating "Seasons Greetings," and a "talking" wishing well. But in *County of Allegheny v. American Civil Liberties Union*,[33] the Court declared unconstitutional a nativity scene standing alone.

McConnell's attack on the doctrine does not discuss the other holding of *Allegheny*, which upheld a menorah accompanied by a Christmas tree and a sign saluting liberty. The decisions are at least consistent with a per se rule permitting a display that unambiguously celebrates pluralism by collecting the symbols of more than a single religion together....

The Court's approach may be the least damaging one that is politically feasible, but it is not costless. The state's involvement with religion, bland as it is, still has a degrading effect. The birth of Christ becomes just one more cultural stimulus for you to go shopping. The price of admission for Judaism is the Christianization of its calendar: The relatively minor holiday of Chanukah is elevated to centrality because it occurs around Christmas. One of the central evils that the Establishment Clause seeks to avoid is thus repeatedly permitted to occur. The mild de facto establishment of religion that the Court tolerates is not one that the religious should be pleased about.

NOTES

The note number from the original article is shown in the parenthesis at the end of each citation.

1. *Stone v. Graham*, 449 U.S. 39, 42 (1980) (per curiam). (3)
2. *Lemon v. Kurtzman*, 403 U.S. 602 (1971). (10)
3. *Epperson v. Arkansas*, 393 U.S. 97 (1968). (13)
4. Ibid., p. 103. (15)
5. *Stone v. Graham*, 449 U.S. 39 (1980) (per curiam). (16)
6. Ibid., p. 41. (19)
7. *Wallace v. Jaffree*, 472 U.S. 38 (1985). (20)
8. Ibid., p. 40. (21)
9. Ibid., p. 56. (22)
10. Ibid., p. 60. (27)
11. *Edwards v. Aguilard*, 482 U.S. 578 (1987). (28)
12. Ibid., p. 585. (29)
13. Ibid., p. 592. (31)
14. Ibid., p. 594. (32)
15. *McGowan v. Maryland*, 366 U.S. 420 (1961). (33)
16. Ibid., p. 445. (35)
17. John H. Garvey, "An Anti-Liberal Argument for Religious Freedom," *Journal of Contemporary Legal Issues* 7 (1996): 285. (80)
18. See Steven D. Smith, "Symbols, Perceptions, and Doctrinal Illusions: Establishment Neutrality and the 'No Endorsement' Test," *Michigan Law Review* 86 (1987): 300. (87)
19. William P. Marshall, "The Concept of Offensiveness in Establishment and Free Exercise Jurisprudence," *Indiana Law Journal* 66 (1990–1991): 374. (89)
20. *Epperson v. Arkansas*, 393 U.S. 97 (1968). (201)
21. Ibid., pp. 112–13 (Black, J., concurring). (203)
22. *Stone v. Graham*, 449 U.S. 39 (1980) (per curiam). (205)
23. *Stone v. Graham*, 449 U.S. 39, 45 (Rehnquist, J., dissenting). (206)

24. *Wallace v. Jaffree*, 472 U.S. 38 (1985). (211)

25. Ibid., p. 88. (215)

26. *Edwards v. Aguilard*, 482 U.S. 578 (1987). (217)

27. Michael W. McConnell, "Religious Freedom at a Crossroads," *University of Chicago Law Review* 59 (1992): 193. (229)

28. Ibid., p. 189. (234)

29. Mark DeWolfe Howe, *The Garden and the Wilderness: Religion and the Government in American Constitutional History* (Chicago: University of Chicago Press, 1965), p. 11. (235)

30. Richard H. Fallon Jr., *Implementing the Constitution* (2001), p. 54–55. (241)

31. McConnell, "Religious Freedom at a Crossroads," p. 127. (243)

32. *Lynch v. Donnelly*, 465 U.S. 668 (1984). (244)

33. *County of Allegheny v. American Civil Liberties Union*, 492 U.S. 573 (1989). (246)

THE PLEDGE OF ALLEGIANCE AND THE LIMITED STATE

Thomas C. Berg

***

II. Current Law and the *Newdow* Opinions

The ... [logic of the Ninth Circuit Court of Appeals decision in the Pledge of Allegiance case] was simple. "The statement that the United States is a nation 'under God' is a profession of a religious belief, namely, a belief in monotheism."[1] Such a profession "is identical, for Establishment Clause purposes, to a profession that we are a nation 'under Jesus,'" or "under Vishnu," or "'under no god,' because none of these professions can be neutral with respect to religion."[2] Teacher-led recitation of the Pledge therefore coerces students by putting them "in the untenable position of choosing between participating in an exercise with religious content or protesting."[3] Even if one assumes that the Pledge recitation is not an "endorsement" of religion ... "yet it does not follow that schools may coerce impressionable young school

Texas Review Law and Politics 8 (Fall 2003): 44–49, 52–53, 58, 62–71.

children to recite it, or even to stand mute while it is being recited by their classmates."[4]

***

A. Tradition and Precedent

An obvious rejoinder to the majority's invalidation of the Pledge recitation is that similar references to God appear in numerous other places such as "the Constitution itself, the Declaration of Independence, the Gettysburg Address, the National Motto, [and] ... the National Anthem."[5] Tradition and precedent make it very unlikely that all these invocations of God are unconstitutional. "A theory of the Establishment Clause that would have the effect of driving out of our public life the multiple references to the Divine that run through our laws, our rituals, and our ceremonies is no theory at all."[6] And the Supreme Court has suggested, in various dicta, that such references are permissible, including "under God" in the Pledge.

The *Newdow* panel first tried to distinguish other references by confining its holding to coercive recitations of the Pledge as in public school classrooms—avoiding the assertion that all recitations of the Pledge are unconstitutional government endorsements of religion. But this fails logically. The majority held that the recitation of the Pledge with "under God" is a religious act because it is a "profession of monotheism." How can a "profession" of monotheism avoid being simultaneously an "endorsement" of monotheism? ...

But the dissenters' arguments that the Pledge is indistinguishable from other religious references do not strike me as very satisfactory either. Judge O'Scannlain's dissent argued that reciting the Pledge, as with the other civic documents above, "[m]ost assuredly ... is a *patriotic* act" rather than a religious one: "[t]he fact that the Pledge is infused with an undoubtedly religious reference does not change the nature of the act itself."[7] But the dissent did not show why the nature of the overall act is determinative, rather than the nature of the God affirmation within it. The panel majority pointed out that to recite the Pledge is to swear allegiance to each value listed in it: "unity, indivisibility, liberty, justice, and—since 1954—monotheism."[8] This logic might distinguish the Pledge from the Gettysburg Address and other civic documents. A few religious references in a larger civic or patriotic document do not turn it into a religious document. But the person reciting the Pledge, the panel majority said, is making a series of affirmations, expressing belief in each value and proposition, including that there is a God above the nation. Since each component in the Pledge is a personal affirmation, courts must evaluate the "under God" reference on its own.

The Supreme Court opinions cited in the *Newdow* dissents offer other explanations why "under God" and other religious acknowledgments in civic documents are constitutional... One explanation is that these references merely acknowledge the historical role of religion in American public life....

[Another] is the ceremonial [deism] explanation. As Justice O'Connor put it... such acknowledgements "serve, in the only ways reasonably possible in our culture, the legitimate secular purposes of solemnizing public occasions, expressing confidence in the future, and encouraging the recognition of what is worthy of appreciation in society."[9] Justice Brennan... said that these references... [are] "protected from Establishment Clause scrutiny chiefly because they have lost through repetition any significant religious content."[10]

Neither of these explanations is convincing as to the Pledge. "Under God" is more than an acknowledgment of a historical fact. As the *Newdow* panel majority pointed out, the speaker is recommitting himself or herself to the ideals in the Pledge, not just acknowledging something about the past. As for the ceremonial argument, it is simply untrue for many people that "under God" has lost its religious meaning. If the phrase had lost its meaning, it is unlikely that so many people would be so angry about taking it out of the Pledge.

More importantly, if "under God" has lost its religious meaning through "rote repetition," that would be a bad thing, a sign of the dangers that such ceremonies pose to the vigor of religious life. It would confirm James Madison's warning that "ecclesiastical establishments, instead of maintaining the purity and efficacy of Religion, have had a contrary operation."[11] ... [This argument suggests] that close association of religion with government can compromise religion's integrity and distinctive mission—including emptying religious phrases of their religious meaning. If that is the price of upholding religious elements in government ceremonies, it is not worth paying.

I fear that if the Court upholds the inclusion of "under God" in the Pledge, it will do so by entrenching further the idea that such phrases have no religious meaning. If "under God" should be upheld, there needs to be a better rationale for doing so, one that does not kill the patient in order to save it....

***

III. THE PLEDGE AND THE LIMITED STATE

A. "Under God," the Limited State, and Inalienable Rights

The positive rationale is that "under God" in the pledge expresses the idea that government is a limited institution, subject to standards of authority higher than itself. "Under God" expresses the idea that the rights of persons—the "liberty and justice" guaranteed to all—are inalienable, stemming from a source higher than the nation or any other human authority.

The 1954 conference report supporting the addition of "under God" emphasized this rationale... The report states:

> ...Our American Government is founded on the concept of the individuality and dignity of the human being. Underlying this concept is the belief that the human person is important because he was created by God and endowed by Him with certain inalienable rights which no civil authority may usurp.[12]

***

Congress's reference to inalienable rights obviously invokes the Declaration of Independence's assertion of "self-evident" truths: "that all men are created equal, that they are endowed by their Creator with certain unalienable Rights, that among these are Life, Liberty, and the Pursuit of Happiness."[13] The natural rights theory of the Declaration rested in religious notions of a higher power who conferred on all human beings a dignity that is beyond the power of any other human being to take away....

***

B. The Limited State and Establishment Clause Doctrine

If "under God" emphasizes the limited state and the higher source of liberties, the phrase nevertheless seems to be a religious affirmation. How then can the recitation of it in public schools be consistent with the Establishment Clause?... [P]ublic schools may not conduct a ceremony that pressures students, even subtly, to engage in a religious act. How, then, can the statement that the nation is under God avoid being a religious act that the government is forbidden to coerce? Moreover, the Court has often articulated even more expansive Establishment Clause tests than non-coercion, requiring that government be neutral toward religion or avoid endorsing it. So how can the "nation under God" qualify as permissible under a standard of neutrality? Can this affirmation satisfy these tests without being stripped of its religious meaning? ...

1. The Necessity of a Religious Rationale for Rights

The first claim is that the statement "under God" must be constitutionally permissible because the vision it expressed—that the state is limited by human dignity and rights of transcendent status—is the only sufficient justification for the rights that the Constitution protects. Religious freedom and other human rights, the argument goes, can only be solidly grounded in a reality or authority beyond any human authority. Therefore, if the Constitution prohibited the expression of the rationale for these rights, it would undermine the very rights it protects and would contradict itself.

***

... Accordingly, even if the rationale reflected in "under God" is religious, it must, by necessity, be a rationale that the state may adopt and recognize. In the words of the Christian Legal Society's amicus brief in *Newdow*, the statement that the nation is under God "is the one type of religious statement with substantive religious content that the government may affirm[,] because it is the foundation upon which rests the requirement that the government must in all other respects be neutral toward religion."[14] ...

Of course, with this subject we swim in very deep philosophical and theological waters. The discussion here has not begun to evaluate all the arguments about whether a religious rationale is necessary to ground human rights in general, or religious freedom in particular.... Philosophers and theologians have debated these questions in some form for centuries....

But strict necessity is not the issue. [Many scholars contend that] ... the religious rationale for rights has been and is uniquely resonant in the United States....

One need not claim that religious freedom or other rights can only rest on a religious justification for the government to act on and express such a justification. It is enough that it was highly important to the adoption of these rights and remains a central justification for them for Americans today.

2. The Permissibility of a Religious Rationale for Rights

Thus, the state can have good reasons for adopting a religious rationale for rights even if such a rationale is not shown to be strictly necessary. The state might choose it as the most convincing rationale, or the rationale most in line with American traditions. The religious rationale might stand not alone, but as an important justification among others. In any case, reliance on the religious rationale should be permissible.

The First Amendment, properly interpreted, permits the government to rely on religious rationales in adopting policies on matters of justice and the common good. Neutrality forbids the government from engaging in religious observances such as prayer, worship, or ritual. But it does not prohibit the government from relying on religious arguments in determining how to legislate on matters such as civil rights, foreign aid, criminal law, environmental protection, or anti-poverty policy. These latter issues are not religious or spiritual matters as such, which the Establishment Clause suggests lie outside government's jurisdiction. Civil rights, environmental policy, and similar subjects are temporal or this-worldly issues, matters "that affect the world here and now."[15] They plainly fall within the government's jurisdiction, and in acting on them the government may be influenced by religious rationales....

That conclusion rests on at least two strong foundations. One is history and tradition. On questions of justice and the common good, religion has historically been deeply involved in American political debate and...legislation. The civil rights laws of the 1960s stemmed from a pervasively religious social movement; the laws also rested significantly on a belief that all human beings are of equal dignity in God's eyes. Countless other religiously grounded movements—from the abolitionists in the 1800s to the Social Gospel early in this century to the antiabortion movement of today—have succeeded in getting legislation enacted. In each case, the legislation presumably rested in significant part on the religious arguments the groups made. American history would be vastly different if legislation could not be based on religious activism and religious rationales....

Second, fairness and equality militate in favor of permitting religious rationales for this-worldly legislation and holding such rationales to be consistent with neutrality. On matters of worship, theology, and ritual, the state need not take a position; for it to do so is therefore, in Professor Laycock's words, merely a "gratuitous statement" that one church (and by extensions, one group of citizens) is better and more fully American than another.[16] But on political, this-worldly matters, government must and will make decisions and take positions. In that context, the fair and equal course in a democracy is for all citizens, including religious believers, to be able to offer reasons for policy and to persuade their government to act based on the reasons that seem most convincing, including religious reasons.

If religious rationales are permissible to ground this-worldly decisions by government, they are permissible to ground religious freedom and other human rights. While questions about religion itself—worship, theology, ritual—may fall outside government's purview, questions about the nature and scope of religious *freedom* fall within it. Government must make decisions about what rights should be recognized, their scope, and how absolute they will be; these decisions plainly fall within government's jurisdiction. Therefore, as with other questions of this-worldly policy, it is fair that religious arguments and rationales may serve as the basis for government's action, just as secular rationales may....

***

How does all this apply to "under God" in the Pledge? It is quite plausible to argue that the inclusion of the phrase is permissible because it does no more than express a religious rationale for the ideal of limited government and inalienable rights. These are political ideals within government's jurisdiction to assert, and the state may adopt and express a religious rationale for them. "Under God" is embedded in a political document, which suggests that the phrase is serving as a basis for political assertions....

***

This argument explains why the overall patriotic and political nature of the Pledge matters. Notwithstanding the overall patriotic setting, "under God" remains a religious statement, but it is one that permissibly operates as a rationale for a political statement about limited government and human rights. Likewise, if this argument is correct, "under God" can be upheld without implausibly viewing it as merely a historical or ceremonial reference and stripping it of its religious meaning. It retains religious meaning—and real force—as the rationale for fundamental concepts of inalienable rights and limited government.

However, this argument has one significant difficulty.... [It is not clear that the] language in the Pledge operates purely as a justification or rationale. The Pledge is a series of affirmations to be said by the individual citizen: "I pledge allegiance to the flag... and to the republic" with various characteristics including being under God. The government does not merely express the religious rationale, it calls on each person to affirm it. Even if the state does not engage in full-fledged coercion, by this call for affirmations the state can be said to be operating upon persons, not merely stating a justification. The *Newdow* panel was right, then, to emphasize that "[t]he Pledge differs from the Declaration [and other documents]. It is, by design, an affirmation by the person reciting it. 'I pledge' is a performative statement."[17]

The Court could uphold "under God" as the expression of a religiously based rationale for fundamental rights and limited government. This is the best ground for harmonizing the Pledge with the idea of government neutrality. But it is certainly not unassailable.

3. Is Removing "Under God" Neutral?

"Under God" in the Pledge may be taken to express ideas that government is limited by higher authority and that rights come from this authority. As I said, the nature of government and the status of rights are matters on which the government must take a position. A possible corollary is that no position the state takes on this question can be strictly neutral toward religion. It may not be wholly neutral for the government to state that God stands above it, for this makes a religious affirmation. But perhaps it is likewise not neutral for the state to omit an affirmation of a higher authority—or worse yet, eliminate the affirmation. In context, people might reasonably take the state to be implying that there is no authority of higher status than itself, or at least no authority that it will recognize and that can bind it.

***

It is true in many situations, of course, that by omitting mention of God the state does not thereby deny God's existence. The very idea of neutrality implies that the state can or must be silent on the existence and nature of a deity, and a person too can make statements omitting reference to God without thereby denying God. But again, in the context of a loyalty oath, many Americans will likely see the issue differently; they may view it as impossible to pledge allegiance without explicitly affirming that the state is limited by God....

Critics of the "under God" phrase may respond again that silence about God in the Pledge does not imply an assertion that God does not exist. Instead, they can argue, silence about God is in fact the way in which the state in America acknowledges its limits. If the state makes any explicit religious affirmation, it ends up defining and limiting the transcendent reality rather than deferring to it. Therefore, the only way for the state to acknowledge its limits is by remaining silent and leaving statements about transcendent reality to the initiative of private individuals and groups. If this objection is valid, then the explicit affirmation of God in the Pledge should be removed; but it then becomes crucial for the state to respect and acknowledge its limits in other ways. One implication of this... is that the state should not view itself as the only or the privileged provider of education. The state should not confine educational assistance to families that attend its own schools; it should provide assistance to families who choose other options, subject to standards of educational quality, so that individuals and families can pursue education in the light of the demands of God as they understand them.

Another implication concerns... what the state should do when its general, secular laws conflict with conduct motivated by religious conscience. If the state is to defer to higher reality, but can only do so by deferring to the higher commitments of its individual citizens, then it follows that the state must accommodate conscientious religious practice in cases of conflict with the law, unless there is a serious reason for refusing the accommodation. In our constitutional scheme such accommodation is mandated through the Free Exercise Clause....

NOTES

The note number from the original article is shown in the parenthesis at the end of each citation.

1. *Newdow v. Congress*, 328 F. 3d 466, 487 (9th Cir., 2003). (13)
2. Ibid. (14)
3. Ibid., p. 488. (15)
4. Ibid., p. 489. (16)
5. Ibid., p. 473 (O'Scannlain, J., dissenting from the denial of rehearing *en banc*). (17)
6. 328 F. 3d, p. 479 (O'Scannlain, J., dissenting). (18)
7. Ibid., p. 478. (26)
8. Ibid., p. 487. (27)
9. *Lynch v. Donnelly*, 465 U.S. 668, 693 (1984). (31)
10. Ibid., p. 716 (Brennan, J., dissenting). (32)
11. James Madison, *Memorial and Remonstrance Against Religious Assessments* (1785). (33)
12. HR report no. 83-1693 (1954), pp. 1–2. (57)
13. *The Declaration of Independence* (U.S., 1776), para. 2. (59)
14. Brief of Amici Curiae Christian Legal Society, et al., *United States v. Newdow* (2003), nos. 02–1574 02–1624, WL 21134177. (108)
15. Daniel O. Conkle, "God Loveth Adverbs," *DePaul Law Review* 42 (1992): 345–46. (115)
16. Douglas Laycock, "The Benefits of the Establishment Clause," *DePaul Law Review* 42 (1992): 380. (119)
17. *Newdow*, 328 F. 3d 466, 489 (9th Cir., 2003). (127)

CHAPTER 10

COERCION AND ESTABLISHMENT

COERCION: THE LOST ELEMENT OF ESTABLISHMENT

Michael W. McConnell

***

One no longer can maintain, as Justice Rutledge did, that the Framers originally intended the religion clauses "to create a complete and permanent separation of the spheres of religious activity and civil authority by comprehensively forbidding every form of public aid or support for religion."[1] Whatever directions our historical research ultimately may lead, it now seems beyond doubt that, as Justice Harlan observed, "the historical purposes of...the First Amendment are significantly more obscure and complex than [the Supreme] Court has heretofore acknowledged."[2]

The Supreme Court's response to these developments has not been encouraging. Essentially, what once was declared necessary because of history now is declared necessary because of precedent.... In the jurisprudential shift from original intention to general principles, however, it seems only right to

William and Mary Law Review 27 (1985/1986): 933–41.

call time out to reexamine those holdings of the Court that were products of faulty history and that have yet to be justified on any other theoretical basis.

One such holding is the Court's statement in *Engel v. Vitale*[3] that "[t]he Establishment Clause, unlike the Free Exercise Clause, does not depend upon any showing of direct governmental compulsion and is violated by the enactment of laws which establish an official religion whether those laws operate directly to coerce non-observing individuals—or not."[4] Before looking to the historical support, or lack of it, for this proposition, three brief observations about how this proposition came to enter the law are appropriate.

First, the Court's statement was without the support of precedent. In *Cantwell v. Connecticut*,[5] the Court had paraphrased the Establishment Clause as "forestal[ling] compulsion by law of the acceptance of any creed or the practice of any form of worship,"[6] and the presence or lack of compulsion, respectively, had been central to the Court's decisions in *McCollum v. Board of Education*[7] and *Zorach v. Clauson*,[8] which concerned release time programs in the public schools. And just one year before *Engel*, Chief Justice Warren had explained the distinction between Sunday closing laws and the release time program in *McCollum* on the basis that Sunday closing laws did not compel religious participation. Finally, *Engel* itself conspicuously fails to supply supporting authority for the Court's position.

Second, the Court's statement was unnecessary to its decision. After informing us that compulsion—or at least "direct" compulsion—is not an element of an Establishment Clause claim, the Court pointed out, in its next breath: "This is not to say, of course, that [school prayers] do not involve coercion....When the power, prestige, and financial support of government is placed behind a particular religious belief, the indirect coercive pressure upon religious minorities to conform to the prevailing officially approved religion is plain."[9] I agree. If I did not agree, I would find it difficult to identify any substantial constitutional right violated by public school prayers.

My third observation is that the Court's decision to abjure coercion as an element of an Establishment Clause claim essentially was without explanation. In *Engel*, the Court stated that the purposes of the Establishment Clause "go much further" than preventing even indirect religious compulsion.[10] The Court's reasons, however, were that a fully compulsory established church in the United States and in England historically had "incurred the hatred, disrespect and even contempt of those who held contrary beliefs,"[11] and that established churches "go hand in hand" with religious persecution.[12] These facts seem merely to reinforce that compulsion—yes, even persecution—had been an element of the established church as our forefathers knew it.

The Court's statement in *Engel*, therefore, is mysterious in many ways. Nonetheless, without precedent, without explanation, and, as the Court admitted, without relevance to the case in which it was announced, the notion has been introduced into the law that the Establishment Clause does not involve an element of coercion. The proposition has been passed down, with an ever-lengthening string of citations, to be applied in cases in which so-called establishments can be found by courts even though nobody's religious liberty has been infringed in any way.

Lest it be thought that only the separationists have disregarded the coercion element of an establishment, then-Associate Justice Rehnquist seems to have done likewise in his dissenting opinion in *Wallace v. Jaffree*.[13] According to Justice Rehnquist, the Establishment Clause "forbade establishment of a national religion, and forbade preference among religious sects or denominations"[14]—nothing more. Despite having quoted Madison's words, Justice Rehnquist failed to mention that under the First Amendment Congress cannot "compel men to worship God in any manner contrary to their conscience"[15] or compel them to "conform"[16] to any religion not of their own choosing. It is easy to imagine forms of nonpreferential aid, short of establishing a national church, that nonetheless would have the effect of coercing a religious observance. While the majority of the justices concern themselves with whether measures favor religion over nonreligion, and their opponents focus instead on whether measures favor one religion over another, the central issue of religious choice is disregarded by both sides.

Let us turn then to the historical record. In the debates in the First Congress concerning the wording of the First Amendment, James Madison, the principal draftsman and proponent, said of the committee draft that he "apprehended the meaning of the words to be, that Congress should not establish a religion, and enforce the legal observation of it by law, nor compel men to worship God in any manner contrary to their conscience."[17] Upon further questioning by those who feared that the proposed amendment "might be taken in such latitude as to be extremely hurtful to the cause of religion,"[18] Madison clarified the point. He stated that he "believed that the people feared one sect might obtain a pre-eminence, or two combine together, and establish a religion to which they would compel others to conform."[19] Is compulsion an element of an Establishment Clause violation? If Madison's explanations to the First Congress are any guide, compulsion is not just an element, it is the essence of an establishment.

Curiously, in all the pages of the United States Reports canvassing the history of the period for clues as to the meaning of the religion clauses, no majority or concurring opinion ever has relied on these words by Madison. Indeed, until Justice Rehnquist dissented in *Wallace v. Jaffree*,[20] no justice ever had seriously analyzed the debates on the framing of the First Amendment in any opinion on any side of any religion clause question. This is not because history was deemed irrelevant, because during much of that time the Court had purported to be judging in accordance with original intent. Nor is it because Madison's views were deemed unimportant. Madison's opinions concerning church-state questions propounded before the amendment, after the amendment, at every time except when he was explaining the meaning of the amendment to the First Congress, have been treated as key to an understanding of the amendment. Under ordinary principles of legislative history, Madison's statements on the floor of Congress are of the greatest weight.

But let us look as well at Madison's famous *Memorial and Remonstrance Against Religious Assessments*,[21] what Justice Rutledge called Madison's "complete, though not his only, interpretation of religious liberty."[22] The Court has relied on the *Memorial and Remonstrance* many times in its search for the original intent of the framers of the religion clauses. What does the *Memorial and Remonstrance* have to say about compulsion and establishment? It states: (1) that the proposed bill for the support of teachers of the Christian religion would be a "dangerous abuse"[23] if "armed with the sanctions of a law";[24] (2) that religion "can be directed only by reason and conviction, not by force or violence";[25] (3) that government should not be able to "force a citizen to contribute"[26] even so much as three pence to the support of a church; (4) that such a government would be able to "force him to conform to any other establishment in all cases whatsoever";[27] (5) that "compulsive support" of religion is "unnecessary and unwarrantable";[28] and (6) that "attempts to enforce by legal sanctions, acts obnoxious to so great a proportion of Citizens, tend to enervate the laws in general."[29] Again, legal compulsion to support or participate in religious activities would seem to be the essence of an establishment.

The result of Madison's *Memorial and Remonstrance*...was passage of Virginia's Act for Establishing Religious Freedom.[30] [The key words to the act state:] "[N]o man shall be compelled to frequent or support any religious worship, place, or ministry whatsoever, nor shall be enforced, restrained, molested, or burthened in his body or goods, nor shall otherwise suffer on account of his religious opinions or belief."[31] It is difficult to see, on this evidence, how an establishment could exist in the absence of some form of coercion.

... [If we look at the issues the Founding Fathers confronted and attempted to solve, we see that] the problems that the Founders had encountered were that the government had sought to compel adherence to one religion or, in some colonies, one of several religions, and that the government had sought to restrain adherence to the others. The Establishment and Free Exercise Clauses arose out of these very problems.

Subsequent history confirms this thesis. Exponents of strict separation are embarrassed by the many breaches in the wall of separation countenanced by those who adopted the First Amendment: the appointment of congressional chaplains, the provision in the Northwest Ordinance for religious education, the resolutions calling upon the President to proclaim days of prayer and thanksgiving, the Indian treaties under which Congress paid the salaries of priests and clergy, and so on. These actions, so difficult to reconcile with modern theories of the Establishment Clause, are much easier to understand if one sees religious coercion as the fundamental evil against which the clause is directed. Even if one would take a different view on the specific issues today, perhaps because of a broader sense of coercions stemming from the pervasive influence of the modern welfare-regulatory state, these examples demonstrate that noncoercive supports for religion were not within the contemporary understanding of an establishment of religion. Strong evidence suggests that discrimination among religious sects also was proscribed by the Establishment Clause, but I have run across no persuasive evidence that the Framers of the First Amendment considered evenhanded support for all religions or religion in general, in the absence of a coercive impact an establishment of religion.

Why does this matter? At the most obvious level, it suggests that the courts are wasting their time when they draw nice distinctions about various manifestations of religion in public life that entail no use of the taxing power and have no coercive effect. The simple answer to most such lawsuits is that the plaintiff has no standing to sue. More importantly, the analysis suggests that the courts should be more hospitable to liberty-enhancing accommodations of religion, like the Connecticut law struck down last year that prevented workers from being fired for refusing to work on their chosen Sabbath.

On the other hand, my analysis suggests that aid to religion must not be structured to influence or distort religious choice. Merely because aid may be neutral among religions does not mean that it is consistent with the non-coercion standard. For example, a program of tuition grants to attend private schools, limited to religious private schools, would be neutral among religions but obviously would interfere with religious choice. A noncoercion standard protects nonbelievers and those indifferent to religion no less than it protects believers.

Doctrinally, renewed attention to coercion suggests that the Court's three-part test [set out in *Lemon v. Kurtzman*] for an establishment of religion[32] should be modified. A rule that forbids government actions with the purpose or effect of advancing religion fails to distinguish between efforts to coerce and influence religious belief and action, on the one hand, and efforts to facilitate the exercise of one's chosen faith, on the other. It is meaningless to speak of "advancing" religion without specifying the reference point. To protect religious freedom against persecution "advances" religion, as does treating religion neutrally if the prior practice had been to discriminate against it.

Recognition of the centrality of coercion—or, more precisely, its opposite, religious choice—to Establishment Clause analysis would lead to a proscription of all government action that has the purpose and effect of coercing or altering religious belief or action. Under this standard, the Court would sustain many worthwhile, progressive social programs that it has struck down in the past—programs such as remedial education for economically and educationally deprived children on the premises of their own schools. The point here is not that the government may undertake to aid religion, but that it can pursue its legitimate purposes even if to do so incidentally assists the various religions.

A noncoercion standard, of course, would not answer all questions. For example, it obviously would not answer the question, "What is coercion?" Enormous variance exists between the persecutions of old and the many subtle ways in which government action can distort religious choice today. This is no less true under the Establishment Clause than it is under the Free Exercise Clause, where the Court has recognized the problem. But while there will be room for continuing debate and disagreement concerning the definition of coercion, at least attention again would be directed to the right question. Not what flunks the three-part test, but what interferes with religious liberty, is an establishment of religion.

NOTES

The note number from the original article is shown in the parenthesis at the end of each citation.

1. *Everson v. Board of Education of the Township of Ewing, et al.*, 330 U.S. 1, 31–32 (1947) [Hereinafter 330 U.S.]. (5)

2. *Flast v. Cohen*, 392 U.S. 83, 125 (1968). (6)

3. *Engel v. Vitale*, 370 U.S. 421 (1962). (9)

4. Ibid., p. 430. (10)

5. *Cantwell v. Connecticut*, 310 U.S. 296 (1940). (11)

6. Ibid., p. 303. (12)

7. *Illinois ex rel. McCollum v. Board of Ed. of School Dist. No. 71, Champaign City*, 333 U.S. 203 (1948). (13)

8. *Zorach v. Clausen*, 343 U.S. 306 (1952). (14)

9. Engel, 370 U.S. 421, 430–31. (16)

10. Ibid., p. 431. (17)

11. Ibid. (18)

12. Ibid., p. 432. (19)

13. *Wallace v. Jaffree*, 472 U.S. 38, 91–114 (1985). (20)

14. Ibid., p. 106. (21)

15. Joseph Gales, ed., *Annals of Congress*, vol. 1 (1834), p. 730. (22)

16. Ibid., p. 731. (23)

17. Ibid., p. 730. (24)

18. Ibid. (25)

19. Ibid., p. 731. (26)

20. 472 U.S. 38, 91–114 (Rehnquist, J., dissenting). (27)

21. Madison, *A Memorial and Remonstrance Against Religious Assessments* (1785). (28)

22. 330 U.S. 37. (29)

23. Madison, *Memorial and Remonstrance*, preamble. (30)

24. Ibid. (31)

25. Ibid., para. 1. (32)

26. Ibid., para. 3. (33)

27. Ibid. (34)

28. Ibid. (35)

29. Ibid., para 13. (36)

30. William Waller Hening, *Statutes at Large*, vol. 12 (1823), ch. 34, p. 84. (37)

31. Ibid., pp. 86, para. 2. (38)

32. *Lemon v. Kurtzman*, 403 U.S. 602, 612–13 (1971). (42)

"NONCOERCIVE" SUPPORT FOR RELIGION: ANOTHER FALSE CLAIM ABOUT THE ESTABLISHMENT CLAUSE

DOUGLAS LAYCOCK

One of the fundamental and recurring controversies about the meaning of the First Amendment's religion clauses is whether government must be neutral between religion and nonreligion. The Supreme Court has always said yes in modern times, but persistent critics have disagreed.

The Court's critics have offered two major alternatives to neutrality. The older alternative is nonpreferentialism: that government may aid religion so long as it does not prefer one religion over another. The more recently proposed alternative is noncoercion: that government may aid or endorse all religions or particular religions so long as it does not coerce anyone to religious practice or belief....

Valparaiso University Law Review 26 (1991): 37, 39–41, 50–53, 61–65, 68–69.

***

I. Neutrality, Nonpreferentialism, and Noncoercion

Nonpreferentialism and noncoercion have common political origins.... Each theory originates from the political desire for government support of religion, and each relies on the historical observation that the founding government did support religion in a variety of ways. Each theory is an attempt to state a principle that will distinguish permissible and impermissible forms of government support for religion. But neither theory produces acceptable results for a pluralistic society, and neither theory captures the practices of the Founders.

It is important to clearly distinguish the two theories. They are not the same and they have very different implications. Under nonpreferentialism, government must be neutral among religions, but it need not be neutral as between religion and disbelief. The essence of nonpreferentialism is that government should be free to encourage or subsidize religious belief and practice so long as it encourages or subsidizes all religions equally....

Under noncoercion theory, the Religion Clauses are not violated unless government coerces an individual to religious practice or belief. Neither neutrality nor nonpreferentialism is part of the noncoercion standard; government need not be neutral between religion and nonreligion, and it need not be neutral among competing religions. Government may endorse generic theism, generic Protestantism, Roman Catholicism, Seventh-Day Adventism, or the Twelfth Street Pentecostal Holiness Church. Congress could charter The Church of the United States, so long as it did not coerce anyone to join.

Under noncoercion theory, government at all levels could take sides in debates about the nature of Christ, salvation by works or by faith, scriptural inerrancy, the authority of the Book of Mormon, or any other religious matter. The President, the Congress or... [a local] School Committee could adopt and promulgate creeds. Noncoercionists believe that "government may participate as a speaker in moral debates, including religious ones."[1]

In theory we might combine the two alternatives to neutrality. That is, we might permit government to aid religion only in ways that are both noncoercive and nonpreferential, if anyone can think of such a way. But so far as I am aware, no one has proposed that, and neither theory leaves room for that.

***

It is ... clear that noncoercionists would not require nonpreferentialism. One of the more visible issues that noncoercionists seek to resolve is the government-sponsored crèche, or nativity scene. The crèche symbolizes the alleged miracle of Christ's Incarnation, a claim that is central to Christianity, heretical or blasphemous to Judaism and Islam, and largely irrelevant to the world's other great religions. If noncoercionists mean to permit government crèches, they plainly mean to permit government to endorse particular religions. One can imagine a practice of noncoercive, nonpreferential religious displays, in which a government would give equal prominence to displays symbolizing central events of all religions. But no government has such a practice, and no defenders of government sponsored religious observances have proposed that government must observe all religions or none.

***

II. The Historical Meaning of the Establishment Clause

***

C. The Protestant Bible Controversy

Government prayer and religious proclamations, and the role of religion in public education, were not real controversies in the Founders' time. There were multiple reasons for this lack of controversy, but the most important was simply that the nation was overwhelmingly Protestant, and no significant group of Protestants was victimized by these practices. If a religious practice was not controversial among Protestants, it was not sufficiently controversial to attract political attention.

Theological and liturgical differences among Protestants were large, but for a variety of reasons, these differences appear to have been bridgeable in the rudimentary schools of the time. Most schools were small, and many served a relatively homogenous local population. Some were run by local governments, some by associations of neighbors, some by entrepreneurial teachers, some by churches. Some of these schools defied characterization as public or private. In some urban areas, parents had many choices.

[As public schools developed over time] ... [t]he common school movement attempted to bridge the religious gaps among Americans with an unmistakably

Protestant solution: by confining instruction to the most basic concepts of Christianity, and by reading the Bible "without note or comment." The Protestant leaders of the common school movement assumed that no one could object to reading the Bible, and by forbidding teachers to explain the passages read, they thought they had avoided sectarian disagreements about interpretation.

That solution was not entirely satisfactory even among Protestants. Conservative and evangelical Protestants accused Unitarians like Horace Mann of secularizing the public schools; stripped-down, least-common-denominator religion was not acceptable to them... But Protestants largely abandoned their disagreements to unite against the wave of Catholic immigration in the mid-nineteenth century.

Catholics fundamentally challenged what seemed to them Protestant religious instruction in the public schools. For one thing, Catholics used the Douay translation of the Bible, and objected to reading the King James translation, which they called "the Protestant Bible."

More important, Catholics condemned the "solution" of reading the Bible without note or comment as a fundamentally Protestant practice. Protestants taught the primary authority of scripture and the accessibility of scripture to every human. Catholics taught that the scripture must be understood in light of centuries of accumulated church teaching. For Catholic children to read the Bible without note or comment was to risk misunderstanding. Protestant practices were being forced on Catholic children.

The controversy over the Protestant Bible in public schools produced mob violence and church burnings in Eastern cities. The resulting controversies were major political issues for decades. The anti-Catholic, anti-immigrant Know Nothing Party swept elections in eight states in the 1850s. Among other things, these issues gave rise to the proposed Blaine amendment to the Constitution, which would have codified the Protestant position by permitting Bible reading but forbidding "sectarian" instruction in any publicly-funded school. This amendment was defeated by Democrats in the Senate....

Thus, in the wake of Catholic immigration, religion in the public schools produced exactly the sort of violent religious confrontation the Founders had sought to avoid. Religion in schools initially had been a nonproblem that raised no concern. Under changed social conditions, religion in schools became a serious violation of the disestablishment principle, which inflicted precisely "those consequences which the Framers deeply feared."[2] The principle of disestablishment did not change, but the nation was forced to confront a previously ignored application of the principle. Just as government could not endorse religion in statutes or state constitutions, neither could it endorse religion in public schools.

The first cases forbidding religious observances in public schools date from the latter part of this period. On the other hand, some schools whipped or expelled Catholic children who refused to participate in Protestant observances, and some courts upheld such actions. Neither side drew the line between coercion and noncoercion. Those who understood the grievance of religious minorities abandoned the offending practice; those who saw no grievance saw no reason not to coerce compliance.

The dispute over the Protestant Bible revealed the impossibility of conducting "neutral" religious observances even among diverse groups of Christians. Protestant education leaders did not set out to victimize Catholics; they genuinely thought that reading the Bible without note or comment was fair to all and harmful to none. What seemed harmless from their perspective was not harmless when applied across the full range of American pluralism.

Today, the range of religious pluralism in America is vastly greater. Immigration has brought Jews, Muslims, Buddhists, Hindus, Sikhs, Taoists, animists, and many others into the country. Significant numbers of atheists and agnostics have been with us since the late nineteenth century; they were little more than a theoretical possibility to the Founders. The possibility of "neutral" religious observance remains a fiction.

***

IV. THE HARM TO RELIGION

It is common to assume that the objection to government-sponsored religious observances comes only from nonbelievers who are hostile to religion. It is easy to see that nonbelievers might object when government adds a prayer service to a secular function. A requirement that government be neutral as between religious belief and disbelief is designed to protect nonbelievers.

But a ban on government-sponsored religious observance is also necessary to neutrality among believers, and it is important to understand that. A nonpreferentialist instinct informs much of the popular reaction to *Lee v. Weisman*: who besides an atheist could object to a short and simple prayer? That question deserves an answer.

... [E]ven if government attempts to sponsor religious observances that are neutral among believers, it will fail. Government-sponsored religious observances hurt believers as well as nonbelievers.

Such observances hurt all religions by imposing government's preferred form of religion on public occasions. It is not possible for government to sponsor a generic prayer; government inevitably sponsors a particular form of prayer. Whatever form government chooses, it imposes that form on all believers who would prefer a different form.

In some communities, government-sponsored prayer unabashedly follows the liturgy of the locally dominant faith in the community. "Sensitive" communities attempt to delete from public prayer all indicia of any particular faith, leaving only the least common denominator of majoritarian religion. But these stripped-down prayers to an anonymous deity are as much a particular form of prayer as any other prayer.

The school teachers who plan the ceremony decide what prayers are acceptable and what not, and what clergy are acceptable and what not. In this process, the schools establish a religion of mushy ecumenism. The clergy for these prayers are determined by the limits of acceptability to the mainstream. In...many...cities, the guidelines for these prayers are supplied by the National Conference of Christians and Jews. The NCCJ's guidelines implement its commitment to minimizing religious and ethnic conflict. The guidelines emphasize "inclusiveness and sensitivity," and they offer a specific list of "universal, inclusive terms for deity."[3] Government adoption of these guidelines establishes an uncodified but generally accepted book of common prayer. This least-common-denominator strategy is the same strategy followed by the Protestant school reformers of the nineteenth century, and it fails for similar reasons. By removing from religious observance all those specifics on which different faiths overtly disagree, the school is left with an abstract impersonal God that nearly all faiths reject. What is left is unacceptable to many believers who take their own faith seriously.

***

Whichever choice government makes, it endorses that choice. Government sponsored prayer on public occasions lends the weight of government practice to a preferred form of prayer. By their example, schools that leave Christ out of prayer endorse that practice as more tolerant, as more enlightened, as government approved. They lend the authority of government to a desacralized, watered-down religion that demands little of its adherents and offers few benefits in return.

The attempt to be inclusive amplifies the message of exclusion to those left out. Because such prayers are carefully orchestrated not to offend anyone who counts in the community, the message to those who are offended is that they do *not* count—that they are not important enough to avoid offending. The message is:

> We go out of our way to avoid offending people we care about, but we don't mind offending you. If you have a problem with this, you are too marginal to care about. This is our graduation, not yours.

It is not just nonbelievers who may be offended or excluded by prayers like those in *Lee v. Weisman*. Such prayers also exclude serious particularistic believers, those who take their own form of prayer seriously enough that they do not want to participate in someone else's form of prayer. There are still millions of Americans who believe that all religions are not equal, that their own religion is better, or even that their own religion is the one true faith, and that their faith should not be conglomerated into something that will not offend the great majority.

Those who would not pray at all, those who would pray only in private, those who would pray only after ritual purification, those who would pray only to Jesus, or Mary, or some other intermediary, those who would pray in Hebrew, or Arabic, or some other sacred tongue, are all excluded or offended by the prayers in *Lee v. Weisman*. Those who object to the political or theological content of those prayers are similarly excluded....

On occasion, religious observances in public schools still produce ugly confrontations between those who object to least-common-denominator prayer and those who support it. A detailed account of such an incident appears in *Walter v. West Virginia Board of Education*,[4] where an eleven-year-old Jewish child was condemned as a Christ killer because he did not appear to pray during a moment of silence. Most contemporary religious dissenters in public schools suffer in silence, and we have had no recent repetitions of the mob violence of the nineteenth century. But reduction of violence is not a reason to relax constitutional protections. Religious dissenters should not have to provoke violence to call attention to their constitutional rights.

The political content of the prayer in *Lee* illustrates another core danger of established religion. When government sponsors religious observances, it appropriates religion to its own uses and unites religious and governmental authority... [to express] an essentially political message—that American government is good, that freedom is secure... et cetera.

...But the school and [the selected member of the clergy] cannot unite the authority and prestige of church and state in support of that message. The school cannot recruit a [member of the clergy] to wrap that political message in religious authority. The school cannot misappropriate the authority of the church to prop up the authority of the state.

It has long been a common observation that religion has thrived in America without an establishment, and declined in Western Europe with an establishment. It is less commonly observed that the established Congregationalist and Episcopalian churches of colonial America declined in numbers and influence, while the dissenting Baptists and Presbyterians, who insisted on rigorous disestablishment, grew and flourished.

These long-term religious trends reflect in part the baleful effects of government sponsorship. Religion does not benefit from public prayer that "degenerates into a scanty attendance, and a tiresome formality"[5]... But the Constitution is equally violated if government makes religion less attractive rather than more so. Government sponsorship of religion is always clumsy, and usually motivated more by political concerns than religious ones. In intolerant communities it tends inevitably toward persecution; in tolerant communities it tends inevitably toward desacralization. One function of the Establishment Clause is to avoid this dilemma....

VII. Conclusion

It is too often forgotten that the Establishment Clause and the Free Exercise Clause both protect religious liberty. They both protect religious believers as well as nonbelievers....

The noncoercion standard would abandon the goal of government neutrality toward and among religions. It would encourage government to denigrate, embarrass, and discomfit nonbelievers. But it would also leave America's many religions exposed to the corrupting intrusions of government. Government could sponsor preferred churches, preferred theologies, preferred liturgies, preferred forms of worship, and preferred forms of prayer. All this is entailed when government undertakes to sponsor a "civil religion."

Government by its sheer size, visibility, authority, and pervasiveness could profoundly affect the future of religion in America. For government to affect religion in this way is for government to change religion, to distort religion, to interfere with religion. Government's preferred form of religion is theologically and liturgically thin. It is politically compliant, and supportive of incumbent administrations. One function of the Establishment Clause is to protect religion against such interference. To government's clumsy efforts to assist religion, several religious amici [in *Lee*] said "No thanks. Too much of such" assistance "and we are undone; the Constitution protects us from assistance such as this."[6]

NOTES

The note number from the original article is shown in the parenthesis at the end of each citation.

1. *American Jewish Congress v. City of Chicago*, 827 F. 2d 120, 132 (7th Cir., 1987) (Easterbrook, J., dissenting). (18)

2. *Abington School Dist. v. Schempp*, 374 U.S. 203, 236 (1963) (Brennan, J., concurring). (76)

3. National Conference of Christians and Jews, *Public Prayer in a Pluralistic Society*, p. 2. (156)

4. 610 F. Supp. 1169, 1172–73 (S.D.W. Va., 1985). (159)

5. Elizabeth Fleet, ed., "Madison's 'Detached Memoranda,'" *William and Mary Quarterly* 3 (3d Ser., 1946): 539. (162)

6. Amicus Curiae Brief of the American Jewish Congress, et al., in Support of Respondents, 8. (174)

RELIGIOUS COERCION AND THE ESTABLISHMENT CLAUSE

STEVEN G. GEY

***

A. The Coercion Standard and Government Endorsement of Religion

The coercion standard is tailor-made for reversing the Court's separationist tendencies in government endorsement cases, which include two of the most frequently litigated Establishment Clause subjects: government-supported religious displays at holidays and prayer in public schools. The placement of passive religious symbols on government property almost always would be upheld under the coercion standard, in contrast to the separationist approach, because it is virtually inconceivable that any religious symbol would "coerce anyone to support or participate in any religion or its exercise."[1] The same result would seem to apply in the public school prayer cases. As Justice

University of Illinois Law Review 1994 (1994): 493–501, 503–507.

Stewart argued in [*Abington School District v.*] *Schempp*, so long as students who do not wish to participate are permitted to abstain from the state-endorsed prayer, their religious views have not been coerced in any noticeable manner.[2] Yet Justice Kennedy takes the exact opposite stance (over Justice Scalia's strenuous objections) in his majority opinion in *Lee v.Weisman*.[3] A comparison of Justice Kennedy's opinions in *Allegheny* [*County v. ACLU*] and *Weisman* indicates that even the coercion standard's supporters recoil from the more oppressive implications inherent in a consistent application of the standard.…

1. Coercion and Religious Displays

The *Allegheny* Court considered two holiday displays. The first, a crèche placed on the grand staircase of the county courthouse, depicted the birth of Jesus, and was accompanied by an angel carrying a banner proclaiming "Gloria in Excelsis Deo!" [Glory to God in the Highest].[4] The second display stood outside the city-county building and included an eighteen-foot Menorah and a forty-five-foot Christmas tree, accompanied by a sign entitled "Salute to Liberty."[5] A majority of the Court upheld the constitutionality of the second display, but held the first display unconstitutional.

Justice Kennedy was willing to find both displays constitutional, arguing that neither display violated the coercion standard, because

> [n]o one was compelled to observe or participate in any religious ceremony or activity.…Passersby who disagree with the message conveyed by these displays are free to ignore them, or even to turn their backs, just as they are free to do when they disagree with any other form of government speech.[6]

The definition of *coercion* that Justice Kennedy employs in his *Allegheny* opinion is the very narrow, common understanding of the term. Under this definition, coercion occurs only when a person is compelled by force or threat to do something that he or she would not otherwise do.

According to Justice Kennedy, a religious dissenter's feelings of discomfort, exclusion, or offense do not, without more, amount to proof of coercion. The government action favoring one religion is constitutional, so long as it does not change the offended person's contrary religious behavior.… This conclusion [that feelings of exclusion by religious minorities are constitutionally irrelevant] is reinforced when Justice Kennedy grumbles at the end of his *Allegheny* dissent that the majority's endorsement approach consigns the country's majority faiths to "least favored faiths so as to avoid any possible risk of offending members of minority religions."[7]

***

From the separationist perspective, this is a radical proposal. Justice Kennedy's interpretation of the coercion standard in *Allegheny* would convert religious practices and symbols into political spoils, and the winner of an election in an overwhelmingly Christian (or, hypothetically, Jewish or Muslim) community would be able to use its political muscle to "recognize and accommodate" its own faith with government resources. This would convey subtly (or often not so subtly) to the religious minority their position in the political hierarchy. Justice Kennedy clearly intended the exclusionary implications of this proposal. His *Allegheny* opinion contains too many references to maligned religious majorities and hypersensitive religious minorities to believe otherwise.

Despite the majoritarian emphasis of Justice Kennedy's *Allegheny* opinion, the opinion also indicates that he might not be willing to tolerate the full exercise of the power the coercion standard would provide an aggressive religious majority. Immediately after he introduces the coercion standard in his *Allegheny* dissent, Justice Kennedy adds the caveat that a government's symbolic endorsement of religion may be deemed coercive "in an extreme case."[8] He then adds an odd example of what may constitute an "extreme case": "I doubt not, for example, that the [Establishment] Clause forbids a city to permit the permanent erection of a large Latin cross on the roof of city hall."[9] The problem with a permanent cross, Justice Kennedy says, is that "such an obtrusive year-round religious display would place the government's weight behind an obvious effort to proselytize on behalf of a particular religion."[10] This seems true, but so what? Under the coercion standard, if no one is coerced into practicing the particular faith represented by the cross, where is the violation of the Establishment Clause?

***

2. Coercion and Public School Prayer: The Kennedy Position

Lee v. Weisman is a distant successor to two of the Court's earliest and, at least at the time, most controversial Establishment Clause decisions. In *Engel v. Vitale*,[11] the Court held unconstitutional government-sanctioned prayers in public school classrooms. In *Abington School District v. Schempp*,[12] the Court used *Engel* as the basis for striking down government-sanctioned Bible reading in public school classrooms. In *Lee v. Weisman*,[13] the Court considered a milder form of government-sanctioned prayer: prayer at a public school graduation ceremony.

In *Weisman*, the Court reviewed the policy of a Providence, Rhode Island, public school system permitting prayer at high school graduation ceremonies. Members of the local clergy conducted the prayers at the Providence graduation ceremonies, guided by school policy guidelines suggesting that the clergy keep in mind "inclusiveness and sensitivity" when composing a graduation prayer.... [A] five-member majority of the Supreme Court held that the prayer violated the Establishment Clause. Surprisingly, Justice Kennedy wrote the majority opinion. Even more surprisingly, he used the coercion standard as the basis for his opinion.

The author of the *Weisman* majority opinion is in many respects a different Justice Kennedy than the Justice who wrote the angry dissent in *Allegheny*. Likewise, the coercion test that first appeared in Justice Kennedy's *Allegheny* dissent is a substantially different animal from the one that appears in *Weisman*. The version of the coercion standard that Justice Kennedy uses in *Weisman* to strike down a brief nondenominational graduation prayer is much stricter than the version he uses in *Allegheny* to approve a large display of the baby Jesus prominently placed in a public building. The root of the difference between the two versions is a very different conception of the term "coercion."

In *Allegheny*, the key indication of unconstitutional coercion is evidence that the government's action has interfered in fact with an individual's religious autonomy. In that case, Justice Kennedy argued that so long as a member of a religious minority retains the right to practice his or her own religion and to disassociate himself or herself from the public display of the religious majority's symbols, the placement of such symbols on public property is not coercive, and therefore is not a violation of the Establishment Clause....

The concept of coercion that forms the core of Justice Kennedy's *Weisman* opinion is much broader, looser, and more indefinite.... In *Weisman*, the Court held that the very fact that the government used its authority to endorse or further the cause of religion is itself evidence of coercion, without regard to the actual effect the government action has on the religious practices of anyone in the audience. Justice Kennedy writes that because school officials decided that the prayer should be given, "from a constitutional perspective it is as if a state statute decreed that the prayers must occur."[14] He concludes that such a statute would be a per se violation of the Establishment Clause.

This conclusion is inconsistent with the broad outlines of Establishment Clause theory set forth in *Allegheny*. In *Allegheny*, Justice Kennedy argued that government speech about religion is not per se suspect, provided the speech does not "place the government's weight behind an obvious effort to proselytize on behalf of a particular religion."[15] He takes exactly the opposite position in *Weisman*, asserting that the Establishment Clause specifically prohibits the government from participating in religious debate or expression. He also rejects the school district's claim (which seems to follow his own suggestion in *Allegheny*) that the government may make generalized references to civic religion, so long as it does not advance the creed of a particular faith. "The suggestion that government may establish an official or civic religion as a means of avoiding the establishment of a religion with more specific creeds strikes us as a contradiction that cannot be accepted."[16] ...

Justice Kennedy's *Weisman* opinion also contradicts his argument in *Allegheny* that the Establishment Clause standard should not turn on an individual's feelings of exclusion from the majority's religious culture. In *Weisman*, Justice Kennedy uses imagery highlighting the plaintiff's feelings of exclusion and religious isolation to demonstrate the existence of coercion, and thus to bolster his finding that graduation prayer violates the Establishment Clause. "[T]he school district's supervision and control ... places public pressure, as well as peer pressure, on attending students to stand as a group, or, at least, maintain respectful silence during the Invocation and Benediction. This pressure, though subtle and indirect, can be as real as any overt coercion."[17]

Three things are noteworthy about this passage. First, Justice Kennedy acknowledges that even a passive demonstration of respect by a member of the religious minority for the government's favored religious practice is tantamount to direct participation in the exercise. Second, he finds coercion even though the government itself does nothing whatsoever to pressure the dissenter to do anything. The existence of conformist religious pressures among the population is sufficient to provide the necessary coercion. Third, Justice Kennedy finds coercion even though there is no evidence that either governmental or nongovernmental actors did anything to pressure or threaten the religious minority to conform. He presumes coercion exists simply because conformist tendencies are likely to flow from the religious minority's feelings of social ostracism. I emphasize that I believe Justice Kennedy's perceptions about these tendencies are correct. It stretches the meaning of the word coercion, however, to apply that term to an individual's decision to modify beliefs that no other person has sought actively to change. Justice Kennedy's description of the constitutional problem in *Weisman* better fits Justice O'Connor's theory that the government should not make nonadherents feel like outsiders in society, a theory which Justice Kennedy criticized at great length in *Allegheny*.

***

... [The fact] that graduating seniors are, in effect, compelled to attend their high school graduation ceremonies [cannot distinguish *Weisman* from *Allegheny*] ... [A] citizen of Allegheny County may also be compelled to transact business in the county courthouse, which would inevitably require that person to pass by the prominent display of the birth of the Christian savior. If the Allegheny County citizen is not coerced by being required to respectfully pass by the religious display, why is the Providence student coerced by respectfully remaining silent during a one-minute prayer? Conversely, if "the act of standing or remaining silent" during a graduation prayer is "an expression of participation" in the prayer,[18] why is walking by an overtly Christian display in respectful silence not also "an expression of participation" in the display?

***

3. Coercion and Public School Prayer: The Scalia Position

If Justice Kennedy is sincere about distinguishing the coercion standard from Justice O'Connor's endorsement standard, then he must take seriously his own *Allegheny* definition of coercion. Under that definition, a person is coerced if he or she is forced by some action of the government "to support or participate in any religion or its exercise."[19] Psychological coercion, which is the focus of the *Weisman* opinion, does not fit this definition because the religious dissenter is not forced to participate in any religious act, and because, in symbolic endorsement cases such as *Weisman*, the main source of the psychological pressure is society as a whole, not the particular government action. Therefore, if the coercion standard is to be a distinctive new reference point for Establishment Clause analysis, it must emphasize legal, rather than psychological, coercion.

Justice Scalia's dissenting opinion in *Weisman* drives this point home with sarcastic force. He labels Justice Kennedy's psychological coercion test "incoherent," and ridicules the idea that it can ever be applied consistently. In place of psychological coercion, Justice Scalia offers his concept of legal coercion, i.e., "coercion of religious orthodoxy and of financial support by force of law and threat of penalty."[20] Justice Scalia's definition transforms *Weisman* into an easy case because "attendance at graduation is voluntary, [and] there is nothing in the record to indicate that failure of attending students to take part in the invocation or benediction was subject to any penalty or discipline."[21] Ergo, state-sanctioned prayer at public school graduation ceremonies is constitutional. If Ms. Weisman does not like it, she can stay home.

***

Justice Scalia's position is a radical departure from the traditional understanding of the First Amendment's countermajoritarian function.... But even Justice Scalia stops short of embracing the full consequences of his argument. Whenever he refers to the general phenomenon of graduation prayer in his *Weisman* opinion, Justice Scalia emphasizes the benign, nondenominational content of the prayer given at Weisman's graduation. This is the type of prayer that Justice Scalia uses as his model in applying the coercion standard. As to other, not-so-benign prayers, Justice Scalia notes only that he is willing to concede that government-sponsored endorsement of religion may be unconstitutional "where the endorsement is sectarian, in the sense of specifying details upon which men and women who believe in a benevolent, omnipotent Creator and Ruler of the world, are known to differ (for example, the divinity of Christ)."[22]

These overtures to nonsectarian tolerance offer some comfort, but if, as Justice Scalia argues, the Constitution permits "the expression of gratitude to God that a majority of the community wishes to make"[23] so long as the community does not coerce others to participate in that expression, then there is no reason to limit the application of the coercion standard to friendly, nondenominational prayers. If dissenting audience members at a state-sponsored public event may walk away from the affair without subjecting themselves to legal penalties, it should not matter whether a prayer given at that function incorporates the tenets of a particular sect, or comments unfavorably on the tenets of another sect. It should not matter even if the government sponsors a prayer overtly hostile to one or more faiths, so long as the dissenters are allowed to ignore the government's advice and practice their own beliefs freely. As Justice Scalia repeatedly emphasizes, the amorphous fear or psychological pressure generated in the minds of religious minorities by such prayers is constitutionally irrelevant....

***

NOTES

The note number from the original article is shown in the parenthesis at the end of each citation.

1. *County of Allegheny v. ACLU*, 492 U.S. 573, 659 (1989) (Kennedy, J., concurring in the judgment in part and dissenting in part) [Hereinafter 492 U.S.]. (132)
2. *Abington School District v. Schempp*, 374 U.S. 203, 316–317 (1963) (Stewart, J., dissenting). (133)
3. *Lee v. Weisman*, 112 S. Ct. 2649, 2658–59 (1992) [Hereinafter 112 S. Ct.]. (134)
4. 492 U.S. 580. (135)
5. Ibid., pp. 581–82. (136)
6. 492 U.S. 664 (Kennedy, J., concurring in the judgment in part and dissenting in part). (137)
7. Ibid., p. 677. (141)
8. Ibid., p. 661. (145)
9. Ibid. (146)
10. Ibid. (147)
11. *Engel v. Vitale*, 370 U.S. 421 (1962). (152)
12. *Abington*, 374 U.S. 203 (1963). (153)
13. *Weisman*, 112 S. Ct. 2649 (1992). (154)
14. 112 S. Ct. 2665. (159)
15. 492 U.S. 661. (160)
16. 112 S. Ct. 2657. (162)
17. Ibid., p. 2658 (165)
18. Ibid. (183)
19. See 492 U.S. 659. (186)
20. 112 S. Ct. 2683 (Scalia, J., dissenting). (190)
21. Ibid., p. 2684 (191)
22. Ibid., pp. 2683–84. (197)
23. Ibid., p. 2686. (198)

LEMON IS DEAD

Michael Stokes Paulsen

I. Introduction

In *Lee v. Weisman*,[1] the Supreme Court struck down as unconstitutional the Providence, Rhode Island school committee's practice of allowing school principles to invite clergy to give nondenominational invocations and benedictions at graduation and promotion exercises at the Providence public schools....

***

III. *Lee v. Weisman*

***

Case Western Reserve Law Review 43 (Spring 1993): 795, 819, 821, 825–34, 846–48, 853–55.

348

A. The Death of *Lemon*

***

... The *only* thing that the *Weisman* majority agreed on was that the Establishment Clause prohibits *at least* government coercion to engage in religious exercise and that the challenged commencement prayer violates this principle. Kennedy, the author of the majority opinion, apparently stands alone (within that majority) in thinking that coercion is all that the Establishment Clause prohibits.

But the four dissenters in *Weisman* joined Kennedy in agreeing that the proper inquiry is coercion. It is clear, then, that the real *doctrinal* majority consists of Justice Kennedy and the four *Weisman* dissenters.... If Kennedy indeed remains in the "coercion" camp, then it may be further concluded that *Weisman* has not only interred the *Lemon* test, but has replaced it with some form of coercion test.

B. The Meaning of Coercion

But if *Weisman* stands for the adoption of coercion as the governing standard in Establishment Clause adjudication, what exactly is meant by "coercion" and is this standard a sound interpretation of the clause?...

***

The first paragraph of section II of the Court's opinion in *Weisman* defines and delimits the scope of the Court's holding:

> These dominant facts mark and control the confines of our decision: State officials direct the performance of a formal religious exercise at promotional and graduation ceremonies for secondary schools. Even for those students who object to the religious exercise, their attendance and participation in the state-sponsored religious activity are in a fair and real sense obligatory, though the school district does not require attendance as a condition for receipt of the diploma.[2]

If the Court had stopped at this point there would have been little warrant for the dissent's howling. Whatever else the coercion test might mean, if it is true to its historical justification, it must prohibit any form of official compulsion to attend a religious worship service. Admittedly, the historical evidence is fairly clear that the giving of public prayers on public occasions as a ceremonial-religious way of solemnizing the event, or the beginning of the day's activities, was not regarded as establishment of religion. At the same time, however, the evidence is also clear that compelled attendance at a religious worship service was regarded as one of the defining characteristics (and most hated features) of religious establishments. Justice Scalia thus gives up half the game when his dissent acknowledges as a feature of historical establishments that "*attendance* at the state church was required."[3]

The other half of the game is recognition that government-induced attendance at a prayer ceremony violates this historical principle. Though the compulsion in *Weisman* is in the form of a condition attached to a public benefit (the right to attend one's own or one's child's public school graduation) and the religious worship service is practically *de minimis* in duration and content (two brief, theologically sterile prayers, opening and closing the ceremony), *Weisman* is little different in principle from laws requiring compulsory church attendance.

It must be conceded that *Weisman* is a reasonably close case on its facts, standing at the intersection of the historical evidence. The coercion is fairly mild when compared to the historical practices against which the Establishment Clause was directed. The result of the government pressure is attendance at a one-time event—a public ceremonial occasion (albeit different from the circumstances where, historically, prayers were sanctioned). A miniature worship service takes place at the event, though it is one lacking serious theological content. It is tempting to scoff at the analogy to compulsory church attendance laws.

On balance, however, *Weisman* is rightly decided. None of these mitigating factors distinguishes compulsory church attendance in principle. The brevity of the religious element does not distinguish it. Surely, the state could not compel attendance at a ten minute Mass or a five-minute sermon. The Regents Prayer struck down in *Engel* was short. The theological vacuity of the prayer also does not alter the principle involved. The prayer in *Engel* was theological slush, too. If compelled *attendance* is sufficient to constitute establishment, it does not matter whether one is offended by the prayers or not. An established "civil religion" is still an established religion. Nor does the one-time nature of the event help in principle. It would be no less a violation of the Establishment Clause if one were forced to attend church only once....

The real issue—and the chief bone of contention between Kennedy and the dissenters—is whether commencement prayer involves actual compulsion. Unfortunately, neither the majority nor the dissent is very clear as to whether the object of forbidden compulsion is *participation* in prayer or mere *attendance* during the prayer. Both opinions address both issues, but the problem of compelled attendance at the prayer is treated as something of a way-station on the route to the question of compelled participation. This is where the analyses of both opinions falter.

A sufficient inquiry, as indicated above, is whether government has coerced *attendance* at a religious ceremony. And it is fair to say that such coercion was present in *Weisman*. One may accept Justice Scalia's definition of coercion as limited to governmental acts backed by force or threat of penalty and yet conclude (with the majority) that a high school student's attendance at commencement is "in a fair and real sense obligatory."[4] ... [A]ssuming that attendance at this social rite of passage is an important benefit for some students (or, more likely, their parents), conditioning that benefit on attendance at the school's theologically debased worship ceremony is a form of compulsion. In a legal world with a meaningful doctrine of unconstitutional conditions, a government benefit to which one is otherwise entitled (here, the meaningful benefit to Deborah Weisman of attending her public school graduation) may not be conditioned on forfeiture of a constitutional right (here, the right not to be forced to attend a religious worship service). To the extent that graduation attendance and attendance at the prayers are "tied goods," a student (and her parents) are compelled to accept the latter as the price of the former. The majority correctly understood this: "It is a tenet of the First Amendment that the State cannot require one of its citizens to forfeit his or her rights and benefits as the price of resisting conformance to state-sponsored religious practice."[5]

If the majority's analysis had rested on the coerced *attendance* point alone, it would have been fine. But the majority went on to suggest that the forbidden coercion is compelled *participation* in the prayers.... It is the majority's clumsy and seemingly desperate attempt to demonstrate coerced participation in prayer that leads it way out of bounds: the majority said that *non-governmental social* pressure occurring in a government-provided forum could constitute coercion forbidden by the Establishment Clause.

The majority noted the heightened "risk of indirect coercion" in the public school setting and asserted as an "undeniable fact ... that the school district's supervision and control of a high school graduation ceremony places public pressure, as well as peer pressure, on attending students to stand as a group or, at least, maintain respectful silence during the Invocation and Benediction."[6] "This pressure," the Court continued, "though subtle and indirect, can be as real as any overt compulsion."[7] The majority also noted that "[r]esearch in psychology supports the common assumption that adolescents are often susceptible to pressure from their peers towards conformity, and that the influence is strongest in matters of social convention."[8] Finally, the Court concluded that "government may no more use social pressure to enforce orthodoxy than it may use more direct means."[9]

It was this discussion that provoked Justice Scalia's acerbic pen. Scalia berated the majority as having taken a "psycho-journey" into amateur psychology in order to come up with a test of "ersatz, 'peer-pressure' psycho-coercion" that treated standing up (or even remaining seated) as an act of compelled participation in the invocation and benediction.[10]

In fairness to the majority, it is not crystal clear that the Court engaged in quite the "psycho-journey" of which they were accused.... [T]he Court's meaning is opaque: "public pressure" could mean *government* pressure (in which case the term is unexceptionable) or it could mean social pressure from private actors that occurs at a state-sponsored "public" event.... The Court seems to glide back and forth easily between private social pressure and a dissenter's "reasonable perception that she is being forced *by the State* to pray."[11]

The proposition that government may not "use social pressure to enforce orthodoxy" is also ambiguous.[12] "Use" implies a deliberate government strategy of deputizing private parties to exert pressure on behalf of the state. If that is what is meant—and this appears to be the better reading of a confusing passage—then the Court is correct in saying that government may not "use social pressure [i.e., employ and deploy pseudo-private actors] to enforce orthodoxy."[13] But if the Court means that private social pressure may be imputed to the government as unconstitutional coercion whenever it takes place in a state-created or otherwise public forum, then the Court has promulgated a dangerous and destructive dictum hostile to First Amendment values.

Social pressure can consist entirely of pure *speech*—the constitutionally protected expression of opinion. The social pressure to conform may come in the form of words—"hey, why aren't you praying, heathen?!"—or it may come in the form of symbolic speech such as disapproving or perplexed glances communicating essentially the same message. In either event, what the Court refers to as social pressure or peer pressure is expression protected under the First Amendment (assuming the listener has not been compelled by government to attend)....

IV. THE COERCION STANDARD IN APPLICATION: RELIGION IN THE SCHOOLS

***

As *Weisman* illustrates, a coercion standard still leaves courts with lines to draw, hard cases to decide, and divisions as to its application....

The public school context supplies several important examples. Ironically (and probably contrary to the expectations of some of its backers), the coercion test is not necessarily more sympathetic to religious activity in public schools than *Lemon*, and may even be less so.

School prayer violates either test, if "school prayer" means government-sponsored religious exercises as part of the school program in a context where the practical ability of students to absent themselves from the proceedings, or the costs visited on them for doing so, render such an opt-out a constitutionally defective alternative. Importantly, however, it is not "peer pressure" that makes an opt-out insufficient. Private pressure to conform does not constitute state action, absent government's deliberate creation or encouragement of social pressure as a means of coercion. Rather, it is the fact that individuals are required by the government to identify and publicly declare their religious beliefs or lack thereof that is problematic, under a "First Amendment privacy" rationale. Individuals have the right to maintain the privacy of their political and religious opinions and affiliations; they may not be required to publicly identify, by word or deed, their positions. In essence, an opt-out scheme asks individuals to "raise their hands" and publicly identify themselves not only as dissenters, but as lacking religious belief. The cost of refusing to so identify oneself is attendance at a religious exercise. The practice, as the school prayer and Bible reading cases themselves recognized, is inescapably coercive.

There is a group of easy cases on the other side. Once it is recognized that the forbidden compulsion is *government* compulsion, it becomes clear that the Establishment Clause does not authorize—and, indeed, the Free Speech and Free Exercise Clauses do not permit—suppression of religious activity by private persons simply because their religious activity makes use of public school facilities and the public school setting. Thus, while "school prayer" or devotional exercises of the type involved in *Engel* and *Schempp* involve government coercion, voluntary extracurricular religious student group meetings involve no such coercion. Such meetings are not rendered suspect under the Establishment Clause by virtue of peer pressure from students or the fact that the meetings occur on school grounds.

***

...A different question is presented where the activity in question is plainly that of the government, but either its coercive tendency or its "religious" nature is disputed. Government speech and public education presents a classic problem because virtually the whole enterprise consists of government speech. May the government engage in religious speech on the same basis as other speech, in the context of public schools?

The paradigmatic case in the school context is *Stone v. Graham.*[13] Decided by the Court under the "purpose" prong of *Lemon, Stone* invalidated a Kentucky statute mandating the posting of the Ten Commandments in public classrooms. Two things make the case troubling. First, the Court has long conceded that public school teaching "about" religion is perfectly appropriate. Why teaching the Ten Commandments does not fit this category is unclear. The problem lies in the incoherence of the Court's concession: It is hard to know where "neutral" teaching "about" religion (is there such a thing?) leaves off and inculcative teaching "of" religion begins.

Second, if schoolchildren are deemed "coerced" in matters of religious exercise by the posting of the Ten Commandments—in the sense of being an indoctrinated, captive audience—it is difficult to avoid the conclusion that they are coerced in their belief structures by everything they are taught in school. It may well be that both propositions are true—that public schools are coercive in *all* that they teach, religious or not—but that the Establishment Clause permits government indoctrination that is "secular" in character and not government indoctrination that is "religious" in character. It does seem strange, however, to think that the First Amendment itself entails a *requirement* of content discrimination in government's own speech, such that public school bulletin boards may not contain the Ten Commandments but can contain the moral code of Robert Fulghum's *All I Really Need to Know I Learned in Kindergarten.*[14] The Court has never owned up to the fact that all instruction conducted by government where attendance is compulsory is coercive; that indoctrination in a secular moral code or values (or lack thereof) is intuitively as problematic as indoctrination in a religious one; and that inculcation of secular values *to the exclusion of* religious ones is the most problematic situation of all.

***

NOTES

The note number from the original article is shown in the parenthesis at the end of each citation.

1. *Lee v. Weisman*, 112 S. Ct. 2649 (1992) [Hereinafter 112 S. Ct.]. (1)
2. Ibid., p. 2655. (114)
3. 112 S. Ct. 2683 (emphasis added). (118)
4. Ibid., p. 2655. (124)
5. Ibid., p. 2660. (126)
6. Ibid., p. 2658. (128)
7. Ibid. (129)
8. Ibid., p. 2659. (130)
9. Ibid. (131)
10. Ibid., pp. 1683, 2684, 2682. (132)
11. Ibid., p. 2658 (emphasis added). (134)
12. Ibid., p. 2659. (135)
13. *Stone v. Graham*, 449 U.S. 39 (1980). (196)
14. Robert Fulghum, *All I Really Need to Know I Learned in Kindergarten* (New York: Villard Books, 1986). (199)

CONSTITUTION OF THE UNITED STATES OF AMERICA

PREAMBLE

We, the people of the United States, in order to form a more perfect union, establish justice, insure domestic tranquility, provide for the common defense, promote the general welfare, and secure the blessings of liberty to ourselves and our posterity, do ordain and establish this Constitution for the United States of America.

ARTICLE I

Section I

1. All legislative powers herein granted shall be vested in a Congress of the United States, which shall consist of a Senate and House of Representatives.

Section II

1. The House of Representatives shall be composed of members chosen every second year by the people of the several States; and the electors in each

State shall have the qualifications requisite for electors of the most numerous branch of the State Legislature.

2. No person shall be a Representative who shall not have attained to the age of twenty-five years, and been seven years a citizen of the United States, and who shall not, when elected, be an inhabitant of that State in which he shall be chosen.

3. Representatives and direct taxes shall be apportioned among the several States which may be included within this Union, according to their respective numbers, which shall be determined by adding to the whole number of free persons, including those bound to service for a term of years, and excluding Indians not taxed, three-fifths of all other persons. The actual enumeration shall be made within three years after the first meeting of the Congress of the United States, and within every subsequent term of ten years, in such manner as they shall by law direct. The number of Representatives shall not exceed one for every thirty thousand, but each State shall have at least one Representative; and until such enumeration shall be made, the State of New Hampshire shall be entitled to choose three; Massachusetts, eight; Rhode Island and Providence Plantations, one; Connecticut, five; New York, six; New Jersey, four; Pennsylvania, eight; Delaware, one; Maryland, six; Virginia, ten; North Carolina, five; South Carolina, five, and Georgia, three.

4. When vacancies happen in the representation from any State, the executive authority thereof shall issue writs of election to fill such vacancies.

5. The House of Representatives shall choose their speaker and other officers; and shall have the sole power of impeachment.

Section III

1. The Senate of the United States shall be composed of two Senators from each State, chosen by the Legislature thereof for six years; and each Senator shall have one vote.

2. Immediately after they shall be assembled in consequence of the first election, they shall be divided as equally as may be into three classes. The

seats of the Senators of the first class shall be vacated at the expiration of the second year, of the second class at the expiration of the fourth year, and of the third class at the expiration of the sixth year, so that one third may be chosen every second year; and if vacancies happen by resignation, or otherwise, during the recess of the Legislature of any State, the executive thereof may make temporary appointments until the next meeting of the Legislature, which shall then fill such vacancies.

3. No person shall be a Senator who shall not have attained to the age of thirty years, and been nine years a citizen of the United States, and who shall not, when elected, be an inhabitant of that State for which he shall be chosen.

4. The Vice-President of the United States shall be President of the Senate, but shall have no vote unless they be equally divided.

5. The Senate shall choose their other officers, and also a President pro tempore, in the absence of the Vice-President, or when he shall exercise the office of President of the United States.

6. The Senate shall have the sole power to try all impeachments. When sitting for that purpose, they shall all be on oath or affirmation. When the President of the United States is tried, the chief-justice shall preside: and no person shall be convicted without the concurrence of two thirds of the members present.

7. Judgment in cases of impeachment shall not extend further than to removal from office, and disqualification to hold and enjoy any office of honor, trust, or profit under the United States; but the party convicted shall nevertheless be liable and subject to indictment, trial, judgment, and punishment, according to law.

Section IV

1. The times, places and manner of holding elections for Senators and Representatives shall be prescribed in each State by the Legislature thereof; but the Congress may at any time by law make of alter such regulations, except as to the place of choosing Senators.

Section V

1. Each House shall be the judge of the election, returns, and qualifications of its own members, and a majority of each shall constitute a quorum to do business; but a smaller number may adjourn from day to day, and may be authorized to compel the attendance of absent members, in such manner and under such penalties as each House may provide.

2. Each House may determine the rule of its proceedings, punish its members for disorderly behavior, and, with the concurrence of two thirds, expel a member.

3. Each House shall keep a journal of its proceedings, and from time to time publish the same, excepting such parts as may in their judgment require secrecy; and the yeas and nays of the members of either House on any questions shall, at the desire of one fifth of those present, be entered on the journal.

4. Neither House, during the session of Congress, shall, without the consent of the other, adjourn for more than three days, nor to any other place than that in which the two houses shall be sitting.

Section VI

1. The Senators and Representatives shall receive a compensation for their services, to be ascertained by law, and paid out of the treasury of the United States. They shall, in all cases, except treason, felony, and breach of the peace, be privileged from arrest during their attendance at the sessions of their respective houses, and in going to and returning from same; and for any speech or debate in either house, they shall not be questioned in any other place.

2. No Senator or Representative shall, during the time for which he was elected, be appointed to any civil office under the authority of the United States which shall have been created, or the emoluments whereof shall have been increased during such time; and no person holding any office under the United States shall be a member of either House during his continuance in office.

Section VII

1. All bills for raising revenue shall originate in the House of Representatives, but the Senate may propose or concur with amendments, as on other bills.

2. Every bill which shall have passed the House of Representatives and the Senate shall, before it become a law, be presented to the President of the United States; if he approve, he shall sign it, but if not, he shall return it, with his objections, to that House in which it shall have originated, who shall enter the objections at large on their journal, and proceed to reconsider it. If after such reconsideration two thirds of that House shall agree to pass the bill, it shall be sent, together with the objections, to the other House, by which it shall likewise be reconsidered; and if approved by two thirds of that House it shall become a law. But in all such cases the votes of both Houses shall be determined by yeas and nays, and the names of the persons voting for and against the bill shall be entered on the journal of each House respectively. If any bill shall not be returned by the President within ten days (Sundays excepted) after it shall have been presented to him, the same shall be a law in like manner as if he had signed it, unless the Congress by their adjournment, prevent its return; in which case it shall not be a law.

3. Every order, resolution, or vote to which the concurrence of the Senate and House of Representatives may be necessary (except on a question of adjournment) shall be presented to the President of the United States; and before the same shall take effect shall be approved by him, or being disapproved by him, shall be repassed by two thirds of the Senate and the House of Representatives, according to the rules and limitations prescribed in the case of a bill.

Section VIII

1. The Congress shall have power to lay and collect taxes, duties, imposts, and excises, to pay the debts and provide for the common defense and general welfare of the United States; but all duties, imposts, and excises shall be uniform throughout the United States.

2. To borrow money on the credit of the United States.

3. To regulate commerce with foreign nations, and among the several States, and with the Indian tribes.

4. To establish an uniform rule of naturalization and uniform laws on the subject of bankruptcies throughout the United States.

5. To coin money, regulate the value thereof, and of foreign coin, and fix the standard of weights and measures.

6. To provide for the punishment of counterfeiting the securities and current coin of the United States.

7. To establish post offices and post roads.

8. To promote the progress of science and useful arts by securing for limited times to authors and inventors the exclusive rights to their respective writings and discoveries.

9. To constitute tribunals inferior to the Supreme Court.

10. To define and punish piracies and felonies committed on the high seas, and offenses against the law of nations.

11. To declare war, grant letters of marque and reprisal, and make rules concerning captures on land and water.

12. To raise and support armies, but no appropriation of money to that use shall be for a longer term than two years.

13. To provide and maintain a navy.

14. To make rules for the government and regulation of the land and naval forces.

15. To provide for calling forth the militia to execute the laws of the Union, suppress insurrections, and repel invasions.

16. To provide for organizing, arming, and disciplining the militia, and for governing such part of them as may be employed in the service of the United States, reserving to the States respectively the appointment of the officers, and the authority of training the militia according to the discipline prescribed by Congress.

17. To exercise exclusive legislation in all cases whatsoever over such district (not exceeding ten miles square) as may, by cession of particular States and the acceptance of Congress, become the seat of Government of the United States, and to exercise like authority over all places purchased by the consent of the Legislature of the State in which the same shall be, for the erection of forts, magazines, arsenals, dry docks, and other needful buildings.

18. To make all laws which shall be necessary and proper for carrying into execution the foregoing powers, and all other powers vested by this Constitution in the Government of the United States, or in any department or officer thereof.

Section IX

1. The migration or importation of such persons as any of the States now existing shall think proper to admit shall not be prohibited by the Congress prior to the year one thousand eight hundred and eight, but a tax or duty may be imposed on such importation, not exceeding ten dollars for each person.

2. The privilege of the writ of habeas corpus shall not be suspended, unless when in cases of rebellion or invasion the public safety may require it.

3. No bill of attainder or ex post facto law shall be passed.

4. No capitation or other direct tax shall be laid, unless in proportion to the census or enumeration hereinbefore directed to be taken.

5. No tax or duty shall be laid on articles exported from any State.

6. No preference shall be given by any regulation of commerce or revenue to the ports of one State over those of another, nor shall vessels bound to or from one State be obliged to enter, clear, or pay duties in another.

7. No money shall be drawn from the Treasury but in consequence of appropriations made by law; and a regular statement and account of the receipts and expenditures of all public money shall be published from time to time.

8. No title of nobility shall be granted by the United States. And no person holding any office of profit or trust under them shall, without the consent of the Congress, accept of any present, emolument, office, or title of any kind whatever from any king, prince, or foreign state.

Section X

1. No state shall enter into any treaty, alliance, or confederation, grant letters of marque and reprisal, coin money, emit bills of credit, make anything but gold and silver coin a tender in payment of debts, pass any bill of attainder, ex post facto law, or law impairing the obligation of contracts, or grant any title of nobility.

2. No State shall, without the consent of the Congress, lay any impost or duties on imports or exports, except what may be absolutely necessary for executing its inspection laws, and the net produce of all duties and imposts, laid by any State on imports or exports, shall be for the use of the Treasury of the United States; and all such laws shall be subject to the revision and control of the Congress.

3. No State shall, without the consent of Congress, lay any duty of tonnage, keep troops or ships of war in time of peace, enter into any agreement or compact with another State, or with a foreign power, or engage in war, unless actually invaded, or in such imminent danger as will not admit of delay.

ARTICLE II

Section I

1. The Executive power shall be vested in a President of the United States of America. He shall hold his office during the term of four years, and, together with the Vice-President, chosen for the same term, be elected as follows:

2. Each State shall appoint, in such manner as the Legislature thereof may direct, a number of electors, equal to the whole number of Senators and Representatives to which the State may be entitled in the Congress; but no Senator or Representative or person holding an office of trust or profit under the United States shall be appointed an elector.

3. [The electors shall meet in their respective States and vote by ballot for two persons, of whom one at least shall not be an inhabitant of the same State with themselves. And they shall make a list of all the persons voted for, and of the number of votes for each, which list they shall sign and certify and transmit, sealed, to the seat of the government of the United States, directed to the President of the Senate. The President of the Senate shall, in the presence of the Senate and House of Representatives, open all the certificates, and the votes shall then be counted. The person having the greatest number of votes shall be the President, if such number be a majority of the whole number of electors appointed, and if there be more than one who have such majority, and have an equal number of votes, then the House of Representatives shall immediately choose by ballot one of them for President; and if no person have a majority, then from the five highest on the list the said House shall in like manner choose the President. But in choosing the President, the vote shall be taken by States, the representation from each State having one vote. A quorum, for this purpose, shall consist of a member or members from two thirds of the States, and a majority of all the States shall be necessary to a choice. In every case, after the choice of the President, the person having the greatest number of votes of the electors shall be the Vice-President. But if there should remain two or more who have equal votes, the Senate shall choose from them by ballot the Vice-President.]*

---

*This clause is superseded by Article XII., Amendments.

4. The Congress may determine the time of choosing the electors and the day on which they shall give their votes, which day shall be the same throughout the United States.

5. No person except a natural born citizen, or a citizen of the United States at the time of the adoption of this Constitution, shall be eligible to the office of President; neither shall any person be eligible to that office who shall not have attained to the age of thirty-five years and been fourteen years a resident within the United States.

6. In case of the removal of the President from office, or of his death, resignation, or inability to discharge the powers and duties of the said office, the same shall devolve on the Vice-President, and the Congress may by law provide for the case of removal, death, resignation, or inability, both of the President and Vice-President, declaring what officer shall then act as President, and such officer shall act accordingly until the disability be removed or a President shall be elected.

7. The President shall, at stated times, receive for his services a compensation, which shall neither be increased nor diminished during the period for which he shall have been elected, and he shall not receive within that period any other emolument from the United States, or any of them.

8. Before he enter on the execution of his office he shall take the following oath or affirmation: "I do solemnly swear (or affirm) that I will faithfully execute the office of President of the United States, and will, to the best of my ability, preserve, protect, and defend the Constitution of the United States."

Section II

1. The President shall be Commander-in-Chief of the Army and Navy of the United States, and of the militia of the several States when called into the actual service of the United States; he may require the opinion, in writing, of the principal officer in each of the executive departments upon any subject relating to the duties of their respective offices, and he shall have power to grant reprieves and pardons for offenses against the United States except in cases of impeachment.

2. He shall have power, by and with the advice and consent of the Senate, to make treaties, provided two thirds of the Senators present concur; and he shall nominate, and by and with the advice and consent of the Senate shall appoint ambassadors, other public ministers and consuls, judges of the Supreme Court, and all other officers of the United States whose appointments are not herein otherwise provided for, and which shall be established by law; but the Congress may by law vest the appointment of such inferior officers as they think proper in the President alone, in the courts of law, or in the heads of departments.

3. The President shall have power to fill up all vacancies that may happen during the recess of the Senate by granting commissions, which shall expire at the end of their next session.

Section III

He shall from time to time give to the Congress information of the state of the Union, and recommend to their consideration such measure as he shall judge necessary and expedient; he may, on extraordinary occasions, convene both Houses, or either of them, and in case of disagreement between them with respect to the time of adjournment, he may adjourn them to such time as he shall think proper; he shall receive ambassadors and other public ministers; he shall take care that the laws be faithfully executed, and shall commission all the officers of the United States.

Section IV

The President, Vice-President, and all civil officers of the United States shall be removed from office on impeachment for and conviction of treason, bribery, or other high crimes and misdemeanors.

ARTICLE III

Section I

The judicial power of the United States shall be vested in one Supreme Court, and in such inferior courts as the Congress may from time to time ordain and establish. The judges, both of the Supreme and inferior courts, shall hold their offices during good behavior, and shall at stated times receive for their services a compensation which shall not be diminished during their continuance in office.

Section II

1. The judicial power shall extend to all cases in law and equity arising under this Constitution, the laws of the United States, and treaties made, or which shall be made, under their authority; to all cases affecting ambassadors, other public ministers, and consuls; to all cases of admiralty and maritime jurisdiction; to controversies to which the United States shall be a party; to controversies between two or more States, between a State and citizens of another State, between citizens of different States, between citizens of the same State claiming lands under grants of different States, and between a State, or the citizens thereof, and foreign States, citizens, or subjects.

2. In all cases affecting ambassadors, other public ministers, and consuls, and those in which a State shall be party, the Supreme Court shall have original jurisdiction. In all the other cases before mentioned the Supreme Court shall have appellate jurisdiction both as to law and fact, with such exceptions and under such regulations as the Congress shall make.

3. The trial of all crimes, except in cases of impeachment, shall be by jury, and such trial shall be held in the State where the said crimes shall have been committed; but when not committed within any State the trial shall be at such place or places as the Congress may by law have directed.

Section III

1. Treason against the United States shall consist only in levying war against them, or in adhering to their enemies, giving them aid and comfort. No person shall be convicted of treason unless on the testimony of two witnesses to the same overt act, or on confession in open court.

2. The Congress shall have power to declare the punishment of treason, but no attainder of treason shall work corruption of blood or forfeiture except during the life of the person attained.

ARTICLE IV

Section I

Full faith and credit shall be given in each State to the public acts, records, and judicial preceedings of every other State. And the Congress may by general laws prescribe the manner in which such acts, records and proceedings shall be proved, and the effect thereof.

Section II

1. The citizens of each State shall be entitled to all privileges and immunities of citizens in the several States.

2. A person charged in any State with treason, felony, or other crime, who shall flee from justice, and be found in another State, shall on demand of the Executive authority of the State from which he fled, be delivered up, to be removed to the State having jurisdiction of the crime.

3. No person held to service or labor in one State, under the laws thereof, escaping into another shall, in consequence of any law or regulation therein, be discharged from such service or labor, but shall be delivered up on claim of the party to whom such service or labor may be due.

Section III

1. New States may be admitted by the Congress into this Union; but no new State shall be formed or erected within the jurisdiction of any other State, nor any State be formed by the junction of two or more States, or parts of States, without the consent of the Legislatures of the States concerned, as well as of the Congress.

2. The Congress shall have power to dispose of and make all needful rules and regulations respecting the territory or other property belonging to the United States; and nothing in this Constitution shall be so construed as to prejudice any claims of the United States, or of any particular State.

Section IV

The United States shall guarantee to every State in this Union a republican form of government, and shall protect each of them against invasion, and, on application of the Legislature, or of the Executive (when the Legislature cannot be convened), against domestic violence.

ARTICLE V

The Congress, whenever two thirds of both Houses shall deem it necessary, shall propose amendments to this Constitution, or, on the application of the Legislatures of two thirds of the several States, shall call a convention for proposing amendments, which, in either case, shall be valid to all intents and purposes, as part of this Constitution, when ratified by the Legislatures of three fourths of the several States, or by conventions in three fourths thereof, as the one or the other mode of ratification may be proposed by the Congress; provided that no amendment which may be made prior to the year one thousand eight hundred and eight shall in any manner affect the first and fourth clauses in the Ninth Section of the First Article; and that no State, without its consent, shall be deprived of its equal suffrage in the Senate.

ARTICLE VI

1. All debts contracted and engagements entered into before the adoption of this Constitution shall be as valid against the United States under this Constitution as under the Confederation.

2. This Constitution and the laws of the United States which shall be made in pursuance thereof and all treaties made, or which shall be made, under the authority of the United States, shall be the supreme law of the land, and the judges in every State shall be bound thereby, anything in the Constitution of laws of any State to the contrary notwithstanding.

3. The Senators and Representatives before mentioned, and the members of the several State Legislatures, and all executive and judicial officers, both of the United States and of the several States, shall be bound by oath or affirmation to support this Constitution; but no religious test shall ever be

required as a qualification to any office or public trust under the United States.

ARTICLE VII

The ratification of the Conventions of nine States shall be sufficient for the establishment of this Constitution between the States so ratifying the same.

THE AMENDMENTS TO THE CONSTITUTION*

The Conventions of a number of the States having, at the time of adopting the Constitution, expressed a desire, in order to prevent misconstruction or abuse of its powers, that further declaratory and restrictive clauses should be added, and as extending the ground of public confidence in the Government will best insure the beneficent ends of its institution;

Resolved, by the Senate and House of Representatives of the United States of America, in Congress assembled, two-thirds of both Houses concurring, that the following articles be proposed to the Legislatures of the several States, as amendments to the Constitution of the United States; all or any of which articles, when ratified by three-fourths of the said Legislatures, to be valid to all intents and purposes as part of the said Constitution, namely:

AMENDMENT I

Congress shall make no law respecting an establishment of religion, or prohibiting the free exercise thereof; or abridging the freedom of speech, or of the press; or the right of the people peaceably to assemble, and to petition the Government for a redress of grievances.

---

*The Bill of Rights are the first ten amendments to the Constitution.

AMENDMENT 2

A well regulated Militia, being necessary to the security of a free State, the right of the people to keep and bear Arms, shall not be infringed.

AMENDMENT 3

No Soldier shall, in time of peace be quartered in any house, without the consent of the Owner, nor in time of war, but in a manner to be prescribed by law.

AMENDMENT 4

The right of the people to be secure in their persons, houses, papers, and effects, against unreasonable searches and seizures, shall not be violated, and no Warrants shall issue, but upon probable cause, supported by Oath or affirmation, and particularly describing the place to be searched, and the persons or things to be seized.

AMENDMENT 5

No person shall be held to answer for a capital, or otherwise infamous crime, unless on a presentment or indictment of a Grand Jury, except in cases arising in the land or naval forces, or in the Militia, when in actual service in time of War or public danger; nor shall any person be subject for the same offense to be twice put in jeopardy of life or limb; nor shall be compelled in any criminal case to be a witness against himself, nor be deprived of life, liberty, or property, without due process of law; nor shall private property be taken for public use, without just compensation.

AMENDMENT 6

In all criminal prosecutions, the accused shall enjoy the right to a speedy and public trial, by an impartial jury of the State and district wherein the crime shall have been committed, which district shall have been previously ascertained by law, and to be informed of the nature and cause of the accusation; to be confronted with the witnesses against him; to have compulsory process for obtaining witnesses in his favor, and to have the Assistance of Counsel for his defence.

AMENDMENT 7

In Suits at common law, where the value in controversy shall exceed twenty dollars, the right of trial by jury shall be preserved, and no fact tried by a jury, shall be otherwise re-examined in any Court of the United States, than according to the rules of the common law.

AMENDMENT 8

Excessive bail shall not be required, nor excessive fines imposed, nor cruel and unusual punishments inflicted.

AMENDMENT 9

The enumeration in the Constitution, of certain rights, shall not be construed to deny or disparage others retained by the people.

AMENDMENT 10

The powers not delegated to the United States by the Constitution, nor prohibited by it to the States, are reserved to the States respectively, or to the people.

AMENDMENT 11

The Judicial power of the United States shall not be construed to extend to any suit in law or equity, commenced or prosecuted against one of the United States by Citizens of another State, or by Citizens or Subjects of any Foreign State.

AMENDMENT 12

The Electors shall meet in their respective states, and vote by ballot for President and Vice-President, one of whom, at least, shall not be an inhabitant of the same state with themselves; they shall name in their ballots the person voted for as President, and in distinct ballots the person voted for as Vice-President, and they shall make distinct lists of all persons voted for as President, and of all persons voted for as Vice-President and of the number of votes for each, which lists they shall sign and certify, and transmit sealed to the seat of the government of the United States, directed to the President of the Senate; The President of the Senate shall, in the presence of the Senate and House of Representatives, open all the certificates and the votes shall then be counted; The person having the greatest Number of votes for President, shall be the President, if such number be a majority of the whole number of Electors appointed; and if no person have such majority, then from the persons having the highest numbers not exceeding three on the list of those voted for as President, the House of Representatives shall choose immediately, by ballot, the President. But in choosing the President, the votes shall be taken by states, the representation from each state having one vote; a quorum for this purpose shall consist of a member or members from two-thirds of the states, and a majority of all the states shall be necessary to a choice. And if the House of Representatives shall not choose a President whenever the right of choice shall devolve upon them, before the fourth day of March next following, then the Vice-President shall act as President, as in the case of the death or other constitutional disability of the President. The person having the greatest number of votes as Vice-President, shall be the Vice-President, if such number be a majority of the whole number of Electors appointed, and if no person have a majority, then from the two highest numbers on the list, the Senate shall choose the Vice-President; a quorum for the purpose shall consist of two-thirds of the whole number of Senators, and a majority of the whole number shall be necessary to a choice. But no person constitutionally ineligible to the office of President shall be eligible to that of Vice-President of the United States.

AMENDMENT 13

1. Neither slavery nor involuntary servitude, except as a punishment for crime whereof the party shall have been duly convicted, shall exist within the United States, or any place subject to their jurisdiction.

2. Congress shall have power to enforce this article by appropriate legislation.

AMENDMENT 14

1. All persons born or naturalized in the United States, and subject to the jurisdiction thereof, are citizens of the United States and of the State wherein they reside. No State shall make or enforce any law which shall abridge the privileges or immunities of citizens of the United States; nor shall any State deprive any person of life, liberty, or property, without due process of law; nor deny to any person within its jurisdiction the equal protection of the laws.

2. Representatives shall be apportioned among the several States according to their respective numbers, counting the whole number of persons in each State, excluding Indians not taxed. But when the right to vote at any election for the choice of electors for President and Vice-President of the United States, Representatives in Congress, the Executive and Judicial officers of a State, or the members of the Legislature thereof, is denied to any of the male inhabitants of such State, being twenty-one years of age, and citizens of the United States, or in any way abridged, except for participation in rebellion, or other crime, the basis of representation therein shall be reduced in the proportion which the number of such male citizens shall bear to the whole number of male citizens twenty-one years of age in such State.

3. No person shall be a Senator or Representative in Congress, or elector of President and Vice-President, or hold any office, civil or military, under the United States, or under any State, who, having previously taken an oath, as a member of Congress, or as an officer of the United States, or as a member of any State legislature, or as an executive or judicial officer of any State, to support the Constitution of the United States, shall have engaged in insurrection or rebellion against the same, or given aid or comfort to the enemies thereof. But Congress may by a vote of two-thirds of each House, remove such disability.

4. The validity of the public debt of the United States, authorized by law, including debts incurred for payment of pensions and bounties for services in suppressing insurrection or rebellion, shall not be questioned. But neither the United States nor any State shall assume or pay any debt or obligation incurred in aid of insurrection or rebellion against the United States, or any claim for the loss or emancipation of any slave; but all such debts, obligations and claims shall be held illegal and void.

5. The Congress shall have power to enforce, by appropriate legislation, the provisions of this article.

AMENDMENT 15

1. The right of citizens of the United States to vote shall not be denied or abridged by the United States or by any State on account of race, color, or previous condition of servitude.

2. The Congress shall have power to enforce this article by appropriate legislation.

AMENDMENT 16

The Congress shall have power to lay and collect taxes on incomes, from whatever source derived, without apportionment among the several States, and without regard to any census or enumeration.

AMENDMENT 17

The Senate of the United States shall be composed of two Senators from each State, elected by the people thereof, for six years; and each Senator shall have one vote. The electors in each State shall have the qualifications requisite for electors of the most numerous branch of the State legislatures. When vacancies happen in the representation of any State in the Senate, the executive authority of such State shall issue writs of election to fill such vacancies: Provided, That the legislature of any State may empower the executive thereof to make temporary appointments until the people fill the vacancies by election as the legislature may direct. This amendment shall not be so construed as to affect the election or term of any Senator chosen before it becomes valid as part of the Constitution.

AMENDMENT 18

1. After one year from the ratification of this article the manufacture, sale, or transportation of intoxicating liquors within, the importation thereof into, or the exportation thereof from the United States and all territory subject to the jurisdiction thereof for beverage purposes is hereby prohibited.

2. The Congress and the several States shall have concurrent power to enforce this article by appropriate legislation.

3. This article shall be inoperative unless it shall have been ratified as an

amendment to the Constitution by the legislatures of the several States, as provided in the Constitution, within seven years from the date of the submission hereof to the States by the Congress.

AMENDMENT 19

The right of citizens of the United States to vote shall not be denied or abridged by the United States or by any State on account of sex. Congress shall have power to enforce this article by appropriate legislation.

AMENDMENT 20

1. The terms of the President and Vice President shall end at noon on the 20th day of January, and the terms of Senators and Representatives at noon on the 3d day of January, of the years in which such terms would have ended if this article had not been ratified; and the terms of their successors shall then begin.

2. The Congress shall assemble at least once in every year, and such meeting shall begin at noon on the 3d day of January, unless they shall by law appoint a different day.

3. If, at the time fixed for the beginning of the term of the President, the President elect shall have died, the Vice President elect shall become President. If a President shall not have been chosen before the time fixed for the beginning of his term, or if the President elect shall have failed to qualify, then the Vice President elect shall act as President until a President shall have qualified; and the Congress may by law provide for the case wherein neither a President elect nor a Vice President elect shall have qualified, declaring who shall then act as President, or the manner in which one who is to act shall be selected, and such person shall act accordingly until a President or Vice President shall have qualified.

4. The Congress may by law provide for the case of the death of any of the persons from whom the House of Representatives may choose a President whenever the right of choice shall have devolved upon them, and for the case of the death of any of the persons from whom the Senate may choose a Vice President whenever the right of choice shall have devolved upon them.

5. Sections 1 and 2 shall take effect on the 15th day of October following the ratification of this article.

6. This article shall be inoperative unless it shall have been ratified as an amendment to the Constitution by the legislatures of three-fourths of the several States within seven years from the date of its submission.

AMENDMENT 21

1. The eighteenth article of amendment to the Constitution of the United States is hereby repealed.

2. The transportation or importation into any State, Territory, or possession of the United States for delivery or use therein of intoxicating liquors, in violation of the laws thereof, is hereby prohibited.

3. The article shall be inoperative unless it shall have been ratified as an amendment to the Constitution by conventions in the several States, as provided in the Constitution, within seven years from the date of the submission hereof to the States by the Congress.

AMENDMENT 22

1. No person shall be elected to the office of the President more than twice, and no person who has held the office of President, or acted as President, for more than two years of a term to which some other person was elected President shall be elected to the office of the President more than once. But this Article shall not apply to any person holding the office of President, when this Article was proposed by the Congress, and shall not prevent any person who may be holding the office of President, or acting as President, during the term within which this Article becomes operative from holding the office of President or acting as President during the remainder of such term.

2. This article shall be inoperative unless it shall have been ratified as an amendment to the Constitution by the legislatures of three-fourths of the several States within seven years from the date of its submission to the States by the Congress.

AMENDMENT 23

1. The District constituting the seat of Government of the United States shall appoint in such manner as the Congress may direct: A number of electors of President and Vice President equal to the whole number of Senators

and Representatives in Congress to which the District would be entitled if it were a State, but in no event more than the least populous State; they shall be in addition to those appointed by the States, but they shall be considered, for the purposes of the election of President and Vice President, to be electors appointed by a State; and they shall meet in the District and perform such duties as provided by the twelfth article of amendment.

2. The Congress shall have power to enforce this article by appropriate legislation.

AMENDMENT 24

1. The right of citizens of the United States to vote in any primary or other election for President or Vice President, for electors for President or Vice President, or for Senator or Representative in Congress, shall not be denied or abridged by the United States or any State by reason of failure to pay any poll tax or other tax.

2. The Congress shall have power to enforce this article by appropriate legislation.

AMENDMENT 25

1. In case of the removal of the President from office or of his death or resignation, the Vice President shall become President.

2. Whenever there is a vacancy in the office of the Vice President, the President shall nominate a Vice President who shall take office upon confirmation by a majority vote of both Houses of Congress.

3. Whenever the President transmits to the President pro tempore of the Senate and the Speaker of the House of Representatives his written declaration that he is unable to discharge the powers and duties of his office, and until he transmits to them a written declaration to the contrary, such powers and duties shall be discharged by the Vice President as Acting President.

4. Whenever the Vice President and a majority of either the principal officers of the executive departments or of such other body as Congress may by law provide, transmit to the President pro tempore of the Senate and the Speaker of the House of Representatives their written declaration that the President is unable to discharge the powers and duties of his office, the Vice President shall immediately assume the powers and duties of the office as

Acting President. Thereafter, when the President transmits to the President pro tempore of the Senate and the Speaker of the House of Representatives his written declaration that no inability exists, he shall resume the powers and duties of his office unless the Vice President and a majority of either the principal officers of the executive department or of such other body as Congress may by law provide, transmit within four days to the President pro tempore of the Senate and the Speaker of the House of Representatives their written declaration that the President is unable to discharge the powers and duties of his office. Thereupon Congress shall decide the issue, assembling within forty eight hours for that purpose if not in session. If the Congress, within twenty one days after receipt of the latter written declaration, or, if Congress is not in session, within twenty one days after Congress is required to assemble, determines by two thirds vote of both Houses that the President is unable to discharge the powers and duties of his office, the Vice President shall continue to discharge the same as Acting President; otherwise, the President shall resume the powers and duties of his office.

AMENDMENT 26

1. The right of citizens of the United States, who are eighteen years of age or older, to vote shall not be denied or abridged by the United States or by any State on account of age.

2. The Congress shall have power to enforce this article by appropriate legislation.

AMENDMENT 27

No law, varying the compensation for the services of the Senators and Representatives, shall take effect, until an election of Representatives shall have intervened.